WHAT IS A BONG TREE?
ARTICLES AND TALKS 1976-2021

MICHAEL ROSEN

Edited by John Richmond

www.michaelrosen.co.uk/books

For Emma

Contents

INTRODUCTION

People ask me to give talks and write articles. Sometimes I write blogs. This book is a selection from these made partly by me and partly by the editor, John Richmond. They are for you to dip into wherever and whenever you fancy it.

A few notes:

1. Anyone reading the whole book will find that I repeat myself. My dear father pointed out this characteristic of mine, starting from about the time I was four till the day he left us. My excuse for doing it here is that as the talks and articles were for different audiences, the audiences didn't notice. Sometimes I've repeated poems. Please take that as a gesture of kindness to you, to save you flicking through the pages to find the page where a poem first appears. One poem is, I think, repeated three times. That's probably a bit excessive. Sorry.

2. This is not a scholarly book, but one essay uses scholarly referencing systems. It might have been possible to put the whole book through that particular formatting mill, but I think if I had tried to do that I would never have got the book out.

3. There are Yiddish words in the book. I have translated them all, but you will notice that they are spelled differently. Yiddish used to be written with Hebrew letters only. In the last few decades more and more people have wanted to write it in 'Roman' letters. There was no agreed spelling so people tended to do it phonetically. And anyway, Yiddish is pronounced differently depending on the regional origins of the users of the words. In recent years

there has been some effort to standardise the spelling. That's a good idea. Sorry I haven't kept up with that.

4. I have written other books and booklets that relate to this book. I'm listing them here:

Good Ideas: How to be Your Child's (and Your Own) Best Teacher (John Murray)

Michael Rosen's Book of Play: Why Play Really Matters and 101 Ways to Get More of it in Your Life (Profile)

How to Make Children Laugh (Quercus)

What is Poetry? The Essential Guide to Reading and Writing Poems (Walker Books)

The Author: Towards a Marxist Approach to Authorship (self-published).

And I've done four self-published booklets for teachers:

Reading for Pleasure

Writing for Pleasure

Why Write? Why Read?

Poetry and Stories for Primary and Lower Secondary Schools.

The poetry teacher Jonny Walker wrote a guide that I have contributed to and published:

Michael Rosen's Videos: How to Get Children Writing and Performing Poems Too.

There is more information about the self-published books at the very end of this book. They're available at www.michaelrosen.co.uk/books.

5. Although the book is roughly divided into four sections, anyone with enough stamina to read the whole lot will realise that the subject matter of one section often overlaps with and bleeds into the subject matter of another section. That's the nature of the work I've done as a writer, the experiences I've had and described, and the arguments I've put forward in my life so far.

6. John Richmond has edited this book. (I told you I repeat myself.) He is a teacher, writer, scholar, poet and great friend. I've known him since I was a writer-in-residence at Vauxhall Manor School in the late 1970s. He pioneered a form of teachers' action research where classroom teachers discussed and wrote up their reflections on the students' and their own work. It appeared as *Becoming Our Own Experts* (now available at www.becomingourownexperts. org). It is a superb example of how teachers can develop their own interests, talents and insights.

John also edited my father's writings, and my family will always be in debt to him for that. The book is *Harold Rosen: Writings on Life, Language and Learning 1958-2008*, published by the UCL Institute of Education Press.

I could not have done this book without John. Like me, he has been critical, and sometimes despairing, of damaging and ignorant interventions which successive governments in England have made in the theory and practice of English teaching, language and learning. He is the lead author of two books, both published by Routledge: *Curriculum and Assessment in English 3 to 11: A Better Plan*; and *Curriculum and Assessment in English 11 to 19: A Better Plan*. These books do three things: they discuss what has been wrong with government policy in the teaching and assessment of English in schools; they remind readers of the best that has been thought and written, over many decades, in these areas; and, most important, they propose an entire alternative curriculum and alternative assessment arrangements for English from age 3 upwards.

John has a website containing his shorter educational pieces: www. languageandlearning.net.

John's book of original poems, *My Proper Life*, and of translations of poems from European languages, *Bring Me the Sunflower*, are available from him at john@myproperlife.com. And his poetry and prose are also at www. myproperlife.com.

AUTOBIOGRAPHICAL

George Orwell on *Gulliver's Travels*

I gave this lecture at Birkbeck, University of London on 6 December 2007.

In 1968, I was at university and some of us thought that the world was changing around our ears. Well, more than that actually: the world was changing and we were helping it change. America was in Vietnam, the Soviet Union invaded Czechoslovakia, there were struggles for civil liberties in the US, for equality in South Africa and something extraordinary was happening in France – there seemed to be some kind of mass uprising going on over there. I don't want to spell out my take on the precise significance of these events or how they inter-related – another time maybe. My point is simply that in 1968 the times felt special, new and genuinely upending or – the word of that moment – revolutionary.

I was studying English Literature at a university where the literature of English was understood to begin somewhere round the ninth century and end at 1900. The word 'English' in this context was not a synonym for 'anglophone' – American literature, for example, was not included – but it was a synonym for British and Irish. And though literature prior to Chaucer required what felt to me like translation, translation of other kinds of text – even of Norman French, a language that had a mighty bearing on the way English was and is spoken and written – was again not permitted.

Over the three years of study, we were taken on what I see now was a trip down a corridor, walking from author to author, noting how one great writer in some mysterious way or another was the father of the next – yes, one or two mothers were allowed in too, notably George Eliot. Occasionally, a door off the corridor was opened and the loud, unruly sound of that author's epoch was allowed to burst in on upon us – at one moment described as, say,

5

'The Elizabethan World Picture', the next as, say, 'The Enlightenment'. Other doors marked, say, 'The English Civil War', 'The French Revolution', 'Industrialisation', remained shut, even though some of the world's most famous scholars of these episodes were running classes on these subjects for students of History, just a few yards away. So, down the corridor, we ran: *Beowulf*, Chaucer, Shakespeare, the metaphysicals, Restoration drama, the Augustans, Jane Austen, the Romantics, Dickens, Hardy and – whoa – we reached those authors who inconsiderately wrote both before and after 1900: irritating people like Hardy and Bernard Shaw.

Incidentally, there was also a phase of study on what was called 'Language' – not 'linguistics', note – which was in essence a parallel corridor to the literary one, because here, down through the centuries, words gave birth to words, 'wroghte' became 'wrought'; constructions bore constructions, 'givest thou?' became 'do you give?'. All this happened seemingly without the agency of people. It was very important to know when these things changed but irrelevant to ask why, or really who was doing the changing.

So, my head was a peculiar place to be. At one moment, caught up in the frantic, impatient discussions about the various ends of Communism, Imperialism and Capitalism, and the next in whether the impact of a metaphysical poem depended or not on the 'yoking' together of heterogeneous images. In the space of minutes I was leaping from Ho Chi Minh to 'Busy old fool, unruly sun . . . ' No bad thing in itself, but at that very moment, in the thick of it all, I didn't feel in my bones that there was any connection that could be made between the two.

Until George Orwell.

Now, Orwell's fiction was of course well beyond the end of the corridor, as were most of his essays. However, as I guess many of you will know, Orwell wrote about *Gulliver's Travels*. A little context here: the pedagogic method of Oxford University was primarily through the means of the one-to-one tutorial.

Somewhere, far off, in an outrageously twentieth-century building, dons put on gowns and gave lectures on whatever took their fancy. I remember one hour on the first word of *Beowulf*, which, as you all know, is 'Hwaet'. However, these lectures were not compulsory. The real meat and potatoes came in writing a weekly essay, reading it to the tutor and entering into a discussion with the tutor until the hour was up. These essays and conversations were not guided by any stated method or theory. You simply wrote and said the kind of thing that people called 'respected critics' wrote. If they leaned towards discovering, say, 'patterns of imagery' – fair enough. If another leaned towards trying to figure out an author's intention, again fine. Some seemed to see the author as a puppet-master, assembling scenes, plots, characters and structures as a means of controlling readers' emotions. Occasionally, we would be taken into the land of genres – tragedy, comedy, the ballad, the novel, though this had to be done either with reference to ancient Greeks and Romans, or to the English. There was no contamination from France, Germany or Italy, though nods were made to authors and texts we wouldn't read. The names of Boccaccio, Goethe, Flaubert were on the corridor doors, but the doors weren't opened.

There was a learned alley we could go down called 'influence', and indeed engage in arguments about who was the greatest influence. Was Keats more influenced by Shakespeare than was Shelley? This was part of the way in which we learnt that one author or even the inert object of one book was the progenitor of another, a birthing that took place in the corridor. Related to this was the practice of mimesis. You could use the space of the essay to say what an image, passage or scene of a book was like.

There was a bloodhound amongst us too, who could sniff out criminal offences, such as sentimentality, cliché, inconsistency, coyness, unbelievability and something that involved what they called 'pandering'. Authors, we gathered, shouldn't have pandered to this or that unsatisfactory, low tendency in us or in society. I can't believe that I was alone in thinking that this bloodhound had a particularly high status, as it was with him that I could prove that Wyatt was a minor not a major poet or that *Measure for Measure* was 'flawed'.

In the midst of this there was also a lengthy dialogue about paradox and irony. Around the time the tanks arrived on the streets of Prague, I remember that a feeling was engendered in me that there was something uniquely English and uniquely brilliant about English Literature's ability to be ironic. As I didn't have anyone else's literature to compare it with, at least not since A-level French and visits to *Candide* and *Tartuffe*, I think I took this at face value. Well, I say that, though my first trip round Jonathan Swift was a disaster. That week's essay was on 'A Letter to a Very Young Lady on her Marriage', where Swift appeared to me at the moment of reading to be telling the woman how to behave, what to wear and even how to think. Accordingly, I wrote my essay, paying close attention to the imagery, structure, contrast and tone and then, with my bloodhound unleashed, I spotted the flaw: a hectoring tone, a tedious repetitious style, a snobbish *de haut en bas* approach to the woman. I read it to the tutor. There! Surely, I had done the job. He looked up. 'You don't suppose that Swift was being ironic, do you, Michael?' Irony! Oh blow. I hadn't thought of it. No worries, next week, *Gulliver's Travels*. See you next Tuesday.

Now, here I was, face to face with one of the great mountains of English Literature, covered in inscriptions like 'classic', 'satire', 'irony' but also 'flawed'. Its surface was crawling with references to eighteenth-century people and events that would reveal the true meaning of scenes in the book. After several days – perhaps interrupted by the cruel murder of Martin Luther King, the Tet Offensive or the call of Women's Liberation – my back was bending under the strain. I went to the bookshop and bought *Modern Judgements – Selections of Critical Essays* (general editor P.N. Furbank) – *Swift*, edited by A. Norman Jeffares, 1968 – yes, 1968.

And here they were, Leavis on the irony of Swift, Kathleen M. Williams on Gulliver's voyage to the Houyhnhnms, W.E. Yeomans on the Houyhnhnm as Menippean Horse and – George Orwell. Didn't he write *Animal Farm*, *1984*, *Homage to Catalonia*, *The Road to Wigan Pier*? Yet here he was talking about 'Politics versus Literature – an examination of *Gulliver's Travels*'. How that phrase, 'Politics versus literature', resonated! Exactly. Would Orwell square the circle for me? Jeffares in his introduction tried to head me off at the pass:

> George Orwell's well-known article [is it well-known? I had no idea], which is now somewhat dated [oh dear, is it?] in its language and approach . . . is based on political assumptions of the 1930s and 1940s [aren't the other essays based on the political assumptions of their time too?] and has all Orwell's originality [that's ok then] – as well as distaste [oh dear] informing its criticism.

Even so, I read the essay. It's hard some 40 years later to recapture the mix of excitement and, I think, the sense of revelation I felt on reading this piece. In a matter of minutes I thought I was being released from the ritual of literary critical game-playing, the one I had learnt to play pretty well – and instead being given the licence to read *Gulliver's Travels* and talk about its ideas. Suddenly, a connection was made between the battle of ideas going on around us in 1968 and what I was studying. Eng Lit could be a place where there was a battle of ideas too.

If you don't know the essay, Orwell's broad thesis is this: in *Gulliver's Travels* Swift attacked or criticised humanity. But this attack came from what Orwell calls Swift's 'perverse Toryism'. This wasn't simply a party-political standpoint, but a cast of mind. So, for example, the book appears not only to attack crank science but all science or even intellectual curiosity itself. In its place, Swift seemed to Orwell to revere the past, especially classical antiquity, uniformity and, above all else, 'reason' – by which Orwell thinks Swift meant his own self-defined idea of 'common sense'.

In the opposition between the Yahoos and the Houyhnhnms, Orwell read a Swiftian contempt of humanity and a refusal of life as expressed through love, friendship, curiosity, fear and sorrow. Politically, says Orwell, this is either Swift's envy of those who can and do enjoy life, or nihilism. In fact, the society that Swift appeared to be commending was in essence totalitarian, as it was uniform and conformist.

Following this analysis, there is a mini-essay on what we would now call literary theory: does the merit of art lie in the work itself, or in the appreciation it arouses? If you feel a book is pernicious, do you dishonestly try to prove that it is aesthetically feeble? Can you disassociate literary quality from subject matter? Is there a way in which the appeal of *Gulliver's Travels*' depiction of, say, the Yahoos is not that we agree with what is implied there about us, but that through an act of recognition we acknowledge that part of us is despicable? Though Swift totalises 'man' as filth, we can respond to this, says Orwell, whilst knowing or believing that human beings can be 'noble' and that life is worth living. So, Orwell asks, can a book be good even if it expresses a 'palpably false view of life'? He claims that the critics of his day believed that a book had to be 'progressive' to be good. He writes:

> This ignores the fact that throughout history a similar struggle between progress and reaction has been raging, and that the best books of any one age have always been written from several different viewpoints, some of them palpably more false than others.

Then, in his closing remarks, he says that all we should ask for in a writer is that he [*sic*] shall genuinely believe in what he is saying. This means that a good book can be written by a Catholic, Communist, Fascist, pacifist, anarchist, Liberal or Conservative, but one can't imagine a good book written by a spiritualist, a Buchmanite, or a member of the Ku Klux Klan. So what we ask of writers is talent and conviction. Swift, he says, did not possess wisdom; he did possess a 'terrible intensity of vision'. The durability of *Gulliver's Travels* goes to show that if the 'force of belief is behind it, a world-view, which only just passes the test of sanity, is sufficient to produce a great work of art.'

I should say here that this last sequence, what I've called the 'closing remarks', seems to me now a powerful mix of the vague and the unsustainable.

As it happens, I have a clear memory of not bothering with the whole of this mini-essay on literary theory. I had an essay to write. But I will return to the closing remarks in a moment.

What grabbed me much more was the notion that a writer has ideas, embodies them in stories, plays and poems and that it's possible to discern the ideas implied by literature and that these ideas can be attached to the author. In fact, it should be possible, following this notion, to deduce attitudes from a knowledge of the author or of the book. There is, I figured, some kind of direct channel between author and text, resulting in a text being a distillation of an author's attitudes, feelings and opinions. What a reader can do, then, is be an Orwell – discern through the conflicts, oppositions and outcomes of a text what these attitudes, feelings and opinions really are. This, I triumphantly felt, is what reading and criticism are about and for. In fact, in a matter of days, I set to work on what I had studied before – *Beowulf*, *King Lear* – and tried to apply the method. *Beowulf* – epic poem. A warrior culture produces a narrative that can comfort and sustain that warrior culture. Thus – key moment, when Beowulf's blood appears on the surface of the pool, at the bottom of which he is grappling in a life or death struggle with Grendel's mother. How do Beowulf's companions behave? They all leave, bar one. It is the one who stays, the one who is faithful and believes in the power of his leader, whose attitude is vindicated by the outcome of that episode in the story. So should we warriors behave! Stand by your leader till the very end! I couldn't make much headway with *Lear* until I found John Danby's *Doctrine of Nature* and felt I could crack that one too. *Lear* became less about old age, forgiveness and the like, and much more about a struggle between attitudes and values of an old order and a new one, highly local and relevant to England, London in the late 1500s, early 1600s.

So now, as I did before this evening, let's return to Orwell's essay and see if it has stood up to the years of theorising about how readers read, interpret and criticise literature. This is, of course, my own highly selective take on the matter.

One of the first moves that Orwell makes is that patrician gesture embodied by the word 'one', but also by 'the reader', and phrases like 'it is difficult not to feel', 'the assumption is', 'no doubt', 'evidently', 'one would expect', 'there is something in . . . ', 'of course no honest person claims that . . . ', 'even the child', 'something in us responds' and so on. This is the process by which critics write highly opinionated pieces but generalise these views into some kind of universal, omniscient reader. The very critique Orwell makes of Swift – that he totalises human beings – Orwell's own critical writing imitates. This to my mind is unsatisfactory. Orwell's writing here and elsewhere bristles with viewpoint, angle and position, and these are his own. He has no need to cloak them in a generalised persona who is supposedly as reasonable as he is. Nor does he need – if that's what the process is about – to recruit unseen millions to his standpoint in order to normalise it. The distinctiveness in a reader's reading is that it can be felt or articulated by a single person. Its generality lies in how it is constituted and constructed out of prevailing attitudes and conditions. In other words, the *Gulliver* essay is Orwell's, but Orwell's views are created out of such matters as his struggles with Soviet Communism, British chauvinism, the class system and so on. What he lacks is what the anthropologists call 'reflexivity', the ability to reveal or at least debate how what you say about a phenomenon has a lot to do (some would say, everything to do) with who you are and where you're coming from. Interestingly and delightfully though, Orwell anticipates this crucial aspect of the politics of response here:

> From what I have written it may have seemed that I am against Swift, and that my object is to refute him and even to belittle him. In a political and moral sense I am against him, so far as I understand him. Yet curiously enough he is one of the writers I admire with the least reserve, and *Gulliver's Travels* in particular is a book which it seems impossible for me to grow tired of. I read it first when I was eight – one day short of eight to be exact, for I stole and furtively read the copy which was to be given me next day on my eighth birthday – and I have certainly read it not less than half a dozen times since. Its fascination seems inexhaustible. If I had to make a list of six books which were to be preserved when all others were destroyed, I would certainly put *Gulliver's Travels* among them. This raises the question: what is the relationship between agreement with a writer's opinions and enjoyment of his work?

Sadly, for me, we don't hear more about the psycho-social outlook of the little George (the little Eric, I should say), nor how later on it resisted being incorporated into the British elite, or indeed if and how it clung to some of its attitudes. I would insist these days that reading *Gulliver* is not simply or only a matter of reading off its apparent or implied attitudes. Some kind of transaction or enmeshing takes place between text and the particular reader in question (realised, constituted and constructed, as I have said, from the prevailing attitudes and conditions of the day), and it is out of this transaction that conclusions, such as these by Orwell, are drawn. However, Orwell also anticipates here one of the basic concepts of modern criticism: the 'implied author' and indeed the 'implied reader'.

That said, when Orwell approaches one of the paradoxes of the reading process, he gives me, reading the essay today, a crucial insight: why, he asks, is it that we (OK, there's the generalised 'we') don't mind being called Yahoos, though firmly convinced that we are not Yahoos.

The answer Orwell comes up with is that we are not (my phrase) unitary beings. We are capable of occupying contradictory positions, of having mutually incompatible ideas and feelings. Writing can exclusively express the one side of a matter without us necessarily believing in or accepting that this is the way life really is. Orwell's idea here hands a good deal of autonomy over to the reader. It allows for the possibility that readers read resistantly; that just because a text appears to be saying this or that, it doesn't necessarily mean that it has the effect it appears to be seeking. Some or indeed all of us are capable of saying to ourselves, 'No it's not like that – I don't agree – I don't believe that,' while still wanting to read on, still deriving pleasure from the process. Pleasure, of course, as Orwell makes very clear, may not necessarily be about enjoying what we say we enjoy – it may well be the enjoyment of feeling disgusted. This is clearly expressed (perhaps disguised by projecting it onto children) when he writes:

> A child, when it is past the infantile stage but still looking at the world with fresh eyes, is moved by horror almost as often as by wonder – horror of snot and spittle, of the dogs' excrement on the pavement, the dying toad full of maggots, the sweaty smell of grown-ups, the hideousness of old men, with their bald heads and bulbous noses.

(Incidentally here, it's not always clear in that little passage whether Orwell is talking about a generalised child's view of things, or his own!)

However, Orwell also anticipates another notion of contradiction when he pursues his idea of what the Houyhnhnms and Yahoos represent. Orwell suggests that:

> . . . Swift's greatest contribution to political thought in the narrower sense of the words is his attack . . . on what would now be called totalitarianism. He has an extraordinarily clear prevision of the spy-

haunted 'police State', with its endless heresy-hunts and treason trials, all really designed to neutralize popular discontent by changing it into war hysteria.

However, when Swift turns to the society of the Houyhnhnms – which in Orwell's view is Swift's ideal – what do they exemplify? Ask Orwell, but a form of totalitarianism? Now, this process of spotting the opposition towards one position at one moment in a book and then the apparent celebration of that same position at another moment has been described as uncovering a text's political unconscious. It's a role that several critics have assigned themselves as a way, I think, of escaping the individualised, personalised trap of making the disembodied self of a reader king of the text, making the text's meanings subject to the king's personal biography – you know the sort of thing: 'I love Juliet because I'm glad she wants to find out if Romeo really loves her before sleeping with him.' Instead, uncovering the political unconscious is a way of incorporating and mixing the politics of the text, the politics of its epoch, the politics of the author, and indeed the politics of the critic.

Problem solved.

But not so fast.

Let's return to those silly old critics and their fetishised games, the essays I used to write, the exams I passed.

What if the Houyhnhnms were not Swift's ideal after all? What if Swift savages the world, then presents the ideal, only to demolish that ideal too? Or maybe we don't even have to commit ourselves that far – but simply hold in our head the possibility that this is the case. Or, and I'll give this a special emphasis if I may, what if we listen to how we feel about the Houyhnhnms, and allow these feelings to be part of the meaning we derive?

Let's take these in turn.

You'll remember that I read Orwell's essay in a collection of essays. Suffice it to say that in 1968 I didn't bother with the other stuff. I was probably more keen to get on and listen to Aretha Franklin. Orwell, it seemed to me, was in tune with 1968 and that was enough for me. However, being a little, but not much, more patient these days, I've read the following two essays in the book. The one by Kathleen M. Williams puts up an extremely good argument for suggesting that Swift presented the Houyhnhnms as a false ideal, and counterposed moments of kindness in the book that show the Houyhnhnms' adherence to reason to be unattainable and unsatisfactory. Meanwhile, W.E. Yeomans anticipates yet another school of modern literary theory when he reads *Gulliver's Travels* in what we would now call its intertextual space – or at least one aspect of it: namely, in this case, its place in the tradition of a particular kind of satire. Informed by this, it's possible to see, says Yeomans, that the Houyhnhnms and the Yahoos are polar, satiric types characteristic of burlesque. Orwell's uncovering of Swift's political unconscious comes crashing to the ground. He has not then uncovered Swift's contradiction.

Perhaps. But maybe the theory of trying to do it has its value. It's just that Orwell didn't get it right in this case.

Meanwhile, what about feeling? What about the visceral, perhaps naïve response that says, 'I like Juliet, I hate her dad.'? Or, 'I don't like either the Houyhnhnms or the Yahoos.'? Though these responses are, I would argue, one of the reasons why so many of us like reading, criticism finds it very difficult to accommodate them. When I'm working with young, inexperienced readers, I try to ask questions that I don't know the answers to. I try to make these ones that help the reader connect what they know about life and what they know about other texts with whatever it is we are reading. Does what you've just read remind you of anything that has ever happened to you or anybody you know? Does this text remind you of anything you've ever read or seen somewhere else? Cunningly disguised here (if I may say so) are links to intertextuality, structuralism and, if you want go that far, social and psychoanalytical analyses. Couple these with the making of a space in which we invite readers to quiz characters, beings, or even objects in a text, or indeed quiz the author, and we have the possibility of raising many of the questions that are customarily delivered up as notes, lectures and hand-me-down pedagogic points. Even the possibility, which Orwell found so hard to understand, that a text has some autonomy from its author and is not identical with him or her, can easily emerge out of such discussions. Perhaps, for example, when you quiz the author (someone in the class is usually keen to give it a go), the author doesn't know why he or she wrote this or that!

My general point here is that it is approaches like this, democratic in spirit, which seem to me to be most suited to the literary impulse, and most in tune with the reasons why we read fiction and poetry, watch plays and films, in the first place. At first glance, this may appear to be a question of the politics of the classroom, but I'd claim more. How we learn to read, and how we learn to discuss and criticise literature, are part of how and why we respond to it in the way we do. So I'd like to suggest that the politics of the literature-reading classroom, right from three- and four-year-olds, through to university, is indeed part of the politics of response. It's my view that our response at this time is controlled far too closely by government. Look closely at the curriculum and strategies for primary and secondary schools, and you'll see specific methods of literary response laid down and enforced by means of inspections, tests, exams and selection processes. These methods turn again and again on the matter of teachers asking questions that they already know the answers to, and, what's more, these questions are not much more than watered-down versions of the very processes I was encouraged to write about at university.

What's even more – I could go on – it is now quite possible, easy and likely for a child to read a whole text, a whole book in school for the last time at the age of eight. From then on, literature is in many schools, in many areas, reduced to passages, extracts and worksheets, where the purpose of the passage is that it provides a context for a school student to answer questions of supposed fact about the passage concerned – questions of trainspotting metaphors or proving why this or that technique is 'effective'. (Strangely, never 'ineffective'!) Meanwhile, we have government (the opposition agrees) deciding that every single child in every single classroom will learn how to read following a particular method of sounding out letters and combinations of letters. This will cost millions. However, nowhere near the same effort or money will be put into getting books into children's and school students' or their parents' hands so that they can get to feel why reading might be worth doing. How mysterious.

In the context of this discussion today, I see all this as anti-literary. It flies in the face of general public statements about the value of reading. It flies in the face of the democratic circulation and open-ended discussion of books. And indeed it flies in the face of the kinds of intellectual struggle over how we criticise books that we see Orwell conducting in his essay on *Gulliver's Travels*.

So, I'd like to say, 'Thank you, George. You were the bridge over which I crossed to help me make a particular kind of sense of literature in a particular time.'

George W. Bush told us that maybe Iraq does resemble Vietnam. Putin deposed himself so that he could become King. South Africa's coal miners have been on strike. Sarkozy tries to fight both the public employees and the *immigrés* of the *banlieues*. Someone has just released a box set of rare and previously unissued Aretha Franklin tracks, and I'm reading and writing about *Gulliver's Travels*.

Re-reading Orwell's essay reminded me of one way in which all this fits together. Listen to the relish, fun and mischief of this:

> [Swift] denounces injustice and oppression, but he gives no evidence of liking democracy. In spite of his enormously greater power, his implied position is very similar to that of the innumerable silly-clever Conservatives of our own day – people like Sir Alan Herbert, Professor G.M. Young, Lord Elton, the Tory Reform Committee or the long line of Catholic apologists from W.H. Mallock onwards – [what did Orwell have against Catholics, exactly? No matter, he goes on:] people who specialize in cracking neat jokes at the expense of whatever is 'modern' and 'progressive', and whose opinions are often all the more extreme because they know that they cannot influence the actual drift of events.

Books of the past, when read now, connect with our lives in ways that could never have been predicted at the time of their appearance. Orwell shows us how we can, if we choose, enjoy outrageous anachronistic comparisons. And I would go further: I don't think we can ever wholly escape from them. They are what we respond with. Some of us have known Penelopes who've waited for their Odysseuses and some who didn't. And even if they're not 'bent double like old beggars under sacks', I, for one, watch the TV and think that '*Dulce et decorum est pro patria mori*' still is an 'old lie'.

The extracts cited above come from George Orwell, 'Politics vs. Literature: an examination of Gulliver's Travels' (1950), as it appeared in Swift (Modern Judgements), edited by A. Norman Jeffares, London: Macmillan (1968), pp. 192-209.

Exhibiting 'Guernica' 1939-2009: Contexts and Issues

This is the introduction I gave at the symposium I organised for the Whitechapel Gallery on 10 September 2009.

I'm Michael Rosen. I'm a writer – mostly but not entirely – of children's books. I'm also a broadcaster – mostly but not entirely – of radio programmes. I'm standing in front of you for a variety of reasons and the best way to explain that is to tell some stories. So I would like to begin by putting you in the picture as to how this symposium came about, before explaining how and why we've arranged the day.

My wife and I put up ideas for radio programmes, and so both of us sometimes follow our noses looking up this and that on the internet. Some of you will have seen on the way in a blue plaque on the wall outside for the poet and painter Isaac Rosenberg. He and a group of painters who came to be known as the Whitechapel Boys are celebrated upstairs in a gallery all of their own. A year or so ago, I reviewed a new biography of Rosenberg for BBC Radio 3's *Nightwaves* and I became interested in the Whitechapel Boys, perhaps as a subject for a longer study on radio.

I've known of this gallery and what used to be the library next door because my father used to speak of it as his university. He was brought up not far from here, living from 1922 until about 1940 in Nelson Street off New Road, behind the London Hospital, in the house his mother, grandmother and great-grandmother had occupied since the 1890s.

So there I was idly looking up things to do with the gallery, when I came across the story that the Whitechapel Gallery had exhibited Picasso's 'Guernica' just over 70 years ago, and that this was done as one of the ways in which people in this part of London were raising awareness of and funds for the Republican side in the Spanish Civil War. This was the last time the painting has been shown in London, and apart from a brief show in Manchester, following straight after Whitechapel, the painting has never been seen in this country since.

So, we started to form the idea of a radio programme that would, we thought, bring together various strands and ask several questions. How did the Whitechapel get the painting? Who organised the exhibition? Who came? What was going on in Whitechapel and the nearby East End of

London leading up to the exhibition?

Now, some of this I knew even before I knew it. I'll explain.

I was brought up in Pinner, in the London suburbs, by a father and mother whose entire childhoods, adolescence and early adulthood had been wrapped up in an intense, personal, social, cultural and political way of life that has come to be known as the Jewish East End. This place and time was for my brother and me a mythic territory. By the time I was, say, 10, in 1956, it had pretty well gone. What's more, it was a territory my parents had left behind and yet constantly referred to, and whatever they said about it, it didn't resemble anything like our life in Pinner. So whether it was in their speech – which would revert to a London Yiddish – or in the stories about, say, horses falling over on the ice outside the brewery, giving away bread to strangers at the beginning of *Pesach* (that's Passover), about visits to the Lane (that's Petticoat Lane or Middlesex Street); or the political stories about defending themselves against Oswald Mosley and the British Union of Fascists, organising support for the Republicans in the Spanish Civil War, or supporting the huge rent strikes that went on in the buildings around this gallery – all this was part of this mythic territory. Mythic for me, real for them but gone.

Much, much later, my father wrote about these things in a book called *Troublesome Boy*, which he updated for his book *Are You Still Circumcised?*. And several times I ended up interviewing him on radio and on TV for *The Culture Show*, when we sat here in the empty library and he talked about what this library meant to him and how he was brought here by his mother and he borrowed a book about whales, and later when he was in his teens he said he would meet people from all over the world, some, like Russian seamen, passing through, others being people from all over Russia and Eastern Europe who had come to live here.

In all these conversations, informal and formal, he had never mentioned the painting of 'Guernica'. As I combed the internet – me living not far from here in Hackney, and he now in Muswell Hill, and very frail from a major operation – I kept discovering new things that could or would go in a radio programme if we succeeded in selling it. There was a quote online from the Spanish Civil War veteran and trade-union leader Jack Jones about the 'Guernica' exhibition. He was originally from Liverpool but lived in Bethnal Green at that time, not far from here, like my mother. He told a story that visitors to the exhibition were encouraged to bring shoes or boots and the solidarity committee would send the shoes and boots out to refugees in Spain. So soon, sitting on the floor of the exhibition, somewhere very near to us now, was a huge pile of boots, which in themselves became something that people came to look at. What extraordinary echoes that has – forward first to the terrible detritus of the Holocaust that speak so silently and awfully of what happened there, but also much less gravely to the kinds of exhibition and installation that we've become used to in the last decade: heaps and piles of objects speaking of randomness or multiplicities where usually there are only singles.

Then, it quickly became clear that 'Guernica' got here as a result of something to do with Picasso's friend and biographer Roland Penrose, and something to do with the local Trades Council. I couldn't piece together exactly how this had happened. I couldn't find out exactly who sat on that Trades Council. For those of you unfamiliar with the trade-union movement, Trades Councils emerged out of the syndicalist movement on either side of the First World War. They were given a formal constitution by the Trades Union Congress, whereby representatives of trade unions in a locality could meet together and discuss matters of mutual benefit to those unions and their members. Their finest hour came, perhaps, in the General Strike of 1926, when it was the Trades Councils that did more than anyone else to sustain the strike and indeed to begin to organise beyond trade-union questions of wages and conditions, on to questions like alternative food distribution.

In the period of the 1930s the local Trades Council, I guessed, would have tried to organise defence against Oswald Mosley and of course solidarity with Spain. But did someone on that Council know Roland Penrose? When the painting first came to London, it was shown at the Burlington Gallery in the West End. So was it always due to come here, or did Penrose and the Trades Council seize the time and get it shown here as a second thought?

Meanwhile, there were the three big stories I've already mentioned that would need telling in such a programme: the anti-fascist action – in particular the Battle of Cable Street in 1936 when hundreds of thousands of East Enders fought with police to prevent the provocation of Oswald Mosley and his blackshirts marching through Gardiners Corner out there and along Cable Street, which was at that time an almost 100% Jewish area; there were all the different kinds of solidarity work for Spain – my mother had talked of what it felt like to go all round the tenement buildings knocking on people's doors asking for pennies for Spain; and again the rent strikes – one of the most brilliant pieces of action ever organised.

I'll explain: Oswald Mosley's argument, if I can call it that, was that the working class was being cheated by Jewish landlords. Now, there were two major flaws with this racist argument: one, that not all landlords were Jews, and two, that most of the tenants round here were also Jews. But the housing conditions were awful. This was multi-occupancy and overcrowding at its worst. My father lived in a two-up, two-down house and for something like twenty years there were twelve people living in that house – one outside toilet, no bathroom. My mother talked of bedbugs, TB and pneumonia. Most of the buildings round here had been put up in the mid-nineteenth century and hadn't been touched since. A rent strike was an act of emancipation and liberation. It was a demand for a better life. And it cut right through the divisive racism of Mosley and his fascists. As I read about this, I found that one of the rent-strike leaders and activists was someone my mother was at school with, Bertha Sokoloff. Had my mother, who died in 1976, ever mentioned Bertha in that light? I didn't think so. My friend Chris, whose mother and father were at school with my mother and father, said that Bertha was living in north-west London, not far from where I was brought up.

So, as you can see, we were piecing together the elements of a radio programme. I came to the gallery and spoke with Nayia, who you'll hear from later, who showed me documents from the archive. I found a historian, now living in Canada – invited today but sadly couldn't make it – whose PhD and later book studied various aspects of the upheavals going on in the East End. He had wanted to work out the relative importance of three aspects of these struggles: the effect of the Communist Party, the effect of this having been a largely Jewish community, and the effect of the rent strike having been largely organised by women.

Then again, I started to ask some questions about Picasso and the painting. He is not only the giant of twentieth-century art who invents and reinvents himself and art several times over. For the left, and for Communists in particular, he was their guy. Or in my parents' view of things, he was 'ours'. As it happens, we didn't have his paintings up on our walls, but they were certainly up in the homes of virtually all the Communist families that I knew as a child. But wasn't there something incongruous here, something contradictory? Many people here will know that in 1936 explicit guidelines were laid down from the Soviet Union about socialist realism, not to be confused with social realism. Socialist realism would be an art, in all forms – music, painting, sculpture, literature and so on – which would express something optimistic and triumphant about the working class in its struggle to make and build a new and better world. This art would show workers as heroes working in factories and fields, overcoming the old order, or beating off enemies of the new. And artists were under strict instructions to produce art of this kind. (You may know the bitter joke that came out of the Soviet Union against this kind of art: 'Impressionism is what you see. Surrealism is what you think. Expressionism is what you feel. Socialist realism is what you hear.') And part of this move to socialist realism was the appearance of a set of critics who got to work attacking other art movements for being variously too individualistic, nihilist, pessimist, anti-social and the like. The experiments of modernism which had given birth to such forms of art as cubism, fauvism, futurism and surrealism, say, were frowned on. How did they serve the working class? Their problem was that they either explored the minutiae of the psyches of the individual painter, or they gave the working class confusing and confused messages where reality was broken into meaningless fragments. And yet somehow, this great weight of opprobrium could exist side by side with a sanctifying of Picasso, of all people, of whom we can almost say that he invented modernism. How did that shake out?

So, we packaged all this up as an offer to Radio 3 and we were delighted to hear that they were interested. It occurred to me that even though my father was very ill, I should tell him about all this in one of our conversations, often interrupted by pain and nursing. In a sense I owed it to him, because if it wasn't for him and my mother, I probably wouldn't have been following up this whole story anyway. I think he was in hospital and coming in and out of an opiates haze when I asked him if by chance he had actually seen 'Guernica' when it was exhibited here.

'Oh yes,' he said straight away. 'I went with Moishe.' Moishe being the old school friend I mentioned earlier.

I thought, why didn't we have this conversation years ago? Or indeed ever?

'Yes, I remember,' he said, 'walking down the stairs from the library with him and into the gallery. It wasn't just the painting. There were some other drawings or paintings showing how he had done the painting.'

I told him what I had found out and that I had put it in as an initial proposal for a radio programme. I think perhaps he thought he had done enough of that kind of talking with me and for me on the radio.

The message came back from the radio commissioners that we must make sure, when we put in the final proposal, to describe the political and social context for it all. We must explain how the bombing of Guernica actually happened. I filled in a lot of what you've just heard me say and off it went. A few months later we got the thumbs down. No, they wouldn't want the programme because, they said, they were doing some programmes on art and the Spanish Civil War anyway. So that was that, and few months later my father died.

I was determined – perhaps it was the death of my father that gave me that extra push – to do something about 'Guernica' at the Whitechapel. So, you're here today because there is no radio programme! We have something better, I think. And that's because the wonderful Whitechapel Gallery was more than keen for today to happen. I think we'll be going on quite a journey, taking in questions of politics, culture, painting, poetry and even the question of what galleries themselves are for. We'll be looking at that extraordinary time of the late 1930s in this locality, Picasso as a political painter, the response of this country, London and the East End to events in Spain. We have a fantastic range of speakers: historians, critics, and we are extremely lucky to have two speakers from that time who I'll mention now; my mother's friend Alice (one of 'the girls', as my mother used to call the group who went to Central Foundation School for Girls when it was in Spital Square) and, last talk today, Sam Lesser, International Brigader, journalist and writer. And we'll finish the day with one of my friend David Rosenberg's famous walks, strolling round the very places where the events I've described – and many others – took place, within earshot of this gallery.

We're hoping that you will participate where and when you can.

Trying to Catch the Moments

In November 2010 I gave the 23rd Helen E. Stubbs Memorial Lecture at the Osborne Collection of Early Children's Books in the Lillian H. Smith branch of Toronto Public Library.

This evening, I want to talk about poems; not all the kinds that I write, but one particular kind I write. But before I do, just a word about chronology, and time, because writers defy chronology in several ways. One way is that they collapse the past, present and future in what they write. You only have to think of someone like Marcel Proust or Henry James, and quite often as you're reading you may wonder actually in which particular time frame you're reading a particular paragraph or, as in the case of Marcel Proust, a particular sentence, and you're not quite sure whether you're in the past or the present, or perhaps you're not in any particular time at all. That's because writing is often a kind of reverie, and reverie doesn't necessarily have to obey the rules of time. And if you're a poet, you're even less compliant to the rules of time because you might not necessarily have a story to tell with one event following another. You might – or you might not.

And the other issue about chronology is that some of you here are librarians, and you're very interested in the chronology in which the strange human beings called writers produce stuff. I'll only speak for myself, but, in a strange sort of way, I'm not very interested in the chronology of what I write, because the poems (in particular the kind of poems that we're reading this evening) don't exist in the time frame of when I wrote them; they exist in a time frame of their own. The poem of the past can be very much about how I feel now, and the poem now can be historical. Anyway, it might take me ten years to write something, so who's to say that I wrote it in 1995 or in 2010? I may have been writing it all the time. So, time and the actual production of the poem might not be totally relevant. And so, when I read tonight, the poems will emerge in an order but it isn't an order that's bound in any way by any form of chronology. I'll be reading some poems that capture moments (plenty of my poems don't do that), so by the end of this evening I hope we'll have some sort of sense of – in a way we're investigating it together – the theory and practice of a particular kind of poetry writing.

Children often ask me, 'How did it begin?' Children are quite interested in that idea – how did your writing begin? – when, where and how? – and their questions are in fact one of the ways in which I write, because children ask me questions and I think, 'I'll have to write about that.' So, quite often a poem will start as an oral answer.

> There was a competition in the paper: Write a
> Story, and the best story would be printed.
> I thought I might go for it. I started thinking about
> *Solomon the Cat*, a book I'd read at school,
> about how Solomon gets thrown out and goes
> from house to house, asking for somewhere to be
> put up. I thought, 'I could write a story like that.'
> I called it 'Solomon the Cat'. And I wrote how
> Solomon gets thrown out and goes from house
> to house, asking for somewhere to be put up. I
> sent it in, and I won the competition, and it was
> printed in the paper: 'Solomon the Cat' by Michael
> Rosen, aged 7. It got printed in the paper's Christmas
> annual, too: 'Solomon the Cat' by Michael Rosen,
> aged 7. Some time later, we got a letter from the
> paper saying that they'd heard from someone who said
> they'd bought a picture book about a cat called
> Solomon who gets thrown out and goes from house
> to house, asking for somewhere to be put up.

> 'See this, Con?' my father says to my mother, 'Someone's
> stolen Michael's story and made a book out of it. Would
> you believe it? The things people do! If I had the
> time, I'd try to get a hold of that book, and sue
> the pants off them.'

> 'No, no,' I said, 'I shouldn't bother, it was ages ago.'

Not long ago I got a letter from a girl in America; she said she'd won a state poetry competition, judged by the poet John Ciardi. She'd won with the poem that went:

> Down behind the dustbin,
> I met a dog called Jim.

He didn't know me
and I didn't know him.

'You wrote that poem, Mr Rosen,' she said. 'What should I do? They want to print it in the paper.' And I said to her, 'Don't worry. I know someone who once wrote a story called "Solomon the Cat".' You know the rest.

So that was an answer to a question. Another question that I get asked a lot of the time, related to that, is: 'What is a poem, and why don't you write them? Because it would be nice if you did write poems.'

And I say, 'Well, you can call what I write anything you like.'

And I mean that quite genuinely, because the issue isn't what it's called, it's whether it's saying anything. So, whatever you decide it to be, judge it on those criteria.

I've often thrashed around and looked at the various definitions of poetry, and what people say poetry is, and you will know 'the best words in the best order' and things like that. You could see W.H. Auden struggling with it many years ago. He put his conclusion in quotes, whether he was quoting somebody else or just himself, when he wrote that poetry is 'memorable speech'. I remember feeling as if he'd constructed a room for me to be in and it felt like a warm and nice place to be. I thought, 'Yes, isn't that what I'm trying to do? Write memorable speech?' But then in a way that just asks another question: what makes it memorable? And anyway, you can't really say all poetry is 'memorable speech', because some are 'concrete' poems, they look like a car crashing, or the word 'apple' is written many times to make the shape of an apple. (Actually, the apple poem I am thinking of is in German so it says 'apfel'!)

Anyhow, I thought, 'What does make poetry memorable?' and of course the one feature of poetry that we're familiar with in the western tradition is rhyme, and, nearly as familiar, rhythm, which sometimes – but not always – go together.

This is something that I can think we can ask children to help us answer. Recently I've been working with children in terms of response to poetry. One thing that really makes me quite angry and tired and fed up is when I go into schools and I see a poem and there's a worksheet attached to the poem which asks questions that either the worksheet-setter, whoever this strange human being is (who are they, do we know?), or this implied examiner-person who hovers over the worksheet, has compiled. It's full of questions that this implied examiner knows the answers to. If you're a child, or one like I was when I was a kid, you're inclined to think, 'Well, if you know the answer, then why are you asking me the question?'

It seems to me that the only questions that are worth asking about poems are the ones that you don't know the answers to. That way, at least we all start off on equal footing. It doesn't matter if you're ninety-three or three or ten, whatever you're going to say in answer to that question (the one that whoever is asking doesn't know the answer to), we'll all be in an equal position. I think that's our job, really: to think of questions about poems we don't know the answers to. I think that one question we can ask is, 'Does this poem, or anything in this poem, remind you of anything that's ever happened to you?' So, there's a question you can't know the answer to. The person might say, 'Having a haircut,' or 'When my cat died.' And they'll both be right.

Or you could say, 'Is there anything in this poem that reminds you of anything that you've ever read, or seen on TV, or seen in a film?' And, if you like, there's a theory behind that as well, which is: what we're talking about here is the children's 'intertext', the texts in their lives. And that's partly what we respond with. Yes, as with my first question, we respond with our experience (the things that happen to us) but also with the text that we've come across. Again, it doesn't matter whether you're three or ninety-three, you have a textual repertoire, and that's what you, in part, respond with. In fact, there's an argument for saying that some or even all our experience is 'textualised', that is, made into texts in our heads as we think, or at the moment of our describing them, but we can leave that to one side here.

Then in this matter of exploring poems with children, trying to find out what's 'memorable' about them, we can say to ourselves, 'Instead of us asking children questions about the poem, why not turn it round the other way and say to the children, or students, "Have you got any questions you would like to ask anybody in the poem, or indeed anything in the poem?"' There might be a tree in a poem and you could ask the tree a question. So then, as teacher or workshop leader, you can group together the children's questions and then say, 'Is there anyone in the room who would like to answer any of those questions?' So, by now, you've dealt with experience, you've dealt with intertext, you're now dealing with puzzles from queries and coming up with answers. But even so, there is still something in the back of my mind that I'm not quite engaging with here: I'm not engaging with what's 'memorable' about the language of poetry or its shape or sound. Quite independently of this work with poetry in schools, I've done a radio programme (*Word of Mouth* on BBC Radio 4 in the UK) where we've looked at the notion of 'cohesion', or how texts 'stick together'. If I say to you, 'A man walked in. He had a funny hat on.', those two sentences are 'stuck together'. They're stuck together with the pronoun 'he'. If I just say to you the single sentence, 'He had a funny hat on.', you're likely to ask, 'Who?' because I hadn't said that sentence before it.

So, that's what sticks it together – in this case a pronoun that refers back to what came before it, sticking the second sentence to the first, giving 'cohesion' to that particular text. And there are many ways in which language sticks together, even just within one sentence. If I say, 'The cat sat on the mat,' that would be different from me saying in English, 'The mat sat on the cat.' I've reversed, changed, the subject of the sentence. In languages (like Latin) where subjects and objects and indirect objects of sentences are marked by their endings, the order in which 'cat' and 'mat' came in the sentence wouldn't matter so much. So, in English, the order of the sentence is again how words stick together and make meanings for us.

Thus, the words we speak or write don't just bob about, like the balls in the lottery bottle, where the guy who calls the numbers pulls the random moving balls out of the bottle. Words stick together. So I found myself asking, 'Is poetry a specialised form of cohesion?' Well, there are things that we do in poems, no matter how 'free' the verse and apparently not poetic-like, which maybe we don't do very much elsewhere. So that's a question I've taken to asking myself and children in order to find out what's 'memorable' about poetry. If I look at the first poem I've read to you, one of the things that I do there (I know it sounds as though I'm a critic of my own poetry, but that's the pain of having been a student all my life, really) is repeat myself. And, by and large in speech, we do some of that, we do repeat ourselves, but usually we do that in speech because we think somebody isn't listening. We do it a lot. We might say, 'Did you go out?' Then, if we don't get an immediate answer, we might say, 'Oh, right, well, did you go out?' But there's a slightly different kind of repetition that goes on in poetry that is very deliberate. And, if it's written, it can't know if someone's listening or not. So, I'll make that, if you like, my first observation for this evening. Repetition is one of the ways in which we make poetry 'memorable'.

There is some kind of repetition and pattern going on here too:

We sit down to eat and the potato's a bit hot
So I only put a bit on my fork
And I blow
Phooph phooph

Until it's cool
Just cool
Into the mouth
Choop
Lip-smack
Nice!

My brother's doing the same
Phooph phooph
Until it's cool
Just cool
Into the mouth
Cccchoop
Lip-smack
Nice!

And my mother's doing the same
Phooph phooph
Until it's cool
Just cool
Into the mouth
Cccchoop
Lip-smack
Nice!

But my dad.
My dad!
What does he do?
He stuffs a great big bit of potato
Into his mouth.
And that really does it.
His eyes pop out, he flaps his hands,
He blows, he puffs, he yells
He bobs his head up and down
He spits bits of potato onto the plate
And he turns to us and he goes,
'Watch out everyone.
The potato's really hot.'

Usually when I introduce that poem to children, I say, 'I had a terrible moment when I was young. It was when I discovered that my dad . . . ' – and I leave a long pause, and you can see the whole room thinking, 'What is he going to say? He ran off with the woman next door? What is he going to say?' And then I go, 'When I found out that my dad does not know everything.' And then I read that poem. And I think sometimes that the job of a poet when we appear in schools – and I got this line from the folksinger Ewan MacColl, who I worked with for a while – is that you have to 'warm the room' for the event that is just about to happen; the room changes, and when the room is changed, there is a right moment for saying the poem. The job for a performer of poems is to do that. It might be the previous poem; it might be that you stroll up and down or jump up and down, or that you tell a joke, but the thing that precedes the poem is important for the meaning of it. Many of us who came through the '50s and '60s education in 'practical criticism' led by I. A. Richards and the so-called 'new criticism' of Cleanth Brooks and others were taught that everything about the meaning of a poem was solely in the poem itself on the page. The idea was that you just looked at the written poem. Now, many of us have found that the more and more that we look at the ways in which all of us, adults and children, respond to poems and to literature, the meaning is also about the 'reading situation', the reading person, and it is these situations and these particular people which combine to make the meaning. So I'm very interested in the moment in performance where you can see some meaning being made, even before I've read the poem. I'm always intrigued by myself asking that question about my dad and the fact that the 'moment' with the hot potato was when I discovered that he didn't know everything. A truly disturbing moment.

Also, you never quite know what starts off a poem. In Britain many years ago, we used to have a Conservative government, led by someone you've not heard of called Margaret Thatcher. Then we got a Labour government which of course was fundamentally different. And then we got what we've got now, which is a Conservative-LibDem coalition which of course is a 'brand new politics', and that's also completely different . . . So we've experienced these massive 'differences'. Anyway, in the days when there was a Conservative government, every now and then, in the way Conservative politicians do, they used to offer us advice on how to run our lives because obviously they were so good at running their own. On one occasion, one of them announced, whilst having an affair, 'The trouble with parents today is that they don't teach their children the difference between right and wrong.' I thought, now there's a really useful piece of advice, because obviously none of us does that, do we? But then I thought, 'Did my parents teach me the difference between right and wrong?' Now my parents were what Hitler lovingly called 'Jewish Communists'. They were parents as well. I thought, 'Did my Jewish Communist parents teach me the difference between right and wrong?' And I found myself doing what I often do – and this is also about capturing the moment – thinking back . . . I should really think of a metaphor for this 'thinking back': what is it that I do? Do I run videos in my head? Roald Dahl describes going into his little hut and becoming seven and eight again, and being able to do it with an intensity which I suspect in his case hurt; bad things happened in his life. I can only think of it in that film-making, video-running way, that something seems to run on the retina which I can watch. So, off the back of this statement about parents and right and wrong, my own parents, this is what came out:

The Torch

I nagged my mum and dad for a torch.
'Oh go on. I'd love a torch.
One of those ones with black rubber round them.
Go on. Pleeeeeeese.'
It was no good. I wasn't getting anywhere.

Then came my birthday.
On the table was a big box
in the box
a torch.
My dad took it out of the box.
'You see that torch,' he says,
'it's waterproof.
That is a waterproof torch.'

Waterproof. Wow!

So that night I got into the bath
and went underwater swimming with it.
Breathe in,
under the water,
switch on

search for shipwrecks
and treasure.
Up, breathe
under again
exploring the ocean floor.

Then the torch went out.

I shook it and banged it but it wouldn't go.
I couldn't get it to go again.
My birthday torch.
So I got out, dried myself off
put on my pyjamas and went into the kitchen.

'The – er – torch won't work. It's broken.'
And my dad says,
'What do you mean, "it's broken"?
It couldn't have just broken.
How did it break?'
'I dunno, it just went off.'

'I don't believe it. You ask him a simple question
and you never get a simple answer.
You must have been
doing something with it.'
'No. It just went off.'
'Just try telling the truth, will you?
How
did
it
break?'
'I was underwater swimming with it.'
'Are you mad?
When I said this torch is waterproof
I meant it keeps the rain off.
I didn't mean you could go deep-sea diving with it.
Ruined. Completely ruined.
For weeks and weeks he nags us stupid that he wants

one of these waterproof torches
and then first thing he does is wreck it.
How long did it last?
Two minutes? Three minutes?
These things cost money, you know.
Money.'

I felt so rotten.
My birthday torch.

At the weekend, he says,
'We're going into Harrow to take the torch back.'

We walk into the shop,
my dad goes up to the man at the counter
and says,
'You see this torch.
I bought it from you a couple of weeks ago.
It's broken.'

So the man picks it up.
'It couldn't have just broken,' says the man,
'how did it break?'
And my dad says,
'I dunno, it just went off.'
'Surely you must have been doing something
with it.'
'No, no, no,' says my dad,
'it just went off.'
'Come on,' says the man, 'these torches don't just break
down.'
So I said, 'Well, actually, I was in the –'
and I got a hard kick on the ankle from my dad.
'I was in the, you know, er kitchen and it went off.'

So the man said he would take it out the back
to show Len.
He came back in a few minutes and said that Len

couldn't get it to work either.
'You'll have to have a new one,' he says.
'I should think so too,' says my dad.
'Thank YOU.'

Outside the shop
my dad says to me,
'What's the matter with you?
Are you crazy?
You were going to tell him all about your underwater
swimming fandango, weren't you?
Blabbermouth!'

So, anyway, that's how I learned the difference between right and wrong from my dad.

They always say about children's literature that there's a core morality to it – that somewhere in our world there's some kind of restitution or redemption and some resolution that you end up with in a real or metaphorical home. No, I don't find it in that poem . . . I keep looking but I never quite find it in there . . .

I've written a book called *Michael Rosen's Big Book of Bad Things*. It's called that because I used to imagine that my dad kept some kind of record of all the bad things that I've ever done, as he was very good at reminding me and my brother of past bad things. As I always tell children, he had a favourite bad thing to remind us of – well, me in particular – which always used to come in a formula, a little oral formula (and oral formulae are aspects of poetry I think which indeed we haven't paid quite enough attention to, particularly in literary criticism of modern texts). A long time ago, someone (Milman Parry) looked at *The Odyssey* and noticed that a lot of phrases kept happening again and again. He and his student, Albert Lord, went on looking and did what was in effect a count. This was in the 1930s, before computers, and the poor chaps just had to keep columns, and every time they came across something like 'big-bellied vessel' they would make a little tick, making five-bar gates, until in the end he found that virtually the whole of *The Odyssey* produced five-bar gates. So, they came up with this phrase 'oral formulae'. Since this incredibly inventive discovery (!), people have been looking at all kinds of folk literature or epic literature with the same attention, and found that it possibly applies to many other forms of literature. Some of you know that the great French critic Roland Barthes got to the point in Balzac's novel *Sarrasine*, where somebody says, 'I love you,' and he said, 'It's already written,' (*déjà écrit*). This has become a famous phrase, making the case that when we write, we write things that have already been written. When I think about my parents, and you've heard they were not only academics, but that they were also great storytellers and singers: my dad had a way of repeating things, particularly as it happens in this case repeating the accounts of the various bad things I had done. One of the bad things he would remind me of went like this:

'Oh yes,'– (I don't know why it always began with that; I don't know who he was talking to with that 'oh yes' – some inner voice, perhaps?) – 'Oh yes . . . like the time you threw your mother's best ring out of the window. It was her grandmother's.'

Well, that's how I tell it the first time, but actually there are two modifications to it. One is that when I say 'window' I have to point out that we did live in a flat, so when it went out the window, it landed in the street, because we lived in a flat over a shop. The other thing is that I used the word 'grandmother' there. The word 'grandmother' didn't pass my father's lips. My father was brought up in a house that mostly spoke Yiddish, the language of Eastern European Jews. He never said the English word. In Britain we called her 'Bubbe', and the grandfather was 'Zeyde'. And so the full phrase goes:

'Oh yes. Like the time you threw your mother's best ring out of the window. It was her Bubbe's.'

For those of you who live in families where people speak two or three languages, when you hop between languages, I think you open another room. So there's the English room which plods along, and suddenly there's this Yiddish room, and, as I say to children, it feels as if it goes back hundreds of years. It's not just one Bubbe that comes out – there are hundreds of them. And all these other Bubbes come out and stand round me saying, 'So, you threw your mother's best ring out the window? And it was her . . . Bubbe's?'

So anyway, I share that little point with children in this book until it reaches an awkward climax when I've been discovered sticking the top of the toothpaste into my father's shaving soap. I then think about it out loud for children, that perhaps this is why I ended up being a writer, because my dad was, in effect, busy making a kind of oral book containing some kinds of oral formulae. I could see, even as a child, that there was something about recording the events of how we lived (even if it was ticking me off) – that there was some way that you could hold all this together. But if you just held it orally, it was harder to hold together because it escaped, so why not write things down as they happened?

My three year-old says to us, 'Put your hand up if you want to be a sandwich.' I put my hand up. 'Good,' he says, 'now I'll eat you.'

That's all there is to it; it doesn't go further.

One of the things I've had to struggle with in writing – and of course you can never predict what happens to you in your life, and a writer is no different from any other human being in this respect – was that my son Eddie died. Eddie was someone I had already written about; I had tried to capture many moments in his extraordinary life, because he was a very funny and clever little chap when he was three and four. Then he went and died on me. I was quite angry about that. I couldn't write about it at all, and didn't want to write about it. I was annoyed that I would even think of writing about it and, as you can see, I got myself into quite a tangle. Until one day I was at the Edinburgh Book Festival, and a child who'd read *Quick, Let's Get Out of Here*, which has some poems about Eddie in, said, 'What's Eddie doing now?' And, there's nothing you can say other than the absolute stark truth on occasions like that. You can't say, 'I'd rather not say,' when there are 400 people sitting there who've just been rolling around laughing. So you just have to say, 'He died.' And it's quite interesting, because in a roomful of children and adults you'll see the adults thinking, 'Oh no, why did that child ask that?' and there's a sense of oh-no-ness going on in the room. But the children don't seem to react at all. It's quite extraordinary. And straight after my answer there's another kid still with his hand up, and he's saying, 'Can you do your one about where you're not breathing in class?' I thought about this, that I'm always reluctant to find differences between children and grown-ups, there really does seem to be such an overlap, that it's not very convenient or sensible to think that there is much difference between us. But I certainly noticed this moment and I thought, 'I ought to answer that question . . . more carefully.' So I wrote an answer to it, and the answer came out as the *Sad Book* and I imagined that child in Edinburgh, and answering in a little bit more detail than 'he died'.

And so, I did write about it, and I thought, 'What I'll do is I'll just write down thoughts that happen,' and occasionally, perhaps, the dreams too. Of course, all of us have known somebody who's died and we dream about them, don't we? In the past, people have mixed the dream with the reality, or maybe they think that the dream is reality, I don't want to enter into the cosmology of it, but the dreams are very powerful. And when you wake up, you have been with that person. There are many stories, wonderful, traditional stories that deal with that. But I just tend to write things as 'Eddie dreams' or some such.

Eddie Dream

It was the one again:
and he's younger than he was
when he died,
but he's got something we both know is deadly
and I think he's had it before
and we're talking about
getting him better
and he's being strange,
old for his age,
but mucking about
and I'm letting him
because
I know that this may be
the last day he's alive
and he knows that I know
that this may be the last day
he's alive,
but neither of us says
that this may be the last day
he's alive.
and I notice he's wearing
the green woollen top
he wore when he was very young . . .

And now in daylight
and the dream is over
I realise I haven't thought of this top
for years.
My picture of it must have been stored away
in my head
without my knowing it was there.
But that's the least of it.
It's sitting on the edge of my bed

knowing that
he's not here
he'll never be here
and that moment in the dream
where I let him fool around
was about loving him being here.

One of the things about poems is that you quite often try to write the poem in the way that represents the way you were thinking, or the way the thing is. One word for it is onomatopoeia – when you say splash, it sounds like splash, and you're trying to imitate the sound of splash. There's another thing: if you say 'stream of consciousness', in a way you're trying to write in a way that resembles your inner speech. We don't actually know whether it is or isn't our inner speech, but that's what you're trying to do. If you're trying to write a poem about a waterfall, you might like to try to make it sound like the waterfall. And so on.

In that poem, I know that I wanted to try to be 'authentic'; I was going to try to be authentic to how the dream felt, in the way that I put the words together, and this is at the heart of this business of trying to be 'memorable'. One of the ways in which you write a particular kind of free-verse poem is that you try to get to the feel of how that feeling felt. You want to try and get to what it felt like having that feeling! And if you take the case of a dream, you want to try and write as if you were in the dream. So that's how that poem came about.

I was brought up in the London suburbs in the 1950s. I often think about that place in that time and ask myself, what was special about them? One of the things was – and this only occurred to me about a year ago – that the war had happened only just before. I wonder why it's taken me so long to get there, as I was born in 1946! So I didn't notice the war much, did I? (It ended in 1945, for those like me who've forgotten.) All those people of my childhood – those teachers and parents and shopkeepers and our parents' friends, they had lived through it, but we didn't know that. They were just people who were being strict or nervous, or anxious, or trying to run our lives in a particular way, but doing it all with the background experience of having been through the war, and before that, the Depression. I often think about all that and little fragments come to mind – many of these poems are fragments. This one's called '1954'.

The wonder of Baker Street Station:

arriving in a train
that's fitted with brass handles and plates
each with curly writing engraved on, saying
'Live in Metroland'
'Live in Metroland'
'Live in Metroland'.

The giant, electric notice boards
with the names of every station
in Metroland,
flashing on and off
electrically
electrically
electrically.

A black bomb
from the Second World War
with a hole in the side
for you to put your money in
for wounded soldiers.

A black bomb.

And a cinema
that shows cartoon films
all day.
In the station
All day.
In the station
All day.

The wonder of Baker Street station.

Anyone been to Baker Street Station? It's not quite as wonderful as that.
    Some people have said that poetry can be a form of journalism, that what
poets do is they go to places, write about it and come back. Or they go places,

come back, and then write about it. And they sometimes tell you about that. Wordsworth's poem, usually known as 'Daffodils', represents this: he went somewhere, he came back, he thought about it, he wrote about it, and he wrote about what he thought about thinking about it! And that's one of the jobs of poetry, which is to make the unfamiliar, familiar. So you go somewhere, let's say something happens like Eddie dying, which may be unfamiliar, and you try to write about it in a way that is possible for other people to understand, so you make it familiar.

The more common aspect of poetry that we've heard of is the opposite of that – 'de-familiarisation' – that is to say there are many familiar things about us, these lights, this room, this microphone, eating an apple, whatever . . . and the job of a poet is to de-familiarise it. To make the familiar, unfamiliar. And possibly, a poet can be doing both at the same time. I sometimes think that what I'm doing with very ordinary things is that: doing both.

The Lift

At the second floor
we heard a voice inside the lift say:
'Second Floor, going up.'
But the Second Floor
was the top floor.
Where were we going?

I treasure all sorts of things about when I was a kid, and one of the strange things about my parents, which they acknowledged after they had left the Communist Party, was that they were strangely libertarian. For most people in Communist parties, as you may have noticed if you've ever known anybody in Communist parties, libertarianism and Communism don't really go too well together. My parents discovered this around about 1956, which coincided not only with some tanks moving westwards, but also with us going to East Germany, which in itself was rather an extraordinary experience for a ten-year-old, I can tell you.

Anyway, so they left 'the Party', and the more I think about it, their lives were resolved at that point as they discovered a particular kind of educational philosophy which couldn't possibly have been contained within that organisation, a form of child-centred libertarian education which they wrote about in their book, *The Language of Primary School Children*.

I often think back to my childhood and the kind of freedom and liberty that they gave us (that's me and my brother), and I often wonder about the roots of it. My dad was born in America, in Brockton, Massachusetts, and came to Britain when he was two, when his parents split. He came to Britain with his mother. He never naturalised to become a Brit, partly I think because, either fictitiously or otherwise, he imagined that he'd never be allowed to as he was a Communist and the Brits weren't too happy about importing Communists. So he never did naturalise, ending up in 1945 in the American army, and his first posting was in England. At this point, he was in what was known as the American University in Shrivenham.

I don't know whether you know about this organisation, but it's a rather extraordinary, amazing and wonderful thing, which I've been researching recently. He only talked about it occasionally. The American Army decided and realised that there was going to be peace, and if they had peace, they would have to work out what would happen to all these guys, some of whom were quite educated, and some of whom were extremely educated, so they set up an American university. Partly out of the war zone, 'the theatre of war', as they called it, they set it up in Shrivenham in England. So my father's first posting, having lived in England for almost the whole of his life, was in England. And it's here that he met someone who some of you may know of: Wayne C. Booth. Actually my middle name is Wayne. In 1946, I think I was the only English-born Wayne in existence – and there I was named after Wayne C. Booth, who at that time had not written an incredibly important book which is a bible to any of us in Literature departments all over the world, called *The Rhetoric of Fiction*.

Anyway, I often used to look at the books my dad brought back from the American Army University in Shrivenham, and they are a wonderful and brilliant set of works coming out of the finest liberal tradition of North America. To see that, you just have to open, for example, Louis Untermeyer's *Anthology of Modern American Poetry* or some of Mark Van Doren's books, or even, say, the philosophy textbooks. They are incredible: each one of them with a number stamped on it along with 'American Army', and inside is this liberal education that was devised at this university that in part helped produce a moment in my dad's and Wayne C. Booth's life. I think of this as one of those moments that 'comes before'. It explains what came after.

Another job of poets is to do archaeology. You can do archaeology on other people, or on yourself. I quite often do it on myself. So, here's me being an archaeologist, trying to figure out why and how my parents were libertarians. It's called 'Staying Over'.

At Malc's flat
there's raisins and tangerine pieces
to have in bed.

At Mart's house
there's a train set in his bedroom.

At Chris's flat
there's a lift to play in till bedtime.

At Malc's
we go over to his Armenian granny's
and she cooks us pilaff.

At Mart's
we make tunnels
for his trains to go through.

At Chris's
we go down to the playground
and play football-tennis for hours.

At Malc's
we talk about places far away
like Czechoslovakia and Bulgaria
where his dad goes.

At Mart's
we talk about two lakes in France
where me and him got lost
in the mud and bulrushes
but got back to the campsite ok in the end.

At Chris's
we talk about Arsenal and Spurs;
he's Spurs
I'm Arsenal.
We imagine what it would be like

if Arsenal played Spurs in the Cup final.

At Malc's
his mum and dad are Peggy and Francis
and I love it
when Francis comes into our bedroom
at bedtime and sings us,
'Barnacle Bill the Sailor'.

At Mart's
his mum and dad are Lorna and Fred
and I love it
when Fred stops wasps stinging me
by grabbing them with his fingers.
'You've got to be quick,' he says,
and Lorna says, 'Oh Fred, please!'

At Chris's
his mum and dad are Rene and Moishe
and I love it
when Rene plays the trick with the plastic egg
that she serves up in a plate of baked beans
and I believe it's real and try to stick my fork
in the plastic yolk.

Not so good at Malc's
when we drew pictures on Armenian granny's doorstep
and she said she couldn't wash it off
and Uncle Felix with the beard
went off in a big huff
and didn't talk to us.

Not so good at Mart's
when I threw Mart's baby brother's
Special Extra-fast Yo-yo over the fence
and when I pretended to put it back
on the shelf,
Lorna saw that my hand was empty

and did a whole 'tut-tut' thing.

Not so good at Chris's
when we came back from
Spurs v. Arsenal
and this group of kids surrounded us
and poked and prodded us and
called us names
and we came back and sat on the sofa
and felt bad all evening.

I love it that my parents
let me go and stay
at Malc's, Mart's and Chris's.

Some part of my parents knew that one thing about parenting is that you cannot control your children all of the time. Some part of them said to us, 'Go elsewhere and find out what other parents are like. You might find them to be better than us or worse than us, but it doesn't matter.'

I've been a parent for many, many years, for thirty-four years; I'm the longest-standing continuous school parent in existence. I've been a school parent for thirty years. I have a thirty-four-year-old and a five year-old, and plenty in between. And I still haven't learned what my parents learned in the forties and fifties, and I don't know why.

There's a part of poetry and a part of writing that we often leave out. Perhaps it's because the world 'writing' has several meanings. Writing can suggest or refer much more to the verb 'to write' than to the thing that has been written. That is to say there is a process called writing – which is what writers do, and yet critics are by and large much more interested in the writing on the page, the writing that's been done. I think there are many fewer people interested in how we actually do the writing, or even in why we do it. Part of the 'how' is that you have to be prepared to investigate. Part of writing is being prepared to ask questions about the things that you're writing about. And here's me now in this talk to you, trying to do that again. In fact, I often say to children, 'The thing about stories is that usually you have to end them; the great thing about poems is that you don't have to.' In fact, a great way to end a poem is with a question because you don't know the answer, and that's okay, that's allowed in poems. A poem could just be one question: it could be

'Why do buffalos eat spaghetti?', which is what my son once asked me and I said, 'Do they?' and he said, 'I don't know.'

Corned Beef

Why does Mum keep cans of corned beef
in the cupboard?
Not just one or two cans –
stacks of them.
Does she think that one day we'll
have a corned beef party?
Does she think that
people will come over
and she will say, 'Surprise!',
pull back a cloth
and there, in front of everyone,
the table will be full of
cans of corned beef ?
And then everyone will sit round
opening cans of corned beef?
And we'll sit and eat it saying,
'Corned beef. This is nice.
Mmmmmm. Nice party.'

Or does she think that one day
all the shops will be closed
and we won't be able to buy
any food, but we'll be all right
because we'll be able to eat
corned beef?
Every day.
For months and months.
And people will be jealous of us
and they'll be queuing outside
our house, shouting,
'Let us in.
We want corned beef.
We want corned beef.'

I don't like corned beef.
I don't like the way
there are these chunks of fat
sitting on it.
And when you eat it,
it sticks to the roof of your mouth.

And now I think of it
I've never seen Mum eating it either.

Why does Mum keep cans of corned beef
in the cupboard?

Once there was a terrible disease in the
country where corned beef comes from.
It was 'an outbreak of typhoid', they said.
In the newspapers and on the TV
they kept saying to us,
'DON'T EAT THE CORNED BEEF.
DON'T EAT THE CORNED BEEF.'
Mum went to the cupboard,
took down one of the cans and said,
'Hmmm. Better not open that
till the typhoid outbreak is over.'

Why does mum keep cans of corned beef
in the cupboard?

And I don't really know why she did that. My mum was meditative, but she
was also mysterious. I know that, because when I ran the thing on my retina,
her pulling out the can of corned beef from the cupboard, saying that about
the typhoid, she's just looking at us, kind of sideways. And she's looking at us
to see whether we know . . . well I don't know why she's looking at us – but
there's a little twinkle in her eye. I never quite figured out whether she knew
that she was saying these things, or whether she only found out she was saying
something like that halfway through, and then wondered whether we had
spotted it. I never knew if it was a deliberate mistake or a something planned.
When the dishwasher broke down, she called it a 'wish-dasher' and she said,

'Put it in the wish-dasher.' And we just looked at her and she looked at us.

I'll read you just one or two other things. I do try to write in different ways, and every now and then an object or a creature or an event seems to demand that you write in a particular kind of way. I've already mentioned an idea about poetry where one of the things it does to make itself memorable is to make itself sound like the thing it's talking about.

OK, a word coming up! And I know this word is problematic in different parts of the world: 'daddy long-legs'. That's what we call a crane fly. So this is a creature that looks like a gigantic mosquito but it's absolutely harmless. It's got a long abdomen and four wings, and it can be about that big or about that big. In Australia, I gather a daddy long-legs is a very large grey spider whose other name is a huntsman.

So I've told you what my daddy long-legs is, something completely harmless, but kids hate them. Dads and mums are sometimes called upon to do things to them. This one's called 'Daddy-long-legs in a Hotel Room'.

Everyone's ducking out of the way
of you, and your furry legs.
You are like eyelashes
with wings,
fluttering and flittering about,
bumping into lampshades:
tutta tutta, ta-ta tutta,
a jerky drum solo.

You feel like a spider's web
when you brush across our faces:
tutta tutta, ta-ta tutta.

– Kill it, Dad.
– Kill it, Dad.

They think your hairs
could bite and sting.
We stare at your
up-the-wall, down-the-wall dancing.
If we're not careful
you could jitterbug down our necks:

tutta tutta, ta-ta tutta.

I switch out the light.
It's quiet.
We lie and wonder if
there'll be a moment
when we'll feel your
whiskers
whisper across our skin:
tutta tutta, ta-ta tutta.

In the morning
the bathroom is white and glarey.
You're flat out on the tiles,
your legs splayed.
The jazz is over.

I will read you one more to finish. In recent years, in Britain, there have been (how can I put it nicely?) some great changes in education. And these have concerned many of us. Basically, the revolution in education that has taken place over the last ten years has involved replacing the humanistic curriculum with something altogether different. And this took most people, like you, completely unawares. Nobody quite thought that it could happen overnight and the work of the previous thirty, forty, fifty years was just swept aside in one move. There was no argument, no debate. For all the previous thirty or forty years, people had thought that what you do is you argue a position and you argue, say, that this kind of thing can go on in the curriculum, and that kind of thing could go on, and there was a debate. No one realised that all it needs is for politicians to say, 'Well actually we won't talk to any of those people who've been working on ideas in education for the last thirty or forty years.' So they were just shunted off the desk, and the politicians said, in effect, 'No, we'll just do it this way.' But nobody could quite put their finger on what 'this' was, or at least on the philosophy of what 'this' was.

And now it is emerging that it was essentially what we can call 'the business model', that what was going on was that every child and every teacher were seen as part of business production. The child was seen as the raw material, the teacher as the worker on the production line, working on the raw material of the child, and everything could be measured: the teacher's input, the child's output, and the smaller the unit of production (that is, the minute-by-minute input-output moment in a lesson), the more efficiently it could be measured. So you could say, 'What are you planning to do in the next hour?' (that's the input), and the child would do this thing, and at the end of the hour the child would be asked, 'Did you get it?', the child would say yes or no as the case may be, and then there's a tick made. Of course, some realised that there were only certain things that fit the business model, and primarily that's what they think are called 'facts'.

So what you do is you teach facts. You don't teach process; you only deal with facts. So if you take fiction, or poetry, this then causes a problem. The only things you could be interested in with a story or a poem are 'the facts'. But fiction and poetry don't seem to be about facts; that doesn't seem to be what stories and poems are. Here's an example of all this: my daughter came home with a worksheet called 'Perseus and the Gorgons'. The heading said, 'This is part of the myth from ancient Greece.' And I thought, 'What's the matter with the whole myth? When did they go out of fashion?' The first line is 'At last Perseus found the Gorgons.' And there's no explanation of where we are or who's Perseus. And who are the Gorgons? Who's telling this story? Why did Perseus 'find' the Gorgons? Why was he looking for them? And then at the end you turn over the page, and there are questions like: 'What has Perseus got on his heels?' 'Who gave Perseus his shield?' and then you have to look back to the story and see that it was Athena. So in a way, that's why that particular moment in the story is there, so you can answer the question on the other side.

I thought, 'Where is this stuff coming from? What is it? What kind of philosophy drives this nonsense?' There is a name for it: pseudo-empiricism. This school of thought imagines that you can describe the world as a series of facts, without ever revealing what joins one supposed fact to another fact. There's no theory, no ideology, no overarching idea. All there is are facts. Logical positivism is the other phrase for it.

We scratched our heads and wondered why or how it had arrived in our schools and we know that someone took the mickey out of it years ago: Dickens, in *Hard Times*. All you have to look at is the chapter called 'Never Wonder', and Mr Gradgrind is saying something along the lines of: 'Facts, facts, facts, must have the facts, everything is facts', and one of the kids says, 'I wonder . . . ' and Gradgrind says, 'Never wonder.' And we thought, 'That's what it is, it's Dickens.' In 1840-something when *Hard Times* came out, he knew the battle was on to defend the rights of children to read, enjoy and understand story and poetry. He knew that there were truths that were there, or – the way I think of it – there's a marriage between ideas and feelings attached to recognisable beings who we care about: human beings, animals, objects, it doesn't matter what. That's what this stuff is about, and we engage with these ideas and feelings, both at the same time. There is a continuum between ideas and feelings. But this other stuff about what Perseus has got on his sandals or who gave him the shield has got nothing to do with feelings. We realised that they're not interested in that. And yet, these people think that this is education.

So I was so enraged by this worksheet, and I tried not to do what my dad did, which was rage – he would go bananas when this sort of stuff came home – and I thought, no, I'll try not to be like my dad, I'll just go out to the garden and kick something, then come back in again and say, 'Okay, let's do the worksheet together.' And then I thought, 'No, no, hang on . . . what else did my parents do? They read to me. Yes, that's what they did to me, both of them.'

One of the people that I learned to love when I was a kid was your author, Ernest Thompson Seton. My mother used to go to libraries and discover books that no one else had ever heard of. It seemed at the time that no one had ever heard of Ernest Thompson Seton in Britain, but there was my mum reading me *Raggylug*. Later, when I was twelve, my dad read us the whole of *Great Expectations* in a tent at night, doing all the voices. So I thought, right, I'll get the book of Greek myths and see if Elsie wants to listen to these.

I started reading the Geraldine McCaughrean version of the Greek myths. Elsie was seven, and I thought the stories were beautifully told, very simple, and we were reading 'Persephone and the Pomegranate Seeds' and when Persephone puts the pomegranate seeds in her mouth, Elsie called out, 'Oh, no! I didn't want her to do that!' and as the story went on we got to the bit where one of the gods takes pity on Persephone and Elsie stopped me and said, 'What's "pity"?' So we talked about what the god might be feeling for Persephone and then we talked about how maybe Elsie might have felt pity when her younger brother cut himself, and we were talking about pity. I've thought about this moment, over and over again, and it's occurred to me what's going on here: the story relates stuff that is concrete enough for you and me and her to think that there are real pomegranate seeds and there is a believable person. It doesn't matter how distant or incredible it is, or that it's from 3000 years ago, and there are believable gods – even though she doesn't believe in gods, and I don't believe in gods– but we believe in them in the story, and, crucially, she cares about Persephone. And then, there's this word 'pity', which is where there is a movement going from the concrete of the story (where there was enough psychic reality, as Freud puts it, in it for her to care) to an abstract: 'pity'. In our conversation, we've related it to her concrete situation, of her and her younger brother. So, what has happened here? We have in the language an abstract word, 'pity', a word which for many young children is almost meaningless – certainly it is if you just lob the word into a room full of kids aged seven or eight. If you or I were to say, 'Today we're going to talk about the word "pity",' we know that we'll lose 95 percent of them, probably by the time we've got to the word 'word'; then we'll lose another 3 percent when we get to 'pity'. Then we've just got one or two who have already come across pity, who think, 'Oh, right, we're doing pity today . . . ' But here, embodied or embedded in a story (however you would like to express it), we're talking about pity. We've moved from the concrete to the abstract: from caring about particular people – in the story and in real life – to something very abstract . . . you're talking about the word's essence and its nature, and the reverberations and connotations that spread out from the word. We've gone all the way along that line and back again.

The point is: these people who devised these syllabuses, who invented this business model, dominated as it is by logical positivism, haven't twigged this. Or maybe even worse . . . maybe they have twigged it but they're saying, in effect, 'We're not going to do it anyway.' One thing that makes me think they have twigged it is the stats that get thrown at them. There's an acronym, and you here will remember better than me what it stands for: PIRLS [Progress in International Reading Literacy Study]. It's an international literacy comparison.

They look at literacy levels all around the world. One of the things they also look at are percentages of children who appear to read for pleasure. And they've noticed there's a correlation between kids who read for pleasure and – however we're going to measure it – school achievement. They've noticed.

If they're right, and, anecdotally, all of you who have worked with kids and stories across a whole year, and two years, you've seen that those kids who are having real trouble will on occasions suddenly fasten on to a particular story or poem or picture book. Or maybe they seem to make leaps and bounds when they're acting in a play. We have that anecdotal evidence. We may or may not take on board that statistical evidence, or even know about it, but if we do and we say, 'How come? How come if we do poetry in the broadest sense of the word, in that Germanic sense, how can it be that if kids are just sitting around reading for pleasure, it can take them from A to B on that academic ladder?'

And then I thought back to that conversation about pity. And I realised that going up that academic ladder depends on moving from the concrete to the abstract. If you sit and talk to eight-, nine-, ten-, eleven- or twelve-year-olds, one of the things you find is there are some kids in that room who can handle abstractions and some who can't. They're not better or worse, but you find it: you hear it in the way they start talking. And as you go a bit older, thirteen-, fourteen-, fifteen-year-olds, you can hear how some kids never quite got hold of it. Yet the school curriculum is throwing abstractions at them, for better or for worse: in geography, in history; in maths it's throwing calculus at them. And some kids never get it. And some kids do. And I just found myself thinking that the conversation with Elsie that night about Persephone and the pomegranate seeds and pity was making the leap for her. And that might happen with kids who read widely and often and for pleasure, again and again and again. It can happen even as they start making comparisons and contrasts between what they're reading and say to themselves, 'That bit is like that bit.' Or, 'He felt that for her, but then she felt that for him in that other book . . . and it wasn't quite the same . . . but it was nearly the same and was that love, or wasn't it?' All this kind of conversation goes on in and around the whole world of books, stories, plays and poetry. And, yes, I thought, wow, that actually is something that we should be fighting for.

As I say, the depressing thing is I think that some of the people who have run education know this, but they don't want to give this world of literature to children. They don't want to give it to everybody. They see it going on, in the fancy liberal arts colleges, they see it going on in the private schools, and they say, 'Terrific. What a beautiful play you do, how great that poetry is!', but when they go into that inner-city school and they see the kids are all lining up doing their worksheets, they say, 'Great. Terrific. That's what they should be doing.' I'm not in much doubt that our task is fighting for the reading of whole stories and poems and for the kinds of conversations Elsie and I had that time.

One other thing: it sends me back to the kind of education I had. I had an education in the fifties, and in England we used to have something called the 'Eleven Plus' exam. They told us that this was an exam which could sort out which of us had heads and which of us had hands – that was the nice way to put it. So they said, 'All of you,' – pointing us out – 'have got heads, and all of you,' – pointing 'them' out, 'have got hands. There's not one better than the other, but you're different. So you're in the 'heads' class and you're in the 'hands' class. But only half of the heads class is going to go to the special school for kids with heads, called the grammar school. Half of this class is going to go to the school that isn't, called the secondary modern school.' So, as I think about the education on offer now, I'm sent back to this moment in my childhood:

The Homework Book

Miss Williams said that from now on
we would have homework
and that we were to bring
a homework exercise book to school.

This was serious stuff:
all about passing The Exam,
The Exam called 'the Eleven Plus'.
Everyone was worried about
The Eleven Plus.
Would I pass?
Would I fail?
Everyone was worried.
Teachers, parents, us.
I couldn't get to sleep.
Mum brought me hot milk.

On Mondays
Miss Williams went through
the homework in our homework books.
While she was talking, I got bored.
I drew a picture in my homework book
of a man with a big beard
right in the middle of my maths homework.
He was carrying a bag.
He put things he picked up off the pavement
into his bag.
I called him Trev the Tramp.

Miss Williams went on going through
the homework with the whole class.
This was really important.

We had to listen or we wouldn't pass

The Eleven Plus.
Everyone was listening.
Everyone was concentrating
so that they could pass
The Eleven Plus.

I bent down behind the boy
sitting in front of me.
I looked across at my friend Harrybo
and held up my picture of Trev the Tramp.
I pointed at Trev the Tramp.
I whispered, 'Trev the Tramp.'
Miss Williams saw me
holding up the homework book.

She was on to it in a flash.
'What's that, boy? What is it?!'
I quickly shut the homework book.
'Nothing, Miss Williams.'
She rushed over.
(She was brilliant at rushing over.)
She grabbed the homework book.
She flicked through the pages.
She found the picture of Trev the Tramp.
Right there in the middle of 23 x 12.

'This is it, isn't it?' she said.
'In your homework book!
I'll tell you what's going to happen
now, boy,' she said.

'You're going to take your homework book
home to your parents along with a
letter from me.'
She pointed at herself when she said, 'me'.
'My goodness, you're in trouble, boy.

Serious trouble.'

For the rest of the day
I was very quiet. I put my feet down
on the ground carefully and I made
sure I didn't bump into anything.
At going-home time, she handed me
a big, white envelope.
'The letter to your parents is in there,
along with the homework book.'

But when I got home
I couldn't face giving it to my mum.
I couldn't face giving it to my dad.
I nipped upstairs and slipped it
under my bed.
All evening I was thinking
about the big white envelope
with the letter from Miss Williams,
the homework book and the
picture of Trev the Tramp.
I didn't want to give it to them.
I didn't want to see their faces
as they read the letter and looked at
Trev the Tramp.

What I did was put the big white envelope
on their bed when I went to bed.

In the morning, my dad said,
'Oh dear, you poor old thing,
you must have been so worried
about that letter, eh? I'll write one back.
I'll say some things in the letter
that will make sure you won't have
to worry about this stuff anymore.
And I'll get you a new homework book.'

At school, my friends said,
'Did you get in trouble?
Did you get the whacks?
What happened?'
And I said,
'My dad said I wasn't to worry.'
They didn't believe me.
And I don't know what my dad wrote
but Miss Williams never said
anything about it ever again;
the head never said anything about it again.

My dad was a teacher
and maybe he wrote in some kind of
special teacher language
that meant Miss Williams wouldn't
ever say anything again.
Some kind of teacher code . . .
that's what must have done it.

Thank you very much. I'll just finish by saying I often hear words like 'privilege' and 'advantage' and 'disadvantage' around education. When I think about my parents, they both came from unbelievably poverty-stricken backgrounds (although I know there's a rumour that Jews are never poverty-stricken); and there they were belonging to this political sect which in the fifties was very much a kind of sect of outsiders, and yet there was something about my upbringing that was incredibly privileged. It was something to do with words and language and curiosity and meditation and jokes and songs and stories, all wrapped up in one. So I think I'll finish by paying a tribute to those educators, the late Connie and Harold Rosen.

Thanks ever so much.

Really Great Expectations

I wrote this piece for the collection Stop What You're Doing and Read This!, *published by Vintage in 2011.*

We are on holiday on the coast of Yorkshire not far from Whitby. It's a campsite and there are two families with a couple of friends added in. This is 1959 and I'm thirteen. Just as it's getting dark we are called to the biggest tent where my father is pumping up the Tilley lamp, a large green light that works by burning paraffin under pressure in a 'mantle' – a white cylinder of cloth that sits at the top of a tube. He loves faffing about doing this, and that's what he calls it when he pretends it's bothersome. 'It's a bit of a faff,' he says whilst adoring the way that it's his expertise with the paraffin can, the funnel and the little brass handle that delivers this hard, white light.

So we sit ourselves down on sleeping bags, blankets and cushions. The Tilley lamp sits on a fold-up wooden chair, my father sits on another in the middle of us. Looking round the tent, I can only see our faces catching the light, as if we are just masks hanging there, our bodies left outside in the dark perhaps. In my father's hands is a book – *Great Expectations* – and every night, there in the tent, he reads it to us. Without any hesitation, backtracking or explanation he reads Pip's story in the voice of the secondary-school teacher he is, but each and every character is given a flavour – some more than others: Magwitch, of course, allows him to do his native cockney. Thinking about it now, I can see that his Jaggers was probably based on a suburban head teacher from one of the schools he taught in; Uncle Pumblechook could have been derived from the strangely pompous shopkeepers and publicans who peopled the hardware stores and cafés of outer London, where we lived in the 1950s. But over the years, as my father tells us about his own upbringing, some of Dickens' characters start to mix and merge with our own relatives.

There is someone called Uncle Lesley Sunshine who, like Pumblechook, turned up in my father's home when he was a boy to offer advice and hold out prospects of betterment. This was London's East End, a terraced house in one of the streets behind the London Hospital in Whitechapel, where my father and his sister were being brought up by their mother, Rose, along with her mother and father, and it's where several (how many? more than we could ever count) of her sisters and brother lived, too. Lesley Sunshine seems to have dropped into this crowded place from some other well-heeled place in order to take the 'boy' to places where he will be improved, like a tailor's, who, because he is a relative, will fit the boy out in a decent bar-mitzvah suit for free.

Rose has plans of her own for the boy. Somehow, in ways that my father never found out, she summons people from another world into their home. On occasions seamen from Russia, Jamaica and America would find their way to their kitchen. At the time, my father didn't know how or why they got there, but looking back, he could see that they were people she had met at meetings, and they would sit in the tiny space of that home talking to her own father, who had arrived from Poland, and to my father, who was of course a boy. It was mysterious and different from his friends' homes and gave him a contradiction to figure out: how come he appeared to be living in such a poor, tiny place, but people from all over the world would choose to come there? It gave him a mix of shame and pride to deal with. His mother would also take the boy to the local Whitechapel Library, which had become a kind of international centre for the uplifting of the masses, and this too was a place that opened a window on the world and a door to a future life away from the area. The air was full of people speaking different languages, whispers and rumour passed around, that this or that great back-street scholar was writing a masterpiece over there; the great painter and poet Isaac Rosenberg had sat just here; this or that revolutionary or preacher or teacher was just over there behind the shelves.

Some of that was true, but a more powerful if more mundane truth was also at work: it was here that poor boys and girls from migrant cultures were finding their route through the literature and science that would take them to the sixth forms and universities they yearned for. My father's journey began with a little book about whales, which he took home and pored over, and ended with Milton. More mysteriously, on one occasion, Rose and the boy got on a tram and travelled north to Belsize Park, a place so different, so luxurious as to appear to him as somewhere foreign. There she took him to a flat, where one room was as big as a whole floor in their house. On the walls were paintings of a woman with no clothes on, her skin yellow, her face still. There were books everywhere and, between the books, pots and carved figures. In the middle of it all sat someone grand, a woman wearing strange clothes who spoke in a voice that came from another place or from another time. This, he was told, was someone important; perhaps there was a prospect that she could help the boy, and he had to be on his best behaviour. So he sat on a chair while Rose and the woman talked about Communism. It turned out that the yellow woman with no clothes on was Beatrice Hastings, their host, and the painter was Modigliani.

Thinking back to the tent and the Tilley lamp, I can see Pip walking up the stairs, following Estella, to see Miss Havisham on what would be his life-changing climb, a moment that would alter his whole perspective on who he was, what he wanted to be and how he would view others. Beatrice Hastings was no Miss Havisham, but there is something swirling around in both my father's mind and mine, mixing and blending, when I think of the lone woman in a room with these haunted ties to a man from the past. In fact, I can't really sort out who's who, real or imaginary, and I think this is how we all read when we have time and space to think about books.

What I mean is that of course Dickens told us about a Miss Havisham whom he created, but when many of us read about that Miss Havisham, we bring her to life with the Miss Havishams we know in our own lives. I think, in my case, this imaginative leap was given an extra kick, first from the way my father read the book, giving the voices and the scenes such a potency from the place and the way he read it to us, but also because both he and my mother filled our minds and lives with such vivid stories and experiences. The slow, measured reading of the book, the talk and replays of the scenes and the accounts of these people, end up as a kind of portrait gallery of pictures that have the ability to change places, so that when I think of Beatrice Hastings – whom I never met – at times she is replaced by Miss Havisham, and when I think of Miss Havisham I can imagine that Modigliani painted her.

My father, back in the tent, packs a lot of power into the moment when Miss Havisham tells Estella to 'beggar' the boy when they play 'Beggar my neighbour'. He seems to especially love Jaggers; the way Jaggers toys with Pip, clearly knowing more than he lets on about Pip's mysterious benefactor. He relishes the descriptions of Wemmick's peculiar house in Walworth – coincidentally, where my father taught at one of the new inner-city comprehensives. These characters have a life beyond the tent. They are quoted and referred to as we go about the campsite. If I'm sent off to buy some eggs in the village, my father puts on a Jaggers voice and says, 'How much do you want? Forty pounds? Thruppence?' When we get up in the morning, my parents are scurrying around looking for the bread or pulling the milk out from under the eaves of the tent, saying, 'Vittles, gimme vittles, boy!' It doesn't have to be an accurate quote. My father's performance had given such life to the characters that their vocabulary became ours, and they could now live with us on the campsite and, it turned out, beyond, for years after. Quite out of the blue, my father or mother would transform themselves into Pumblechook, calling out: 'And three! And nine!' as if I was Pip and they were calling after me through the railings of Miss Havisham's house.

The character that my father brought most vividly to life was Trabb's boy, a young chap who works for the local tailor and who is the first to spot Pip's efforts to distinguish himself from his lowly background, mocking him for his apparent snobbery. To be honest, at the time I didn't understand the significance of Trabb's boy. I couldn't really see the humour in this little chap walking down the street with a pretend cape over his shoulders, calling out, 'Don't know yer!' For my father, this seemed both incredibly funny and especially poignant in ways that I couldn't see or reach. Why, when he was quiet, prodding the fire, or if we were walking on the moors, would he suddenly say, 'Don't know yer!'?

Years later he gave a hint as to why this might have been. He said that there was a boy at school called Rosenberg – David Rosenberg, I think. He showed him to us on his class photo. Rosenberg was, he said, his best friend. But the Rosenbergs were poor. Quite how you could be even poorer than my father, his sister and his mother I could never understand. After all, Rose had on occasions taken my father to various charities in order to ask for school boots. Both my mother and father talked of the tenements and flats that surrounded them while growing up as being full of bedbugs and grime. My mother hated dirt and could spot it a mile off, whether it was under a table, along the top of a cupboard door or on my face. So I thought, listening to my father, that maybe the Rosenbergs had bedbugs and dirt. Even on their faces. Rosenberg, it seems, had been my father's friend, but then at some point someone else became his best friend, Moishe Kaufman. Indeed, not only did Moishe Kaufman become his best friend, but Moishe Kaufman's girlfriend, Rene Roder, became the best friend of my father's girlfriend, Connie Isakofsky. They were a foursome and David Rosenberg wasn't part of it. In the shuffling of the pack of these East End boys, each in their different ways got what they needed to leave this place, to move northwards or eastwards to get out of this poverty and foreignness, to become less 'heimish', as it was called – the *Heim* being the mythical far-away place in Eastern Europe where everyone looked and talked like their grandparents, lived in tiny houses and kept chickens. At some point David Rosenberg got frozen out. But something went deeper than that. There was some moment, some event, some incident, which I never fully heard about or understood, where it seems as if, to my father's great regret and shame, he did something or said something to David Rosenberg – perhaps he pretended not to know Rosenberg, cold-shouldered him, looked down on him. It was a Trabb's boy moment and I can now see that my father must have recognised himself in Pip, trying to leave his past behind and better himself.

So, wrapped up in that gesture that my father did when he played out Trabb's boy was a mockery of himself. Trabb's boy was doing what I presume David Rosenberg didn't do, which was act out the snobbery that he saw in my father. To do it on a campsite in Yorkshire in 1959, some twenty-five years after that scene or event that had taken place in a dingy, inky 'Foundation School' on the Mile End Road, may, I suppose, have helped him banish the guilt – well, at least for a few seconds.

In the end, my father did a Pip on nearly all of his family. We used to visit Rose – a tired figure he called 'Ma'. We saw his sister Sylvia, but that was about it. In their place was a set of names, the kinds of names you never heard in the London suburbs of the 1950s – Raina, Lally and Busha – only as real as characters in a novel. We were in John Lewis; this wasn't somewhere we went very often. In fact, I think it was the first time I had ever been there, though I understood that there were places my parents thought of as rather special: quality places where you could buy tasteful things. John Lewis was one of the places you could go to get such things, and Heal's was another, and as a result chairs and carpets and curtains appeared in our flat in the suburbs with patterns and designs and colours that I never saw in other people's houses. Perhaps there was a touch of the Beatrice Hastings about the things they tried to acquire: the long arm of my father's own Miss Havisham determining how he thought about curtains. Anyway, in this place, John Lewis, a woman stopped my father and said, 'Is it Harold?' They talked for a few moments. She seemed tall and posh and imposing and then off she went. Who was that? That was his Aunty Rene – her real name was Raina. My father looked bothered and distracted by it.

So, perhaps in Trabb's boy's 'Don't know yer!' were Raina, Lally and Busha. I never knew exactly why we weren't part of them, or they not part of us. There was a suggestion that some of them were locked in an old religion, full of what he thought were pointless beliefs. But there were times when he would show regret that he hadn't kept on with *Chanukkah*, *Purim* and *Seder* nights, and he would talk longingly of dishes we had never tasted, strudel and *charoseth* and *humentaschen*, and fun things like giving away bits of bread before *Pesach* or hunting *matzos*.

So as *Great Expectations* got read and re-enacted, and these re-enactions were absorbed and re-absorbed into our family life down through the years, I could see various characters and situations in the book intertwine with these missing people. Alf, whom we didn't ever see, was lovely. My father loved Uncle Alf. He talked of his kindness and the special treats. He was a lovely man, he would say. So was he a Joe Gargery figure to my father? Or, in his mind, was his loving grandfather the Joe figure who kept the stern aunts at bay, those aunts who seemed always in my mind to be frowning at the boy and complaining that he was getting the tastiest bits of the chicken – the *fliegel* or the *pulke*. These women were all at once Pip's sister, bringing him up 'by hand'.

Of course there doesn't have to be a like-for-like match between people. Part of the power of stories is the way in which we can see facets of this or that fictional person in the people we know, and scenes from the fictional world have echoes in the events of the real world. As the book, and my father's reading of the book, and my feelings about the book developed, I felt from him a sense of yearning. Pip is desperate to get away from his old home and, once he's had a sniff of what Miss Havisham appears to offer, he follows the dream of a better life. My father had some kind of dream. It was that his father would turn up and take him away from these horrible aunts. His father would arrive from America in his swell car, in his swell suits and say, 'Hey, Harold, let's make tracks.' And he would drive down Nelson Street in a convertible while all the family and the kids with their bedbugs and dirty faces would watch open-mouthed. But his father never came. Morris Rosen stayed in America. Rose never said bad words about him. He had special things to do. He was a union organiser. He was standing for the State Senate of Pennsylvania for the Socialists. He was organising support for Sacco and Vanzetti, who had been framed and would be executed. He was busy. So he never came. But the yearning stayed until my father was old enough to realise that he never would. By then, like Pip, he had become what one of the relatives had called a 'psy-college boy'. He had studied English literature – books like *Great Expectations*. When I too came to do the same thing, I saw how so many things had ended up getting intertwined here: my father's performance of the book; how the scenes became part of our daily lives and language; how all this spoke to me about the kind of family my father had come from and the changes he had been through before I was in this world. Books can do this. I'd also say that there is an added dimension, when books leave the page and become spoken out loud in a room full of people; of course they become live and vivid, but they also become social, they end up belonging to everyone in the room (or tent) at that moment. My father also read us *Little Dorrit*, Walter Scott's *Guy Mannering* and, much later, most of

Catcher in the Rye and *Catch-22*. Even more memorably, he also read out loud his own memoir, which he called *Are You Still Circumcised?*.

A few years ago I went to Boston because I had found out where Morris Rosen was buried. It was on a long road out through the north of the city. I walked out past tattoo parlours and empty car dealerships until there were no more buildings, just waste depots and cemeteries. It was November, cold and raining, and I found the graveyard, the 'Jewish Workmen's Circle Cemetery'. And there was Morris Rosen. On his grave it said 'Beloved father'. Beloved father? Beloved?! As one of my relatives replied, 'Haven't you heard of Jewish humour?' There was also a number on the grave: the number of the branch of the Workmen's Circle, the self-help organisation that Jewish workers set up. It was number 666. For several days I scanned pages on the internet trying to find where branch 666 was. In the end I found it: Mattapan. Boston's biggest mental institution, where Morris died as a patient.

So there in the graveyard was where all that misplaced yearning had ended up, with a number representing the name of an 'asylum' on it. No Magwitch came out from behind any gravestones while I was standing there, but in a way all my cemeteries are Magwitch cemeteries. That's how my father in the tent in Yorkshire goes on working.

Beyond Recitation – Poetry and the Arts in the Curriculum

Since my father, Harold Rosen, died in 2008, people and organisations who admire and have been influenced by him and his work have instituted a series of lectures in his name. I've given two of these, including the first, in June 2012, at the invitation of the National Association for the Teaching of English.

First, I would like to thank NATE for setting up this Harold Rosen lecture. Harold wasn't shy of writing or talking – far from it – but he was perhaps reluctant to gather together his thoughts and ideas into an accessible form. I think he thought – I'm only guessing here – that someone else could or should have done that. I've created a blog in his name which includes a couple of bibliographies. Various people have suggested putting together some of his key works, including several memorable essays published by NATE. The setting up of this lecture will spur me on to get this done – or as Harold himself would say to our mother, Connie, 'Must press on, Con! Must press on!'[1]

Secondly, I must thank NATE for asking me to give this first lecture in what I hope will be a long series. The tradition of memorial lectures is that they should reflect some aspect of the named person – whether it be their work or their life. I've never hidden the fact that I know something of both; indeed, there were occasions when we used to do a double act. In the morning, Harold might give a talk to a gathering much like this one, on the meaning of narrative, and then in the afternoon I might be asked to read some poems. Some of my favourite poems featured him – not as Professor Harold Rosen – but as 'my dad', 'the old man', 'the O.M.', or just 'Harold' as he rather liked his sons to call him. He would sit at the back of the room and halfway through my reading a poem he would shout, 'Lies! It's all lies!' So, I'll do one now, and we can imagine him, right now, sitting at the back – in fact, when I get to the end, you can be him, and call out, 'Lies, it's all lies!' both by way of remembering him, but also in the spirit of what he believed in, argument, discussion, counter-culture, and the questioning of received wisdom.

So, here goes – a scene in a flat in Pinner in around 1956.

> We sit down to eat and the potato's a bit hot
> So I only put a bit on my fork

And I blow
Phooph phooph
Until it's cool
Just cool
Into the mouth
Choop
Lip-smack
Nice!

My brother's doing the same
Phooph phooph
Until it's cool
Just cool
Into the mouth
Cccchoop
Lip-smack
Nice!

And my mother's doing the same
Phooph phooph
Until it's cool
Just cool
Into the mouth
Cccchoop
Lip-smack
Nice!

But my dad.
My dad!
What does he do?
He stuffs a great big bit of potato
Into his mouth.
And that really does it.
His eyes pop out, he flaps his hands,
He blows, he puffs, he yells
He bobs his head up and down
He spits bits of potato onto the plate
And he turns to us and he goes,

'Watch out everyone.
The potato's really hot.'

And you say:
'Lies! It's all lies!'
Thank you.

As John Richmond made clear in his wonderful obituary, Harold's work shifted focus from his early days as a classroom teacher, to being a head of department in a south London comprehensive, to being a teacher-trainer at what was then Borough Road training college, to being a lecturer at the Institute of Education, on to being a professor and head of department, and in retirement pursuing several scholarly interests as well as gathering together his poems and autobiographical writings. Alongside this, he joined with James Britton and Nancy Martin in the forerunner to NATE – the London Association for the Teaching of English – memorably now written up by the present NATE chair, Simon Gibbons, in a recent book. During this time, he investigated and talked about such matters as poetry in schools, the home languages and cultures of school students, the orthodoxies of the exam system and its criteria of assessment, the politics of central government's interventions into the English curriculum, language use across all the curricula in secondary schools, the centrality of narrative in knowledge and learning (or the marginalisation of it in education), the power of storytelling, the functions of language and the patterns and purpose of autobiography – including his own.

Out of all this work, it might seem odd or 'churlish' (a word Harold loved) to quote something as far back as 1958, long before he became or even thought of himself as an academic. Thanks, I think, to Simon Clements, the English syllabus devised at Walworth Comprehensive School by the English staff themselves, with Harold as head of department, has come to light. It contains this passage:

> The teaching of English at Walworth calls for a sympathetic understanding of the pupils' environment and temperament. Their language experience is acquired from their environment and from communication with the people who mean most to them . . . However narrow the experience of our pupils may be (and it is often wider than we think), it is this experience alone which has given their language meaning. The starting point for English work must be the ability to

handle effectively their own experience. Oral work, written work and the discussion of literature must create an atmosphere in which the pupils become confident of the full acceptability of the material of their own experience.

It's cited in *A Curriculum in its Place: English Teaching in one School 1946-1963* by Peter Medway and Patrick Kingwell.

In a chattier article from the same year, Harold writes:

Without hesitation I would say the home is the first source of supply. Keep sending them home – to mum, to dad, to the family; at meals, quarrelling, having a laugh, getting up, going out, buying something. Then what happens? They are dealing with a situation, rich in first-hand feeling, charged with association and personal relationships, alive with people they know extraordinarily well, down to the last foible. Because they know and feel about these things they have the language to write about them. The springs of language are being tapped, and all the writing skill can be directed towards the experience. From the home we can branch out into other autobiographical material, friends, the district, and school.

And in Medway's and John Hardcastle's 2004 interview with Harold – also cited in the book – Harold talked about a lesson on *Great Expectations* and the first chapter in which we find, of course:

the encounter with Magwitch, the convict, which is a fantastic piece, I've always thought it was quite incredible. And we read the big chunk of where he gets him to promise he'll bring a file and something to eat. And so we read it, I read it once, and then I had them read it as a drama, skipping the intervening bits, just, it's full of dialogue. And then we explored the idea of being frightened, and being frightened of certain kinds of adults. Well, I can remember being fantastically chuffed because . . . they couldn't stop talking about frightening adults, quite different kinds, of course, and I was surprised at how often they were people encountered in the markets, and who grabbed hold of them and so on, tried to get money from them. And then, of course, they could, if they wanted to, write about that, and they did, and there were a lot of good pieces . . .

As we know now, though, it took the interventions of such people as Kenneth Baker in 1988 and Michael Gove in 2014 to allow all students in comprehensive schools to read Dickens. Or not.

Some people here will not only remember some of the things Harold said and wrote, but also the way in which he said them: his provocative questioning perhaps, or the anecdotes from his childhood, classrooms and staffrooms. Of course, as his children, we got another view of it. If you can imagine the way in which a dog harasses an old glove you might get a sense of it. He would fasten on to a word or phrase or whole subject and argue with it out loud. As a teenager, I can remember him sitting at the table with us having our evening meal, he with papers and books all round him, getting enraged about something called T-units. He was doing his PhD on a system of defining a student's quality of English based on a supposedly objective measure called T-units. Many years later, long after I had left home, I would come to the house and almost as I was walking through the door he would be offloading his fascination with, say, Bakhtin on 'subversive laughter', feminist analyses of autobiography, or Frederick Bartlett on memory. In case this conjures up a vision of someone locked helplessly in a prison of theory, I should add that the particular fascination he had to share could just as easily be with the previous week's Arsenal performance, the miners' strike, or the state of mind of the cats.

In more ways than I can know myself, I have learned from Harold not only in the 'what' of what he talked about but also in the 'how' and the 'why'. You all know better than me that his specific area of interest and work – English teaching in schools – is a matter of intense scrutiny and control from politicians. Right up to his death in 2008, we would talk about this, and in some ways the regimes imposed on English teachers since 1988 represent a defeat of ideas that he and many others believed in. One conversation that I didn't ever have with him, though (perhaps I was worried that it might be too painful), was over the matter of tactics.

Let me put it this way: the predecessors of the people in this room believed – and acted on the belief – that the teaching of English would develop and progress through the active participation of classroom teachers, working hand in hand with university-based teachers. Through a network of conferences and the production of papers and books, ideas would be produced, contested and adapted, and traced to actual encounters between teachers and students. And – this is the important political bit – this would be enough. It would be self-evident that such teacher-based ideas would have the stamp of reality on them. What's more, in the process of developing these ideas, teachers would be developing themselves as thinkers, as professionals and as people, enjoying doing the work.

What all this missed out is the politics of education. That's to say that since at least 1988, politicians in many countries – Finland would be an exception – have taken on the role of knowing more about teaching than those who teach and those who study teaching.

Now, English teaching is particularly susceptible to this kind of intervention because, in some ways, we are all experts in it. Most of us under the domain of the British government speak and write English. It's very easy to make broad, general statements about, let's say, a whole generation of people who (it is suggested) can't write and only speak in grunts. This seems to be the tenor of what Michael Wilshaw likes to say over and over again. The fact that this generation is now in their 20s, 30s and 40s ought to give pause for thought. After all, the supposed failure of the 'failed generation' is often linked – without evidence – to why Britain is falling behind and failing. Yes, it's true that the thing we were allowed to refer to for a short while as 'British capitalism' did come very close to collapse, but we've been told that the only thing that can save us is lower pay and less money spent on public services. So, was this collapse, this failure, caused by bad English teaching, or not?

If Michael Wilshaw is worried about a failed generation and the failings of British capitalism, shouldn't he nip down to the City of London and do some hard questioning of the educational backgrounds of the hedge-fund managers, debt-sellers, rate-fixers and speculators? And then he could apply his findings back to the kinds of schools these folks came from and he could, perhaps, conjure up the kind of educational input that he might imagine would put a check on such people and such activity.

But of course he won't.

Instead, we get talk about generations being failed by you and your predecessors being linked to what are indeed tough times for many people, tough times for which you are not responsible. But it's more than talk. It's legislation, tests, exams, inspections and league tables. I don't think anyone – my father included – could have imagined how centralised, how Napoleonic, the Department for Education could become in its micromanaging of syllabuses and teaching methods. In short, I'll put this bluntly, successive governments have behaved as if teachers are too stupid and too lazy to be trusted to think about education. More particularly, English teachers are too stupid and too lazy to know about literacy, language and literature. Or worse, you have been involved in a conspiracy to deprive those particular children who come from backgrounds where Standard English is not regularly written, and where the shelves are not laden with great books. The fact that you have repeatedly jumped through the hoops that successive governments have put in front of you, the fact that you have consistently adapted previously held beliefs to fit the requirements of tests, exams and inspections, is ignored. The fact that there is a long line of talks, articles, books, textbooks and conferences, perhaps dating from those words of my father in 1958, showing an almost obsessive commitment to working-class education, is seen as part of the problem and not as part of the solution. The fact that the system now in place embeds failure, failure and more failure at the heart of education, more than ever before, is just an inconvenience that we can overlook.

A good deal of this, I think, involves what Freudians call 'displacement'. That's to say, we live in times of panic about the general state of affairs, with humanity's ability to cope with real or concocted fears about climate change, war, terrorism, antibiotics, migration and debt. What politicians are expert at – in fact I sometimes wonder if they go on special courses to learn how to do it – is to displace these anxieties onto things that are neither the cause nor the remedy. One of these is English teaching and, within that, the English language itself. So, for example, I'm beginning to doubt if I can read. After all, I was taught to read without an hour a day's-worth of systematic synthetic phonics implemented according to the principles of 'first, fast and only'. Even worse, Harold and Connie Rosen read to me every night and shared with me the writing on the pages of Beatrix Potter books and Picture Puffin Books, none of which was written according to the approved graded methods of systematic synthetic phonics. Heaven knows how I picked up the 'alphabetic principle' given that I learned to read using a multi-cuing system.

And so to grammar.

Or, more particularly, to the grammar of written English. I don't need to tell you that a grammar syllabus based on the total language use of the students you teach doesn't meet with the approval of those who lay down what you teach. Indeed, the implication at the heart of these guidelines and regulations is that the way many students write and speak is faulty. And presumably, once they've scored less than a C at whatever the exam is to be called at 16, which will prove that they have failed, they will go out into the world knowing that they are faulty users of English. More than that, having been told that everyone should be able to get an A-C grade, and having not got one, such people will know that they have only themselves to blame. And presumably whatever setbacks befall them later in life, like, say, being sacked, will be their own fault too. Well, it's one way to make sure that people, when sacked, go quietly.

So, if it's not easy, not possible or at least highly unlikely that there is time to run a grammar course for under-16s which has at its heart the students' own language use, spoken and written, is there any wider interpretation of language use which includes at the very least the variety of English that students come across?

One of the futilities of prescriptive grammar is that it takes as its implied or actual sample the grammar of one specific kind of writing – the writing of continuous non-fiction prose – and, within that, single, isolated, out-of-context, specific sentences. So leaving behind, albeit reluctantly, the varieties of spoken language in use, what happens if we ask ourselves, 'What varieties of written language in use can we spot?' After all, a scientist or a sociologist would take it as read that a given field of study would and should involve spotting varieties, creating distinctions and categories and classifications. So let's put on our anoraks and go language-spotting.

Better still, let's start with an experiment: you are going to write a puff for a place – road, village, town, city, country – as you wish. This is in order to say that the place in question is a desirable place to visit. This is not the part of the ad which commands your reader to come or to visit. That's in another part of the ad which says things like 'not to be missed' or 'come to . . .'. This is the box inside which you tell us, as expansively as you can, what you've got. One restriction: you've got to do this in 30 words and you can lay it out how you like. Your box of writing can be wide or narrow. You can use letters and punctuation how you like.

Over to you.

Let me read one I saw on an ad in the London Underground this week:

Centuries [with a capital 'c'] of naval history, [comma] waterfront shopping, [comma] superb dining, [comma, new line] soaring sights [no comma] and miles of amazing beaches. [full stop] Ideally [with a capital 'i'] situated on [new line] the beautiful south coast, [comma] only 90 minutes from London. [full stop]

This presumably should fall into the category of defective and incorrect writing. Capital letters and full stops are used here without the phrases being true and correct sentences. Stylistically, there are problems with the adjectival present participle 'soaring' and the adverb 'ideally'. It's far from certain how, in a piece of factual writing, a 'sight' can be 'soaring' or why or how this place can be 'situated' 'ideally'. Conveniently, maybe, but not 'ideally' surely?

But in reality I don't give a fig. I may not love this writing, but it's doing its job: without finite verbs between its capital letters and full stops. Now, an hour reading ads and notices will reveal hundreds of examples like this. Quite clearly, this world of signs – away from continuous non-fiction prose – operates according to principles not devised in school grammar books.

We might ask, who invents these principles? And once invented, how come we're able to read what's written? Just to take the full stop in ad- , poster- and sign-land: it seems to have functions other than those of continuous prose. It can be dropped even when a full so-called true sentence is given to us:

In an emergency [new line]
Use [capital 'U'] the red emergency [new line]
button to alert the driver [no full stop]

In fact the capital 'U' but not capital 'b' has a principle all of its own. I don't know what that principle is, but perhaps it's best to ask the executive of Transport for London, headed by Boris Johnson, who I know is a stickler for such things.

Or the full stop can be used like this:

'One Water. [capital 'O', capital 'W', full stop] One Difference. [capital 'O', capital 'D', full stop]

In fact, the more you look at ads, even quite complicated, language-dense ones, the more you realise that it has become a kind of playground for graphic designers and copywriters who have in effect invented or re-invented ways of writing. Yet, as I say, we can read what they write.

I think there are important lessons here.

Written language is not static, unchanging and conservative.

Some very public, appropriate, highly communicative written language does not follow the patterns and conventions of traditional continuous non-fiction prose.

Some of this very public writing is commercially successful. People make a living inventing it. Firms rely on it in order to sell their products. Official bodies and authorities use it in order to pass on messages, some of which are a matter of life and death.

When talking about grammar – which is often a synonym for what people imagine is 'correct grammar' – it's uncommon for this kind of writing to be included. Within the terms of 'correct grammar' this kind of writing is incorrect, though clearly it's doing its job correctly enough to satisfy people publicising Portsmouth or delivering life-and-death instructions on the London Underground. I think we confuse, baffle and deceive children and school students if we talk about written English as if there is only one way to write it, as if it is static, unchanging and conservative.

What do grammarians say about this?

R. L. Trask taught linguistics and wrote *The Penguin Dictionary of English Grammar*. It's arranged along dictionary lines, in alphabetical order listing grammatical terms. So we find here a term I hadn't ever come across before:

BLOCK LANGUAGE The distinctive type of language used in public signs, typically consisting of PHRASES, rather than complete SENTENCES. Examples: No Parking; Left turn only; Stage door; EU passports; Birmingham and the North; Open Sunday. Compare HEADLINE LANGUAGE.

When we go to 'headline language' we find:

The rather special variety of English used in writing newspaper headlines. In the following examples, the first form illustrates headline language and the second ordinary English: President denies misconduct (The President has denied misconduct); Universities feeling the pinch (Universities are feeling the pinch); PM to visit China (The Prime Minister is going to visit China).

If like me you're obsessive enough to be the kind of person who would read a whole dictionary of grammar, we find some other terms:

the 'minor sentence', where a piece of language doesn't have the form of a complete sentence but, I quote, 'which is normal in context'. Examples: Why not do it now? Any news? All aboard! No smoking; This way, please; As if I would know;

the 'pro-drop' – 'the property of a language in which a sentence does not require an overt subject'.

(Here Trask suggests that English is 'not a pro-drop language', but I would suggest that there are plenty of examples of 'pro-drop' in English, as in, say, 'See you soon'.)

the 'fragment' – 'an incomplete piece of a sentence, used by itself. Examples: Ted: Where's Susie? Mike: In the library. Ted: Can England win the World Cup? Mike: Probably not.'

the 'pro-sentence' – 'a single word which can take the place of a complete sentence'. 'The most familiar English examples are yes and no. Here is an example. Jan: Would you like some tobasco [sic] sauce? Larry: Yes. Here Larry's response is equivalent to the sentence 'I would like some tobasco sauce.'

 And of course our old friend 'ellipsis'. 'The omission from a sentence of material which is logically required to complete its structure.' Examples: 'Nough said ('Enough said.'); Seems we have a problem ('It seems we have a problem.') – which should feature as an example of pro-drop which, according to Trask, doesn't occur in English.

So, what should we make of all this?

My first reaction is to be mildly delighted. Of course other grammarians visit this territory – our hero David Crystal gives it a couple of pages in his *Rediscover Grammar* book. With Trask, we are given more terms than Crystal gives us in that particular handbook, though of course they're spread out and diffused through the whole dictionary. There isn't a consistent effort to describe and analyse the kinds of signs and posters that we see every day.

I have another problem. The usage in question is mostly seen in the light of whatever it is that a 'complete sentence' is. Though Trask tells us that such usage is 'normal in context' – thank goodness for that – there is the suggestion that lying behind all these signs and utterances are more complete forms. In other words they are defined in terms of what they are not, rather than what they are. I don't buy this. The first rule of descriptive grammar should start out from the principles of who is doing the speaking or writing; who are they talking or writing for. In other words, it has its own force field, if you like, and can only be explained in terms of structures outside that context if it can be shown that they derive from that context.

I'm not sure that the examples I've given derive from what Trask calls more 'complete' forms. I think they come from somewhere else. For example, some of the language in question might be described in terms of its proximity to a good deal of speech. Advertising copywriters and sign-writers frequently try to imitate the questions, commands and phrases that we use or might use in speech, albeit in a very exhortatory, get-up-and-go sort of a way.

All the following come from ads and signs in the Underground:

The command: 'Go miles further with our best ever Skywards Miles offer'

The coax: 'Let's get it done'

The statement that sounds like an answer: 'Helping London grow for the future'

The question as if in speech: 'Going on a hot date this weekend?'

or:

'Got an opinion? Then share it with us'

The famously ambiguous command that isn't a command: 'Dogs must be carried', to which we can reply, 'But I haven't got a dog.'

The request: 'Please stand on the right.'

The statement as in speech, followed by the informal exclamation: 'Delays cut by 40% (Whoosh!)'

The pseudo-poetic or proverbial: 'Cold drink Warm heart'

Again: 'From everyday potentials to future spouse essentials' followed by announcements: 'Brands you know. [full stop] Rewards you'll love. [full stop]

Telegram or text-message-type descriptions: 'Floor slippery when wet'

Punctuation-free zone: 'This is a residential area please leave quietly'

The hidden request or command – embedded in the use of 'to fill' as in '700 empty bowls to fill this Christmas'

. . . or a simpler statement but more complex grammatically:

'Coffee to go' where I think 'to go' is probably a highly specific adjectival phrase but which we can only understand if we know American usage.

And even more compact, with yet another function for the word 'to':

'SMINT
Fresh to impress'

. . . meaning, I think, that it 'will impress', rather than a command or an adjectival description.

The right of titles of books, films, plays, songs, poems to use language that implies that something is unfinished, unsaid or indeed incomplete:

'London Grammar If you wait'

Inventing new vocabulary:

'Whole food revosmooshon
Fruit and nuts smooshed together'

Invented punctuation.

'Mortgages. [full stop] Courtesy of our savers. [full stop]

or

'Planet. [full stop] Sized. [full stop] Brain. [full stop]'

The conventions of the press recommendations, including single words, the title of the newspaper, or even an accepted sign:

'dazzling'
Metro

***** [five stars in a row]
Evening Standard

'a beauty of a show'
The Telegraph

The strangely non-referential:

'Manchester for just £19'

. . . so, the 'for just £19' doesn't refer to Manchester but the journey to Manchester.

A different sense to the grammatical term, the 'dangling participle':

'Closing down, everything must go!!!'

. . . where what is being referred to is a place not the word for a place.

Grammatical ambiguity: 'Lower window for ventilation'.

Is it a command or a description? Should I lower the window, or look for a lower window? Context explains all. I should lower the window.

Or similarly:

'Look right' – well, I look fine, thanks.

A complex and, dare I say, poetic utterance: 'Eat up. [full stop] Feet up. [full stop] Catch up. [full stop]'

. . . two of which are verbal commands ('eat up', 'catch up') but one of which ('feet up') sounds as if it could be or should be, but is actually a description. So it's a kind of grammatical pun.

The feigned correction:

'It's the thought that counts' where 'the' is crossed out but still visible, so we read both 'It's the thought that counts' and 'It's thought that counts'

. . . invoking mistakes, corrections, re-writes, edits. Or, it is the pseudo-palimpsest – the text written on another text?

'Travel alerts on twitter
(OMG!)'

. . . using a quotation without having to reference it, because it's colloquial digital language shared by those that the ad wishes to address. A fine example of how an implied reader is inscribed in the language of every piece of text.

Highly complex but simple:

STOP
WORKS

. . . which, as we know, does not mean, say, this bus stop is working. Or that stopping works in life, but that we should stop because there is a building site or some such nearby.

Even more simple but even more complex:

STOP

. . . written on the button on a bus, where it does not mean that we should stop anything. It means, if I want to send a message to the driver to stop the bus, he or she will. But not that he or she will stop the bus immediately. He or she will stop the bus at a bus stop. I can't think of a better example of how language can only fully signify when we know the context.

So within the context of ads and signs, we have a complex range of language use and grammars. Interestingly, I think, we learn how to understand them without being told how. We pick them up through looking, reading, re-reading and talking about them with family and friends. I would argue that they offer us in education a rich resource for describing and understanding language in use. People like R. L. Trask give us some of the means by which we can pin this down, but it may well be that we have to invent our own – a truly liberating thing for school students to do, I think.

Now, of course, I am by no means the first person to draw attention to this idea of varieties of written English – and there are many more than the ones that I've talked about so far. Some of you may know *Variety in Written English* by Tony Bex, published in 1996 and, I would suggest, subsequently largely ignored by those who want to tell us how to talk about language with children and students. More technical is *Text Types and the History of English* by Manfred Görlach, from 2004.

Bex reminds us that Standard English, even within the context of continuous non-fiction prose, has variety, and he draws attention to such things as the language of letters informing people of their rights, descriptions of a gas boiler, printed messages on Christmas cards, legal notices, lists of ingredients, Psalm 24 in the King James Bible of 1611, information about lost telephone cards, recipes, letters, bills, an announcement of a conference on linguistics, notices of sale of second-hand items, a spoof scientific document on temperature and geography, and finally, in a surprisingly short section, poems and novels.

Görlach attempts a classification of text types going back to Old English and forward to such things as hymns, jokes, representation of a standardised dialect in Scots, and what he calls 'Indian English'. In the central section of the book he has a glossary of over 2000 examples of text types.

Before I look at a few more examples I've collected, let's just stop for a moment and consider how a minister of education who was seriously interested in children and students of all ages understanding language might behave. With the kind of work done by Bex and Görlach, a minister might start up a commission, under the auspices of NATE, say, in which teachers and teacher-educators might develop potential fields of study and investigation for students and teachers to look at in the field of text types, or 'varieties of written English'. What might be the most appropriate types, what might be the most appropriate terminology, what would most help children and students to understand the language they see, read and try to use when they're writing?

This wouldn't have to be limited and held within what have been called 'genres'. It wouldn't have to be limited by criteria derived from outside language, on the basis that one genre is more powerful than another. I know the argument which claims that the language of administration is more powerful than the language of, say, subjective accounts of what I did today. Meanwhile, the language of, say, advertising, leads us to believe that the word 'fat-free' indicates that it's healthy even if the food in question is stacked up with refined sugar. In a previous NATE talk, I suggested that helping students discover the strategies by which people lie – when speaking as well as writing – might be just as powerful as being told that this or that genre is powerful and that you become powerful when I dictate to you how to write like that: a strange contradiction in terms, I've always thought.

So, let's return to one or two more text types: the press are often on teachers' backs for failing to instil what they often call the rules of English. Here's the sports writer, Patrick Barclay, writing in the *Evening Standard* on June 23 2014:

> There was no shilly-shallying, no retraction that time would be taken to absorb the lessons (in other words, assess the determination of the media to have a head on a plate). Just a grasp of the international game. And it will get better.

The phrase 'Just a grasp of the international game' is given a capital letter at the beginning and a full stop at the end. Likewise, 'And it will get better'.

What's going on here?

This is the development of Standard English writing. As we can tell from the phrases 'no retraction that time would be taken' and 'assess the determination of the media', Barclay is a writer who can draw on highly formal ways of writing. And yet he is quite happy to break what children and students will be told is a rule about sentences, and indeed marked on in tests and exams. In short, you are required to fib to children that there is only one way to write continuous non-fiction prose in Standard English. Clearly, even the sub-editors at the *Evening Standard* were quite happy for Patrick Barclay to write like that. In other words, there is a new – what shall we call it? – informal-formal writing. Any curriculum based on language in use would enable students to find, investigate and write about a development like this. I would suggest that we don't even really know why or how it has come about. Interestingly enough, it's come about at precisely the time that the bookshops are full of books by people like John Humphrys, Simon Heffer or the ubiquitous Gwynne, telling us what correct writing should look like.

Again, something to investigate.
Meanwhile, like Tony Bex, I've left the best till last.

Swallows?

Dark air-life looping
Yet missing the pure loop . . .
A twitch, a twitter, an elastic shudder in flight
And serrated wings against the sky,
Like a glove, a black glove thrown up at the light,
And falling back.

Never swallows!
Bats!

from 'Bat' by D.H. Lawrence, 1923

Many of you will know the layout on the page, done according to the principles of free verse, namely that the line breaks are guidelines to how the poet would like us to read it. Some people have said that the line in a free-verse poem is the equivalent of the foot in a metrical poem; it is the marriage of a unit of sense with a measured-out unit of language.

Lawrence, like thousands of other poets, writes in what appears to be a standard form of language, except that he doesn't, in this section, use finite verbs. He bounces between questions, descriptions and exclamations. He not only uses exclamation marks, but also italics with exclamation marks: a kind of double exclamation, then. He uses double line breaks as if there are verses or stanzas. He uses them irregularly. He uses traditional capital letter systems at the beginning of lines, for, I suspect, no other reason than he wanted to call this kind of writing 'poetry'. He uses repetition, done, as we used to call it, 'in apposition', listing terms, adding descriptions as he goes. It's hard to resist the temptation to say the lists gather descriptions to give the impression of the looping of the flight of the swallow. A musician will explain that if you say 'a twitch, a twitter, a shudder', there is no change in the tempo.

If you add in 'elastic' but keep the beat, and squeeze in the extra words, you speed up the speech to fit the beat, thus: 'a twitch, a twitter, an elastic shudder'.

Poetry and poetry-with-music, as with rap, can teach us how to do these things. And we can unpack it grammatically to see how it was done.

Lawrence didn't invent this way of writing. Let's try Shakespeare. Hamlet is in quite a state. He wonders whether it's worth going on. He says:

To die, to sleep,
No more; and by a sleep, to say we end
The Heart-ache, and the thousand Natural shocks
That flesh is heir to: 'Tis a consummation
Devoutly to be wished. To die, to sleep,
To sleep, perchance to Dream; Aye there's the rub.

This is of course 'written speech' – another text type. Grammatically, Shakespeare has written this part of the 'To be or not to be' speech with what Trask has called 'minor sentences' and 'fragments'. Though the first part of the speech that I have quoted is enclosed with full stops, the first finite verb in sight is the colloquial ''Tis', and then off we go with the inversion of 'to die, to sleep . . . Aye there's the rub'. You could perhaps put up an argument that, grammatically, the whole thing refers back to 'that is the question', but either way this soliloquy is what some people might foolishly call 'highly irregular'. But we don't call it 'highly irregular'; we call it Shakespeare, or a great speech . . .

What we can do is investigate it; we can see if grammarians have given us ways of describing what we find, or if we need some new ways. We can see if looking into it releases some meanings that we hadn't thought about before. So, we might see that the grammar is different from the first part of the speech:

To be, or not to be, that is the question:
Whether 'tis nobler in the mind to suffer
The slings and arrows of outrageous fortune,
Or to take arms against a sea of troubles
And by opposing end them.

This part sounds coherent, is written in standard grammar, subject, verb, alternative but equal clauses as subjects. This involves a classical balance of opposites, with a view to possible consequences – very rational. Do we say that the grammar produces the rationality? Or that the rationality produces the grammar? Interesting question.

We might say that the passage with the minor sentences and fragments represents a process whereby Hamlet's rational thought and standard grammar break up. Could we say that the passage gives us another kind of thought process: the ruptures, self-questionings and self-interruptions of inner speech – or what we think sounds like inner speech? Again, do we say that the grammar produces the impression of confusion, or the impression of confusion produces the grammar?

That's a question to ask a writer. And I get from that, that it's something that we can invite students to try themselves. We can say, 'Can you convey in writing a slide from coherent thought into confusion? One minute you're planning for your GCSEs and the next minute you slide into panic. How do you write that? Or the other way round, one moment you think of your parents in a state of rage and the next, you have an insight into what kinds of childhoods they had, and this enables you to make allowances. We can investigate what kind of grammatical constructions we find ourselves using in order to do that.'

And we can make comparisons between what and how we write, and how Shakespeare wrote that passage.

Finally, we can take a well-known example from a novel. This is from chapter 1 of *Bleak House* by Charles Dickens, written in 1852 and 1853.

('aits' is an old word meaning little islands that are in rivers;
'cabooses' are the 'kitchens' or 'galleys' on a boat;
'collier-brigs' are ships that carry coal;
'gunwales' (usually pronounced 'gunnels' to rhyme with 'funnels') are the upper edges of the side of a boat;
'nether' means 'lower';
'divers' means 'diverse' or 'various' or 'different kinds of . . . '
'husbandman' means 'farmer' ;
'hoary' means 'grey-haired' or simply 'old';
the 'Lord High Chancellor' was in Charles Dickens's time the most senior of all judges; it was the highest position in the running of the law.)

> Fog everywhere. Fog up the river, where it flows among green aits and meadows; fog down the river, where it rolls defiled among the tiers of shipping and the waterside pollutions of a great (and dirty) city. Fog on the Essex marshes, fog on the Kentish heights. Fog creeping into the cabooses of collier-brigs; fog lying out on the yards, and hovering in the rigging of great ships; fog drooping on the gunwales of barges and small boats. Fog in the eyes and throats of ancient Greenwich pensioners, wheezing by the firesides of their wards; fog in the stem

and bowl of the afternoon pipe of the wrathful skipper, down in his close cabin; fog cruelly pinching the toes and fingers of his shivering little 'prentice boy on deck. Chance people on the bridges peeping over the parapets into a nether sky of fog, with fog all round them, as if they were up in a balloon, and hanging in the misty clouds.

Gas looming through the fog in divers places in the streets, much as the sun may, from the spongey fields, be seen to loom by husbandman and ploughboy. Most of the shops lighted two hours before their time – as the gas seems to know, for it has a haggard and unwilling look.

The raw afternoon is rawest, and the dense fog is densest, and the muddy streets are muddiest near that leaden-headed old obstruction, appropriate ornament for the threshold of a leaden-headed old corporation, Temple Bar. And hard by Temple Bar, in Lincoln's Inn Hall, at the very heart of the fog, sits the Lord High Chancellor in his High Court of Chancery.

Never can there come fog too thick, never can there come mud and mire too deep, to assort with the groping and floundering condition which this High Court of Chancery, most pestilent of hoary sinners, holds this day in the sight of heaven and earth.

This piece of writing defies the neat categories we like to give to literature. It is descriptive, poetic and figurative, it's social in that it shows us a range of social class, but it's also political (or *engagé* as the French would say), and ultimately passionate and angry. This range is represented in the grammar which begins with the syntax of a free verse or prose poem: short descriptive strokes as if it had been written by one of the imagists, T. E. Hulme, or H.D.; extends into phrases with present participles as it includes people at work, and ends with complete sentences sculpted into patterns of repeated finite clauses piling on top of each other just as a political speaker or priest might use to grab and hold the attention of an audience. Incidentally, the first part of this passage uses a dance of punctuation, between full stops, commas and semi-colons, employed apparently arbitrarily by Dickens – unless we can detect a subtle attempt to mark pauses between cadences as a composer might do with minim rests, semi-breves and breves. Why not?

The term 'Standard English' cannot contain writing like this. Nor should it. It's the job of grammar to describe what writers and speakers do. It's not the job of writers and speakers to do what grammarians or politicians tell us to do.

I'll finish with a Harold-like suggestion. Perhaps we can take R. L. Trask, Tony Bex and Manfred Görlach along with, say, Michael Toolan's *Language in Literature* and break their work down into something accessible for 10-year-olds or 14-year-olds, which would enable them to investigate (not enforce) varieties of written English in use. Yes, Ronald Carter and his colleagues in the Language in the National Curriculum project have produced books in that zone, but I'm suggesting something simpler and, dare I say, more fun than that. Perhaps NATE could produce a resource for teachers and students like that.

And while I'm on the topic, has NATE ever thought of asking, say, twenty published writers how and why they write; and what suggestions would they give to students and teachers on how to do it?

If not, no worries, that's another idea for another time. Harold always believed there was another idea for another time.

Note 1: *Since I gave this lecture, John Richmond has gathered together many of Harold's writings – a large sample of his educational work, and some of his stories and poems – in* Harold Rosen: Writings on Life, Language and Learning, 1958 to 2008, *published in 2017 by the UCL Institute of Education Press. Available at https://www.ucl-ioe-press.com/books/language-and-literacy/harold-rosen.*

Doing and Thinking

This is a talk I gave at the Royal Society of Arts in 2013. It's available at https://www.youtube.com/watch?v=mdjec8H9dGw.

My mother was a primary-school teacher, but when she was in her early forties she took study leave to do a diploma in primary education at the Institute of Education with a person who, for us at home, seemed unfathomable and mysterious: a man called Christian Schiller.

I was around 16 and the first immediate consequence of my mother's studies was that I found that I had to get my own tea a lot more than I had done previously. The next was that my mother started to talk in unfathomable and mysterious phrases. These would surface sometimes after she had spent half an hour or an hour or so staring into the middle distance. I remember coming home from school once; the house was dark and I thought no one was in. I opened the door to the living room and saw that my mother was sitting there and she hadn't turned the light on. I asked her if she was OK and she said she was fine. Later I heard her say to my father (I quote), 'It's all a matter of doing and thinking.' My brother, the family satirist, had tuned into this way of talking and he'd started a new comedy routine where he would pretend to be my mother, look into the distance and say, 'Harold, it's all a matter of "being and seeing",' 'No, Harold, what it is is "talking and walking",' and so on.

At the time, I had no idea what she was talking about. My notion of what ideas or knowledge were was wrapped up in senior-school-type problems like the downfall of Antony and Cleopatra or the unification of Italy. Or again in, say, the politics of banning the bomb. To my mind-set at the time, a phrase like 'doing and thinking' wouldn't or couldn't capture anything that I thought worth knowing.

And yet, for the last fifty years, I can see that whether I knew it or not, the phrase has been some kind of pole star for me. I grant straight away that there is a problem in the idea that you might be locked into following a guide that you don't know you're being guided by, but let's leave that for a moment.

So, from the vantage point of now, what do I think my mother was on about? (And I should say that neither my mother or father is alive to ask.)

I think my mother was expressing what might be called the activist thesis, which in summary – or 'in my own words', which the best teachers always encouraged us to use – goes something like this:

In activity of any kind – imagine throwing a ball, or squeezing a sponge – we get our minds and bodies to go through actions. The way this involves our minds seems to involve such things as memory, recall, observation, response, reflection, interpretation, evaluation, as well as a synthesis of some or all of these. Yet none of them is entirely separate from whatever it is that our bodies are doing. So even as we say a word like 'observation', we need to understand that it means observing something from the inside of what it is our body is doing.

As my mother was a primary-school teacher, she was much concerned by the environment of the classroom. This I know because whenever we went on walks, she said she'd 'collect bits' to take into school. She was of course interested in the collective of children she was in charge of for the year, and how they could all make advances in that time. For her, I know, it was especially important that it was 'all' the children.

So, as anyone knows who has been in that situation or anything like it, a teacher has to address the matter of how this group of children co-exist and co-operate. At which point another of my mother's principles comes into play: a crucial part, as expressed by her or my brother, or both, as 'talking and doing and thinking'.

And as she sat in the dark and amalgamated what she was learning from Christian Schiller and from her fellow students with her twelve years or so of teaching experience, she included in the mix that her flock had to feel that they were allowed or entitled to experiment with what they could do, with what they could talk about and with what they could think.

So let me cut to the chase. For her, and people like her, the route to learning – or, if you prefer, to understanding – involved the idea that children would try out things, talk about them, do them, discuss them, think about them; and though I've separated these processes out, children might do them simultaneously or in conjunction with each other.

Now I should say that I didn't ever have the conversation with my mother where we talked about all this. I left for university and got involved with trying to solve the problems of the world. I have no regrets about that, though I regret that I think there was a part of me that thought that my mother wasn't as wise or as quick-witted as my father, and so when I came back in the holidays or on visits after I had left home, it turned out that I ended up getting into a talk-huddle with my father. Then, by the time I was 30, she was gone.

She left behind papers, stories, poems and a book she wrote with my father about the education of primary-school children, but I didn't ever have a real face-to-face chat about all this, and she didn't live long enough to see what has happened to education.

Even so, when I look back, say, all the way to when I was at university, I can see that there must have been part of me that knew that if I wanted to understand something, I had to 'do', I had to co-operate and I had to talk. To take one obvious example: Shakespeare. I loved reading close textual examinations of Shakespeare plays. I still do. And there are thousands of them. But I have to concede that very few of the very scholarly ones are about what it means to make a production or what it means to sit in a theatre (or any space) and watch a production. It's as if there is some kind of invisible hierarchy between a gold standard, bona fide analysis, which is about the written form of the play, and there is something below that which is less serious, and this is about such things as how you might turn that script into a live play, or how and why a person experiences the passing of events and thoughts in the play in the real time of a performance. Interesting, but less important.

To give you one small glimpse of what I mean: a few weeks ago, my wife and I went to see *Othello* at the National. I have to say that I found it an overwhelming experience. Looking back on it, I can see that bit by bit I was being wound up tighter and tighter so that when we reached the final unravelling at the end, after the killings, and Othello realises that Iago has engineered the whole situation (or, depending on how you look at it, Othello realises that he was only too willing to believe what Iago suggested to him), it became unbearable. Then, just as Aristotle suggested thousands of years ago, as a consequence of that explosion of feeling, and in reflection afterwards, it's possible to ask questions like, 'What if Othello hadn't believed Iago?' or 'What if the bit inside us all that's a bit like Iago, or a bit like Othello, could be suppressed, or avoided, wouldn't we and the world be better?'.

But – and this is crucial – for all this to work as I've suggested, it took a particularly brilliant production. When Othello looked across at Iago and realised what he realised, and when in the physical real time and space of that moment we realised that he realised, the script could do its work. Or, as my mother would say, doing and thinking.

Now, that wasn't me out there acting (if only . . .) but at university I did quite a lot of 'doing' around Shakespeare and other plays, and the more I did it, the more I reckoned I could get to a level of understanding about plays and drama that I could not get only or purely from reading the scholarly stuff. What any performer knows is that the script can be as good as can be, but it has to work on the night. Voice, movement, looks, glances and a hundred other elements. Did I absorb that from my mother?

Around that time and for a few years more, I started to write poems. I thought I was writing wry little pieces about my childhood that adults would find amusing. The trick I was playing with is that the narrator in the poem doesn't know as much about himself as the reader. Again, I had arrived at this point by churning up what I was reading into things that I wanted to write. Writing (or doing, if you like) was in a way a kind of criticism.

In fact, there didn't seem to be many adults who were interested in what I was doing, other than a schools radio producer and an editor of children's books. These were for children, they both said. So the poems became a book, whereupon I started being invited into schools, libraries and on teacher-training courses to read the poems. To start off with, I did this in a rather non-doing way. On one occasion I arrived at a school, Princess Frederika in north London, and the deputy headteacher said that the children were very excited and they were all waiting for me. I thought he meant a class but he took me through an arch and there was the whole school, three hundred of them. Mr McErlaine, the teacher, said, 'Boys and girls, here's the moment you've all been waiting for,' and they all roared. I suspect that they roared not so much because it was me but that they liked roaring. So I hid. I hid behind my book and started to read, in my reading-a-poem voice.

> The ship in the dock was at the end of the trip
> The man on board was the captain of the ship
> The name of the man was Old Ben Brown
> And he played the ukelele with his trousers down.

Now, when you perform in front of three hundred children, you usually have about thirty seconds to prove yourself and if you don't or can't, it's not that they're rude or start heckling, they just start getting interested in other stuff – their shoes, their hair, their teeth, their ears.

And it had started happening.

I looked across to Mr McErlaine and he looked horrified. He had read the poems off the page and interpreted that I was some kind of live wire, who could electrify his school.

So, he seized the moment and said to the children, 'Noooo, it doesn't go like that, does it, children?' And they roared back at him, 'Nooooo.'

And then he did something I've never forgotten; he danced the poem.

He read it with the whole of his body and the whole school joined in moving and singing the poem:

> The ship in the dock was at the end of its trip
> The man on board was the captain of the ship
> The name of the man was Old Ben Brown
> and he played the ukelele with his trousers – down
> he played the ukelele with his trousers – down.

In that one moment, I learned that if I was going to make contact with a live audience with the words I had written onto a page, I would have to do some serious doing, I would have to dance the poems too. And if I did that, children would do that too. They wouldn't just read poems. They would 'do' poems.

Much more recently, I've been involved in writing a book about a particular aspect of language: the alphabet. Now, another side of being a child of my parents is that language was treated in our home not only as something functional, something expressive, and something reflective, but also as something endlessly provisional and endlessly malleable. My parents exchanged English words with words, expressions and songs from Yiddish, French, German, Latin and Italian. They exchanged their accents with experiments in American (my father had been in the US army) and Welsh (my father had been evacuated there when he was studying at University College, London). They implied in how they spoke that language was a resource; no, more than that, it was a playground. When our dishwasher broke down, my mother called it a 'wishdasher'. When she saw what a mess our bedroom was, she called it a 'mishadamonk'. When we asked her what a 'mishadamonk' was, she said it was our bedroom. When either or both of my parents heard or read or said something that seemed to them pithy or ironic or significant, they cut and pasted it into their conversations. My mother said, 'Ask your father what he's doing and tell him to stop it.' It was requoted a thousand times.

I learned that I could think of language this way too. I could make it and remake it, quote it and edit it, make substitutions and additions, switch between accents, dialects and languages. And all this activity was not a matter of being clever-clever. It was again a matter of doing and thinking. By doing all that stuff, it was a way of thinking about language. At the heart of it is a question about who language belongs to.

A good deal of education implies that language belongs outside of yourself; it belongs to the invisible know-alls who set and mark tests and exams; to invisible writers of dictionaries; to the invisible writers of the scripts that teachers appear to be using in order to teach, especially when they say things like, 'I would prefer not to be doing this, but we have to . . . '

It's a nonsense. Language belongs to all of us because we're the ones who use it and change it. It is at times a battleground with all kinds of instructions and demands being issued; some contest these, while millions carry on regardless. At times it's a place of exchange, borrowing and lending between groups. The activity of people leads them to put language to use as part of those activities. Doing and thinking and talking.

And yet, even if I know all this, I can find myself caught out. As I started work on the book about the alphabet, my first feeling was that the alphabet was something fixed. After all, people call the alphabet which I've used to write this talk 'the Roman alphabet', and there it is carved into stone on Trajan's column in Rome. You can't be more fixed than that . . . other than that the Romans wrote the word 'Julius' as 'IVLIVS', all in what we would call capital letters. We don't write like that any more. So unchangeable, but changeable. And who did the changing? Who thought up the little letters, and the letters 'J', 'U' and 'W'? Julius Caesar? Elizabeth I? Napoleon?

Well, it took me four hundred pages to find out, but these changes and many more happened because, more often than not, the doers in the actual material business of getting writing onto paper and screens – scribes, printers, compositors and people sitting at terminals – decided, through doing, talking and thinking, that change was a good idea or even a necessity.

Maybe my mother would like that.

So I believe that we not only all make and change language, but that we have the right and necessity to find out how it works by playing with it. Most classrooms I go into have a poster on the wall of specially good words. I am always curious about this. Where do these words come from? What's so good about them? Why do good words come from outside the children? Again, perhaps informed by my mother, I always suggest that teachers could create a magpie wall, where children and the teacher put up words and phrases, things that parents have said, lines from songs, stories, poems, newspaper headlines that show interesting, exciting, odd or intriguing use of language. As I say, poets may or may not be people with imagination – whatever that means – but we are also people on the hunt for a good way to begin a poem. Looking for things said, written or sung out there is as good a way as any. It's a way of doing language instead of just receiving it.

Yesterday I was at a teachers' conference. We were talking about reading for pleasure. It seems to be a good idea. There are vast quantities of research from all over the world which show that when children have the opportunities to choose what they want to read and have time to read it, the benefits are enormous. So, though we call it something soft and cosy – reading for pleasure – it has gloriously serious consequences. Governments know this. They even put it into the kinds of documents they turn out to show that they are not entirely dominated and obsessed with measuring, classifying, selecting and segregating children. Then they do nothing about it and get on with spending millions on not reading for pleasure.

Reading for pleasure is a kind of doing too. The reader is active about choosing, browsing and selecting, and then active with playing with the possibilities in a text. More often than not, readers for pleasure will talk about what they read. They pass on their enthusiasms and raise queries.

That's why it gets banned. At the teachers' conference yesterday a teacher told us that she had been told not to spend time doing such things because it was a 'waste of time'. Another told us that if she went on doing role-play around stories she would be graded as 'unsatisfactory', which is a short cut to being slung out.

This week, I decided that I am going to stop calling myself a poet or a writer or a broadcaster. I'm going to call myself a literature activist. I hope my mother would like that.

No, I'll rephrase all that. I'm going to suggest that children and teachers become literature activists. I'm sure that my mother would like that even more.

How I Learnt to Read (and Became a Reader) and Learnt to Write (and Became a Writer)

Here's a piece about how I became first a reader, then a writer, what that led to once I began to visit schools and work with teachers, and where we are now in relation to attitudes to learning to read and learning to understand what we read. It's a talk I gave to the United Kingdom Literacy Association in July 2014.

The other day I got a tweet from someone called Cath Beard. There was a photo of a very young child sitting with a board book. The tweet said:

> 5yr old read the 1yr old 'We're going on a bear hunt' this morning. Here she is reading it to hrslf

My first thought was, 'Well, that's nice.' And then I thought some more. Surely there's some mistake here. Assuming all the facts are as stated, then a five-year-old reading *We're Going on a Bear Hunt* is either wrong or misguided or both. *We're Going on a Bear Hunt* is not phonically regular throughout, the 'tricky words' or 'red words' are not clearly marked, the book is much too heavily illustrated, the words are much too easily learned off by heart, the final page has no words on it at all. I think we should assume that the children in question are not only not decoding but that they are in great danger. They are in great danger of what ex-schools minister Nick Gibb told me happens: namely of being confused by multi-cueing strategies, which will let them down later on when they try to decode words that they haven't come across.

I will assume that this room is full of people who learned how to read. While we were learning to read, there were some children who did not. According to present orthodoxies, there is one reason and one reason only for that. Or to nuance it a little, there would have been only one remedy for that. On account of that position – that there would have been only one remedy for some of our companions not learning how to read – this lone remedy should be applied to all children, including the child reading *We're Going on a Bear Hunt* to her baby sister. I understand this as a marketing ploy. I'm not sure I understand it as a piece of educational policy. After all, one of the watchwords of educational policy is choice. But not in learning how to read, it seems.

So we should ask, I think, 'Is there any other part of the school curriculum that applies a one-size-fits-all method quite so rigidly?' If, as I think, there isn't another part of the curriculum being treated in that way, can we ask, 'What is so special about learning to read that it requires this one-size-fits-all method?'

Meanwhile, back with the people in this room learning to read. If we weren't taught by:

i at least a half-hour a day of systematic synthetic phonics,

ii readers graded according to these principles

and

iii taught on the principle of 'first, fast and only'

. . . how did we manage?

I learned how to read in several ways – simultaneously. I say 'simultaneously' in that rather sententious, loaded way, because the word is itself highly controversial. I am told on a daily basis that it's either impossible or undesirable for children to learn how to read for meaning and learn how to decode at the same time. I am told over and over again that first you learn how to decode, then you learn how to understand. Meanwhile, I am now being told that, in fact, I am wrong when I have said in the past that 'decoding' and 'reading with understanding' are different. Apparently, there are some now who say that, for most native speakers of English, to decode is to 'read with understanding' because they know the meaning of all the words they are decoding. And that is because the words in the phonics schemes are so simple that it can be assumed that the readers will know what they mean anyway.

And then.

The snag with all talk of learning how to read is there is always an 'and then'. Well, several actually. One of the big 'and thens' is what happens when you meet a word you can't decode. What do you do then? And another 'and then' is the question of what happens when you meet a word, a phrase, a sentence, a paragraph, a chapter or a book that you can 'decode' but can't understand. What strategies will you use? What strategies are available? What strategies work?

Have the five-year-old and the one-year-old in that tweet got anything to offer in this conversation? Or are they in danger? And wrong?

So I go back to my own first reading experiences.

I was born in May 1946, and the first schooling in reading that I remember happened in September 1951 in Pinner Wood Primary School. I was on what was called the 'Old Lob Approach to Reading'. In the picture book *Old Lob and his Family*, along with the matching cards, I was introduced to 61 words. In the following book, *At Old Lob's*, I was introduced to 14 more.

In *At Old Lob's* – I quote from the preface –

> . . . every story about Old Lob and his animal family is presented in two forms. First, the story is told in a sequence of pictures wherein new words are introduced. The pupil thus connects a new word with a specific picture, and can refer back to the picture if he fails to recognize the word subsequently. In its second form the story is presented as a little play which uses the vocabulary of the preceding sequence pictures, but in a slightly different form. The play thus becomes a test of work done through the pictures and an opportunity for the child to use his new reading vocabulary in an interesting, conversational way.
>
> It is assumed that while the pupil is reading *At Old Lob's* and using the individual material to accompany it, his phonic powers are being developed so that by the time he is ready for Book One (*The Move*) he will be able to recognize as wholes the one-syllabled words containing a short vowel sound which occur in the context of that book . . .
>
> Teachers who prefer an approach to phonics through single letter sounds will find the material for this in the Teachers' Manual . . . The phonic tables at the end of this book can be used for phonic practice in connection with either of these methods.

Meanwhile the theory behind this practice is spelled out in *The New Beacon Readers, Teachers' Manual*. My copy dates from after the original edition of 1926, so I can't sure that my teachers were trained in exactly the same way.

I would like to read you a chunk of this because there is quite a lot of misinformation passed around about the theory and practice of the good old days. I come from the good old days, so I think this is very relevant. Please note, I'm not reading this out because I agree or disagree with it. I'm reading it out for the historical record, which is much disputed.

> The act of reading – getting meaning from the printed page – is dependent

upon two factors: (1) a mastery of the tools or the mechanics of reading; and (2) the ability of the reader to interpret the thought of what is read. The success and efficiency with which small children are taught to read depends upon the development of these two factors, and the maintenance of an adequate balance between them. Although the way in which reading is taught in some instances may seem to suggest that these factors are incompatible and incapable of development one with the other, a careful consideration of the reading habit can lead to but one conclusion – both an ability to recognize words in [*sic*] the printed page, and an ability to understand the meaning that lies behind them, are at the very basis of correct and efficient reading habits.

The author is James H. Fassett.

In practice, I was learning how to read by reading the following, which is what the preface to *At Old Lob's* called 'a little play' ('Miss Tibs' is a cat):

Miss Tibs Up a Tree

Percy: Mother Hen! Mother Hen! Miss Tibs is up a tree. She is afraid to come down. What can we do?

Mother Hen: Run for Mr. Dan, Percy. He will help Miss Tibs.

Percy: Mr. Dan! Mr. Dan! Miss Tibs is up a tree. She is afraid to come down. What can we do?

Mr. Dan: Run for Old Lob, Percy. He will help Miss Tibs.

Percy: Old Lob! Old Lob! Miss Tibs is up a tree. She is afraid to come down. Come and help Miss Tibs.

Old Lob: I will come. Where is Miss Tibs?

Percy: Look up, Old Lob. Miss Tibs is up the tree.

Old Lob: I see you, Tibs. I will come to you. Here I come — up, up, up.

Percy: Old Lob has Miss Tibs. Down he comes. Miss Tibs is safe.

I remember liking my *Old Lob* books.

By the way, it rather seems as if people in government think that learning to read by 'look and say' methods was something invented by dope-smoking hippies intent on tricking poor children out of the right to read. Let me show you *The Merry Readers: A Whole-Word Method of Learning to Read* by H. Ada Beeny, published in 1915. Here's the contents list from Book 1:

Jack and Jill Went Up the Hill
Hickory, Dickory, Dock!
"Baa Baa, Black Sheep"
"Pat-a-Cake, Pat-a-Cake, Baker's Man"
Little Tommy Tucker
The North Wind Doth Blow
Little Jack Horner
If I Had a Donkey
My Little Pussy
Old Chairs to Mend!
Girls and Boys, Come Out to Play
Little Boy Blue
"Pussy-Cat, Pussy-Cat, Where Have you Been?"
Three Blind Mice
Hey, Diddle, Diddle
Tom, Tom, the Piper's Son
There Was a Crooked Man
Jack and Jill
Hush-a-Bye, Baby
Humpty Dumpty
There Was an Old Woman
The Five Little Pigs
My Little Pony
Ride a Cock-Horse
See-Saw! Margery Daw!
Little Polly Flinders
Little Miss Muffet
Ding, Dong, Bell
Simple Simon
Robin Redbreast and Puss
"Where are you Going, My Pretty Maid?"

Looby Loo
Mary's Little Lamb
Little Bo-Peep
Cock a Doodle Doo!
When the Snow is on the Ground
Here We Go Round the Mulberry Bush
Three Little Kittens

I can't speak for my friends of the early 1950s, but in my case this wasn't the only way in which I was learning what James Fassett calls the 'mechanics', or again what he calls 'interpretation'. What else was helping me to do what Fassett calls 'understand the meaning that lies behind' the 'words in the printed page'?

My father sang a lot of songs, which we learned. Most of these were in English but some were in French and German and one or two were in Yiddish or had Yiddish words in them. My mother read every night to me from as early as I can remember. As I am a younger brother, I suspect that I was that younger child who snuggles in with the older ones and hears what is sometimes called 'older material' but, incredibly, doesn't mind. Amongst these books are the Beatrix Potter range, most of which we owned, the first in the series of Puffin Picture Books, which were a mix of fiction and non-fiction, the *Orlando* books, *Babar the Elephant*, and the English versions of the Père Castor books from France, much influenced by Russian and Czech artists and which were hybrid fiction/non-fiction books with a libertarian undertow linked to an educational system founded by Paul Faucher, known as 'New Education'.

Incidentally, anyone interested in the cross-fertilisation between Soviet, French, English and American books from the early 1930s through to the early 1950s should look at *Drawn Direct to the Plate: Noel Carrington and the Puffin Picture Books* by Joe Pearson (2010) – a remarkable account of how the idea of producing cheap, multi-coloured, imaginative, creative, large-format picture books for very young children spread around the world. I am in part a product of this movement – and it was a movement – just as much as I am indebted to my teachers who used the Beacon Readers, Mrs Hurst and Miss Thomas of Pinner Wood Primary School.

I also learned to read at the meal table, in the street and on holidays. I have a clear memory of wanting to know what it said on the food packaging on our table – one good reason for not dispensing everything into jugs and serving dishes. My brother in particular was keen to decipher and explain everything. In the streets, I would go shopping with either or both of my parents and they were keen to help me read shop names and signs in shops. I was particularly fascinated by a shop where we lived called Payantake. I'll spell that. All one word. I now realise that this was one of the first serve-yourself supermarkets. But there was also Maynards the newsagents, Sketchley's the dry cleaners, Swannell and Sly the estate agents, Pat's Pantry for toys, the Old Oak Tea Rooms, Beaumonts the newsagents, Vassars the newsagents, Ellements for funerals, the Oddfellows Arms, The Queens Head, the Red Lion, the estate agents we lived over, Norman and Butt, the caff next door, Cosmo's, the Midland Bank, the Electricity Service Centre, Greatbatch the cobblers, the Co-operative Wholesale Store and of course Woolworth's. I learned to read all these names.

I was particularly fascinated by all the words on the station, the signs, the directions, and the ads for things like Virol, a rather delicious sticky tonic. On the handles of the trains it said in curly writing engraved into brass, 'Live in Metroland'. We lived in Metroland. This was the name for where we lived.

On holidays, from 1950 onwards, we alternated between camping on farms, and going to France. My mother kept scrapbooks of train tickets, bus tickets, boat tickets, sweet wrappers, food boxes, leaflets from museums and ancient sites. We pored over these when we came back. I learned to say the words in French. My brother kept a logbook which he read to me.

When we visited my father's sister, her daughters did puzzles. They always had puzzle books which they showed me how to do. When we visited my mother's parents, her mother would tell long stories about how either she, or my mother's father, or my mother's brother, had been cheated. When I went to the park with my mother's father, he met up with other men in dark blue suits like him and they spoke a language I didn't understand – Yiddish.

On all our holidays, my father had maps. He was always pointing out the names of places, sometimes making up rhymes about them. He also made up songs about the people we went camping with.

At home, my parents read the newspapers, one of which was the *Daily Worker*. In the corner of one of the pages there was a 'Children's Corner'. Here's a poem about it:

> There was a competition in the paper: Write a
> Story, and the best story would be printed.
> I thought I might go for it. I started thinking about
> *Solomon the Cat*, a book I'd read at school,
> about how Solomon gets thrown out and goes

from house to house, asking for somewhere to be
put up. I thought, 'I could write a story like that.'
I called it 'Solomon the Cat'. And I wrote how
Solomon gets thrown out and goes from house
to house, asking for somewhere to be put up. I
sent it in, and I won the competition, and it was
printed in the paper: 'Solomon the Cat' by Michael
Rosen, aged 7. It got printed in the paper's Christmas
annual, too: 'Solomon the Cat' by Michael Rosen,
aged 7. Some time later, we got a letter from the
paper saying that they'd heard from someone who said
they'd bought a picture book about a cat called
Solomon who gets thrown out and goes from house
to house, asking for somewhere to be put up.

'See this, Con?' my father says to my mother, 'Someone's
stolen Michael's story and made a book out of it. Would
you believe it? The things people do! If I had the
time, I'd try to get a hold of that book, and sue
the pants off them.'

'No, no,' I said, 'I shouldn't bother, it was ages ago.'

When I was seven this happened:

When I was seven
David Kellner came up to me at school and said,
You are aren't you?
What?
No, you are, I know you are, you are aren't you?
I'm sorry, I don't know what you mean, I said.
My mum says you are and she knows,
she says she knows you are from your name.
What?
You're Jewish aren't you?
I think so, I said.
There you are then, David Kellner said . . .
well, my mum says you should come to the synagogue

and do Hebrew classes.

So I went home and said,
Er David Kellner says I should go to synagogue
and do Hebrew classes.
I see, mum said.

Hebrew classes were run by Mrs Kellner
but there wasn't a synagogue yet.
It was a corrugated iron Methodist chapel
without any Methodists in it.
Zeyde thought it was hysterical:
So Michael's going to *kheder*! Michael's going to *kheder*!
Zeyde didn't go to *shul* either,
he went to Hackney Downs instead
and stood around with a lot of old men in dark suits
with shiny bits on the *tukhes* of their *gatkes*.

At Hebrew classes Mrs Kellner who was very small
and had a huge and very wonderful bosom,
taught me the letters.
I could only remember two of them.
They both looked like the letter seven
but they each had a dot in a different place.
One of them had a dot over the top
and the other one had the dot in the middle.
How do you tell the difference? said Mrs Kellner.
I'll tell you.
(I never told David Kellner
that I loved his mother's wonderful bosom.)
What happens, she said
when you get hit by a football over your head?
You say OH!
And what happens
if you get hit by a football in your belly?
You say OOOH!
There you are
that's how you tell the difference.

One says OH! And the other says OOOH!

This, I remember
but I left Hebrew Classes
after they shouted at me on the outing to Chessington Zoo.
You don't have to learn Hebrew
from people who give you *tsurres* at Chessington Zoo.

zeyde = grandfather
kheder – Hebrew classes
shul = synagogue
tukhes = bum
gatkes = trousers or long johns
tsurres = bother

Through all these activities, not just one of them, I learned that reading was not something you did purely and only in school with a Beacon Reader. I learned that English was not the only language in the world. I learned that letters could be used in different ways for different languages. I learned that there were letters other than the ones used in school and you could read using them. I learned that you could borrow language and use it for yourself. I learned that you could play with language and unpredictable and funny meanings came out. My father sang:

The higher up the mountain
the sweeter grows the grass
the higher up the donkey climbs
the more it shows its face.

He said his mother had taught him that and that she had learned it from when she and the family lived in America. That means it dates from before 1922.

On Saturdays we went to the local library. There was a children's room and we were allowed to borrow two or three books at a time. My parents would let me browse through books on my own while they went off to choose books for themselves. I would lay books out on the table and if one of my friends happened to be there, we would look at them together. As it happens, I've come to think that this is one of the most important activities that parents and teachers can provide for children. It enables us to find what we want to read. We do it by scanning many different kinds of texts, selecting and rejecting – each of these being as important as the other, and it implies in its practice that texts belong to the reader.

My brother and I got comics. I think I was most interested in my brother's one which was called *The Eagle*. It was a mixture of British science-fiction heroism (Dan Dare who battled the mighty Mekon and the Treens), comedy with a character called Harris Tweed, various kinds of information about wonderful British inventions, pets and good Christian deeds. He would read these to me and we talked about them.

Somewhere around this time, my best friend and I discovered *Winnie the Pooh*. His father was a painter and decorator, his mother was what we used to call 'the lollypop lady' – that's to say she helped children cross the road on the way to and from school. I have a strong memory of walking down the street, chanting some of 'Pooh's Hums', especially the one about his nose being cold. I can also remember talking with my friend about the Hefferlump episode and laughing as we tried to explain to each other the absurdity of the story. I can see now that we were trying to get to grips with dramatic irony: that we knew more about what was going on than the protagonists.

At school, we were read to at the end of every day. The first of these readings that I distinctly remember was *Emil and the Detectives* and the one I was most enthusiastic about was *Hue and Cry*, a novelisation of the film of the same title. Our head teacher read to us once a week on a Friday. He would read a chapter and then snap the book shut. We would shout out how cruel this was, and how he should read it to us more often. We tried to get a copy of the book from the library but he seemed to have the world's only copy. More important than I can explain, we would talk about the book in the time between the Friday readings. This is a great example of the social production of meaning – something that Dickens is celebrated for. That's to say that the meaning of a text is not something produced in some kind of private, isolated, individual way. Meaning comes out of social interaction. On the playground we played out *Hue and Cry*, which incidentally has strong links to *Emil and the Detectives*.

There was a good deal of learning of hymns, carols and songs at school right from the first years. We had songbooks, hymn books and carol sheets. We got these through music lessons, morning assemblies, hymn practice, carol concerts, and what used to be called RI – religious instruction. This was a text-heavy experience, with hundreds of words that I, for one, didn't really understand. The music often – not always – compensated for the boredom of not knowing what I was saying or singing. I can remember asking what was the meaning of 'There is a green hill far away, without a city wall'. I said that hills don't have walls. It was a good example of being able to read without understanding what I was reading. Not in itself particularly bad – it was part of the textual variety that we were offered. We recited prayers every day – the Lord's Prayer and one other. I had no idea what the Lord's Prayer meant – again, in itself no bad thing necessarily.

We also recited poems. At the age of seven – I can remember the teacher – we were asked to perform poems. One boy learned his off by heart – 'Autumn Fires'–but the rest of us read ours 'with good expression'. I think I read 'When icicles hang by the wall' and everyone laughed at the phrase 'greasy Joan' because there was a girl in our class called Joan.

When I was a little bit older I was in the choral speaking group – other children were in the choir or other groups. We recited 'Adlestrop'. There was a good deal of discussion about whether 'unwontedly' meant not wanted. We were told by Mrs MacNab that it did not, but at the end of the discussion I still thought that it kind of did.

By this time, I was reading historical fiction by authors like Geoffrey Trease, who was a kind of compulsory curriculum for left-wing parents, Rosemary Sutcliff, Henry Treece, Cynthia Harnett, animal novels by people like a French author called René Guillot and a Canadian author Ernest Thompson Seton, other novels like *Raff the Jungle Bird* – a story that obsessed me about two New York naturalists who looked after a mynah bird.

These two tastes came out of what my parents had read to me, but I have the memory of hunting down books and authors by myself, asking in the library, for example, if they had any more by, say, René Guillot or Ernest Thompson Seton, who weren't published by Puffin Books.

When I was ten my father brought back from a conference a book called *There's no Escape* by Ian Serraillier, which Serraillier signed 'For your ten-year-old'. I thought that there was something magical about the author of a book signing it and I badgered my father to tell me about what he looked like. I still have the book.

Throughout this time, I was also reading what I was writing. Surely, one route to being able to read, understanding what we read, is to write things that we say? If there are things we say but can't write, again, surely it's wonderful that there are people who can do it for us? I have no memory of this being done at school – it may well have happened, though – but my mother did plenty of it. She did it in two ways: she wrote down things we said and showed us; also, she had trained to be what used to be called a 'shorthand typist' and she would type things that we said to her and we would read them together.

From 4 November 1952, I still have what we would now call a 'trail'. It's 'My Visit to the Geffrye Museum, Kingsland Road, E2'. I was six. I remember the visit. I went with just my father, who would have been 33 at the time. I filled in the sections with him, 'Christopher Wren was a . . . "famous architect" who lived in the . . . "17th and 18th" century'. Under 'Find the names of four people living now who are helping to make the world a better place to live in, I have written, '1. Harry Pollitt', who at the time was General Secretary of the Communist Party. I have a memory of my father laughing that I had written that.

After the trip, we came out to the bus stop and my father pointed over the road and said, 'Look, there's your shop.' I looked and the shop was called 'M. Rosen', written in large red letters on a white background. I had always had a sense that hardly anyone was called Rosen and certainly there were no other M. Rosens in my world. Now here was a shop with my name on it. It was again magical that just a few letters could have such a powerful effect.

At school, a group of us asked if we could make a class magazine, and we made it, duplicated it on a Gestetner and sold it for school funds. We each wrote articles, jokes and puzzles.

In sum, put all these activities together, say between the time I was born and the age of ten, and they made me a reader. I understand that by saying that, I have said something controversial. Someone – let's call him Dave – showed a conference how the children at his school learned how to read. They learned to read doing SSF, he said. He showed us his timetable and it included, I think, about an hour a day, right from the very start, a lot of storytelling, singing, listening to poetry, learning it, listening to teachers reading stories. I made the fatal error of saying that this was also teaching the children how to read. He got very angry with me and said that it didn't.

So, let's forget for a moment what this hour a day of storytelling and poetry is called. Why did they do it? What was the purpose of it? Dave's not here to answer that question, so I'm going to give it a go. Quite apart from the fun and delight that I hope was going on the room doing songs, poems and stories, quite apart from whatever these songs, poems and stories say about personal and social experience, hopes, desires, fears, loves, hates and the rest, presumably something else was going on. The children were hearing language used in ways that by and large they wouldn't hear or use themselves. Just to be clear, this is not because they are backward, benighted, underprivileged children, in the words of West Side Story 'depraved on account of being deprived'. No, simply because most written texts are organised in ways that are not the same as the way we speak and talk. We all speak in what have been called 'minor sentences' – 'fragments' with 'ellipses', corrections, repetitions, fade-outs, self-interruptions or interruptions from others, speech with visual cues (gestures, facial expressions), speech with expressions which can indicate the exact opposite of what the word apparently means as with, famously, 'Yeah right' and 'Yeah, right'. Speech often relies on pronouns which do not specify each time who the person is talking about.

The literature and non-fiction that was going on in Dave's school, as he described it, would have been made up of continuous prose, interspersed sometimes with the constructed dialogue of stories and novels. And it would also have included the strange, specialised language of poetry, which is often a thing unto itself, but also picks up on language from a wide range of sources as its raw material.

If we think that learning to read can be expressed in the phrase 'learning to read with understanding', then this hearing and acting out of the written word is part of how we learn to read with understanding. We get how the complicated systems of the written language work. We get how to derive meaning from these systems. We learn that learning how to read with understanding is not a matter of reading letters and not even a matter of reading words. And this is where the arguments can get the fiercest. Reading with understanding involves getting the units of meaning across several or many words, linked as they are by the grammar of the language.

We learn the grammar of the spoken language by hearing and using it thousands of times. One of the key ways to learn the grammar of the written language is to hear it and use it thousands of times. The most pleasurable ways to do that are to be read to, to learn songs, poems and plays that please us and to have what we say scribed for us so that we can read it back.

Dave must have known that. He proudly showed us authors visiting his school, who, as far as we could see, were also teaching the children to read as they read their works to the children and followed it up by doing writing workshops with the children, where the children read what they wrote.

I'm not one of those authors at Dave's school, but it is what I do. I go into schools, I do poems that the children can read for themselves, as they are in books. I have put performances of my poems – by me – up on my website so that children can see them over and over again and, as I've discovered, learn them without having to learn them.

I hope that many children get to make the connection between the language coming out of my mouth in these performances, the language that they can find on the page, and language that they themselves can write and say.

It's a very simple circle: writing, reading, performing (or call it reading out loud), writing, reading, performing, but, sadly, not one that is necessarily or universally given emphasis. Here's an example.

Last year, some musicians and I put together a show called Centrally Heated Knickers. It was based on a book of poems of the same name that I wrote several years ago. All 100 poems have a link to science, technology and design. It was a commission from the Design Council with co-operation from the Institute of Physics and the Royal Society of Chemistry. We had several meetings where I met the scientists and we discussed whether the poems did or did not open up questions about science and its application in the world around us. In the book, the links between the poems and science are mentioned in the headings and the Association for Science Education produced a lengthy book with links between the poems, the science in question and what they called 'literacy'.

The show was a piece of theatre involving me performing the poems, along with a sax player, a guitarist and a percussionist who played drums and vibes. A dance and mime artist acted out the poems or choreographed them. We focused on the poems that were linked to the production and reception of sound and in the middle of the show there was a partly improvised section where I played the scientist demonstrating a machine called the 'earstrument', which was a mock-up of a cross-section of the ear.

At most of the venues where we did the show, there were copies of Centrally Heated Knickers on sale. Sometimes, I went out front-of-house to sign copies. Most of the shows were daytime ones for schools; some were at the weekends for families.

Now, I don't know how the adults at these shows conceive of reading and literacy – and for me to talk about this particular show is a matter loaded with my own bias. But, put it this way, when I've taken my children to shows, I've very consciously thought of ways in which the show can have an afterlife, in part through text. It may well have an afterlife in, say, putting on shows, dancing or singing or whatever . . . but I've always thought that if we want to make texts *as texts* matter, then we have to grab every possible link with occasions that are fun, exciting or interesting to that child.

So, if we go to the Tower of London, we go to the shop and whatever things the children buy, I will get some piece of written material that links to it and that will lie about in the house following the visit. I can remember going with my oldest child to see David Wood's play and his own direction of *The Gingerbread Man*. On the way out there were copies of the play and a cassette tape of the show. Surely here was a perfect way to make a link between the show that Joe had enjoyed, the songs and the dialogue.

So, there am I, sitting in the foyer of a theatre, having done a show that the children have joined in with. As they go out, some of the adults seem to know exactly the fun and worth of making a link between what the children have just seen and heard and the words on a page. We have conversations about that as I sign the books. I see parents or teachers opening the book straight away and saying things like, 'And here's Boogy Woogy Buggy.' They make the connection between what for a young child possibly looks like instant invention – Michael Rosen plus a jazz group doing a performance – and here, laid out on the page, again, as if by magic, is the frozen representation of that performance, the poem in a book. Alongside some other poems that Michael Rosen didn't perform, and some that he did, and some that are very similar but in some key ways are different.

I'm not surprised that some parents might not know how useful it would be to make the link between the live words of a show and the frozen words on the page. Many have come to believe that the best ways to get their children to be literate is to buy those grammar and spelling booklets on sale in newsagents. The daft thing is that the jokes and puzzles in comics often did the same thing but in fun, sharing ways that we could enjoy together.

In the case of the teachers, I think it's a matter of how, in the last ten years, the different sides of reading, writing, performing (or saying out loud) have been separated off. So, the occasion of the visit to see Centrally Heated Knickers was for some of the teachers clearly in the category of 'seeing a show', and had no direct or explicit connection to, say, reading or writing.

As I sat there, I found myself wondering, 'What other ways are there of interesting or exciting children in the written language?' There are of course many and I just hope that the schools in question tried these. I hope that the schools weren't like the one the poet Andrew Fusek Peters wrote about on Facebook recently. He recounted that he had performed his poems in a school and did writing workshops with the children. He had brought some of his books to the school and asked the head teacher if he wanted any. The head replied, no, as they had spent all their money on a new reading scheme.

So, though the school had spent money on inviting a poet in, though the poet had entertained the children – knowing Andrew's work, they would have joined in and participated in the performance – and though they would have written and read things out loud, one part of the circle would have been missing, namely that no child in the school would have been able to make a link between what Andrew said and what might appear on a page.

In case this sounds what in Yiddish is called '*kvetsh*' – a moan or whinge on behalf of we poor poets – I think we do have a serious question here about how we initiate and, just as importantly, carry on an interest in written language.

It is clearly not sufficient to announce that this or that child or school student is proficient in reading. If we are interested in the education of the whole child, we have to be interested in whether the child or student is intrigued and delighted by written things.

Maybe in the future we will encode our most precious, powerful, wise and indeed most evil ideas in forms other than the written language. We do a lot already of course via radio, TV and film and the digital platforms now available to us through PCs, laptops, tablets and phones. These are all highly oral and visual forms. However, those that have the power or wealth to produce these forms actually encode nearly all of them in their first stages through the written word. So there is an irony going on here in that we the masses imbibe this stuff orally and visually, while those that produce it do it, more often than not, through the literacy of scripts, written offers to producers, and the whole thing is surrounded by blurbs, puffs, crits, contracts, law cases, articles in magazines and newspapers, text-rich websites.

Meanwhile, powerful ideas – whether those of power or those who wish to critique that power – are still largely expressed through the written word, whether that be in traditional forms in printed newspapers, books and magazines, or in online blogs, Twitter, Facebook, on-line newspapers, websites.

I'm not sure that what goes by the name of literacy in schools is universally keeping up with this. In one school, I'll see children blogging their stories or accounts of the trip to Kew Gardens to schools in the USA or Australia. In another school, I'll see children writing their stories and accounts in their exercise books, where they get marked and forgotten. In one school, I'll see children making performances out of songs and poems, partly written by themselves, partly written by teachers, partly written by published authors. In another school, I'll gather that children hardly do any of this because it's not 'literacy'. Literacy in some cases is doing literacy exercises and only literacy exercises, because the exercises are good rehearsals for the literacy tests.

Just to be clear, I am not blaming or even criticising those teachers and those schools which do this. In a system which is centrally controlled through the tests, league tables and inspection systems, schools will do whatever they think is the best way to get through the hoops. If dry runs of high-stakes testing appear to get the least able through the tests, they will do it. If the same authorities then blame them for teaching to the test, they'll take the insult and carry on so that their school doesn't get closed or turned into something else that no one in that school's community asked for.

Of course, I – and I suspect most people here – will try to say that exciting children so that they are interested in reading and writing has to be a multi-faceted, multi-dimensional process in which we look out for hooks to catch different children in different ways. One child gets hooked on comics and graphic novels, as three of my children have. Another one gets hooked on fairy books – one of my children. Another one on poetry – as none of my children has. Another one on song and performance – as I did. Another one on puzzles and science – as my brother did. For some, it might be the fact that a child has a younger brother, sister, cousin or neighbour who wants to be entertained . . . as in the tweet I mentioned at the very beginning.

So, I'll mention one other powerful motor in my life that has affected me since my childhood. My brother discovered the Molesworth books. These take place in a Hogwarts sort of a place – a private school, called St Custards, where Molesworth, a thirteen- or fourteen-year-old, has sussed what's going on: the corruption, the senseless testing, the overblown rhetoric. The school itself was absolutely nothing like my primary school, though some of it could be related to the grammar school that my brother went to and where I would go a few years later.

Over a long period, my brother read the Molesworth books to me. They are written in non-correct English, as if Molesworth, who tells the stories, is only semi-literate. He read these to me many, many times. We sometimes sat next to each other laughing at the spelling, marvelling at Ronald Searle's drawings and caricatures. Sometimes we would weep with laughter at these books. Eventually, we would be able to quote whole sections at each other and expressions from the books started turning up in our speech, and in our letters to each other if were apart – on holiday or whatever.

Nearly 60 years later, we're still doing it.

Most people in this room, I suspect, might be able to point to analogous activities to do with comics, songs, poems, theatre clubs, where the social activity drove the attachment to this or that text or part of a text. Sometimes it's only intermittent or fragmentary. In my case I'm lucky enough to say that it was intense, frequent and repeated. As it happens, in my case, it went on at home.

But I've been to schools where it goes on through stories, poems, songs, plays, pantomimes and whole-school projects on, say, *The Tempest*. This calls for teachers, children, parents and school workers to co-operate on a huge joint enterprise. In the process and the evaluation, teachers find out areas of practice not covered by words like 'lesson' or 'assessment', but which nevertheless have everything to do with – for want of a better word – literacy.

In the last school I was in, where the school were embarking on a whole-school project about Noah and the flood, I got into a conversation with a teacher about how the children could each contribute to a narrative performance poem about the flood, whilst at the same time putting in solo pieces written and performed by the animals and by Noah's family, along with choruses from, say, the rain, the clouds, the sky, God, the water, the ark. 'I am king of the clouds,' wrote one boy. The rain chorus warned that they would rain and rain and never stop. God said that nothing frightened him, nothing at all. I showed them that simply by repeating a word or phrase you set up a rhythm. I had a conversation with a teacher saying that repetition is the basis of most poetry, whether that's through metre, rhyme, alliteration or patterns of images; even opposites and contrasts are a form of repetition. All the teachers and all the children were active planners in the devising of the texts and performances of the show.

[To end the talk, I ad-libbed about some of the other experiences, books and people who have helped me, and who continue to help me, to be a reader and a writer.]

Life, Death and the Prose Poem

I wrote this piece as a chapter for British Prose Poetry: The Poems without Lines, *edited by Jane Monson and published by Palgrave Macmillan in 2018.*

In 1999, my 18-year old son died. It was overwhelming. The first way I dealt with it was to pretend it hadn't happened. I would lie in bed in the mornings and come up with stories of where he was. As I started to realise that he was dead, I found myself making a conscious decision to not write about him, not write about how I felt. I had written about him often before and earlier on the very day he died I had told some children how small he was when he was a baby but now how huge he was, so huge that he could lift me up and whirl me round on his shoulders. I loved the fact that they thought this was funny, especially when I acted it out, shouting, 'Put me down! Put me down!'

But now, with him dead, I decided I couldn't and wouldn't write about him.

Several months went by and I stuck to my plan. But then I read 'Locking Yourself Out, Then Trying to Get Back In' by Raymond Carver, in his *All of Us: The Collected Poems*, in the paperback edition published by Harvill in 1997.

I read it over and over again, sometimes performing it to myself in a faux, specially dry, Robert Frost-like voice. It is in part about death, the persona's death. He can see his death because he's not in his house. As it happens, I had once done a radio interview with his last partner, Tess Gallagher, and she had talked about Carver's last days. In a way, I was on the other side of the poem. He had written about what had now happened. He wasn't in his house.

I loved the way Carver had said these things without being obviously metaphorical or emotional until the end of the poem when he talked of a 'wave of grief' and being 'violently ashamed'. It felt as if the topographical detail of standing outside the house earned the right to have this outburst later on.

I started to write about what had happened. I started to describe things like my son's body bag slipping down the stairs, or the way in which it looked as if hair grew out of his forehead several days after he died. I recorded the things that people said. Carver laid his poem out according to the conventions of free verse: a line break representing a speech-pause. I had written hundreds of poems like that. For some reason, and quite spontaneously, I decided that I didn't want to put that patterning over the words I was writing. I wanted them to be even less rhetorical than that. I wanted what I was writing to be more prosaic, more factual than the free-verse format implied. I was hanging onto the idea that I wasn't writing poetry. I was writing paragraphs.

The moment that I had that word 'paragraphs' in my head, I knew what to do. I could write short, medium or long ones . . . but not too long. No longer than Carver's poem. What came out were anecdotes, reveries, meditations, considerations about what had happened. I saw them as fragments of a whole, just as the segments of a stained-glass window, or the pieces of a mosaic, make up a whole. But I wasn't pretending or claiming them as poems, I kept saying. If other people wanted to call them that, that was fine. I was writing paragraphs, segments and mosaic pieces.

They weren't the whole truth. They weren't even the essence or the 'inscape' of Gerard Manley Hopkins. They were moments.

There was even the satisfaction of seeing how they looked on the page. I engineered tiny cliffhangers at the ends of lines, so that they were the opposite of the free-verse pause. The ends of lines were anticipations demanding that the eye and meaning were suspended in the hope that they would make the reader go on. I liked the chunkiness of the paragraphs too. I started to have an ideal length in mind, somewhere around 18 lines.

The more I wrote about my son, the more a uniting principle started to appear. This loss, this hole in my life, had connections with other losses. But in writing, I discovered that it wasn't only a matter of loss. There was something incongruous and bizarre about what had happened. Something so big and all-encompassing had taken place in the ordinariness of home. He went to bed. I went in the morning to tell him I was going off to work. He was dead. It was all so simple.

This strangeness, I felt, was in its own way like surrealism: the unlike in amongst the like; the unfamiliar stuck in the middle of the familiar. Thinking along these lines produced more paragraphs, some excavated from my past, others spun out of the present. I came back again and again to a postcard I had bought in Paris. It was an 18th-century engraving by Jean-Baptiste Oudry, illustrating one of La Fontaine's fables: 'Les deux aventuriers et le talisman, Fable CCII'. In the picture, a man in knee breeches and shirt is carrying an elephant up a mountain. I have it on my window sill in front of me as I write even now.

I decided I was the man in knee breeches. I am carrying the elephant, I thought. And he became another paragraph, an 18-line one that became the core of the collection which came out under that name, Carrying the Elephant, published by Penguin in 2002.

I went on to write two more books in that vein, This Is Not My Nose

(Penguin, 2004) and *In the Colonie* (Penguin, 2005), and I digested all three into *Selected Poems* (Penguin, 2007).

The prose poem form enabled me to tell stories that seemed at the moment of writing important. Because I took from that form its apparent prosiness, I felt I could inhabit the kind of detachment that a narrator of a novel has at the moment that narrator appears to be telling the story. I like the way the author hides behind the narrator, just as Michael Rosen could hide behind 'I'. Michael Rosen could invent some qualities of 'I' that didn't belong to Michael Rosen.

Of course, the prose poem doesn't dictate any of this sort of thing. A prose poem can be as metaphorical, rhythmic, non-syntactic, ornate and poetic as it wants to be. I think that I'm saying that the apparent prose format of a paragraph suggested to me a non-fiction quality: not inevitably or essentially attached to that form, just the one that I took from it. So I used it to write three autobiographical mosaics.

At the core of *This Is Not My Nose* is the experience of having consumed my own thyroid gland. I didn't do this voluntarily. My immune system identified my thyroid as a foreign being and digested it. The result was a change of body and identity. When I started to take replacement medicine, I became someone else. The format that had served me so well in describing the extremes of death seemed to be just right for describing many different ways in which I wasn't who I appeared to be. Again, the detachment worked for me.

Finally, in *In the Colonie* there was a core experience which I was and still am haunted by: a six-week stay, at the age of 16, as the only English person in a French *colonie de vacances* (kids' summer camp) on the dry plateau of the upper Ardèche. In my head was a set of scenes. I had tried on several occasions to knit the set into a narrative until I realised one day that there wasn't one. There wasn't a slowly developing sense of jeopardy, or an unresolved conflict that swelled to a climax, no hubris that took six weeks to work its way through to a denouement. It was a series of scenes, vignettes, cameos which sat in my mind, untold but affecting, scenes that I had returned to over and over again in the fifty years since their happening. A mosaic for paragraphs, I felt, would serve me well. The idea of being away, estranged, on my own but being initiated, politicised and forced to acknowledge my own culture released other analogous stories before the spell in the *colonie* and after.

In digesting them for *Selected Poems*, I think now, in retrospect, I lost something of the three uniting principles. Indeed, the uniting principles (or is it symbols?) behind each of the books had had the effect of holding these detached paragraphs together in a way that I hoped would result in the books being more than the sum of their parts. There was an invisible string running between the prose poems in the three books that was much less evident in the selections from them.

Defensively, I can feel myself acknowledging here that sometimes these prose poems – I'm most certainly not speaking for any others – need each other. Where the secret string is absent, the detachment that I am so fond of can sometimes tend towards the ordinary. That tone that I picked up from Raymond Carver needs support. That's how it feels to me.

There was a pause between *Selected Poems* and a rush of writing that I did in 2012, 2013 and 2014. This time, instead of the trigger being a poet, as it was with Carver, it was new technology. I've found that two digital spaces feel just right – snug, if you like – for writing prose poems or paragraphs: Facebook and my blog. I found that I could respond in direct, surreal, absurd, satirical ways to events as they happened, rather as if I was just saying them to someone sitting next to me. I could dash off a paragraph – a comment on what George Osborne [the Chancellor of the Exchequer] had said, a reply to someone on *Question Time*, a story of something that could have happened on the bus today, that is if a whale had got on the bus. One moment these paragraphs could be in the voice of, say, Adrian Mitchell, another more like Eddie Izzard or Russ Noble, another more like Bertolt Brecht. I don't say these names because I fancy myself as being them; more that I'm saying I was talking as if I was their echo.

This time the paragraph quality told me that I was writing short monologues. When you open the old 'Reciters' much loved in the Victorian and Edwardian period, you notice that they are full of non-rhyming monologues that people would perform in 'parlours' or by way of home entertainments. In fact, looking back to my university days, I remembered that I had written and performed some monologues which we called 'sketches' for 'cabarets'. All a bit self-satisfied perhaps, but an interesting form all the same. In fact, all sorts of performers, from Joyce Grenfell to Michael Crawford, Harry Enfield or Rik Mayall, do something very similar. As I'm not on the road or knocking on the door of TV to let me in, I found that I could do my monologues on Facebook and my blog. I could even video them and put them up on YouTube.

On the page, they are prose poems, they are paragraphs. As I started to collect them, I found myself looking at everyday events and turning them into everyday encounters with the surreal. A man tries to sell me a washing machine that de-shrinks clothes, I lose a cucumber and try to get it back from the Lost

Property Office, Bear Grylls gives a course in poetry, and so on. Surrealism is not only a means to investigate whether we have an unconscious or not. It can also be a means to investigate the meaning of our random encounters. If I can meet a man who I've never met before and within a second he tells me he hasn't been to the toilet for a week (true), why shouldn't Michael Bublé be in the next door loo compartment on Euston Station? And if *The Guardian* says that the Israeli government put out a directive that no one should mention the names of children killed in the latest round of wars going on, why shouldn't I extend that directive in absurd and totalising ways?

Again, I was pleased to see that the paragraphs found their secret strings again. Events that are to all intents and purposes 'real' sit alongside the whale on the bus and an invisible tattoo. The act of deconstruction, in a critical sense, is to reveal the power relationships behind the texts and utterances we come across (not, as some say, to separate a statement or work into its constituent parts). Poetry of any kind has a tradition of revealing powers and reasons that lie behind what is said or shown. Its old 'defamiliarising' process can do a lot of that. Paragraphs seemed to be very useful too. One moment they could be mini-essays, as if I was some kind of modern-day Montaigne, and the next a stand-up peering into an audience trying to fool them that an odd thing happened on my way to the theatre. This collection appeared as *Don't Mention the Children* (Smokestack, 2015)

So, this format has served me well. I am grateful to it.

Shelley's 'Lost' Poem

This is a talk I gave to the Keats-Shelley Memorial Association on 29 April 2019.

Thanks very much indeed to the Keats-Shelley Memorial Association for inviting me to be the final judge for this year's competitions, and indeed for hosting this lovely event.

Special mention to all the finalists in the competitions – essays and poems. Remarkable standard. I enjoyed them all very much indeed.

For this little talk, let me first take you back to November 2015.

For nine years, the world of scholarship and those interested in the works of Shelley had been put in a very strange position.

In this period of time (nine years), we had known that a work by Shelley (that had been described for a long time as 'lost') had been found. Let's think about that for a moment. What do those words mean: 'lost' and 'had been found'? More on that in a moment.

What had happened was that in 2006 the scholar H.R. Woudhuysen announced in an article in the *Times Literary Supplement* that Shelley's poem 'A Poetical Essay on the Existing State of Things' had been 're-discovered'.

'Re-discovered' from where? From when?

The 'when' question is easy to answer: from 1811.

On 9 March 1811 a poem, 'Poetical Essay', was advertised in the *Oxford University and City Herald*.

It was published by, but not in, this newspaper, as a 20-page pamphlet, written by a 'gentleman of the University of Oxford'. This was in fact Percy Bysshe Shelley, then aged 18 in his second term at University College.

It's not known for certain how many copies were printed or how many sold other than that they all seem to have disappeared – bar one. This single copy seems to have been the one that Shelley gave to his cousin Pilfold Medwin, who took it to Italy.

Notice my use of the word 'seems'. Anything in the murky world of the history of manuscripts and lone single editions has to use words like 'seems'.

(Digression – anyone interested in this world should spend some time looking at the fates of the manuscripts of John Clare, Franz Kafka and James Joyce.)

Let's come forward again to November 2015.

For nine years, this poem had only been seen in full, had only been allowed to be seen, by a tiny group of people. The only person to have both seen it and written about it at any length was H.R. Woudhuysen in the article in the *Times Literary Supplement*.

So where had it been for these nine years?

We'll come to that in a moment.

How about in the period between 1811 and 2006?

According to the Bodleian Library, the poem wasn't officially identified as being by Shelley till 1872. It was at this time that two nineteenth-century scholars talked of 'valuable information as to the library wherein a copy of Shelley's "Poetical Essay on the Existing State of Things" is affirmed to exist', yet neither of them or anyone else at the time thought the matter was worth pursuing.

A 'library' – what does that mean? What kind of library?

And why didn't anyone pursue the matter in the 1870s? (I don't have the answer to that question.)

The poem itself is highly political – both in what it says and in its purpose. The purpose was to raise funds on behalf of a journalist called Peter Finnerty.

Here's Woudhuysen:

> Finnerty's reports on these events [that is, the conditions facing troops in wars against Napoleon] in the Morning Chronicle led to his arrest and transportation back to England. In January 1810 he accused Lord Castlereagh of trying to silence him and compounded the offence by repeating accusations against the politician about the abuse of United Irish prisoners in 1798.
>
> Finnerty was tried for libel in February 1811 and sentenced to eighteen months in Lincoln Gaol. It was not the first time he had gone to prison as a result of clashing with Castlereagh: he had previously spent two years in prison in Dublin for printing a seditious libel and had been made to stand in the pillory. This second libel case was reported in great detail and Finnerty's plight attracted widespread support, prompting a debate during the summer in the House of Commons and a public subscription, initiated by Sir Francis Burdett, which reached Pounds 2,000 on his release. Among those who contributed to a fund to maintain the journalist while he was still in prison was Percy Bysshe Shelley, then an undergraduate at Oxford in his second term at University College. His name appears in a list of four subscribers, each pledging a guinea, printed in the Oxford University and City Herald on March 2, 1811.

The poem itself, in the words of Professor John Mullan, is 'A verse denunciation of oppression in the colonies and corruption at home . . .'

Nevertheless, it had been lost. Well, if you think about it, not exactly 'lost'. More 'out of sight' for nearly everyone.

But where had it been? How was it out of sight? All we have is this image of an unnamed 'library' . . .

But we're a gathering here tonight interested in Romanticism, so let's feel free to run our Gothic or Romantic imaginations over this story: all through the nineteenth and early twentieth centuries, most copies of this 20-page pamphlet have ended up being used to start fires, tipped into rubbish bins . . . bar one. And this sits in a library . . . Where is this library? In a country house, perhaps? You've seen these, I'm sure. As we stroll through them, we see shelves rising from floor to ceiling, behind glass doors, jam-packed full of ancient books. Let's make this country house a bit mouldering, a bit Castle Rackrent. The pamphlet, we might imagine, is where? Tucked between two other books, nothing to do with Shelley. One is, let's say, *Grantham's Voyages to the South Seas* (1758) (I've made that up) and the other is a book I heard mentioned on Radio 4's *In Our Time* about *A Midsummer Night's Dream* the other day: an Elizabethan book on the interpretation of dreams. (I haven't made that up. Really.) This stately home we're imagining now has a catalogue of all the books and pamphlets in its library, but this pamphlet is only listed as, let's say, ('Poetical Essay', 1811, Anon.). No one out of whoever lives in the house or who visits this house thinks a publication with a title as dull as 'Poetical Essay' is worth pulling off the shelves.

Come forward to the twenty-first century.

The mansion and the shelves are getting damp. Money is short for the aristocratic owners of the mouldering mansion. It's time to bring in a valuer to see whether funds can be raised.

At which point enter one Bernard Quaritch. Based on that name alone, perhaps switch here from Gothic-Romantic to Dickensian.

Let's imagine old Bernard Quaritch invited into the country home (inhabited by Miss Havisham of course). As Quaritch is poring over the old damp books, he suddenly finds the 'Poetical Essay'.

It is now in the hands of Bernard Quaritch, the 'antiquarian bookseller' of South Audley Street, London W1. We know this because it was announced in July 2006 that Quaritch had put up for sale what seemed then to be the sole example of the 'Poetical Essay', the sole source for the poem.

Again, let our imaginations run free – note the Romantic image there of something called 'the imagination' that has a capacity, free of the mind or reason, to 'run free' . . . taking us . . . where? A dark, musty bookshop, stacked up with books, thousands of them, with slips tucked in and protruding, men in dark overalls with pencils tucked behind their ears, moving silently about, one lone woman at a cash register reading one of the books herself? Old Quaritch is upstairs, dozing, an open bottle of port on his desk in front of him.

In actual fact, this is miles from the truth, because Quaritch says on its website:

> We have been buying and selling rare books and manuscripts since 1847. Our founder, Bernard Quaritch, was born in 1819 at Worbis, a small town near Göttingen in Germany. After working for booksellers in Nordhausen and Berlin, he set off for London in 1842, aged 23.
> On his death in 1899 The Times wrote 'It would scarcely be rash to say that Quaritch was the greatest bookseller who ever lived.'

Quaritch is 'now owned by book collector and investor John Koh'.

Switch image – let the imagination run free again – smart, shiny, immaculate office, every book carefully shelved, brushed, polished. Moving swiftly and purposefully around the offices are smart, suited, recent Oxbridge graduates, equally distributed women, men, culturally diverse, trans, and John Koh . . . who bears a remarkable resemblance to George Clooney.

It's July 2006. The phone rings.

It's Michael Rosen.

Michael says that he has read the article in the *Times Literary Supplement* and asks if Bernard Quaritch (at this point Michael still thinks that Quaritch is alive and well and living in South Audley Street) will be making the 'Poetical Essay' available. Michael mutters confusedly about how easy it is to make digital copies these days, saying how the British Library was at this very moment digitising swathes of its collection on-line. In fact, he was at the library talking to a curator at the very moment they were working on the *Beowulf* manuscript . . . Michael's voice tails away.

No, says the person on the phone, the 'Poetical Essay' is not available to the general public to see and it's not going to be digitised until a buyer is found.

The conversation gets awkward. Michael is asked if he wants to view the copy but he thinks that would be dishonest because he can't imagine for a moment that he has the money to buy it. And anyway that's beside the point. The point is, surely, that Shelley enthusiasts (and the world) should be able to read the poem. Who, after all (asks Michael rhetorically), does literature belong to?

Bernard (or whoever it is on the end of the phone) politely points out that digitising the poem isn't going to happen.

Cut to Michael in his own workspace. Think now, more BBC 4 profile . . . (I'm making this up too. More imagination.) Alan Yentob is dawdling round Rosen's books and picks up a 1954 copy of the Communist *Daily Worker*'s *Christmas Annual* for children. He flicks the pages and finds a story . . . written by Michael aged seven.

'Is this . . . ?' Yentob says.

'Hang on, Al,' interrupts Michael, 'don't you see? They think they can own Shelley. It's the capitalist paradigm. Purely because history has determined that there is only one copy of this poem, this copy has value. Because it has value, it becomes private property. Because it is private property, it can be withheld from view. But why, Alan, why?'

'Yes, Mike, why?' says Alan.

Close up to Michael.

'In order to raise its price in the market place!' says Michael as if he thinks he has discovered the meaning of life.

'Yes,' says Alan slowly – as is his wont – 'but do we know if the poem is any good?'

Michael is waving his arms about and his eyes are popping.

'That's beside the point, Al.'

'What is the point, Mike?'

'The point is that literature belongs to all of us. And come on! How ironic that Shelley – yes, revolutionary Shelley of all people – should be hidden from us so that the price of his words can increase!'

Cut to Michael walking past Alexandra Palace in Muswell Hill. Michael stops to look out over London. We hear Jeremy Irons as voice-over saying, 'Look on my works, ye mighty, and despair . . . '

(This gave the impression to viewers at the time that Michael thought he had built Alexandra Palace, but perhaps it was ironic in a post-modern sort of a way.)

Back to reality: between 2006 and 2015, Michael (this bit is true – no imagination involved) writes letters to the *Times Literary Supplement* and *The Guardian*, and writes articles on his blog about . . . why is Shelley's poem not available, and why aren't Shelley scholars causing a fuss? Rosen claims contentiously that Woudhuysen's scholarly article has in fact served the purpose of raising the value of the object (not the poem itself but this lone physical copy of the 'Poetical Essay').

On one occasion Michael finds himself co-examining a PhD – the oral examination or 'viva'. His colleague, it turns out, is a Shelley scholar.

Cut to: Book-lined room in a university – think *Educating Rita*. The colleague is, let's say, the one played by Michael Caine. I'm, let's say . . . er . . . an English version of Elliott Gould as campus radical teacher in that film *Getting Straight* (1970) . . . Caine and Gould-Rosen are chatting before the PhD student comes in. Gould-Rosen asks Caine about the 'Shelley thing', as he calls it. Caine says, 'Believe me, we're following this closely. We're cheering you on.'

Gould-Rosen says, 'Are you? But why aren't you out there complaining? Where are the petitions? Why . . . isn't there a collection on behalf of the Shelley poem?'

'I don't know,' says Michael Caine.

'This could go on for years,' says Gould-Rosen. 'It's locked away out of sight. To all intents and purposes it's in a bank vault. We should liberate Shelley.'

(Minor interlude here while we reflect on how the Romantics in their very different ways absorbed and recycled previous forms of poetry: Coleridge taking the old ballad form for the *Ancient Mariner*, Wordsworth taking the *reverdie* and the *aventure* for 'I wandered lonely as a cloud', and Keats absorbing Shakespeare. All texts are intertextual, including this little talk with its references to films, but, we reflect, all this is rather un-Romantic, not leaving much room for the 'imagination'.)

Anyway, back with the fate of the 'Poetical Essay' between 2006 and 2015 – the lost nine years.

In this time, as I say, the poem is deliberately hidden from view, concealed, occluded.

(One sadness as a digression. The poet Adrian Mitchell died in 2008. Though William Blake was Mitchell's great hero, he was also a Shelley enthusiast and if any living poet of the late twentieth, early twenty-first centuries could claim to have written in the tradition of 'The Masque of Anarchy', it's Adrian. At the memorials for Adrian, I ponder on how wrong it is that he lived but also died in a time when the poem had been discovered but not revealed.)

The story gathers pace. Rosen gathers at some point in his phone calls with Quaritch that Quaritch has moved on from being the seller of the 'Poetical Essay'. Quaritch has bought it.

The 'Poetical Essay' has become an investment.

But is it now available to be seen and read? No.

Next: the pamphlet is displayed at an exhibition. But as it's only the title page, it seems more like a tease than anything else.

Then comes The Big Day: the Bodleian Library announces in November 2015 that it had . . . 'acquired its 12 millionth printed book: a unique copy of a pamphlet entitled "Poetical Essay on the Existing State of Things" . . . '

It goes on . . .

> The acquisition is a momentous event for the public, for scholars, the University and the Bodleian Libraries. Known to have been published by Shelley in 1811 but lost until recently [there's that 'lost' word again], Shelley's Poetical Essay is, thanks to the generosity of a benefactor, now freely available to all in digitized form.
>
> The Bodleian Libraries are extremely grateful to Mr Brian Fenwick-Smith and Mr Antonio Bonchristiano for their generous support of this project.

Yes, the Shelley One was released. The whole strange nine-year-long episode came to an end.

The poem is now available at archive.org, or with full commentary at poeticalessay.bodleian.ox.ac.uk.

You can find Woudhuysen's original article at the *TLS* archive, as well as articles about the poem in various places by, for example, Alison Flood, John Mullan, Michael Rossington, Michael Caines or Michael Rosen.

I'll finish with a few lines from the poem, to give you the flavour of what John Mullan called Shelley's outrage. Here's the opening:

> Destruction marks thee! o'er the blood-stain'd heath
> Is faintly borne the stifled wail of death;
> Millions to fight compell'd, to fight or die
> In mangl'd heaps on War's red altar lie.

Later . . .

> Ye cold advisers of yet colder kings,
> To whose fell breast, no passion virtue brings,
> Who scheme, regardless of the poor man's pang,
> Who coolly sharpen misery's sharpest fang,
> Yourselves secure . . .

> The fainting Indian, on his native plains,

Writhes to superior power's unnumbered pains;
The Asian, in the blushing face of day,
His wife, his child, sees sternly torn away; . . .

End of the poem:

Man must assert his native rights, must say
We take from Monarchs' hand the granted sway;
Oppressive law no more shall power retain,
Peace, love, and concord, once shall rule again,
and heal the anguish of a suffering world;
Then, shall things, which now confusedly hurled,
Seem Chaos, be resolved to order's sway,
And error's night be turned to virtue's day.

Oracy and Literacy in Education and Life

Here's the second Harold Rosen lecture I gave, to the United Kingdom Literacy Association on 4 July 2021.

I love the idea that UKLA have a Harold Rosen lecture. Just in case some people don't know, professionally he was at various times in his life a classroom teacher, a head of department, a teacher-trainer, a writer, a scholar and a university professor. He was also a son, a brother, a husband and then father to three children, one of whom is me. Now I've just done that customary thing of separating the professional life from the domestic, but for anyone who knew Harold, things weren't that simple. And this is rather relevant to the matter of oracy and literacy. (By the way, the spellcheck on my computer corrects the word 'oracy' to 'Tracy', making the word 'oracy' much easier to say than to write, even if not quite on the subject in hand.)

Back to Harold and the two worlds. People who knew him professionally will know that he scattered his talks and writings with reminiscences and observations from his non-professional life. Here's one.

(There are several Yiddish words in the passage: '*zeider*' means grandfather; '*der Heim*' literally means 'the home', but I'll return to that later; '*bubbe*' means grandmother and '*meshuggene*' means 'a crazy person'.)

> We would stand by the edge of the grubby old public swimming pool drying ourselves, my *zeider* and I. As likely as not he would tell me once again about how he would go swimming back in *der Heim* somewhere in Poland. I would listen to this fragment of his boyhood. Always I saw him in some Arcadian setting of endless pine trees and velvet grass sloping down to a still lake. It was always early morning. He would emerge from a log cabin, run to the water and fracture its stillness with strong strokes. He would go on swimming till he was lost to view. There were no other people, no other houses, no other movements. It was an idyll I clung to from which I had banished pogroms and poverty and the fearful little community huddled over their prayers and sewing machines. That was my story not his. And when we went on day trips to Southend, east London's seaside, in his sixties he would set out to swim the length of the pier and back, a mile or so each way. My *bubbe* without fail went through the identical torments of anxiety.

'The *meshuggene*! He's gone out too far again!' I was free from all such fears. For he was always the intrepid boy swimmer in the pure lake who always came back. And he did. And even in death still does.

In passing, let me draw your attention to a few things. As a piece of writing, there's a mix here of memory, myth, commentary and observation from the moment of writing. The memories themselves are a mix of description, reported speech, dialogue, and general views. The myth comes in the form of Harold's self-interrogation of his memory in which he reveals the difference between reality and the 'idyll' in his boyhood mind. The commentary tells us of a wider community that he and his grandfather belong to. And the observations come in his narration as with 'an idyll I clung to' or 'the identical torments of anxiety'.

Of particular interest to us today might be some features of language: he uses four words that he knew primarily from the oral environment of his childhood: *zeider, bubbe, meshuggene* – and let me return to '*der Heim*', a simple phrase to describe something quite complex. It literally means 'the home' but what it signified in London's East End where Harold was mostly brought up in the 1920s and '30s was the Jewish communities of Poland and Russia. So it wasn't Harold's home, it was his grandparents' home. These oral words, then, are doing a lot of work: full of feeling, self-awareness, along with some primary cognition to do with his kinship group, and his communal awareness. Something else going on that you wouldn't necessarily be aware of as it's only a very short passage: you might wonder where his mother and father are in this story. His father was in Massachusetts in the US. The last time Harold saw him was when Harold was two, and he would never see him after that. Harold's mother may have been with him that day, but she was hampered by the effects of polio so possibly not. I say this because his affection and interest in his grandparents was coloured by such matters. In other words, Harold's use of his vernacular – the oral language of the home – is doing a lot of work in this passage and indeed elsewhere in his writings. I'm drawing attention to this because the words and phrases our students use when talking or writing may well be just as laden with social and communal significance.

Can I draw your attention to something else? Several times in the passage, the register changes. On the one hand Harold writes what we might call formal, classic complex sentences full of additional phrases and subordinate clauses. At other times, he uses snappy short expressions that I sense have an oral feel about them: his opening sentence has an oral feature, expanding the main subject of the sentence by inverting it – putting it at the end:

> We would stand by the edge of the grubby old public swimming pool drying ourselves, my *zeider* and I.

He interrupts his flow with 'That was my story, not his.' And he closes with 'And he did. And even in death still does.' Let me put it this way: these thoughts or comments are inflected with orality. Partly as a joke, at other times I've called this 'oral writing' (oxymoron) and I want to come back to that later.

Another way of looking at this passage is to think of it as a conversation Harold is having with himself. From my own experience I can sense that there are several aspects to this kind of 'inner speech': formless sensations, feelings, images; words or phrases that express these and other thoughts; queries and questions about the significance of what happened, how and why; memories of snatches of dialogue. These can exist in our mind for years, interesting us, obsessing us, bothering us, upsetting us. The process of writing may well do several things at the same time. Because it is writing (and writing like this is linear and consecutive) it forces an order onto the thoughts. I won't say that the thought had no order, but it was much more fluid than a paragraph of text. In fact, one of the things we can do with the thoughts is move them about at will: one day in one order, another day in another order. We may also discover what we might call invasions: material that suddenly appears – people, dialogue, sounds, smells. And there is something repetitive that may well go on, things that recur. Writing is a fixer, though. It won't necessarily fix the flow of thoughts but it is itself fixed on the page or screen, in an order. Again, you can change it, but if it ever gets published it will become fixed in an evidential sort of a way at the very least. Think Shakespeare's quartos and folio.

Often, I find that writing is a relief from what I sometimes see as the pressure of the experiences in the mind. But of course, there's another arm to how we handle all this: talk. We can write something or talk something or both. And Harold did plenty of both himself.

One last comment on this passage: Harold is interrogating memory, a subject he was fascinated by, often referring in his conversations with me to the psychologist Frederic Bartlett (1886-1969). I didn't ever read Bartlett, even though Harold would often say to me things like, 'Old Bartlett was on to this, you know, Mick.' Or, 'You really should read Bartlett, he was saying some of this stuff, long before anyone else.'

Which brings me to another point. I want to flip my observation that Harold brought the domestic into his professional life and tell you that he also brought the professional into the domestic. Oh boy, did he! There was hardly a time in all my times with Harold and my mother – and, after she died, with Harold and his great wife Betty – that his professional interests weren't played out in our conversations. It is no exaggeration to say, for example, that he did his PhD at the kitchen table. I can see him sitting with his leg crossed, several books laid out amongst the crockery and food, a notebook on his knee, jotting notes from the books, looking up, interrupting the chat going on between my brother, mother and me, with cries of outrage at this or that villain in the sphere of linguistics, or delighted eureka moments when he felt he had cracked a conspiracy going on in the undergrowths of pedagogic theory. I can hear him saying, 'Listen to this, Con . . . ' (my mother's name was Connie) and then him reading out what was to me a completely incomprehensible passage from the linguist Michael Halliday. For better or worse, it made one aspect of domestic life a kind of home university. Why did he do this? I think it was an extreme version of what many of us do when faced with challenges and difficulties: we try to talk it through. Harold by his own estimation had scraped through university, being more interested in politics than Old English (or Anglo-Saxon as it was called then) and Old Norse – about which he said:

I know two things about Old Norse.
I have forgotten them of course.

As he moved into teacher-training, he took it upon himself to do that PhD, and again, by his own estimation, it was a big change and a big effort. I'm guessing that his extemporising at the kitchen table was part of how he coped. I notice from parents' evenings that I've attended – I mean, as a parent – that they are often about teachers inviting my children to voice what's bothering them, or what they think about the course or what they've found difficult. The best examples of these are when the triangle has been a genuine exchange of viewpoints: teacher, parent, student. The not-so-good ones – if I might put it like that – have been when the triangle has been broken by a lengthy reference to a line of marks across a term's worth of tests. Yes, as we all know, conversations – oracy – are very variable things.

Back to oracy at home: both my parents were – and indeed so is Betty – great storytellers. They were storytellers in several ways: stories from their pasts, political stories about Churchill, Stalin and the rest, stories from their workplaces, formal stories told at bedtimes or on long walks plucked (I now realise) from Chaucer, Shakespeare and the Odyssey, story-jokes – more often than not long Jewish jokes, and also a kind of storying of the everyday.

Harold in particular took it upon himself to turn events that happened in our lives into what I can only describe as routines. Things that I had seen unfold in front of me would get told to friends in our living room and I could watch them becoming shaped, re-shaped, refined, exaggerated as the story was told and re-told to the next group of friends who came through the door. One example: one camping holiday in Yorkshire, my teenage brother was to leave our campsite to go on a holiday somewhere else. To do this, we would take him to the station in our car, he would go to our home in London, pick up some of his stuff and head off on his holiday. So we dropped him at the station, but the moment we waved him goodbye, my mother remembered that she hadn't given him the key to the house. There was a moment of panic. Then my father figured out that we could drive over the North York Moors and get to Pickering station and meet the train and my brother there. So that's what we did, with my father asking me to look and see if I could see the train in the gaps between the hills. We got to the station, the train was there, my father ran down the platform, looking in the windows, found my brother, and handed him the key. My brother then said something to the effect that he had already figured out what to do, either ask the neighbour who had a key or borrow a ladder and climb in through our kitchen window, which was upstairs.

Now, over the weeks following, I watched Harold turn this into a saga, full of gesture, mimes of him in the car, urging me to spot the train and bit by bit inserting completely invented bits, like how he had run down the platform shouting, 'Stop the train! Stop the train!' And of course he loved closing off the frenetic energy, tension and crisis with an impression of my brother just shrugging and saying, 'I was going to get the key off Mrs Townsend.'

As some of you know, Harold's academic speciality was narrative and talk. He returned to it again and again, in different forms over most of his professional – and, as I'm telling you here – his domestic life. You can follow this line of thinking, practice and research in the book that John Richmond edited of Harold's writings, published by the UCL Institute of Education Press.[1]

Now, I want to draw out of this introduction some elements that I think might be of interest:

the flow between the oral and the written;
a hinterland which is not really expressed by such a rigid division;
the conversation we have with ourselves;
the power of what it means to find words to say what we are thinking;
the power of shared talk, discussion.

To illustrate all this I want to reflect on the last 18 months of my life.

In brief, I got ill. I was treated by people who used their knowledge, training and kindness to make me better. Since coming out of hospital I've gone back to doing many of the things I used to do before, but a lot of it now through this medium, the remote talk and conversation. This has alerted me to a question about how we frame this matter of oracy and literacy. I've already touched on it in describing how Harold used material taken from his oral world in his writing, how he shaped and re-shaped his oral storytelling.

I'll begin this section with something I wrote in my book *Many Different Kinds of Love: a Story of Life, Death and the NHS* (Ebury, 2021):

> A doctor is standing by my bed
> asking me if I would sign a piece of paper
> which would allow them to put me
> to sleep and pump air into my lungs.
> 'Will I wake up?'
> 'There's a 50:50 chance.'
> 'If I say no?' I say.
> 'Zero.'
> And I sign.

This is of course a memory, though I've done that writing trick of pretending it's happening now. When I read it, I think there's a lot missing. For whatever reason, I've left out what I was thinking when the doctor tells me that I have a 50:50 chance. I can locate it by concentrating very hard on that moment. I'm lying on my back looking up at the doctor. When he says 50:50, one thought comes into my mind is that he's joking. Another thought is that 50:50 is not bad. Actually, it's not bad. It's quite good. So what I can do is catch words and sensations I experienced and which sit in my head but which I can express now in sentences, as I've just done. Since then, as I read this poem and replay the scene, I become horrified and upset. I was told much later that in my ward 42% of the Covid patients died. So 58:42, not 50:50, but not far off. I am now putting into words on a page and telling you more of that experience than is in the first piece. It has emerged out of reflection, writing, more reflection, hearing things that doctors have told me, storytelling this in interviews and now writing it down, and reading what I've written to you.

We used to talk of speaking, listening, reading and writing. I liked that, so long as we could hold in our heads that we can, and often do, free-flow between these categories – as I've just done here. I'll say in passing that I try to suggest to children, young people and teachers that thirty seconds or a minute of daydreaming is a great way to start writing.

Anyway, back to me! I was sedated and stayed in that state for about forty days. I know nothing of this time from my own mind. I know about it from two sources: hospital staff and my wife. The main way the hospital staff have told me things is through what's called a 'Patient Diary'. It's an exercise book, in which nurses and volunteers wrote letters to me at the end of their shifts.

I mention this because letters are very interesting when it comes to considering the relationship between the oral and the written. And we can add to letters texts, emails, tweets, chat rooms, social-media posting, comments threads and the like. A study of these shows us that we free ourselves from the constraints of written Standard English and produce many features of our spoken language as written – that's in addition to the many text-specific things like abbreviations, emojis and the like. Lols. TBF. FYI. FFS.

So the letters in my patient diary include phrases like: 'Keep fighting', 'Keep going!', 'You've got this!!', 'Happy birthday for tomorrow', 'It's Claire the physio . . . again', 'Take one day at a time'; and Emma, my wife, sent emails to the family saying things like: 'Quick update:', 'Evening guys', 'Bloody hurrah!' and 'Looking forward to a glass of wine later!' This kind of informal language, obviously written – because it's written (!) – but not formal Standard English, has become for many of us the landscape of our lives. Glance at your phone while I'm saying this. Look at the text messages and see this genre of writing in abundance. Here's the first one I can see on mine. Son to me: 'Big result'. This is of course heavily contextual writing . . . he knows that I'll know what he's texting about and produces a non-formal sentence to say it.

None of this is inferior or second-class writing. It's to the point, intimate, knowing and written with strong reference to the receiver and what the receiver knows or might appreciate. It's not for me to say how we might harvest and benefit from this in educational settings but I know that teachers can and do. When I put up on Twitter the other day the suggestion that Romeo and Juliet could text each other after Romeo has been banished, there were immediate replies telling me that they did that last year, or the year before.

But how about my encounters with doctors? There's a nice paradox about medicine, in that it requires the trained practitioner to have absorbed vast amounts of written knowledge, to have acquired the art of accessing information from relevant sources – most of which is written; but in face-to-face encounters with patients, a good deal of it is oral. In fact, to match the practitioner's knowledge to the case before them, this oral encounter may well be crucial. The patient usually has to say what's wrong, the practitioner has to be able to interview the patient without leading them, and then possibly has to explain what's going on and what a possible remedy might be. It may well be a life and death matter. I've had hundreds of these over the last eighteen months and several have been very difficult. For example, I've had to try to describe what's wrong with my left eye. I groped for words like 'foggy', 'misted over', or I use similes: 'It's as if there's a shower curtain over my eye'. In return, doctors have said things like, 'Your optic nerve is buggered,' 'Your eye was dilated, we didn't know if you would be brain dead.' It's earthy. Direct. But I also got glimpses of how the practitioners were talking to themselves. Professor Hugh Montgomery told me how at the beginning of the pandemic, patients were arriving with respiratory problems but getting strokes. When they took blood samples, they had the experience of the blood being 'sticky'. His word. What did they do? Doctors called each other up across the world. They quizzed each other about what they had observed. They shared what they had found. And yes, they discovered that this respiratory virus was killing people because it was somehow affecting the clotting of the blood. 'You, Michael,' Hugh said, 'had clots in the "saddle".' Notice the nickname he used for the bifurcation of the pulmonary arteries where the blood clots were.

It all reminded me of how in 1981 I was diagnosed as being hypothyroid. I arrived in the Renal Unit – that's kidneys – for suspected failing kidneys. I sat in front of the consultant and he started getting me to talk about what I had been up to that week. As I talked he stared at me very closely. Eventually, he interrupted me, pushed my notes to one side and said, 'I think this is rubbish. You're hypothyroid.' It was only me doing that everyday thing – talking – that revealed what was wrong. Note it was HOW I was talking (part of oracy, of course), not WHAT I was saying. What a powerful thing it is, the 'how' of our talk! He then called in his students and told them to diagnose me. He left the room. One student whispered in my ear, 'What you got?' I said, 'I don't think I'm allowed to tell you.' The consultant came back, 'What's he got?' he said. 'Kidney failure, sir,' said one. Mr Baker the consultant exploded, 'You haven't taken his pulse, you haven't tested his reflex, you haven't touched his skin, you haven't asked him to walk across the room. If you had done these things, you'd've known.'

Notice how Mr Baker was teaching medical practice: orally. As I found out later, this was indeed a matter of life and death. When I came back with my blood test a few days later, another doctor met me, Dr Gesundheit (no, I didn't make that up), opened up my notes and said in his American accent,

'Technically, you're dead. Or at the very least, you should be in a torpor.'

These moments, these words, these oral encounters have stayed with me ever since. I've written them down, I've told them and re-told them. They are part of who I am. That's another way oracy works: as milestones, powerful indicators, signals, symbolic moments, crux points in our lives, statements about identity, strange ironies, contradictions, meaningful, powerful utterances and more.

I'm also reminded here of Harold talking about Sir Peter Medawar. Somewhere buried in his writings or lecture notes is his citation and analysis of how Sir Peter Medawar described getting his medical students to learn how to diagnose – through discussion, talk or what we now call oracy. In fact, it's a model for what we also call, thanks to the work of Robin Alexander, Neil Mercer, Fiona Maine, Lynn Dawes and others, 'dialogic learning'. If anyone finds the piece where Harold wrote about this, do get in touch!

As I've already indicated, I spent some time between June and September trying to understand what had happened to me. My way of dealing with this has been to write about it. But saying that oversimplifies the matter because a lot of what I write and how I write, I call – oxymoronically – 'oral writing'. Or, as I say to school students, 'talk with the pen'. I imagine I am talking to a reader, and write things in that voice.

> I've forgotten my shoes.
> I don't know what my shoes were.
> I try to remember my feet in shoes.
> The only shoes I know
> are the ones I have here:
> black plastic crocs.
> But what shoes did I used to wear?
> I've forgotten my shoes.

OK, I'll be a bit more precise about this kind of writing. It's made up of oral segments. Each line or part of a line is something I have said, or could have said, or might say. Partly what distinguishes it from actual speech is the repetition and the shape of the piece as a whole. It is of course framed with the sentence 'I've forgotten my shoes'. It's a literary device which can have the effect of indicating something that runs invisibly through a whole piece. That is, whatever is stated in the opening of the frame continues, while the actions, thoughts and feelings unfold and then reappear at the end. It never went away.

I often think an analogy is the way in which the chalk of the Chiltern Hills runs under London and comes up in the south of London as the North Downs. The chalk is there under London all the time.

This kind of oral writing can be a powerful educational tool. In my book *Did I Hear You Write?* (Five Leaves Press, 1998) I tried to flag up many different ways the oral language and oral cultures of children can be harnessed for writing, drama, and spoken-word poetry. To be more accurate, it isn't so much a matter of one oral language, but that our lives in the oral world are full of oral genres: narratives (of which there are many kinds), also repartee, proverbs, idioms, jokes, songs, rhymes, imitations, recipes, advice, commands. As I would say, one of the easiest ways to capture this is through poetry and spoken-word work. A good deal of my adult life has been devoted to doing this through the medium of my own poetry, using it as models that can be used, adapted, recycled by children and school students. I often say that one of the most fertile one-line things you can say to help children and school students write is 'You could write like that'. That's to say, face to face with a poem that you've read or heard, 'You could write like that,' where 'like that' can mean: sound like that, look like that, have similar feelings, have similar pictures, similar phrases or even just be triggered by something in the poem – a memory, an echo, a thought, or something that springs out of the well that's in the daydream that I spoke of.

I should say in passing that of course I didn't invent 'oral writing'. I begged, borrowed and stole it from poets like D.H. Lawrence, Carl Sandburg, Langston Hughes. In a sense, they gave me permission to use my spoken voice and the spoken voice of others in my writing. Years ago, the teacher David Jackson and I thought that we were on to an immensely productive genre and produced an anthology called *Ways of Talking* (Ward Lock, 1978) – a deliberately provocative title for a book that was of course full of 'ways of writing'. It was an anthology of poems told in these particular ways. And, appropriately, we produced a cassette tape to go with it. The vagaries of the capitalism of publishing brought the venture to a speedy and sad end. David had based his input in the book on work with students at his school in Nottingham: using poetry, drama and improvisations to harvest their oracy for writing. In *Did I Hear You Write?* I added in the fact that writing down what children actually say is a very well known and useful aid to teaching literacy. It seems to be a practice that comes and goes in waves: in my lifetime, teachers have sometimes done a lot of it, sometimes not at all. Sometimes parents have been encouraged to do it with their children, sometimes it's not mentioned. I've always thought that there is a powerful message to give to young children when we say, in effect, that the stuff that comes out of your mouth can be represented by these squiggles on a page. Look! I can read back what you just said! Again and again. It's still there. Unlike speech, it hasn't gone away. And we can put it in an envelope or in an email and send it thousands of miles to someone else, who can read it too. The process of scribing what a child says seems to me to hold within it great power. The more often we do it, I have thought, the better! Whether that's still appropriate is a matter of policy, so I'll leave it with you.

Now, while I've been musing about all these things (and trying to get better) several other things have been going on: my 16-year-old has been doing his GCSEs and my wife has been doing law exams.

I guess all of us here are very familiar with this sort of thing: genres of language. The basis of a good deal of work in preparation for exams, and the exams themselves, is a written genre all of its own: the essay. Or, in the case of exams and tests, should I say, the essay produced under the very special conditions of not using reference, not conferring with others, under the conditions of a fixed time and staying in your seat throughout.

This genre is de facto the litmus test for whether they, you or I can or could pass to a next level in education, until we can get to a point where we don't ever have to do such things again. A strange apprenticeship: getting to be good at something that you don't ever have to be good at. Yes, we may have to write reports, be succinct, work to deadlines, but to a clock? And not consult anything or anybody? Remember stuff, yes, but remember everything that someone else tells you to remember, and then have people who don't know you judge you on that ability?

But this kind of extreme writing – or what my tutor at university called extreme journalism – is to my mind remarkable in itself, and also remarkable for being the main way we judge everyone in our education systems.

With that in mind, I've been very interested to observe how people I've seen at close hand – members of my family and indeed myself – prepared for this.

I note that it involves more often than not a form of translation or transformation: there are sequences of information, whether they come in the form of paragraphs in textbooks, teachers' notes, primary material like experiments, or literature texts. The trick for me and them is of course packaging this up into parcels. But not any old parcel. They have to be the parcels you guess that examiners will want to receive. So a degree of intuition, mind-reading and teachers' tips come into play here. And perhaps we should add in the canny trick of being able to understand the questions being asked.

Back in the day when my youngest son was doing his Key Stage 2 SATs, there was a question which asked the children to look at a passage of writing from a book called *Comfort Herself* by Geraldine Kaye (Scholastic, 1997). The passage described what Comfort saw in the market in Ghana. The question was 'Explain the description in the passage.' I'll say that again: 'Explain the description in the passage.' Now one way or another I've done a lot of what is loosely called 'literary criticism', but for the life of me I couldn't figure out how to answer this question. I couldn't decode the code. As it was a rehearsal question for the SATs and not the exam itself, I was able to go in the next morning and ask the teacher what it meant. In the playground. 'Oh come on, Mr Rosen,' he said, 'it's author intention.' 'Is it?' I said. 'You mean we were supposed to do a bit of mind-reading? Guess what Geraldine Kaye was thinking when she wrote that?' 'Yep,' he said, 'you've got it.'

Interesting for me, and perhaps for us in the context of this talk, is that the means to understand that tiny piece of writing – the question about writing – was done orally. The process of decoding was done through talk. I'll leave to one side the relative worth or lack of worth of doing such a thing, especially as there is a whole theory that 'author intention' is a pointless activity because we can never know what the author intends. Even so, it is something we all like doing and it does give us a chance to speculate about texts.

Back with essays and exam preparation: how to do the packaging? One method we've all used is the reducing trick. Start long, and edit down in stages, from chapters to pages to paragraphs, to bullet points to single words, and even to single letters and mnemonics. Another trick is to create formulaic dialogues with friends, family or even oneself: this involves turning the bullet points, say, into questions which we fire at each other or ourselves. This is where an oral element creeps in, where we hope that by mouthing and speaking out loud, these slabs of written knowledge will 'stick'. Perhaps, when we go into the exam hall, we'll remember the sounds of, say, the difference between sedimentary, igneous and metamorphic rock. And here the art of rote learning kicks in. Is this oral? Written? Both? A hybrid?

I noticed that my son did these things, mostly at about one in the morning, but with an additional factor that was missing from my days at school. He learned what might be called the protocols of the language of essays. He learned, partly orally, that group of words like 'however', 'furthermore', 'additionally'. He was keen to pick up the jargon of things like 'it could be said that', 'there is some evidence for', but I got lost in the matter of whether paragraphs are PEC, PEE, PPE. When I said that I thought that the best thing you can do in a paragraph is make some kind of statement or point and illustrate that point with an example, I got pushed angrily to one side. I didn't dare go there again.

Now ask me what these late-night conversations were for. I don't know. I did them. I'm a parent. I bent my mind as hard as I could to doing all I could to make helpful suggestions. To use oral language to make things stick. But no, I don't know what it was for. I mean I know it was for the exam. What I don't know is what it's for existentially, or beyond that, for the sake of the universe. Even so, though this is a world saturated with writing, it is circumscribed by oral interventions.

Of course, the last eighteen months have restricted the kinds of practice that I've understood to be valuable in itself: face-to-face talk, discussion, dialogic learning or what John Yandell has called 'the social construction of meaning'. (That's the title of his book: *The Social Construction of Meaning: Reading Literature in Urban English Classrooms*, Routledge, 2013.) This is the co-operative learning through talk which enables us to give voice to what we know, what we don't know, to hear what others like ourselves know and don't know: that mix of statements, questions, suggestions, hesitations, interruptions which enables us to arrive at judgements, evaluations, conclusions. We can read about this in great detail in a book like John Yandell's but also in books such as *Exploring Talk in School, Inspired by the Work of Douglas Barnes*, edited by Neil Mercer and Steve Hodgkinson (Sage, 2008), *Classroom Talk: Evidence-based Teaching for Enquiring Teachers* by Rupert Knight (Critical Publishing, 2020), *Talking About Oracy: Developing Communication beyond the Classroom* by Sarah Davies (John Catt, 2020) or *The Noisy Classroom: Developing Debate and Critical Oracy in Schools* by Debbie Newman (Routledge, 2020) and many others, e.g. by Fiona Maine and Lynn Dawes, and older books by e.g. Nancy Martin, my father, Douglas Barnes, Robert Protherough, or recent papers by e.g. Kristina Kumpulainen, and so on.

But we can also act as our own observers and researchers. Consider this: a common-sense view of the legal profession is that it's one of the most heavily laden with literacy – legal documents, law books, written judgements, prepared scripted speeches, articles of criminology, statutes and so on. Yet, get involved in a case and something else emerges. Without going into details, I got embroiled in an unfortunate matter. I received what is called a 'letter of claim'. I felt that I couldn't handle the matter myself and turned to a solicitor. So, what then happened is of interest to us today. I had many, many conversations with my wife, and this solicitor, his assistant, and in the end with another lawyer. The conversations ranged over who I am, what I thought, how we interpreted specific words in the original letter, how we might phrase this or that reply, what we should draw attention to, what we should emphasise, what would be the best thing to do next . . . and many, many more examples of more nuanced stuff. All done through speech. Oracy. Of course this got synthesised into documents, letters which were then in themselves subjects of discussion between me and my wife and/or the solicitor, translated into clarifications, emails, postscripts to emails and the like. It would be possible to analyse all this into various levels of oral work: reasoning, digressing, logical thought, intuition, anecdoting, exegesis on specific words or phrases – hermeneutics if you like, planning, strategy, research, gossip. Within the dialogues themselves there was the matter of how to make a point, how to disagree, how to take turns, how to accept a counter-argument, how to suggest, how to accept that this or that might be desirable but was probably not appropriate. Behind that, there might well have been questions of ego, whether this or that toe had been trodden on or could be trodden on, so a good deal of chat about what we might expect; in other words anticipatory and predictive . . . and much more.

Where do we learn how to do this? Autobiographically, I can say that I learned a lot of it at home. I was very lucky to have had Harold and Connie Rosen as my parents and Brian Rosen as my older brother. Between them they spent hundreds – probably thousands – of hours drenching me in this kind of analytic dialogue: clarifying what things meant, asking me or others to talk things through, experimenting with other ways of saying things, illustrating arguments with quotes, anecdotes, comparisons and contrasts, referring to authorities who might also have views, drawing attention to how people said or wrote things as an indicator of hidden or deliberately concealed intentions.

Some people aren't so fortunate. That said, I'm often very interested when listening to people who seem to have had no higher education but who have been through many years of seeking justice. I'm thinking of people like those involved with miscarriages of justice or enquiries like Hillsborough, or Grenfell. They've learnt the differences between facts, accusations, defences, delays, procrastinations, justice, truth and lies. They appear in interviews on TV and radio and talk fluently, clearly, analytically, reflectively about what they've been through. They are able to reflect on how the system has worked against them being heard, or getting justice. I can't know for certain, but there are occasions when I've got the impression that many of these people learn this sort of thing on the job. Again, I can't be certain, but I've suspected that this has largely come about through hundreds of hours of talk with lawyers, loved ones and friends to – as we say – get to the bottom of what was going on.

This idea of decoding what people say lies at the heart of several professional activities, one of which is forensic linguistics. On BBC Radio 4's *Word of Mouth* I've had the benefit of being able to talk to several forensic linguists. One put in front of us the transcript of what Edward 'Ted' Kennedy said in his statement in relation to the events at Cape Chappaquiddick on 18/19 July 1969. Here's some of it:

> On July 18, 1969, at approximately 11:15 p.m. in Chappaquiddick, Martha's Vineyard, Massachusetts, I was driving my car on Main Street on my way to get the ferry back to Edgartown. I was unfamiliar with the road and turned right onto Dyke [*sic*] Road, [Notes 5] instead of bearing hard left on Main Street. After proceeding for approximately one-half mile on Dyke [*sic*] Road I descended a hill and came upon a narrow bridge [Notes 6]. The car went off the side of the bridge. There was one passenger with me, one Miss Mary___, [Notes 7] a former secretary of my brother Sen. Robert Kennedy. The car turned over and sank into the water and landed with the roof resting on the bottom. I attempted to open the door and the window of the car but have no recollection of how I got out of the car. I came to the surface . . . etc.

> (Taken from the Wikipedia entry for 'Chappaquiddick incident', accessed 3 July 2021)

The forensic linguist drew our attention to something I hadn't noticed: most of the clauses in the first part of the statement begin with the word 'I'. 'I' is the subject and theme of these sentences. Then, quite suddenly, the subject changes and becomes 'the car' and the statement, 'There was one passenger'; not, for example, 'I was with . . . ' Then again there's another sentence that begins with 'The car . . . ' but then the statement returns to 'I' with 'I attempted to open the door . . . ' and on beyond my extract to Edward Kennedy notifying the police. The forensic linguist left me with the problem of trying to figure out why Kennedy removed his agency from the passage in the story where he is at the wheel as the car goes into the water and remains as a non-agent until he gets free.

How we speak (or how we prepare statements to be read out) says more than we say. But where and how do we (or can we) learn such things? Some years ago, I was asked to give a talk to NATE, and one of the aspects of linguistics that I thought might appeal to teenagers would be to ask how might we know whether people are telling the truth or lying. What linguistic clues might we find? I'll repeat it: to my mind it's of crucial importance. Forensic linguistics is only the tip of the iceberg: lying, dissembling, pretending, exaggerating, insincerity, hypocrisy, deceit, fraud, concealment – these are potentially fascinating areas for us to investigate when we talk of oracy.

Now, another part of my life in the last eighteen months has been teaching. I co-teach an MA in Children's Literature at Goldsmiths, University of London, and when we were devising the course, we put in a module that I don't think exists anywhere else in the country: Children's Literature in Action, where we lay aside our rights to be critics of children's literature and invite students to research and investigate how children respond to literature. This immediately invites the question, yes, but how? One old and familiar way is to give children questionnaires. These have the drawback of being formulaic (in order to standardise the answers), are often closed-ended, written, and very much part of the adult-to-child relationship rather than the child-to-child one. Other possibilities lie in front of us: inviting children to interpret the texts they encounter. They might do this through drama, storying, painting, the making of objects – e.g. art, model-making, sculpture, writing. But what about talk? And this could be in such situations as: teacher and whole class, adult and one child, two children talking, a group talking. As you will know, these are very different situations, particularly if you're seeking out what you hope will be authentic views of what children actually think of a text. What's more, how do you collect such data? Film? Audio? Each has its advantages and disadvantages. And then if you collect it, how do you analyse it? These are the kinds of problems we have faced in the five or six years we've been running the course, and to help us or guide us are those who've gone before – names I've mentioned already: Alexander, Mercer, Maine, Dawes, Protherough, Yandell, Davies, Newman, Knight, but now with these years of work behind us, previous years' students, including one who you've already met today (introducing this talk), Richard Charlesworth.

So, one way or another these authors all suggest ways in which we can figure out what speakers are saying, and why, in relation to texts. For example, Robin Alexander in his chapter 'Culture, Dialogue and Learning' in *Exploring Talk in School* talks of the 'learning repertoire' which would include the ability to:

narrate, explain, instruct, ask different kinds of question, receive, act and build upon answers, analyse and solve problems, speculate and imagine, explore and evaluate ideas, discuss, argue, reason and justify, negotiate . . .

to which he adds: 'listen, be receptive to alternative viewpoints, think about what they hear, give others time to think'.

This is a very helpful and fertile guide. It immediately invites us to think about what conditions we can set up in classrooms which might enable all this happen. What role might a teacher have to play to enable it? What kinds of questions, or comments or body language, might enable it? And indeed, writers and our students reveal such strategies as echoing, holding back from explaining, taking part as a parallel contributor, e.g. as someone speculating, reflecting, offering anecdotes, or sometimes just through body language: nodding, looking, indicating that you're attentive, gesturing approval, showing that you want to hear more, and so on. Aidan Chambers in what is now called *Tell Me* with *The Reading Environment* (Thimble Press, 2011 – other editions are available) is a rich source for open-ended questions in this area, but some of it comes from intuition and surrendering the role of instructor for the length of time of this kind of encounter.

However, all this leaves open another level of analysis: the content of what a child might say in relation to a text. For a while I looked through these excellent references for descriptions of e.g. where a child makes a discovery of what they think is the meaning in a text, or where they interpret through the means of telling an anecdote. One guide for this was a little known book, *Young Readers, New Readings* by Emrys Evans (University of Hull Press, 1992). Evans proposes a matrix of response ranging from intuitions to evaluations:

Unreflective interest in action; empathising; analogising; reflecting on the significance of events (theme) and behaviour (distanced evaluation of characters); reviewing the whole work as the author's creation; consciously considered relationship with the author; recognition of textual ideology; understanding of self (identity theme) and of one's own reading processes.

This brought me closer, but in the end I thought I would start to assemble a matrix of my own to approximate the kinds of thought we all have, children too, in response to literature. It's evolved into some 25 ingredients, but I hope others can refine, adapt or add to it. It's in my booklet *Poetry and Stories for Primary and Lower Secondary Schools* (self-published, available through my website www.michaelrosen.co.uk) along with another matrix provided by James Durran from NATE in response to the matrix. These are what he calls 'trigger questions'.

So this (my matrix) has arisen out of the teaching of this module, and from our MA students – a mix of teachers, librarians and others working with young people – as they've brought to the class transcripts of children talking about texts. I've named each of the ingredients, but they're explained in my booklet. They are: experiential, intertextual, intratextual, interrogative, semantic, structural, selective analogising, speculative, reflective, narratological, evaluative, eureka moments, effects, storying, descriptive, grammatical, prosodic, effect of interactions, imaginative, emotional flow, author intention, contextual, representational or symbolic, extra-textual, causation.

You might immediately see that these are not discrete, watertight categories, but that they overlap and that any utterance by a child responding to a text might be in several of these categories. No matter, it gives us a language with which to analyse children's discussions in relation to children's literature.

One of our students this term has brought to the class transcripts of conversations she's having with a 13-year-old boy about *Lord of the Flies*. There are several conversations about which characters he – let's call him Peter – likes or dislikes. In session one, he said, 'I feel like I can relate to the characters and if I don't like some of the characters, if I really hate some of the characters, I think it's good then 'cos then they make, they make characters I actually have feelings against or towards.'

So this is a comment about 'effects', if you like. He is assessing how he is affected by the characters. In session three, Peter expanded on this. The researcher asked him, 'Do you think author Golding is successful at achieving effect?' Peter says, 'Yes, I think so, because you feel affected by what's happening in the book, like even with characters like . . . he makes good characters, like you don't like, generally you don't like Jack and that shows his, I don't think you're meant to like Jack so that's good. And I think you're kinda meant to be on the fence with Ralph, which I am and with Piggy you're meant to feel a little sorry for him which I do . . . '

So there's a lot going on here to do with 'effect' but also author intention. Going back to Alexander's matrix, there's 'discuss', 'argue', 'explain', 'explore and evaluate ideas'.

And in Richard Charlesworth's Master's essay 'Does Critical Discussion of Refugee-Themed Picture Books "Scaffold" Children's Understanding of the Refugee Experience?', Richard discusses and analyses numerous transcripts of pupils' conversations in response to picture books about refugees, including this conversation about Sarah Garland's *Azzi in Between*. The pupils are in Year 5 in a primary school in west London.

Transcript from *Azzi in Between* (session 1, group 1) Pupil-pupil context	Researcher Notes (linked to theory, if relevant)
Tom: It's the same as Refugee Boy. It explains about the border between Eritrea and Ethiopia. It says they're fighting over a pile of rubble and dust. Which is kind of what they're doing there (indicating image A). They're just fighting in piles of rubble and dust. There's nothing to fight over. **Kate:** (Continuing point) . . . and they're still fighting. **Tom:** Even if you did win the war you'd have to pay for . . . **Kate:** (continuing point) . . . for all of that. **Tom:** For all of that to get rebuilt. To take over the country. **Zara:** So really there isn't a point in fighting. You don't get anything out of it. **Kate:** You get land, but haven't you already got enough land?	Example of collaborative, dialogic discussion. Links to Vygotskian principle that understanding can be co-constructed by children building on previous comment. The children here are discussing quite adult concepts of economics, politics and geography in relation to the refugee experience.

So, if we choose, we can set up situations in which children can and will do the things that Robin Alexander and many others say they can do.

Note 1: Harold Rosen: Writings on Life, Language and Learning, 1958 to 2008, edited by John Richmond, *was published in 2017 by the UCL Institute of Education Press. Available at https://www.ucl-ioe-press.com/books/language-and-literacy/harold-rosen.*

Conscious and Unconscious

In July 2021, I was asked to write this piece for The Lancet.

Being ill can take you places you didn't know existed. If we're not medically trained, we rely on everyday words to describe our states of being. For as long as I can remember I've been happy with a pair of opposites: conscious and unconscious. People who've spoken English over the last few hundred years have developed and used that prefix 'un' to do a lot of work: happy-unhappy, lock-unlock. It's so familiar to us that we don't always think of the un-word as one of a pair. Untoward? Unmatched?

In early April 2020 I was sedated to help me survive Covid. If you throw me a date in April or May of that year, I can tell you that in that time I wasn't conscious, or that I was 'in a coma'. From my notes, I gather that I was in this coma for 40 days. After a few more days in the ICU I was taken to a geriatric ward to recover. I was in this ward for another ten days or so. I say all this as if I know what I'm talking about, but I only know it by consulting my notes. That's because the old dividing line between conscious and unconscious that I had in my head before is blurred.

Let me complicate it further. I appear in a film, *2020: the Story of Us*, that was broadcast on ITV. It showed three Covid patients with and recovering from Covid. I can watch myself in intensive care. Some of the shots show me as if I'm asleep, limp and inert. Others show me sitting up in bed, listening to Professor Hugh Montgomery and responding to him. He asks me, 'You've got children?' I pause, looking at him, and say, 'Apparently.' I have no memory of this conversation. I don't know whether I was trying to be ironic, facetious, obstructive or what. I suspect it was an attempt at wry humour but I have no connection with this moment at all. Similarly, my wife tells me of coming into the hospital, meeting me on the fourth-floor atrium, in a bid by Professor Montgomery to shake me out of the coma. I gather the team was getting worried about getting me back to full consciousness. There was even a suggestion that I might have been 'brain dead', in his words.

Emma held my hand, played me recordings of our children, and of my older offspring talking to me. I responded. Apparently, this encounter was transformational. The 'prof' said it was a 'game changer'. When they wheeled me back into the lift to return to the ICU, I had become 'lucid' and didn't stop talking. Did I? Again, I have no recollection of this.

My first memories are, I think, in my last few days in the ICU before going to the geriatric ward. By my reckoning, I think that must be around day 45, but possibly earlier. I can remember chafing against the mittens that were given to me to prevent my pulling out tubes. I can remember the way the nurse said the word 'energy' as if she was a tai-chi teacher and I have the recollection that I was in some kind of correction camp or training camp, but didn't know why. By the time I'm in the geriatric ward, I have memories of many conversations with nurses, doctors and physiotherapists.

All this tells me that the binary of conscious and unconscious is insufficient. The language is not doing the job it should do to help me describe the state of mind – or states of mind – I was in from about day 30 to about day 48. Some of these days involve me in responding and talking, but these are not accessible to me now. It's clear that I engaged with people. I was thinking and possibly reasoning. Was I 'conscious'? I must be wary here of linking consciousness to my present state of mind demanding of me that I should recall these times. There is presumably a kind of consciousness that is 'conscious' but lies submerged or hidden from full consciousness. (You'll sense that I'm groping for ways to describe this and turning to a metaphor like 'submerged' to help me.)

This is complicated further by the fact that my ability to remember things improved the further I got away from the sedation. In the weeks immediately following, I had a good deal of short-term memory loss along with strange 'holes' that I hadn't had before: the most notable being unable to retrieve the names of famous Hollywood film stars. Tom Cruise, George Clooney and Meryl Streep's names proved impossible to find without using Google. I also resisted Emma's accounts of what had happened to me, repeatedly asking her to tell me what she had told me the day before. And the word 'tracheostomy' proved impossible to remember, as I tried to apply my rudimentary medical knowledge to pull it forward: 'brachio . . . something? bronchio . . . something?'.

All this would be totally new for me if it wasn't for something else. When I was 17 I was knocked down in the road by a driver who left the scene, called in at a police station about a mile down the road, returned with the police and pointed to where he thought he had knocked someone down. It was dark, there was no pavement, and there was no sign of me. They were just about to leave the scene when they heard a voice. It was me. I was lying away from the road in a kind of hollow – this was in a patch of green belt between Northwood and Rickmansworth, just in Hertfordshire. When the police got to me, I appeared to be awake, eyes open, and responded to questions. I told them the name of my doctor – well, actually, it was the old doctor. We had moved house about a year previously. I went on talking while they took me to the nearby hospital (Mount Vernon). All this was around 10 or 11 at night. At the hospital we had to wait till 4.00 in the morning before the radiographer arrived and then I was put on an orthopaedic ward because my pelvis had come apart at the front.

What of my memory? I can remember leaving school following a basketball match. The next thing I can remember is sitting up in bed in the hospital ward to talk to a colleague of my father's who had come to see me. Apparently, I had been talking to the other patients about rugby.

So here is another example where the two words 'conscious' and 'unconscious' don't cover all my states of mind. In the past I've talked of this time following the accident as a 'blank' and have tidied it away like that. Following this episode with sedation and Covid, I feel that I want to probe these transitional states further. What are they? What do they tell us about how the brain works?

LITERATURE AND CHILDREN'S LITERATURE

Are Books for Children Worth Reading?

This is the inaugural lecture I gave in 2005 at Middlesex University when they made me a Visiting Professor there.

What a strange question to ask! Most of us in this room have spent years making, reading, teaching or studying children's books. We've devoted great chunks of our lives to this matter. So surely it's a question that doesn't even need asking. We just know that they're worth reading.

Well, perhaps that would be the case if it weren't for some problems. Problems that make it harder for us to answer the question. I mean, if you say, 'Are books for children worth reading?' I sometimes feel like saying, 'Well, when you think of the way they're treated, you might think not.'

Let's begin with education. It's in schools that most people not only learn to read, but learn how to read. For many people, outside of the regularly book-reading minority, this is the one place where they will learn what reading feels like; and what reading is for. It's the critical moment when either the reading bug might bite or give up trying. Now, the world of children's books has always existed in a symbiotic relationship with education, with schools looking to children's literature for books to read; and children's literature looking to schools to buy their books for its libraries and classrooms and for schools to create active readers who come back over and over again to read more books. So, no apologies for beginning with education.

But what's going on with books in schools? Many of us here have been witness to the fact that the way books are read in schools has, over the last four or five years, changed. We are full of anecdotal evidence of, say, Years 5 and 6 classrooms where whole books are not being read; where books are being chopped up into fragments which are then turned into worksheets;

and these fragments are then used as examples for exercises on spotting verbs and similes.

We can offer eyewitness accounts of how the word 'literature' has been abolished. It is, as you know, now called 'literacy'. So this has turned the act of reading into a performance to be assessed. How well is he reading? Is she reading accurately? Is she reading fluently? How can we test this reading performance? How can we create a set of classroom activities around reading that will be testable so that we can show that a child is reading at this or that level?

For those of us who write children's books, let alone for the hundreds of thousands of people who enjoy the business of reading books with the children they know, we're pretty sure that this is not why we got involved. The reasons why we write books for children are complex and diverse but amongst them you can find a notion like: wanting to say things that matter to young people. And when I say 'matter', that can take in such ideas as wanting to intrigue, entertain, educate, amuse, excite, stir up and challenge our audience. I don't know many writers of books for children who would say, 'I write children's books so that a class of Year 5 children can count the adjectives on page 43 of my latest novel.'

But let's leave the anecdotal evidence to one side, and even my wistful complaints about what's happening to our precious books in schools. In fact, looking at the people in this room makes me think we should set up an open and independent commission to look into exactly how books are being read in schools at the moment. And before that, to set the field, we could invite people who have thought long and hard about why we read and enjoy literature, to offer some thoughts. And then we could match these thoughts with what is actually going on. I have a picture of taking, let's say, A.S. Byatt, Derek Walcott – I don't know – John Carey, Germaine Greer into a set of primary schools to see a classroom preparing for a SAT reading paper and asking our visitors if what's going on matches up with what they think literature is for. Come to think of it, it might make an interesting documentary . . .

In the meantime, we either have the anecdotes and the speculation, or we can look closely at the ideas that have come to dominate how teachers and children read books in schools. Where should we look for these ideas? Compressed into the hundreds of anonymous foolscap booklets that have landed up on head teachers' desks over the last ten years? You know, the ones full of phrases like 'research has shown that' without ever telling you whose research, or what the results of the research were.

Or should we look at the part of the process where a model of reading is put before teachers as the most valuable, a model that has the currency that really counts?

Let me read you a story. It's called 'You Can Do It' by Theresa Breslin. (And, just to be clear, what I say following this story is in no way a criticism of Theresa Breslin or the story.)

'Fiona, for goodness' sake, hurry up!' Her mother's voice, sharp with annoyance, sounded all the way up the stairs to the attic. Fiona scowled and stuck her chin out. 'Do this, Fiona. Take that, Fiona. Bring this downstairs. Carry that upstairs. Don't slouch about, Fiona. We don't have much time.'

Fiona picked up the last of the boxes she was bringing down from the attic, and as she did so, it burst. Without warning it gave way, spewing bills, old photographs, postcards and letters all over the floor. She gazed down in bewilderment at the mess.

She disliked change, she decided, as she gazed at the chaotic pile of papers at her feet, and this change she especially hated. Moving Grampa out of his big old house into that flat. There was never going to be enough space for all his things, and hardly enough room for her to stay every weekend with him as she had done ever since she was small. As she knelt down and began to gather up some of the bits and pieces, she heard her mother's voice again.

'Fiona! Come down this minute!'

Fiona dropped the papers she had in her hand and went to the door.

'Coming,' she shouted.

She trudged down the narrow attic stairs. She could see her mother's face peering up at her from the stairwell.

'Whatever is keeping you up there? We'll have to leave now. I don't want to have Grampa waiting too long on his own at the new flat.'

Fiona walked down the next flight of stairs to the bottom hall. She passed her father on his way out to the back garden.

'Are you going with your mum?' he asked.

Fiona shrugged. 'Looks like it,' she said.

She went out of the front door and helped bundle some boxes and carrier bags into her mother's car.

'You won't be able to get in here now, Fiona. You'll have to stay with your dad and come on later,' her mum was saying.

Fiona watched her mother drive off and then went slowly back upstairs. Her dad must still be sorting out the contents of the shed. She had time to go back up to the attic and gather up the broken box. It was mainly photographs which had spilled out. Memories of her Grampa's life and family.

There was an old one of him in uniform. She picked it up and squinted at it.

He smiled out at her. A strong face with a dark moustache. Fiona sighed. He wasn't like that any more. Not since a stroke had left him with shaky legs and quivering muscles.

She decided to get a box to put the photographs in. She twisted round and ran to the stairs.

'Those who hurry fastest are the first to fall' was one of her Grampa's sayings, and it was as if she heard him saying it now, right out loud in her ear as she stumbled on the top step. Seconds later she landed with a crash at the foot of the stairs. Her head hurt, her bottom hurt and her legs throbbed painfully.

Fiona was quite alone in the big empty house. She started to get up. Her legs were caught underneath her body and she tried to heave herself up and straighten them out.

'Oww,' she yelped. A stabbing pain flared in her knees. She moved again, this time more carefully.

The pain was terrible. There were tears crowding in behind her eyelids and her hands were shaking. When she tried to move, both legs hurt badly.

'Now what am I going to do?' Fiona asked herself, looking at the steep, uneven stairs below. She couldn't stand up. She was a prisoner.

Both her parents were so busy at the moment with Grampa being unwell and moving house, that they might not realise anything was wrong, not for a while anyway. But then, Fiona thought, there was someone who usually noticed immediately that she wasn't around. Grampa. Well, he used to, anyway. Things were different now.

The first day he had come home from hospital she hadn't recognised the sick old man whose clothes seemed too big for him. She had pictured herself helping him get better, sorting his cushions, picking flowers for his room. She imagined him smiling and saying, 'Thank you, Fiona'. Then they would play cards and she would win most of the games. But it hadn't been like that at all. He sat slumped in his chair by the fire most of the day, his eyes were vague and sometimes he dribbled his food. Just like a baby!

She didn't want to sit on the little stool beside his chair and talk. His eyes were always sad, and he hardly ever answered anyone anyway. 'He's not even trying,' Fiona's mum complained. 'He's supposed to exercise his fingers and practise those words, but he just sits all day.'

As the weeks passed and he didn't get much better, he finally agreed to sell the big house and move closer to the rest of the family.

Fiona looked at her watch and groaned. She might have to wait ages before Mum or Dad came. She moved her position. Something was pressing into her back. Something hard with sharp corners. It was a photograph album. Carefully written on the front in her Grampa's writing was 'Photo Album – Fiona Growing Up'.

Fiona made a face. She hated baby photographs of herself. Still . . . it would pass the time, and take her mind off the pain. She flicked it open. There was one of Grampa with his arm around her as she stood in the swimming pool. It seemed silly now she was older, but she had been scared to stand by herself in the water. Her legs had trembled as she stepped away from the tiled side.

'You can do it, Fiona,' Grampa's voice whispered in her ear. 'You can do it.' And he had steadied her until she was confident enough to stand on her own. 'Thanks, Grampa,' she'd said. And he had pulled her hair and said, 'What are friends for?'

What were friends for? Helping each other, she supposed. She could do with some help now . . . and so could he, she suddenly thought.

A friend to help him now that he had trembling legs, now that he was unsure, with no confidence, maybe a little scared of trying. Fiona felt more tears coming, and this time she didn't stop them.

And she was still tearful, with a grubby, streaked face, when she heard the back door open an hour or so later.

'Dad! Dad!' she yelled frantically as he ran up the stairs.

'You poor thing!' he cried when he saw her.

They got back from the hospital at six o'clock.

Grampa was sitting in his chair, hands resting on each knee. He looked up as Fiona came in. His eyes followed her as she limped slowly across the room.

'I suppose neither of us will be able to manage stairs for a while.'

Fiona sat down beside him. 'How about a trade?' she suggested. 'I borrow your wheelchair, and you get a turn of my crutches?'

The old man looked at her uncertainly. Fiona giggled.

'We could have races,' she said. She looked at him, full in the face, the first time she had done so since he had been in hospital.

'Where's your mirror?' she asked.

'Mirror?' he repeated.

'You're meant to have a hand mirror by your chair and do your vowel sounds every day,' she said. 'You've not been doing them, have you?' He shook his head slowly.

'Well, it's not good enough,' said Fiona. 'We'll have to make a start right away.' Then she winked at him, and leaning forward close to his head, she whispered.

'You can do it, Grampa. You can do it.'

Now, I wonder if you could help me here. I want you to imagine that you have that story in front of you and you're in the company of a group of children. Can I ask you to talk to the person next to you about what kinds of things you might do with that story? Before, during or after reading it.

[Which they did . . .]

Well, as some of you may or may not know, this was the story that was set in the Key Stage 2 English Reading SAT for levels 3-5 last year.

[In the illustrated booklet, 'a stroke' is explained as 'a sudden illness affecting parts of the brain, which can cause speech difficulties and loss of feeling in the body'.]

So let's see what kind of activity that exam is, what is the purpose and meaning of a SAT paper in relation to a story. And you can compare that with the kinds of activities you've just come up with. But before we get on, just so that there's no misunderstanding, I'll explain why I'm doing this. It's because it's my view that within and behind the questions asked on a SAT paper is a whole outlook that implies a way of reading. But more than that: without stating explicitly that this is the approach teachers should take when reading stories to their children, the sheer institutional power of the SATs creates a dominant discourse. Something is being dictated here. Very few of us need reminding how much pressure there is on teachers, parents and of course the children themselves to do well in the SATs, to get the school a good place in the league tables, to show the Ofsted inspectors and the local press that this isn't a failing school, and so on. That's the institutional power that lies behind the questions that I'm going to look at now.

So, having read the story, the children begin. You might like to try too. I won't be marking your papers.

The first group of questions you're asked goes like this:

> Choose the best group of words to fit the passage and put a ring around your choice.

Then there are five multiple-choice questions, along these lines:

> When Fiona waited she remembered how Grampa had 'saved her' / 'helped her' / 'played games' / 'read to her'.

What the children are being asked to do here follows rule one of all exams: that your best chance of being able to answer a question lies in the extent to which you know the game, the extent to which you've been initiated into the procedures and jargon of the exam itself; and it's much less a matter of knowing the answer to what is actually being asked. It's hard to think of a more opaque way of saying what they're asking than with the sentence: 'Choose the best group of words to fit the passage . . . ' Can words 'fit' passages? And what's a 'passage' anyway? We should remember that it is at this very moment, in the difficulties of decoding the code of exam questions, that children are graded and selected, rewarded and failed. For some of us, it's particularly distressing to know that it is the things we write that can be used in this way. Once again, I can say that I don't know of a writer of books for children who came into the business thinking, 'I hope that one day I'll write something that examiners will be able to use to dub some children failures.'

And then there's the mess of multiple choice to think about. It's thought that multiple-choice questions are more objective and therefore more informative about the candidate than open-ended questions about such fuzzy things as feelings and emotions. In fact, hidden in every multiple-choice question is the snag that the wrong answers are not all as equally wrong. Some are more obviously wrong than others. Some wrong answers could at a stretch be kind of right. The marks given never reflect this. In other words, it's not very objective at all, and tells you very little or very misleading things about how a child is thinking.

So, in the question I just gave you, the right answer, says the booklet invitingly called 'English tests, Mark schemes' is that Grampa 'helped her', but the way he helped her in the pool, you may remember, was in a way to play games with her. No marks for using your intelligence and giving both as answers.

We are also asked about what Fiona found after she fell downstairs: 'a photograph album', 'some old letters', 'a photograph of Grampa in uniform' or a 'letter from Grampa'. This is a trick question, because, yes, she did find a photo of Grampa in uniform but that was earlier in the story. The right answer is a photograph album.

What is going on here? It's a crude attempt to impose a rightness on the way a child should read. That there is some kind of correctness and that this correctness is linked to identifying facts about a story in their right order, in the right time frame. We should remember here that Theresa Breslin's story is not a whodunnit, where our reading will in part depend on remembering who did what to whom and when.

It's a story, I would suggest, that is very much about shifts in feeling. The significance of whether Fiona found the photo album or the photo of Grampa after she fell is minute. It is what I'll call a 'spurious facticity', an unnecessary and falsely based obsession with what are perceived to be the 'facts' of a story, in lieu of its shifting tone and feeling.

Interestingly enough, for a mode of examining that pretends to be objective and factual, the next two questions offer a correct answer that introduces ideas not stated in the story. After her spell in hospital, we are asked if Fiona and her dad went to 'watch television', 'see Mum and Grampa', 'collect the old photos', or 'help Mum with the packing'. Well, we know that Fiona went to see Grampa but there's no certainty that Mum was there too.

What is this kind of trickery for? It's for whose benefit, exactly? What does it prove? Again, and excuse me for repeating it, I think the function of this kind of interrogation is to control teachers in the way that they read stories with children. In order to get your class to do well at the tests, you the teacher should spend time each week, perhaps each day, interrogating children along these lines after you've looked at a story or a passage from a story. Once again, we are talking about a process here of showing this model of reading and talking about reading as the one with the most value.

By the way, I've got some questions here for SATs setters in case they use passages from some well-known books.

'On what side of the road was the good Samaritan walking?'

'On what leg is Long John Silver's wooden leg?'

'In which way did Odysseus turn the stake in Cyclops' eye, left, right or both ways?'

'How sharp was Hamlet's sword to go through an arras tapestry, Polonius's clothes and in sufficiently far to kill him?'

As with all systems that draw attention to their own correctness, SATs frequently contain errors and misleading information.

We are asked, 'Why did Fiona's mother feel annoyed at the beginning of the story?' And we are offered page 9 as a place to look. In fact, at least one possible answer is stated quite clearly on page 10 . . . Mother is calling up to Fiona with various words like, 'What is keeping you so long?' and then, 'I don't want Grampa to be waiting too long.'

Because the examiner and child are locked into this ballet of correctness, when misleading or unhelpful or not-helpful-enough information is given us, we never have the courage to defy what we're told. If it says 'see page 9', they must be right. The answer won't be on page 10, and even if it looks like it is, it can't be, because they've said it's on page 9. This is, in its own way, an example of the classic psychologists' test of conformity. Better to conform than to be right. Better to risk nothing than to be right.

Then we are asked what Grampa's proverb means: 'Those who hurry fastest are the first to fall.' 'Explain what he meant.'

Now, let me begin to look up from this dreary business for a moment. Faced with a story that has an old person passing on his thoughts to a young one in the form of a proverb, just think of the interesting directions you could take. You could ask the children to collect proverbs and sayings that their own grandparents and parents say. You could ask what it feels like to be told these things. And you could even ask whether Grampa's one, or any of the others that the children collect, are in their view true.

In this way, we would make the children equal to the story, not part of a process that rewards and humiliates. We would also, and I'll be coming back to this, be treating story as something open-ended. A place where we acknowledge that the reader brings a knowledge that he or she responds with and that this is one of the unavoidable and utterly delicious things about reading.

(By the way, you get two marks if you say something like 'People who rush things never get them done.' But only one mark if you say something like 'He meant don't rush what you're doing, take your time.')

In direct contrast to an approach to response that makes children equal to the story, the next question crystallises all that's wrong with the test's approach to literature:

. . . pain flared in her knees. (page 12)

Why is this an effective way of describing how Fiona felt after she fell down the stairs?

We are so indoctrinated into this way of talking to children about literature that it's sometimes hard to see what's so appalling about it.

Who says that 'pain flared in her knees' is 'effective'? Where is the author of this opinion? How does the author of that opinion justify it? No, we have the pure silence of authority, embodied in the dull voice of the examiner. The exam states that it's 'effective', so it must be. Conform, children, conform.

The question also reveals an obsession that lies behind the teaching of literature, and in particular of poetry – that's to say, 'metaphor'. For quite complicated reasons, metaphor shoots up the league table of priorities in the teaching of literature and is considered much more worthy of close examination than, say, repartee, mimesis, intonation or lying. Again, we have here an example of indoctrination of teachers disguised as exam-question: teach the children metaphor if you want them to pass their exams. Why? Where's the justification for this? Where's the intellectual rationale that makes metaphor king of the castle? Nowhere to be found.

I've got nothing against metaphors, but even within the parameters of their given high status, consider the possibility of asking children to come up with their own ways of saying what it felt like when they hurt themselves. Did things 'flare', as Theresa Breslin writes, or did they explode, rip, stab, etc.? The reading of literature shouldn't be someone forcing you to your knees at the feet of authors in praise of their effective metaphors.

The next question likewise reproduces one of the classic misleading notions that lie deep in the heart of old-school literature teaching: 'Why do you think the author included these details about how Grampa used to look?' The details in question are the photographs that spill out of the box, him in his uniform, his strong face and dark moustache.

This is the process whereby the correct answer is the one in the examiner's head, who for some magical and mysterious reason had a direct channel of communication with the author's mind. So what you now have to do is not include any random or Freudian reasons that you might come up with like, say, Theresa Breslin likes men with dark moustaches. Nor should you suggest that it might be for any ideological reasons to do with this family being quite well off with Grampa's 'big old house', and that such people often mark out their lives with nicely kept photo albums. Nor should you suggest that this is a story that relies on two kinds of flashback, the one in the narrative and the one in the objects that are referred to, sometimes both at the same time.

No, the correct answer is, 'I thought it was because using details makes stories come alive,' or something like that. I don't think I would have got a mark for that. Two marks for pointing out that it's a way of comparing the state of Grampa now with what he used to be like, but only one mark for saying that 'It shows that people change as they grow up.' To be honest, I think they got out of their depth with this one and can't distinguish between questions about author intention, questions about rhetoric and questions about what is thought by these people that a bit of writing will do to you.

Again, we could say, 'Why not first ask children about what it's like when they go through photo albums and see pictures of what their grandparents and parents looked like when they were younger?' And the thoughts you might have here would inform you about Fiona's reactions. But the snag with that is that we wouldn't know what they would answer, and the children wouldn't go through this bit of pretend mind-reading that is always thought to be so important. Instead, they would spend a moment guessing what was in their own heads. They would be the authority of their own experience, rather than novices in the process of becoming experts on examiners' heads. As it happens, in my experience, exam-setters are amongst the least able to divine what authors are up to.

By the way, I have noticed the pseudo-liberal 'Why do you think the author included these details . . . ?'

It's pseudo-liberal because there are only two kinds of right answer allowed. This leaves teachers in their daily practice with the job of setting children this kind of question so that the children can learn how to make their mind-reading guesses fit the examiners' requirements more and more closely. Under 'Assessment focus 6', this is known as 'Identify and comment on writers' purposes and viewpoints, and the overall effect of the text on the reader'. (All that took about a term on my MA on children's lit at Reading.) By the way, this has nothing to do with encouraging children to respond to what stories feel like to them, nothing very much to do with daring and experimenting with what they might think a story might be about. Nothing to do with investigating story for all its possibilities. And it's this readerly sense of indecision, wonder and experiment that many writers deliberately play with. Vital to active writing and reading; irrelevant to SATs examiners.

We have another question now, which is surely one of the most mysterious in the whole exercise. It quotes a line:

'But it hadn't been like that at all.' (page 12)

> What does this sentence tell you about Fiona's feelings after Grampa came out of hospital? Explain your answer fully.

I love that 'Explain your answer fully'. More exam-ese, a phrase that is hermetically sealed into the language of testing and never emerges to see daylight in everyday speech.

But back to the question . . . What does this sentence tell you about Fiona's feelings? I'm sorry, but the sentence, ripped from context, as the examiners have done both by quoting it, and by referring to it as 'this sentence', tells you absolutely nothing whatsoever about Fiona's feelings. As a sentence, it is entirely un-freighted with the language of feeling. It merely sounds, on its own, like a sentence of contradiction of some sort, which might imply anything from fussy pedantry, to anger, disappointment, mockery, irony, irritation, good humour, contempt, horror, surprise. As you might expect, though, there are three marks up for grabs if you ignore the instruction to look at the single sentence and pour into it all the contextual stuff about Fiona hoping that Grampa would be the same old Grampa and what he was like in reality. Knowing how to do this wins you three marks, but if you write 'Everything she had dreamed of did not come true' will only get you one.

This part of the story interestingly includes some examples of what's known as free indirect discourse, much loved of writers probably since Jane Austen but certainly since *Madame Bovary*.

> Then they would play cards and she would win most of the games. But it hadn't been like that at all. He sat slumped in his chair by the fire most of the day, his eyes were vague and sometimes he dribbled his food. Just like a baby!

The phrase 'Just like a baby!' is probably not the same voice as 'sometimes he dribbled his food'. Now I'm not suggesting that we should be firing questions about free indirect discourse at children. However, when we can get away from interrogating children in the ways that we've seen so far, there might be times when we could invite children, particularly when they're doing some writing themselves, to think of narrative sometimes as a bit like a game, where you can be in one person's head and speak their feelings, then in another person's, sometimes in everyone's head, sometimes only in one person's.

And that there are different ways of speaking from inside a person's head. Or sometimes you can avoid being in anyone's head. And that stories nearly always mean that somebody or something is the centre of attention, but you can shift this around and, indeed, play with it. But 'play' and 'games' are not on the agenda here.

Then, and I suspect that this is as a reaction to the kind of criticism I'm making here, we have two questions that suggest that someone somewhere deep in the heart of test-land has realised that stories are indeed often largely about how people's feelings change and why.

> How does Fiona's accident change how she feels about Grampa?

And:

> What do you think Fiona might have written in her diary after visiting Grampa two weeks after he had moved to his new flat?

Needless to say, it's not as open-ended a question as all that, because the candidates are then told what to think:

> Think about:
>
> what she thought of the flat;
>
> her friendship with Grampa.

What?! Why? Fiona the diarist might not want to mention the flat. Her diary could be about a programme that they watched on the telly together, a story that Grampa told her about when he staggered down the market to buy some carrots, a story about Fiona's mother when she was young, an article in the paper about a fire in the flats next door . . . or anything! That's the whole point of asking this kind of question. Well it should be, but not in these folks' hands. It seems as if even as the examiners give with one hand, they take away with the other.

Finally we are asked:

> a) What made Fiona remember things that happened in the past?

Which I answered with 'She was good at remembering catchphrases like "what are friends for?", "you can do it" and "those who hurry fastest".'

I'd have got no marks for that.

Why are Fiona's memories important to this story?

I answered that by saying 'Because the story is about change', which would have got me one mark but not two. I should have said 'Because the story is about Fiona realising that in the past her Grampa helped her and so now she must help him.' Or 'Because you need to know what happened before and compare it with the present.'

So here we tie the whole story up with a bit of liberal moralising, which to tell the truth passed me by. We are told, then, by 'English tests, Mark schemes, key stage 2, levels 3-5 2004' that there is a right meaning to this story, a nearly right meaning and a whole load of wrong ones; and in so doing, we learn that that's what stories are: things that have an overall right meaning that some clever people like SATs-setters get, and other dullards like me don't.

This is a model of reading that, as I've suggested, worms its way back into teachers' practice through the institutional power of the compulsory SATs system.

And it's a model of reading literature that I reject, for the simple reason that it makes books for children not worth reading.

It makes them dull, tiresome and irritating. It draws attention away from what moves us, or even from questioning why things move us or don't. It centres the facticity of story and de-centres the importance of changing feelings – and it takes the meaning of stories away from you into some strange, slightly frightening and abstract place occupied by Those Who Know Better And More Than You. They know the meaning. 'Play this game and you might be able to join them. Get it wrong and you won't.'

When we remind ourselves that in many schools the reading of whole books has come to an end, we face the fact that many children don't get to know how things turn out in a story, so they will never feel the experience of change when they read. They will never feel what I think is the most important thing about story, the presentation of possibles – possible behaviour, possible scenes and possible worlds. And you need to feel the sensation of how these possibles work out, to get it.

In short, you won't ever get the buzz of reading the stuff. So why bother to do it when, say, you're on your own? Or when you're bored? Or when there's something else to do?

Which brings me to the second reason that suggests that books for children might not be worth reading.

It's one of the curious ironies of our time that though children's literature has just been discovered, it's precisely at this moment that large sections of the public arena are intent on avoiding a discussion about children's books that treats them just as we might talk about books for adults.

First a little anecdote: I'm very lucky to work for the country's main public-service broadcaster, the BBC. For ten years, it ran a programme called *Treasure Islands* which for 18 shows a year looked exclusively at books aimed at children. It wasn't a children's show. It was aimed at people who would probably be looking for books for children they knew, but not entirely so. The programme had to be sufficiently interesting in its own right to engage people who were once children themselves, or who might become one while listening to the programme, or even for people to wonder what kind of place or what kind of time it is or was that produces or produced this or that kind of book.

It was taken off the air for the explicit reason that there wasn't room for ghetto programming. Children's books would be now looked at as part of arts and book magazine programmes or in separate features.

Yes, children's books appear more frequently for children with Go4It and BBC 7, but the question remained: do we need a place where a conversation goes on about children's books, just as we have conversations about children's minds or children's behaviour? About children but not always in the language of children themselves.

Meanwhile, TV finds almost no time for this kind of conversation about books for children, unless it involves an author who sells prodigious numbers of books (hooray for that); unless there's a scandal; or unless there's what is described as a crisis in childhood, a crisis in literacy or a crisis in parenting.

The popular newspapers are utterly uninterested, and the broadsheets stutter along: I see that *The Guardian*'s pages for children's books, where I'm an occasional reviewer, often has to justify itself with a quarter page ad, whereas an interview with an adult fiction writer can, quite properly, spread to three pages, or a page of fiction reviews goes without an ad entirely.

I know that editors like Julia Eccleshare, Nicolette Jones and Jill Slotover struggle to get regular reviews in, paragraphs here, interviews there, but all of them (and others) can tell you how hard it is to get the stuff noticed and taken beyond brief reviews and news.

So what's going on here? Why is there, in the midst of weekly announcements about literacy standards, schooling, constant heart-searching analyses of children's behaviour and parenting problems, an unwillingness to open a conversation about children's books? A conversation about the ideas embodied in the books and the social conditions and traditions they come out of?

It's hard not get conspiratorial about it. Or should I say, structural? It can't be an indifference to literature in general because books are getting as good a whack from the media as they've ever got. It can't be to do with a lack of interest in what, as adults, we think we're doing with our kids. So where's the problem? To tell the truth, it's a problem this culture has with children themselves.

The difficulty surrounding books for children is that they are unashamedly on the side of children. They also suggest that children should be taken seriously. That's not to say that they are serious, though they may well be, but that how children think, feel and behave is something that matters. This is implied both in what the stories seem to be about, but also in the very manner in which they are presented, the very fact that they are presented at all; we say, 'Here is something that you may well enjoy, you are someone worth entertaining, have a laugh, get scared, be amazed, be bewildered. See if you can follow this.' What's more, on close examination different children's books imply different kinds of reader; and flip that over, we find different kinds of children reading in different kinds of ways. Behind the 20 millions and 50 millions of readers that hit the headlines are complex and interesting patterns of reading going on . . .

Now that's a cluster of ideas that is hardly on our culture's dial. Children, our culture seems to suggest, are often a problem – we have ASBOs and curfews and off-site units; we have anguish-laden articles about children with problems of the body or mind; we have programmes proving that they are more stupid now (never more clever), their education is worse, their materialism and sexuality are out of control.

Our culture also tells us that children are often best left at home with baby-sitters, it's hard to travel and eat out with them; we find it difficult to create mixed-age occasions.

We have governments who make detailed and expensive plans on how to contain, control and grade children inside educational institutions, but very rarely take any notice of places where children play and could or actually do entertain themselves. That's left to low-paid youth workers and librarians and constantly closing play facilities on one side, or Hollywood and the TV moguls on the other.

In other words, what children do, think and feel is well below the radar of the prevailing ideas of the powerful. It doesn't feature as part of public discourse. A possible reason for this is that though children rate as consumers (or their parents do on their behalf) they don't rate as producers. Rather like old-age pensioners. They don't make anything, so they matter less for what they are, only for what they will become; they're not a state of being, they're a state of being on the way to somewhere else, called adulthood. Again, an ironic state of affairs considering the massive rise in therapies that place our adult lives in the grip of our childhoods. It's as if we're saying, 'Children are boring, but my childhood is fascinating . . . let me tell you about it . . . '

So, this thing we're in, books for children, has to struggle with this structural indifference. A structural indifference that always mouths that books for children are worth reading, but rarely puts its money where that mouth is.

Meanwhile, within higher education, the fledgling of university courses on children's literature is beginning to take flight. For the public conversation about children's books to be thoughtful and helpful, we need people doing first degrees and post-graduate work to have some time to look at the ideas and theories surrounding children's literature. For example, children's literature has always played an important, sometimes central, part in how Western societies have constructed ideas about gender, race, class and identity in general. Think of the power and position in the making of consciousness of such books (and their film and TV adaptations) as *Little Women*, *Treasure Island* or *The Wind in the Willows* or, more recently, *Where the Wild things Are* or, of course, *Harry Potter*. Again, it is around the reading of books in classrooms and bedrooms and in the talk surrounding those books that we learn how story works: how to pick up on sequences, patterns and symbols; how to see points of view represented by people; how to see consequences; how to allow ourselves to be deceived by narrators and protagonists; how to be disappointed or delighted with the way things turn out. University courses have the time to look at the kinds of satisfactions offered to readers in terms, say, of wish-fulfilment, yearning and desire, projection and transference, and indeed to look at those books that appear to run against the grain and defy, subvert and challenge prevailing ideas of gender, race and class. And they can look at traditions within the literature, how writers have tried again and again to address such matters as coming of age, transgressive and subversive behaviour, redemption, bravery, in-groups and outcasts, loneliness and solidarity, and how and why these themes have changed according to the epochs in which they were addressed.

Yesterday, on the semester on children's literature Piers Bilston and I teach at London Metropolitan, we looked at Benjamin Zephaniah's *Refugee Boy*. It's a book that puts the outsider on the inside. It makes someone who comes from the least important, most outcast group in society, a child refugee from an African country, into the lynchpin of the narrative, the focal point of your attention. The students on that course will go their various ways into a mix of teaching, librarianship, therapy in this country and in other countries, having seen that the very narrative method itself, the book's own narratology, has a politics. We speculated whether the book's main protagonist is a 'hero figure', whether stoicism is heroic, and whether the heroic structure dissipated when the collective that supports the lead character becomes more important than him, and what that said about the ideology of the book. We touched on the question of what kind of reader was implied by this text: was it calling for empathy in its readers or something cooler? Wouldn't we need to talk to some young readers of the book to know? Could reader-response surveys and studies be the final arbiter of the value of a book? And quite coincidentally, one of the students said that at her local synagogue, three boys had chosen a passage from the book as their presentation pieces for their bar mitzvahs. We were just about to wind up, when a student from Nigeria said that she was reminded of parts of Chinua Achebe's *Things Fall Apart*, sometimes dubbed the first post-colonial novel, and we were able to finish with questions about this post-colonial tradition. Was Benjamin an inheritor of the idea of 'writing back'? You, the white writers of the West, used to write about us, now we write about ourselves. With Achebe it was within Africa, with Benjamin it's here. I think that the world of children's books needs people out there who can engage with children's books on all these levels.

My third problem lies with the publishing industry. What? How can that be? Surely, they are the champions. They're the ones producing the stuff that you, Michael Rosen, are rooting for.

Yes, but.

To tell the truth, I think the publishing industry is not simply interested in publishing books, but primarily, not entirely, primarily interested in publishing new books.

Excuse me while I become economistic. It was about fifteen years ago that some huge upheavals took place in the world of publishing books for children. These upheavals had a very specific intention but it was one that was never fully spelled out.

Most of the small independent publishers were taken over by multi-nationals. The multi-nationals brought in a very logical ethos that said that if the commodity of the book – that's to say the number of copies – wasn't selling at a certain rate, it wasn't making money for the company and so should be deleted, remaindered, junked. This could be measured quite objectively by the speed with which it disappeared from its highly expensive-to-rent shelf in the warehouse. Indeed, if it went below a certain rate, it wasn't just not making money, it was losing money. Go, book, go.

The problem with this is that you would soon end up with only a few book titles on your list and that could lead to the law of diminishing returns: fewer books, less noise, less hype, and indeed less money-making. The way to solve the two problems was to create an entirely new publishing policy. It would be to treat the book-making business much more as if it were the magazine trade. Publish books for what in your heart of hearts you would know was a fixed term of about twenty months, then pulp. Every book has a graph of sales, and for most it looks like an inverted tick, a short quick rapid rise to a peak and then a fairly rapid tail-off. The trick, surely, is to publish all books so that they are only half a tick. Pulp them before the down stroke descends too far. The best publisher would be one who produces the most number of steep upward ticks, and who pulps at a time that anticipates the plunge. Shelf life twenty months or less.

Now, I would suggest to you, who, like me, may think of books as places of ideas, feelings, possibilities, strange knowledge, intrigue and incredible laughs, that this half a tick process is a bit chilling. Might it not be possible that some incredibly brilliant books might just disappear? Of course, all authors think that it's their own book that falls into this category and are very sore about it: 'My best book went to the shredder in 1999.' That sort of thing.

But what is the real structural consequence of this? Well, I think it contains dangers and the dangers are in what is or is not hazarded, what models are replicated, what sequences are repeated. Yes, it's a familiar cry, that the engine of capitalism squeezes out the oddball, the divergent, the subversive, the minority, the small. I think there's an element of truth in that, but of course the warehouse watchers have got a perfect riposte, haven't they? The democracy of the market place. 'If the kids don't wanna read your book, then why should I publish it? I'm not a charity. You write something they wanna buy and I'll sell it for you . . . '

Well, there is an alternative, and it takes us back over all three of these impediments to our believing that books for children are worth reading.

And I'll call this, after the strange titles of some old folksongs and broadsheets: the grand conversation.

You see, there is a democracy about books that runs along different lines from the publishing production lines. It lies in the talk and writing that we all have about books for adults, but only flickers and splutters along when it comes to books for children. It got stamped out when all over the country local authorities said that they couldn't afford to sustain the relationship between libraries and schools. It got sidelined when teacher-training courses found that they didn't have time to run modules or semesters on children's literature. Same again, when courses for teachers got so tailored to the curriculum and the Literacy Strategy that the only way in which schools could get money to second teachers onto courses was if it was for literacy, spelling, grammar, handwriting, behaviour management, gifted children, special-needs children and how to run an assembly. Anyone who has worked in and around teacher-training and INSET knows how hard it is to get a course off the ground that might be called, let's say, 'Having a laugh, great books for Friday going home time,' or 'What to do when the whole class is crying: books that move the heart.' Or 'Any old books – teachers and students on this course will talk about books that they've read to their class and what happened when they did.'

But a democracy of reading requires a different way of talking about books. In the first part of today we saw one model of how to have a conversation about books. It is, I'm arguing, a highly un-democratic one, even in the fact that the people who ask the questions are represented by nothing more nor less than mysterious initials: QCA. Who are these people? Why are they so shy? Most authors I know love their names to be on the books and articles they write. Why is it so hard to get hold of SATs papers? It must be about the only public document that you can't get on the internet. You have to bribe, cajole and shmooze a head teacher to get hold of one.

I think you only know if books are worth reading if you have a chance to find out what you think of books – and it helps a lot if you have a chance to find out if anyone else wants to hear what you've got to say. I suggest that the starting point for this is a curriculum that puts the reading of whole books back on the agenda. It also suggests that the best way to ask children questions about books is either to ask none, or to ask questions that the questioner doesn't know the answers to. Questions like: does this book remind you of anything you've met in real life? Or remind you of anything you've read elsewhere? When you compare the book with these things you know from your life and from your reading, what similarities and differences do you spot? Is there anything about this book that puzzles you? Is there anybody in the room who thinks they can help with this problem? Is there anything you like or dislike about this book? Why's that then? Is there anything we would ask any of the characters in this book? Is there anywhere we can go to find out answers to any questions we have about this book? Thanks to the writer and critic Aidan Chambers for some of these.

But there are also ways in which we can enter a story without interrogating children . . .

I suspect many of you came up with interesting ideas after I read the story used by the SATs examiners.

I want to finish by looking at a book called *The Gardener*.

[We looked at the book together. It's a wonderful book by American author Sarah Stewart, illustrated by her husband David Small. Published in 1997, it's about a young girl and her rooftop garden in the city. It's set in the Depression era and told through letters. The girl goes to stay with her uncle in the city. He's a grumpy baker. She slowly brightens up the shop and cheers up the customers with the flowers she grows. But her most important and secret achievement is the rooftop garden, which she hopes will make even her uncle smile.]

Every time I read this, I get the feeling that it's worth reading. I don't ask, 'Worth reading for children?', or '. . . for adults?' I just think it was worth reading it.

I've been making a pilot for a programme that may go out on the new teachers' channel *[which became Teachers TV]* and whaddyaknow, it's about reading. Not 'reading' in the literacy sense (you know, are synthetic phonics better than plain phonics?). No, not that sort of thing, but reading in the sense of 'reading books'. This is how I got to know about *The Gardener*. I was asked to interview a teacher who had been reading the book with her class. I asked her how.

She told me that they read the book in stages. And at each scene, each tableau that we've just seen, the class would re-create the moment. When Lydia stood on the station, they acted out a scene of them standing on a station. They wrote letters to Uncle Jim, and when Lydia gets to the city, they wrote letters back home. When Lydia planted bulbs, they planted bulbs. They made bread, they decorated cakes, they made a secret place, and at a crucial moment, someone, an adult at the school, dressed up as Uncle Jim, appeared with a birthday cake, covered in flowers, and like Jim didn't smile. They debated the question of why some people smile and why some people don't and what that's about and they talked and talked about the picture in which Uncle Jim is saying goodbye to Lydia. I'm not doing either the teacher or her class justice here, but I hope you're getting the drift. One of the ways in which children find out if a book is worth reading or not is to live it.

For most of us in this room, as I said at the outset, the question is hardly worth asking. Are books for children worth reading? We know it. For many children though, this is not self-apparent. We have to prove it to them. To do that, we need an education system that encourages teachers to find all sorts of different ways for children to live in books. We need a public discourse that can go beyond treating children's books as scandals, sensational sales figures and symptoms of some crisis or some 'seismic shift' in something or another. And we need a publishing industry that remembers that books are not only or simply commodities, but carriers of ideas and feelings. But the industry can only do that if the public discourse and the reading of books in schools wise up.

Many thanks to Theresa Breslin O.B.E. (Services to Literature) for permission to reprint the version of her story You Can Do It *which appeared in the Key Stage 2 English SAT in 2004. This version was adapted from Theresa's original story, which appeared in the anthology* Best of Friends, *published by Mammoth in 1995.*

'General, Your Tank has One Defect . . .'

This is the introduction I gave at the 2006 conference Owners of the Means of Instruction? Children's Literature: some Marxist Perspectives.

I'd like to begin with a bit of a negative definition – that is, saying what we're not, or at least saying what we never intended this conference to be.

It's not been called in order to found a political party, group, tendency, fragment, faction, or, as the French would say, '*groupuscule*'. No one behind this conference has called it with the intention of putting over what is sometimes called 'a line' that must be adhered to. It has been called with the intention of exploring the possibility that children's literature can be investigated fruitfully and interestingly using what we've called 'some Marxist perspectives'. If it turns out that there is some running in this, then we have the opportunity to do any or some of the following: publish a book based on today's proceedings, start a journal, carry on having conferences.

That said, I would like to put us on the map in the following way: you are attending what I think is the first ever conference with these terms of reference and the programme on offer.

Let's do a bit of situating. We're a group of what I suspect is a mix of teachers, librarians and writers meeting together in a university in one of the wealthiest countries of the world. It seems to me that we're positioned on a cycle that repeats itself all over the western world. Social-democratic governments (like Clinton, Blair, Mitterrand and Schroeder) alternate with explicitly neo-liberal governments (like Reagan, Thatcher, Chirac and now Merkel) in trying to privatise whatever is left of these countries' state-run welfare systems. This is called 'modernisation' and directly affects the standard of living, care and education of the children we write for and teach. Governments of either hue show themselves to be unable or unwilling to do anything about staggering inequalities at home or between the rich and poor anywhere else in the world. In the face of this, for us to talk about 'the child', as if he or she is one uniform entity with common experience, cannot be sustained.

Somewhere here, we also have to factor in the way in which these inequalities alter the cultural make-up of countries: in the West, the old fantasies (some would say 'lies') about a homogenous race or homogenous national culture can't be sustained because of ever-increasing diversity. Again, the question, 'Who is the child?' can't be answered simply. Not that it ever could be, but that's another matter.

Meanwhile, we know that a massive geo-political crisis is coming over the horizon in the forms of humanly made climate change and a humanly made energy shortfall. The semi-permanent state of war that we now find ourselves in seems to be a consequence of how our leaders try to handle this. Again, this is something that has a direct impact on children, schools and parents, in particular in and around the many battlefields across the world and away from the battlefields in the minds and consciousness of all children. Yesterday, my five-year-old asked me why was the woman's head put on a pole. She had overheard the report from the Congo on the *Today* programme on BBC Radio 4.

If this is our epoch, where are we in it? Economically, some of us are employees in the institutions (schools, colleges, libraries and the like) that the state has asked to deliver to the economy the workforce that the economy says it needs. Others of us are earners of fees and freelance payments in the leisure and entertainment industry [open brackets] 'book section' [close brackets]. These two sides (the institutional and the freelance) have relationships with each other, as expressed by such processes as writers in schools, teachers reading books, or indeed examiners using literary texts, but we also have relationships with the institutions we find ourselves in: on the one hand, education and on the other, the publishing business.

Each of these two institutions has been directly affected by the epoch we are in and people like us working in them have responded. So, it's not hard to see that the publishing industry in this country has moved from being dominated by small family units to one dominated by massive world units. Meanwhile, education all over the West has come under greater and greater pressure to dispense with humanistic and liberal ideas and adopt instrumental approaches (of which the rush to synthetic phonics is only one) policed by systems of testing, inspection, grading and selection.

The day-to-day matter of what books are written, get published and indeed read is, as I see it, not only held within this matrix. Also, the strands of power or lack of power, and the environments created by this matrix have an impact on what gets written, what gets read and how it's read. I'm not sure that this area has ever been fully theorised or explored. I hope we can have a go at it. So, for example, it's always been my argument that the way in which literature is examined and tested has an impact on the way it's taught and the way it's read. It's examined and tested in a certain way now because education has been re-structured in order to deliver more accurately the segregated sections of the labour force that industry is asking for, and that, in turn, is a consequence of the increasing desperation of those in charge of the economy in the global environment.

Thus, open a KS2 SATs English paper and you'll find that very nearly all the questions involve the child re-stating the chronology, logic and empirical sense-data-type facts of the story. There is no space for the child to relate aspects of his or her experience and feelings to those that appear to be manifested within the story, no space for the child to speculate about the ebb and flow of feelings that the story appears to engender. The kind of questioning the tests demand has had a knock-on effect on how stories are read in class, and indeed, what kind of role children's literature is now seen as having within the curriculum. In essence it is being pushed more and more into the role of being the handmaiden to something called 'literacy' – a manageable, instrumental entity which the powerful think can be measured and thus, in their terms, can be given an economic value. Again, this is an area that could be explored much more.

As 'literacy' has become increasingly regarded as being culture-free (so, for example, the bilingualism of a Bangladeshi child doesn't register anywhere on the evaluations of literacy that the state demands or publishes), so we have moved towards an education strategy that has removed the being of the child from the learning process. The education documents that have landed in teachers' lockers over the last twenty years do not include anyone who we could identify as this or that child in this or that mode of thinking, or anything other than a creature who is acted on. It is the final perfect match of the industrial production line that begins with raw material, is acted on by processes and emerges as a car or a biscuit.

If this were the total picture we would be living in a totalitarian state and human beings would have become automata. But we're not. As Bertolt Brecht put it:

General, your Tank is a Powerful Vehicle

It smashes down forests and crushes a hundred men.
But it has one defect:
It needs a driver.

General, your bomber is powerful.
It flies faster than a storm and carries more than an elephant.

But it has one defect:
It needs a mechanic.

General, man is very useful.
He can fly and he can kill.
But he has one defect:
He can think.

(from *A German War Primer;* see *www.public-domain-poetry.com/
bertolt-brecht/from-a-german-war-primer-1502*)

Editors, authors, teachers, librarians, parents and children have resisted many
of the processes I've described and I'll be so bold as to suggest that we here
are in part evidence of this too. There have been many attempts to assert
the humanism in literature for children (think of the interventions of people
like Philip Pullman and Michael Morpurgo), to talk subversively (as it now is)
about an activity known as 'reading for pleasure' and to resist the regimes of
selecting and testing.

But there is also the matter of what is written, pictured, edited and
published. How or where precise works fit (or don't fit) in this picture of the
epoch that I've given is, I suspect, one of the many matters we'll debate. So,
by way of introduction I'd like to ask the question, 'What can Marxism or
"some Marxist perspectives" offer us by way of explanation, critical power,
methodology and even, perhaps, suggestions as to what is worth doing?'

I acknowledge that we may never reach some kind of neat agreement as to
what consists of 'a' or 'the' Marxist approach to children's literature. And to
tell the truth, I don't think we need to. However, I would like to pick out what
I think are amongst the most interesting and useful observations that Marx
and Marxists have made.

I think these centre on class, the base-and-superstructure question and
ideology.

Following from these, my own inclination leads me to value the questions
raised by Raymond Williams and his notion of dominant, residual and
emergent cultures; Frederic Jameson and Pierre Macherey and the political
unconscious; Pierre Bourdieu on reproduction; various writers on race and
post-colonialism; and again various writers on how (and indeed why) gender,
patriarchy, childhood and sexuality are constructed.

I'll begin with class. Sadly, this is an area full of misunderstandings. The

Marxist approach is neither one that relies on what individuals think nor one based on a league table of incomes. People often talk subjectively about what class they think they or others belong to. Again, we are often given what is supposed to be a more objective analysis of class by rating people according to incomes or expenditure. A Marxist approach says that there is a different way of looking at class, which is suited to explaining how the great wheels of society grind away. It says that the underlying structure of society is not static; it is a process in which one class which owns and controls the vast majority of a society's or indeed the world's resources and systems of production and distribution is in perpetual conflict with a class of people who own very little more than their ability to sell their labour power.

The needs and requirements of these two classes of people are not only in conflict with each other; they are in contradiction with each other and create further contradictions. Put simply, it is in the interests of the class that owns to keep what it calls its 'labour costs' at a minimum. Meanwhile it is in the interests of the class that sells its labour to keep those same costs (which it prefers to call 'pay' or 'wages' or 'salary'!) as high as it can. However, this conflict is not always as bald or as plain as this. We can see it at work in the upheavals going on in the UK over pensions (a classic case of what the owning class sees as a 'cost') or in France over youth-employment laws. Again, when we look at what are sometimes called communal upheavals, like the ones that have taken place over the years in, say, Brixton or Blackburn, then again, it's clear that the fact that those communities are made up of people trying to survive on what are in effect labour costs kept low by the owning class is the underlying reason for their difficulties. Yet again, when we look closely at our own field, the main indicator of educational success and failure has been shown over and over again to be income. However, by putting it in this language, using the word 'income' we are thrown back onto the conventional causes of what makes people rich and poor (luck, merit, innate idiocy and the rest) and not as the process of class.

I'll say here that class (in the sense that I'm talking about) delivers a massive differential in income through a process whereby the value of what a workforce produces is greatly in excess of the total value of what they earn. This differential or profit is not, as is sometimes claimed, beautifully and elegantly recycled for the benefit of all, but, as all statistics show, is appropriated by and within the class that owns and which continues to acquire more and more of the world's wealth.

But where in all this are the people we think we all know so well and who are of immense interest to the world of children's books: the middle class? Isn't this the group who are neither the people who own the resources from which they can benefit greatly by employing others, renting off vast swathes of property or plant, or from lending millions of dollars, nor the people who earn income solely through the sale of their labour power?

Well, to start off with, a lot of the people who are subjectively called 'middle class' are indeed people who live solely by selling their labour power – a lot of teachers, social workers and, if you like, educated employees. There may be a whole host of indicators that suggest these people see themselves as different from blue-collar, less educated folk, but economically and structurally they're in the same boat. However, that said, there are some people who are, if you like, in a different boat – people who use small amounts of capital or property to generate income, people who employ a few people to generate profit, people who control sections of the workforce or make big decisions within the legal system and so acquire sufficient income to generate yet more income from property or capital. It is clear that structurally these people are neither substantial members of the owning class nor of the class that lives solely by selling its labour. Perhaps we can indeed call these people, within this schema, 'middle class'.

When we look at the history and indeed the present state of affairs with children's literature and education, we can see that it is from within the class that occupies either this middle position or from those educated sections of the class that lives by selling its labour that most writers have arisen, and which in turn has generated the outlook of most children's books and, by definition, the people who've done the most teaching and directing of children's reading.

As Bob Leeson showed us in *Reading and Righting: The Past, Present, and Future of Fiction for the Young* (1985), the origins of what we call children's literature are full of struggles between those who thought they were upholding the values of this middle class against the low habits of the class below them, reading their penny chapbooks and the like. The marks of this struggle can be still be found within the world of children's books, in something like the distinctions made between the *Beano* and the picture book. More seriously, we can see it at work in the nature of education itself.

In the 1970s, people began to ask what we might call 'class questions' about education itself. Are there ways in which we could say that class is built into education? I will suggest that I think this work is unfinished and has an immense relevance to the world of children's books. We can ask: are there ways in which the very process of education, its language, its structures, its day-to-day goings-on, its culture, is in some way or another encoded in ways that suit children of one kind rather than another? The coincidence of poverty and educational failure is based on what precisely? That the children don't have enough or the right food to eat? Enough time and space at home? There isn't enough time given by hard-pressed parents?

Or is there something more subtle going on that is intimately linked to what we're about? Pierre Bourdieu's theory of reproduction suggests that the educated, yes, middle-class family creates what he calls a 'habitus', a linguistic and cultural disposition that matches the language, values and ideology of education. So, we know in this room, don't we, that there is in effect a private, informal, middle-class curriculum that we offer our children – in particular by choosing the 'right' mix of books, but also by visits to the museums and art galleries (with their guides for children – a kind of children's literature in itself), and of course by holding the kinds of conversation we have with our children about values, about their homework, about the place we live in, about the TV programmes we watch, and the like. It is a potent mix of culture, values, abstract thought, outlook, which matches perfectly what is on offer in school. There are historical and social reasons for this which can be spelled out and it's not a process that has gone on without struggles and resistance within the world of children's literature. The argument over Leila Berg's reading scheme *Nippers* (1971) some years ago was precisely in this zone. I would suggest that a new hierarchy is emerging exacerbated by the government's educational programme. That's to say, schools are being coerced into offering a bread-and-butter minimum literacy for all. The effect of this is that those children who would not in their lives easily or usually come across the full range of books on offer from the world of children's books (and there are economic and educational reasons for this) are now less and less likely to come across them in school, whilst middle-class children will acquire the full range of books at home, thereby further enabling them to benefit from what I'll simplistically call the 'education code'. Children's literature has always been consumed hierarchically and by class. In the past there have been times when schools were places that tried to erode that hierarchy. I fear that the present situation restores it. A variety of writers, publishers, teachers and librarians have been contesting this for many years and in a variety of ways. I think there is a good deal of fruitful work we can do in this field, charting what's been done, what's been successful, what's failed, where we are now and the like.

Let's move on to 'base and superstructure'. For those who've read in this field, you'll know that there's a long and winding path that has struggled with the concept. This is not going to be a review of the literature. I'll just make a few observations that I hope will be productive.

First, the concept is a metaphor not an abstraction. A better translation would have been something like 'foundations' and 'upper building'. What is being referred to here concerns an understanding of ideas and the whole field of institutions concerned with producing ideas and indeed putting them into practice institutionally. Both in idle usage and sometimes more theoretically, we often consider a process like education, or the work of an artist, or the operation of the law, as if they exist in an autonomous world, self-governing, influenced only by its predecessors and contemporaries within that field. Thus, we might say idly, 'Keats was influenced by Shakespeare'; 'Surrealism grew out of Dada'; 'The 1870 Education Act paved the way for the 1944 Education Act'. If that sounds too crude a representation of what gets said, then there is a modification that treats 'discourse' as if it too had this kind of autonomy. So, it is seen as legitimate by some to explain an artistic movement, the inspiration for a novel, or a legal judgment as if it is sufficient (I use that word advisedly) to treat these events simply and only as interventions within their ideological or discursive field. Thus, we might say that the work of Anthony Browne is 'in conversation with Magritte'; or that 'no anthropomorphic children's book of the twentieth century can quite escape the shadow of Beatrix Potter'; or that 'Hans Christian Andersen was above all else part of Romanticism'.

Of themselves, these statements aren't to my mind wrong. The problem with them is when they become, as I've said, sufficient explanations. For that sufficiency, I suggest that we need something else.

So back to the Marxist metaphor: base and superstructure. The idea here is that human beings must organise themselves co-operatively in ways that enable them to satisfy their material needs: primarily food and shelter. The Marxist argument is that whatever structures a society devises for this to take place will in the final analysis (a phrase that may cause some of you to smile) shape and determine people's consciousness. In shorthand, the base will determine the superstructure. The material base or foundations of a society (economic arrangements) will shape its laws, its education system, the components of its dominant ideology, and its artistic output. However, in Marx's writings and indeed in many others since, people have been at pains to modify this schema and save it from what has been described as its vulgarity. Firstly, Marx himself spent some energy pointing out that one of the contradictions I referred to earlier is that in any given society there is often a mismatch between what the dominant ideology is saying and what developments might be taking place in the material base. So, for example, the ideological demands of the rising bourgeoisie in the sixteenth and seventeenth centuries (for example, in relation to a lack of democratic representation in government, but also, say, with the representation of Hamlet as a prototype modern, secular, expressive, illusorily self-creating individual) were often in conflict with the economic arrangements of the time. It was, in Raymond Williams' terms, the 'emergent culture' coming into conflict with the material base of late feudalism.

So whatever determinations are going on, they can't simply be along the lines of formulaic statements like 'feudalism produced illustrated manuscripts', 'capitalism produced the Beach Boys'. And here we need to return to what we were saying about class. Class is, I suggested, a dynamic, changing relationship, full of conflict and contradiction. At any given moment, societally there is some kind of uneasy balance of class forces. At any given moment, for any given individual, this balance of class forces is in some way or another played out in the consciousness and body of that individual. In other words, the foundations or 'base' are not some rocky firmament but a shifting set of demanding forces acting on the ideational field and on individuals.

Take the case of the rise of the 'folk tale' and in particular someone like Hans Christian Andersen, born like the rest of us into a time and place not of his own choosing. He found himself in a Europe of immense turmoil but was living in a backwater on a rural island in Denmark. Of all the writers to have ever produced children's literature he is one with perhaps the poorest origins. His father was one of those people we now see more and more clearly in the nineteenth-century European picture: the impoverished tradesman hungry for knowledge, eager for change, freedom and democracy; many such people were emerging as part of the American and French revolutions, events that broke as a consequence of the rise of a new class. Meanwhile, HCA's mother, part-time worker and washerwoman, was, it seems, embedded in the traditional ideology and so-called 'superstition' of the pagan, peasant culture of the previous several hundred years. When Andersen gets himself to Copenhagen he meets a world full of the old and new: the Danish fragment of Europe's aristocracy brushing shoulders with a local bourgeoisie. The form he is sometimes credited with inventing, the literary folk tale, is in fact being invented simultaneously in Germany by such people as Clemens von Brentano, E.T.A. Hoffman and of course the Grimms, with connections to the aristocratic French tales of Perrault, Mme Aulnoy and the like. It is now clear that for the Grimms, the latent ideology behind their tales is the hope that they are producing a form that appeals to the whole society, the whole 'Volk'. Meanwhile, Andersen, he of the humblest of humble origins, finds that his tales offer him a calling card in the most exalted of homes. Somewhere in all this, I detect the invention of a form that is concerned, consciously or not, with flying in the face of the social and economic upheavals and divisions going on all around: the creation of something unifying and consoling, that gives succour to the needs and desires of the lower orders for a better life whilst maintaining the institutional and structural status quo.

It's my view that we've reached a point in the writing about children's literature where some people are quite at ease conducting a discussion in this way without necessarily acknowledging that there is something Marxist about it. Jack Zipes's work on the Grimms (*The Brothers Grimm: From Enchanted Forest to the Modern World*, 2002) is full of this kind of observation and much more, without necessarily tracing the reason why he is saying what he's saying back to quotes from Marx. Interestingly though, Jackie Wullschlager's biography of Andersen (*Hans Christian Andersen: The Life of a Storyteller,* 2000) is also a book that probes some questions of how the material stresses and strains of the time go towards shaping Andersen's life and work, again with no acknowledgement that Marx and Marxism had ever existed.

There is another qualification to the base-and-superstructure metaphor. Marxists of the non-vulgar kind have always understood that the ideological field is not without some impact on the material. Limits on human action are not only set by how you earn your livelihood. More satisfying is to understand this dialectically. That's to say, the material (with all its contradictions) shapes the ideological while the ideological is able to some degree to arc back on the material. The law on homosexuality is a case in point. Here in post-war Britain was a law founded with the full intention of sustaining heterosexuality as the enforced norm, flying in the face of what was the day-to-day reality for a sizeable segment of society. The testimony of many gays from that period is that that law prescribed the shape and form of their lives, culture and, in some cases, their art. It was a law embedded in attitudes to the body that are in turn embedded in the ideologies that sustained the rising bourgeoisie in its assault on aristocratic power. It is these ideologies, also concerning family, childhood, gender-specific roles and heterosexuality, that we find running right through the history of children's literature. Ideology, I suggest, has the power to affect and influence but will in the final analysis be traceable back to material interests and contradictions.

In recent years, it seems to me that several productive insights have emerged that owe a debt to at least some of the ideas I've outlined here. So, for example, of the many ideas that pour forth from the mind of Frederic Jameson, his work on what he called 'the political unconscious' (*The Political Unconscious*, 1982) presents us with an interesting starting point. In fact, he borrowed and adapted the notion from Pierre Macherey (*A Theory of Literary Production*, 1978). If, as I've suggested, the contradictions of society are manifested within an individual, then we can also say that they are manifested in an artist or writer and so by continuation in that artist's work. One kind of contradiction I'm talking about here concerns what we might call 'positioning'. I think it was the writer Julius Lester who asked what was the historical difference between the field slave and the house slave. He suggested that if the slave-owner's house was on fire, the field slave said that the master's house was burning, whereas the house slave said that it was 'our' house that was burning. Though the two kinds of slave were materially in the same relationship with the owner, the house slave perceived his or her position in a way that is in contradiction with that reality. If we take Hans Christian Andersen again, and one of the first, if not the first literary folk tale he wrote, *The Tinder Box*, we see a story about a figure who strode across the European stage, the penniless soldier. He achieves what many folk tales allow their penniless heroes to achieve: relief from his wretched state – upward social mobility through cunning and luck. However, his route to this involves bizarre scenes of sexual molestation carried out on an inert, prone upper-class woman. No matter what these scenes tell us about Andersen's sexuality, it seems to me that they also express the ambiguous contradictory position he found himself in: a member of the rural poor (who had in Europe been kept at subsistence level by the aristocracy for nearly a thousand years, occasionally relieved when the men were put in arms and received some cash and plunder if they weren't maimed or killed) but also someone who materially needed the attention of the middle and aristocratic classes if he was to sell his work. At one and the same time part of him yearned for that upper class to be prone and inert (or indeed flung into the air and dismembered by huge dogs) while another part of him yearned to be, how shall I say?, conjoined with it.

Another of the key contradictions that Marx draws our attention to is that the very methods the owning class use to further its interests create the conditions within which they are resisted and, Marx hopes, will be overthrown. Thus, for capitalism to work, it needs to constantly bring many people together in one place in order to get them to produce the goods or services that will deliver the profit. However, in order to sell these goods and services, it is necessary for the owning class to repeat over and over again how these goods will satisfy our individual needs, or indeed will construct our individuality. A particular hair dye will make me look younger and I will have a better relationship with my lover as a result. I will also have my own bank account, my own mortgage and a choice of holiday, school, health-provider and patio doors. However, as I've said, the process of production keeps bringing people together in large numbers in order to get things made, serviced and distributed. In those conditions people have often found that as their needs are in contradiction with their employers, so are they in contradiction with the dominant ideology's way of dividing us up into castes, groups, cultures, and ultimately into seemingly individualised consumers, defined by what we buy. It seems to me that schools are also places that in some respects guy this process, bringing together people (pupils and teachers) in large numbers, who some of the time appear opposed to each other, sometimes united, as the demands of the society keep trying to segregate and select those being educated. Teachers are often placed in the role of those who do the bidding of those who would have pupils divided in this way.

Some of you will be familiar with Robert Cormier's two *Chocolate War* books (*The Chocolate War*, 1975 and *Beyond the Chocolate War*, 1986) which use the microcosm of a school (in this case a Catholic boys' school) to indicate what can and might happen when there is collaboration between corrupt power and popular thuggery in what one might call the 'masses'. As with all dystopias and indeed Gothic horror stories, there is inevitably an onward momentum towards what I've jokingly called in the past the 'anti-Boris' (that is, Karloff as Frankenstein's monster); that's to say, someone, some thing, some force somewhere which will relieve us of the monster. If you saw *The Blob* (1958) you'll remember it was the discovery that the Blob didn't like cold, so members of the air force dropped it on either the North or the South Pole.

Interestingly, in the *Chocolate War* books, Cormier offers very little in the way of anti-Boris other than the growing awareness by the focaliser of what's happened. Powerful enough, you might say. However, the key speech at the end of *Beyond the Chocolate War* is made by the arch-villain when he explains that in reality he is only what is inside all of us. What is this about? It seems to me that this expresses perfectly the contradiction born out of talking about a class-free notion of evil. In this denouement in the book, evil is de-located from time and place and person; made universal and in a way value-free, the implication being that evil just exists everywhere unless you as an individual take up arms against the sea of troubles and vanquish it. However, this notion, which seems to suit the dominant ideology as it tries to explain everything from Saddam Hussein to paedophilia via hoodies and Pol Pot in the same way, sits in the *Chocolate War* books in contradiction with Cormier's brilliant exposé of the Machiavellian methods of corrupt power. It's Jameson and Macherey who offer us an insight into how such contradictions are manifested in literature through what they've called the political unconscious.

However, let me take a step back and make a cautionary comment. One severe challenge to these approaches has come to us from the critical field known loosely as 'reader-response' and its sister 'reception theory'. Put baldly, the problem is this. It's all very well me or you or anyone saying that this or that text says this, or shows this, or manifests this, but the truth of the matter, says reader-response theory, is that it is only my or your construction. A book's meaning, the argument goes, doesn't lie in some immanent way in the text. It lies in how the reader constructs that meaning. I have some sympathy with this. As Stanley Fish reminds us (*Is There A Text In This Class?*, 1982), writing is only a set of material squiggles on a page. We take those squiggles and turn them into words, ideas, concepts, plots, characters, meanings and values. This has given lots of fun to Fish who, he thought, had demolished the whole of criticism and critical theory with one stroke. Interestingly, he doesn't seem to have succeeded, as people, myself included, continue to talk about books as if we have unlocked key meanings from a text rather than simply saying that we have found stuff that interested or amazed us, given that we are prejudiced or biased or constructed in this or that way. In fact, a vast amount of what we call criticism continues to be little more than saying over and over again, 'The text I've just looked at reminds me of something else I read or something that happened to me ten years ago.' If not that, then you can get away with a series of intended-to-be engaging re-enactments of moments from the text. How do I know? I've done it many times. Perhaps it's not a particularly insightful activity but it is one of the ways in which we enjoy books.

However, Fish may be more than a spoilsport. He also stumbled on the fact that readers are not like random molecules bouncing around in boiling water. Certain groups of readers appear to respond to a given text in one way and other groups respond in other ways. Thus he gave birth to the notion of what he called 'interpretive communities'. I think we can and should take this further. Much further. Fish said that readers construct texts. We can and, I believe, should ask, 'What or who constructs readers and how?' And indeed we are in a better position than many in academe to ask that question because we work at the very point at which people become readers and develop as readers. I think that it's possible to escape from Fish's rather vague and elitist idea of 'interpretive communities', which is full of the suggestion that the main thing that defines readers is their reading. I think that some of the observations of Marx and Marxists would give us a far richer, far more complex notion of what a reader is, and what reading does for them. However, Fish and someone working in a related field, Tony Bennett (*Outside Literature*, 1990), have put an important check on the kinds of statements that claim infinite certainty about meaning without reference to real readers. As any of us in this room knows, this is particularly dangerous when it comes to interpreting books written for a young audience. In short, no matter what we think a book is about, or for that matter what its 'political unconscious' is, there is no certainty that any child will agree. Indeed, they might turn out to be that fascinating object, the reader who reads to the end of the book, refusing to be won over to what we might have thought were its ideological siren songs; in short, 'the resistant reader'.

Which leads me neatly to questions of post-colonialism and gender because some of the most interesting work I've come across in relation to young readers reading across or against a text have been in these fields. Gemma Moss (*Un/Popular Fictions*, 1989) and Beverley Naidoo's work (*Exploring Racism: Reader, Text and Context*, 1992) come to mind. Now, it's quite possible to approach children's literature from the perspectives of race, gender, sexual orientation or physical ability without any acknowledgement that Marxism has got or should have anything to do with it. The question I'd like to raise though is whether some Marxist perspectives (as we've put it) can contribute something to these discussions.

At first glance, it might appear not. Classical Marxism places the dynamic model of class that I've represented here at the centre of its world view, whilst each of the areas I've mentioned here – race, gender and the like – often appear to be talking of a world centred somewhere else: variously in, say, issues surrounding racial domination, patriarchy, heterosexuality or indeed the use (or the meaning of the use) of the human body. Hovering over and through all this is the use of the word 'power', particularly as used by Foucault who himself looked at most of these areas. Thus, very relevantly for us, Foucault brilliantly showed how one of the methods the modern period used in order for the bourgeoisie to seize and hold power is through what it did and does to contain and control the human body (*Discipline and Punish*, 1975), in particular the young human body in school. This offered us a viewfinder with which to look at a great deal of children's literature in terms of, say, the libidinous desires it unleashes or forbids; the transgressions it admonishes or appears to licence; the punishments it lends authority to or undermines; the racial and sexual segregations it supports or resists; the idealisations of the human form it supports or subverts, and so on. I find much of this kind of analysis fascinating and irresistible; it raises important and troubling questions for us about children's books from, say, the imperial period; the construction of, say, motherhood or the feminine ideal throughout children's literature; or indeed the support of certain kinds of masculinity through adventure books, and so on. The other side of the coin is in my delight in reading books such as Benjamin Zephaniah's *Refugee Boy* (2001), Mary Hoffman's *The Colour of Home* (2002) or David Levithan's *Boy Meets Boy* (2005), all of which seem to be informed (at least partly) by a wish to break the power and certainty of such notions as nationhood, the dangerous 'other', and the heterosexual norm. But surely none of this can be simply subsumed under the heading 'Marxist perspectives'.

Well, I see that I've used the word 'power'. My first observation is a criticism of the criticism. Yes, indeed these Foucauldian approaches have been massively illuminating and part of that has been because they dissect in minutiae the means by which power and dominant ideology are sustained in society. But again, I'll ask, do they do so 'sufficiently'? I don't think so. The problem is that I don't think it is sustainable to suggest that power is wielded simply or only for its own reasons. I suggest this mystifies and reifies power. The most dominant power in all societies is what's wielded by those who own and control the resources and the means by which those resources are turned into useful things, and in so doing end up (a tiny minority) owning the vast proportion of the wealth. Yes, it's absolutely true that down through society, through its groups, clubs, schools and on down to the most intimate relationships between two people and into the struggles within one's own head, there are indeed what we call 'power struggles'. The question we have to ask though is whether these smaller group and psychological questions of power are projected onto society or whether it's the origins, shape and determinations of power in society that reach down and into the groups, institutions and intimate relations we live in. Or perhaps both. Freud's model of the super-ego, ego and id was one way in which the reaching-down into the individual was conceptualised, though I've always thought his writing about totalitarian leaders suggests the reverse: the projection of psychology onto society. But there are others such as Reich and Erich Fromm who've struggled with it too.

Children's literature poses some interesting questions here: children have very little power in any society and it could be said that children's literature, whilst appearing to support and sustain children over and beyond what they

183

are often not allowed (identity, autonomous thought, culture, self, transgressive ideas, adult-free action and the like), is also a process by which adults in the form of writers, editors, publishers and critics wield some kind of ideological and emotional power over children. Children's literature might well be a form of nurture but it has historically been a suitable site from which it could apply torture. It has in its time offered a binary choice: 'nurture or torture'. In very general terms, I think we can say that its broad aim has nearly always been to improve the lives of its readers, but what if that was merely in order to make adults' lives more bearable? If any of this is true or only partly true, are different kinds, yes, different classes of children treated in different ways by children's literature? If so, to what ends? I've a feeling that it's possible to detect that power over children is wielded through children's literature and through the uses to which children's literature is put. However, and this links in part to Bourdieu's 'habitus', the power is wielded for a social purpose and that social purpose will in the end take us back to the dynamic, Marxian model of class.

It seems to me that we have an area of fruitful discussion and debate here. Can we enlarge and demystify Foucauldian criticism by linking power to what classical Marxism would say is its function? After all, the very fact that we bandy about the term 'dominant ideology' stems from Marx's idea that the prevailing or dominant ideology of any time is in essence the ideology of the class that owns and rules. For much of the time, the criticism that I read looks at the dominant ideology but unhinges it from this class and has it hovering over us unattached. This doesn't make the criticism uninteresting or invalid. I just find myself wishing that it could do more.

Meanwhile, I hope we all have a fascinating and insightful day and that this is just the beginning.

Children's Laureate

I was honoured to be asked to be the fourth Children's Laureate, following in the footsteps of Quentin Blake, Anne Fine, Michael Morpurgo and Jacqueline Wilson. I did the job from 2007 to 2009. This is my acceptance speech.

I wouldn't be standing here if it hadn't been for the work, help and kindness of many, many other people. This will be a constant reminder to me that whatever work I get into as the Children's Laureate, I should cooperate with all the other people and organisations pushing in the direction of making reading a delight and inspiration for young people. Part of the great achievement of Quentin, Anne, Michael and Jacqueline is that they've created paths and networks throughout the world of books for children which the laureates coming after them can use.

A special word for my immediate predecessor: Jacqueline is someone who writes books that fascinate millions and millions of readers. Her appearances make waves. She has created characters, scenes, moments and plots that have taken the thrill of reading to children of every kind. To pursue her aims of getting everyone to enjoy reading, all she needs to do is go on writing. The fact that she spent time and energy doing so much more than that has benefited everyone involved in writing, publishing, distributing and of course reading children's books.

It's a fantastic privilege to be following her and the previous laureates who I hasten to add haven't hung up their laurel crowns in the shed but go on and on drawing, writing, talking, visiting and helping new projects like the wonderful Seven Stories Museum in Newcastle or the forthcoming Museum of Illustration in London.

Another privilege I have to mention is that I was brought up by two special people. It's that moment when one of my children says, or the older sons and step-daughters said in the past, 'Read to me, Dad,' that I have felt most acutely how it was the hours and hours my parents spent sharing stories, poems and plays with my brother and me that got me into this whole malarkey. They were both teachers and a two-way street ran between our bedroom and their classrooms. My old copy of *Peter Rabbit* has the stamp of Harvey Road Primary School on the endpapers, not because my mother nicked it from the Harvey Road store cupboard but because she filched it off my shelf and took it into school. It was she who took me to see the folklorist Alan Lomax take us on a trip across the USA with the songs of working people in Joan Littlewood's stage show *The Big Rock Candy Mountain*. She took me to the world of British Columbia with the stories of Ernest Thompson Seton, to Latin America with a book called *Miskito Boy* and to the fight against the nobility in Geoffrey Trease's *Bows Against the Barons*. And it was also she who, in the midst of her daily work in a primary-school classroom, started to write and present poetry programmes for BBC Schools Radio. And it was me who used to look over her shoulder and wonder if I could have a go at writing this poetry stuff.

It was my father who pumped up the Tilley lamp one night in a tent on a campsite on the North Yorkshire coast, called us all in, sat us down, opened a book and began:

> My father's family name being Pirrip, and my Christian name Philip, my infant tongue could make of both names nothing longer or more explicit than Pip. So, I called myself Pip, and came to be called Pip.

And went on night after night until it was finished.

It was the pair of them kneeling on the floor alongside that wonderful teacher and anthologist Geoffrey Summerfield as he laid out on the carpet of our front room hundreds and hundreds of poems, proverbs, songs, litanies and jokes from all over the world for what would become the great *Voices* anthologies that helped me realise that I really could do this poetry stuff.

It was my brother in our bedroom at night waving his arms and doing all the funny voices of Geoffrey Willans's subversive *Down With Skool!*; the whole family in tears of laughter watching Peter Ustinov; or us going to see my father's productions of school plays that helped me make the connection between writing and performance.

And it was two women formed in that 1940s and '50s intellectual tradition that loved and championed serious literature for children who first found a space for me in schools radio and children's books: Joan Griffiths and Pam Royds. I remember their work and their commitment to new and old, popular, high-quality, multi-cultural children's literature when I look at where we are now.

This historical moment for us in our work is at one and the same time inspiring and difficult. Two facts: the sales of both children's picture books and original single-authored collections of poetry for children are dropping fast.

Why should this be? I suggest that the root cause is the same: many – not all – primary schools feel that they are no longer able to make reading a matter of free, wide-ranging exploration. Instead, reading in many but not all schools starts off by being something that has to be done quite explicitly without the use of books, followed by being something that is done when you read a reading book, not a book, followed by being that thing you do when a teacher has some questions to ask you about what you have just read.

I think there are many consequences. Here's one tiny indicator: the spinners in the corners of newsagents used to be full of Ladybird books and tie-ins from movies. They are now full of spelling, punctuation and grammar drills.

I hope in my time as laureate to go on doing what I've been doing for thirty years: going into schools, libraries and theatres to share with children what I've been writing; working with children helping them to write; meeting teachers on courses to talk about ways of writing and ways of enjoying reading poetry; teaching children's literature in universities.

I would like to look at how the reading of poetry can be saved from the vice-like grip of the Literacy Strategy. Please let's remember: poetry can take us to places of our deepest misery, our greatest joy, to the exceedingly silly, to the foot-tapping heart-stopping wonder, to moments of unexplained melancholy. It can make the familiar unfamiliar and the unfamiliar familiar. It can be chanted, sung, yelled, whispered, read quietly to yourself, mimed, illustrated, danced to, filmed or accompanied by sounds that charm the ear. If you don't believe me, come and see hundreds of London children working with squads of poets year after year in the Barbican Education's 'Can I Have A Word?' project.

I'm hoping to work with all the agencies that provide live poetry experiences for children and perhaps add to them: so, for example, from the head of my son Joe comes the idea of using the technology of YouTube to create a website where poets and children in schools could share their poetry performances; to work with the Book Trust to create a page on their website where we can all contribute ideas on how to make poetry-friendly classrooms free of closed-ended questions about similes, and why the effects created by the poet are effective; to get some kind of show on the road round the country packed full of poets. Why not *The Poetry A-Z Show*, from Agard to Zephaniah?

I'm hoping that I can convince the British Library and other libraries round the country to put on exhibitions that celebrate the fantastic history and present-day diversity we have in our books of poetry for children. The BL, after all, has in its possession a unique gem: the world's only complete copy of what is the world's first collection of nursery rhymes.

I have a provisional slogan for all this: 'Diverse verse for all'.

Again: the picture book is a unique, intricate and massively various art form. It offers families and classrooms a space in which ideas and emotions can be pored over, questioned, discussed and felt. Picture books are the fuse that lights our awareness that reading is full of intense pleasures. If schools aren't the places where a huge range of these small works of art are to be discovered, many children will never find their way to this pleasure. With this in mind, I'm looking forward to working closely with the Book Trust's initiative 'The Big Picture'.

On a broader canvas, I'm hoping to kick off something which I'm provisionally calling 'Children's Literature Trails'. Hans Christian Andersen came near to where I live in Hackney to have a row with the woman who first translated his tales into English. Did he get what was owing to him for *The Tinder Box*? Down the road Anna Laetitia Barbauld fought against slavery and wrote one of the first reading books for very young children for her own son, whilst Anna Sewell grew up in my street and nearby before moving back to the county of her birth, Norfolk, where she would write *Black Beauty*. Did Anna Sewell read Anna Barbauld?

Every area has its connection with books and writers for children. I'm hoping to work with the Book Trust, Tourist Boards, libraries, education authorities and anyone else interested in coming up with some lively materials that will give families and schools places to visit all over the country, books and poems to read and fun activities to get involved in.

In just a moment, I have an important announcement to make, but before I do so, can I say that the next two years will involve all kinds of sacrifices and extra work from one person I haven't mentioned: my wife Emma. I'm hoping that there'll be some occasions when our two children will be able to have some fun on laureate days too. Come to think of it, if they're not enjoying themselves then there's a good chance that others won't be either. I owe them and my older ones a great deal for the way in which they've given me motivation, a first audience, devastating criticism and – it must be said – ideas.

It's also my job today to make an announcement:

The Department for Education and Skills (DfES) is funding a new national programme called Booked Up, aimed at encouraging Year 7 children to read for pleasure.

Every 11-year-old in England in autumn 2007 will be able to choose their own free book from a list sent to their school. The scheme will also provide an accompanying website, children's magazine and a range of add-on activities. The books will be delivered to schools in partnership with distributors Red House. If you want to know more, please talk to Katherine Solomon at the Book Trust.

Meanwhile, the DfES is also supporting the expansion of the current Booktime programme for every reception child in England, giving children the gift of a book pack shortly after they start school, with a guidance booklet for parents and carers on shared reading.

The book for this year is *Funnybones*, by Allan and Janet Ahlberg, published by Puffin.

I'm more than happy to support the handing out of good books for free.

Thank you for listening.

The Bigger Picture: Celebrating our Picture Books

I gave this lecture to the Children's Book Circle on 31 October 2007, in memory of the celebrated children's book editor Patrick Hardy.

We know that the picture book is in difficulty. And by that we mean that because sales are down, it follows that publishers will take fewer risks, and the creative potential, room for experiment by both established book-makers and newcomers, declines. It goes without saying that the health of any art form depends both on the continuance of traditional features intermingled with the arrival of the new.

Now, anything that takes place in the world of children's books never takes place in isolation. For those of us who work within its frameworks, or indeed for those of us who study children's literature, it's very easy to be seduced by the idea that children's books simply breed more children's books, and don't depend on some vitally important institutions that reach right into the children's book world. So, rather obviously, the publishing of children's books goes on within the world of publishing as a whole, and that in turn depends very much on the rates of profit in national and multinational companies. You'll be relieved to know I'm not today going to attempt to trace the links between the difficulties faced by children's books and what's going on in Wall Street and the London Stock Exchange.

No, it's the effect of another institution that children's books interrelate with that I want to look at: education. In truth, children's books have never been entirely independent of education. Whether it was the reading of cheap ballads and chapbooks, or the forbidding verses and admonishments of the Puritans, even at its outset children's literature needed readers, and readers were mostly taught by teachers in schools. No teachers, no books. Interestingly, many of those early teachers and schools were themselves very strongly influenced by the Puritan tradition too. Schooling and book-making were very closely related, though it would also be quite true to say that the scurrilous and sensational and fantastical chapbooks came from a much more underground, carnivalesque, extra-mural tradition, as we see when Shakespeare satirises the street trade of ballads when Autolycus turns up and sells them in *The Winter's Tale*.

Over the following two hundred years or so, as a children's book market emerges, we know that it relies on the growth of an educated literate class with time to sit with children and read *to* them and *with* them – or, in the case of Anna Laetitia Barbauld in the 1790s, say, to write books specifically for the children in their care. At the beginning of the nineteenth century, just as the Puritans get a second wind, and produce hundreds of little, improving, moral books in the style and format of the street literature they wanted to exile from children's lives, the enterprising John Harris, writing, printing and publishing in London, realises that even the cautious, morally minded middle classes can enjoy unalloyed fantasy. Books, seemingly very little to do with what was understood then to be education, started to appear. At this very moment, we can celebrate the 200th anniversary of the appearance as a kind of picture book of that morally dubious, little guy versus big guy, decidedly un-didactic tale, *Jack and the Beanstalk*.

But again, of course, the formula remains: no teachers, no books.

However, we have to wait some time before schools become places that want and buy books produced for that open family market. When you look at, say, the sales figures of *Alice's Adventures in Wonderland*, you can't help but think that this seminal book was in fact read by remarkably few people, and almost certainly outside of school. Quite right! After all, it satirised certain aspects of education anyway.

And coming forward to my own classroom in the fairly prosperous suburb of Pinner in the years 1949 to 1957, I can tell you for certain that my book-loving parents gave me and my brother more books than were ever to be seen in our classrooms. Of course, in the classrooms there were readers, encylopaedias and hundreds of various kinds of books full of exercises, questions, tests and the like. What there wasn't were story books, poetry books, picture books produced for that open market. We didn't even have a school library. There was a warm, cosy, squeaky linoleum public library by the bridge where I remember reading the *Mary Poppins* picture books, but it took enterprising parents like mine to bring, say, Puffin Picture books into our lives. Teachers read to us from books that they seemed to own themselves and we could sometimes step up to their desks and take a look at them. The children's book market didn't rely on schools as an important means by which they survived.

Something changed in my lifetime, and schools did indeed become places full of books, with whole-school and class libraries. School bookshops sprang up and parents were actively encouraged to go into their local libraries and borrow books, and indeed to go into a bookshop and buy books for their children too.

Now, let's take a break from this historical rundown. I want you to picture a scene from now.

We are in a school that has come in for a bit of a beating from Ofsted. Never mind the reasons, but a set of what are called 'measures' is being put in place. Words like 'targets', 'delivery', 'monitoring', 'expectation', 'outcome' and 'agenda' have become very frequent. In fact, there are a lot of 'initiatives' being 'put in place'. As part of this, people now known as 'KS1 parents' have been invited to a meeting to talk with all the teachers concerned with the 'delivery of the KS1 curriculum'.

A very attractive Powerpoint display shows the parents what is going on in school in the areas of Numeracy, Science, Literacy and ICT, in that order. In fact, the Numeracy and Science presentations whizz by, but when it comes to the Literacy section, some of the parents' hands go up:

'What's the school's attitude to synthetic phonics?'

'At my child's other school, they did it another way.'

'I think it's wrong that you let children spell wrongly.'

The teachers explain how they adopt different strategies: phonics for simple words, learn-cover-copy-check for what they call 'tricky' words, phonetic spelling for free writing. Several teachers say that it cannot be 'stressed enough' that parents should read to their children, with their children, and hear their children read. One parent says that she's very pleased that her child is coming home with more interesting books this year. Last year, she says, it was all book after book from the same reading scheme and her child got bored. Another person says that she doesn't know whether her grandchild should say the names of the letters or sound them out when she's spelling the 'tricky' words. There's a consensus amongst the teachers that either will do.

The teachers are kind, helpful and thorough. They demonstrate how you can show children the way to break words into their sounds: 'ter' 'rer' 'ee' to make 'tree – 'three phonemes', one says.

The parents are thanked profusely for coming. A word about them: they are an interesting inner-city mix of professionals and first- and second-generation descendants of migrants. The room is full of people whose first acquired language was not English. The main earners in the households of these people do jobs that range from postman to MP. The languages and cultures represented were acquired in places all over the world.

Scenes like this are going on all over the country. They are snapshots, if you like, of where this country has got to in its approach to the written word in the very early phases in the human development of this country's people. What could I possibly say is wrong with such an approach? How could I possibly have anything but praise for the holistic and humanistic way in which the teachers presented their work and engaged with the parents? In truth I don't. My problem is located elsewhere.

Schools want and need parents to be partners in the education of the children. The Powerpoint display emphasised this. But in this matter of reading – how should parents be partners? When? Where? And with what? Is the parents' role to be confined to reading the book a child comes home with? More times than not, in more schools than not, I have a pretty strong feeling that this book isn't actually what I'd call a book. It's more a kind of pamphlet or booklet that tells some strange inconsequential tale about a group of people who don't say things in any kind of recognisable or even utterly fantastical way. They seem to talk mostly in short statements in the form of instructions, intentions and conclusions: 'I am going out.' 'I am happy.' Is this what the teachers mean by reading with your children? The after-school meeting doesn't make that completely clear.

It was also suggested at the meeting that parents could, and ideally should, come into school to hear the children read when they have their shared or guided reading sessions. The teachers are delighted to tell the parents that the school has got in some new books. They don't tell the parents what these books are and don't appear to have any on hand for this session. Some posters are up in the school telling the parents and children that the Scholastic Bookfair will be coming soon.

So what I sense is missing from this event – and indeed from many schools in the present climate – is any sense of *urgency* that schools could or should be places that ought to be creating what I'd want to call a 'book-loving culture'. It's my thesis that if you want to look at the reasons why the picture book in this country is in difficulties, this is the main factor. Those crucial years of four to six are when the picture book is the ideal reading and sharing material. These years have become clogged with anxiety, reading schemes, programmes, panic and the obsessive attention to individual letters. In saying that, I am more than aware that the people who are the most enthusiastic advocates of whatever scheme is in vogue (we are of course on the crest of the synthetic phonics wave at the moment) will say over and over again that their schemes are not, repeat not, a substitute for real books; the schemes – they say – are the most efficacious bridge to them. My experience is different and it works like this.

Governments are very good at passing on a sense of urgency – some would say a sense of anxiety – around the matter of education. This is nearly always directed towards scores in literacy and numeracy tests, along with the permanent background noise about what is known as 'behaviour' – a word nearly always applied to children as if what adults do to or with children isn't 'behaviour' too. Curious!

Don't let me digress.

The knock-on effect of the literacy-scores urgency is that there is an assumption that the way to address literacy in an urgent sort of a way is to develop literacy programmes, schemes and strategies. I would like to stress that this never can and never will be enough. And I'd go one step further and say that if a school, local authority or government puts such a programme or regime into place (as indeed has been in place since the arrival of SATs and more recently the directions stemming from the Rose Report), it is a discriminatory regime.

How so?

Surely it is just the opposite – it enfranchises the semi-literate and the illiterate? I'll suggest it does something else. It fails to address the fact that amongst the many social divisions in our society, there is one that is marked out by the presence or absence of books in the home. There isn't time to go into reasons here, but let's just observe it. What's more, we know that purely in terms of school success (which may or may not be related to success in life, love or leisure), book-reading and book-loving children do well at school. What follows from this is that if schools don't get books into the homes of children whose homes don't usually see books, then no one else will. If, on the ground, in the exact playing out of priorities, schools put much more emphasis on the kind of session I've just described, and sit back from intervening in the matter of getting books into book-free homes, then, unknowingly perhaps, they participate in the very process by which the book-loving children do best at school and the book-less children do worst.

So I've become more and more interested in looking at how schools do or don't help create this book-loving culture. Here's my checklist of questions to ask of a school, to see if it really is serious about books.

1. Does the school have in place any kind of home-school liaison where someone talks with individual parents about specific books, libraries, book departments,

magazines, book clubs, book shows, that might interest this specific child and his or her carers? Interestingly, the great synthetic phonics research example, cited by government and everyone else – the Clackmannanshire experiment – did have one such home-school liaison scheme in place, generously funded. However, this wasn't regarded as a crucial intervention in the matter of drawing the conclusion that 'synthetic phonics works'. How odd.

2. Does the school hold book events all year round, with writers, illustrators, storytellers, librarians, book enthusiasts coming in and talking and performing for the children and parents?

3. Does the school not only invite a syndicated book fair, but also invite local and specialist bookshops, and has it books available for borrowing or buying to support the visiting writers, speakers, performers and storytellers?

4. Is there someone in the school trained and interested in running the school library and who is on hand to give advice to every teacher to help them with their class libraries?

5. Does the school run book clubs for teachers, parents and children?

6. Does the school give every parent information – perhaps in the form of an attractive pack – on the local library, the local bookshop? Does the school take children and parents to these venues?

7. Do the school and individual classes adopt an author or illustrator for the week or month or term, and investigate, explore and do creative work around that author and illustrator?

8. Do the children make books of their own? Are these readily available for everyone in the school and for parents too? Does the school encourage parents to come in and make books with the children? Does the school celebrate and cherish these books as much as it celebrates its most important activities?

9. Does the school encourage children to pass books between each other by means of book swaps, prominently displayed reviews, assembly presentation of 'this week's good read', book posters and the like?

10. Does the school seize every possible moment – e.g. visits to museums, visits from specialists of any kind, school trips – to support these events and activities with books, eliciting from all and sundry what their favourite books are or were when they were children?

11. Are there regular whole-school projects (like, say Black History Month, or 'The Sea') where a topic or theme can be supported by books of all kinds, all genres and all ages? Is the school on these occasions inundated with books?

12. Are assemblies and classrooms frequently a place when children are encouraged to become fascinated by something – anything! – to do with a book or what's *in* a book?

13. Are the head's study and teachers' desks places where special, intriguing, exciting, ever-changing, odd, old, weird books lurk?

14. Does the school keep and use book reviews of children's books from *Books for Keeps*, *Carousel*, *Times Educational Supplement*, *Child* and *Junior Education*, *The School Librarian*, the broadsheet review pages and the internet?

15. Is there at least one time every week where children will have nothing else to do with a book other than to read it, listen to it, and chat about it in an open-ended way?

This series of points should not be a utopian wish list. It should be addressed with exactly – yes, exactly – the same urgency and attention to detail that the whole panoply of reading strategies is given. For every sounding out of 'per' and 'ther' there is an equivalent attention to detail that can be given to any of these fifteen points.

And the obvious, mind-blowingly simple fact stares us in the face: in the very area where the book-loving culture begins – nursery, reception, Years 1 and 2 – there is, if you like, a world-class range of 'materials' (!). No, I'm not referring to the Oxford Reading Tree or the Jolly Phonics books or to *any* all-in-one, solve-all literacy pack. I'm talking about – the picture book.

There it sits, like some massive inflorescence, budding and flowering and reproducing in all its delightful, complex and beautiful ways, all freighted with the same impulse – how to please, intrigue and amuse young children and their carers and teachers. When we look at who makes these books, we are talking here about some of the best people to go through art school, some of the funniest, cleverest, most thoughtful people we have, and I'm talking here about the whole team – whoever it is who makes up the words, makes the pictures, designs the books, edits, publishes and prints them.

They produce what is a complex art form that passes on its meanings, makes its suggestions, in ways that call on readers to make many, many creative leaps, many, many investigations, many, many connections between parts of pages, different pages, forwards and backwards through the book.

And it does this inviting in many different ways: visually, orally, textually and in any combinations of all three. Eye and ear are constantly challenged to look and listen here, there and everywhere. The narrative is in truth a multi-narrative: one moment told in words, next in pictures, simultaneously in both, sometimes complementing each other, sometimes in contrast with each other, sometimes even in contradiction with each other. There are often more and more details to be found, there are rhythms to be remembered and re-found, there are shapes, patterns, tones, visual rhythms and compositions to be made sense of.

The strategies that we all adopt as older children and as adults in order to read, stick with and unlock stories are all to be found in picture books: plot and sub-plot, goodies and baddies, mysteries to be uncovered and guessed about, heroes on quests, heroes being tested, loss, compassion, achievement, solidarity, pain, intrigue, subversion, scheming, psychologising, resolution and much more.

What's more, these books address a complex, multi-faceted audience. Picture books are not solely for or about children. They are artistic interventions into the many different kinds of relationships between children and adults. The reading situation itself is nearly always one shared by at least one carer and at least one child, or at least one teacher and, nearly always, several children. The books are both for and about these relationships. In the books, parents comfort their children, or get the wrong end of the stick, or are indifferent. Surrogate children in the form of animals and soft toys get lost or face tremendous ordeals. These open up moments of talk between adults and children as the book is read on many disparate occasions afterwards. How many times have I been asked by parents who've been asked by children, 'Is there a mummy in *We're Going On A Bear Hunt*? Is that larger female figure a mummy or an older sister? Is the bear sad? Did he just want to play?' These are the brilliant gaps left by Helen Oxenbury (nothing to do with me, I hasten to add), where talk between children and adults arises spontaneously. And these are serious questions from the child, and about that child itself. The child who asks about the missing mummy is a child who, like all of us, wondered what life would be like without mummy. The child who asks, 'Is the bear sad? Did he just want to play?' is the child who at one time wanted to play or join in and couldn't and was left out.

Meanwhile, adults, as they read these books with their children, wonder about their own childhoods and about their own parenting, caring and teaching. If you've ever been a carer of any kind, it's impossible to read *Not Now Bernard* without knowing that you've been a not-now-Bernard person. It does the work of a hundred guides on parenting, a hundred TV programmes on why you are an inadequate parent. *Peepo* is not just a book. It's a game and, if this doesn't sound too dull – it's not meant to! – it's a social document. There are a hundred details of the way people used to lead their lives, and any number of unquantifiable feelings attached to those people and objects. This is the stuff that history books leave out: what it felt like to look in a mirror at the moment that a family faced up to the fact that the man was going off to war. Imagine a whole-school project on, let's say, how we used to live, or World War Two. As the school gears up for visits to the local museum, visits by old people, and children go home to quiz their grandparents, a host of books come into the school, from Nina Bawden's *Carrie's War* through Michael Forman's *War Boy*, to archives from the local library or town hall, so *Peepo* can take its place amongst it all. Perhaps the Year 1 children will perform it, which will be videoed, and there'll be copies of the book for them to buy so that they never need forget what it felt like to look through those holes and find the next picture. Grandparents can say how they remember their parents talking about bomb shelters and rationing . . . You would be hard pushed to find any other artistic form that has the power and potential to help create conversations like this.

This is something far too valuable to be let go into decline or restricted to privileged reading situations.

All this is what I'll call the 'literacy of literature', not 'literacy' per se. This is not just a matter of *how* we read, it's *why* we read.

I suggest that the question 'why we read' should be addressed with just as much attention as schools are giving to the question of how we learn to read.

And so to point 16: I don't think any meeting held by teachers to help parents understand what literacy is should ever be without the presence in the room, and the time to look at them, of such books as Trish Cooke's and Helen Oxenbury's *So Much*, Tony Ross's *I Want My Potty*, Shirley Hughes's *Dogger*, books by Anthony Browne, Penny Dunbar, Michael Foreman, Mick Inkpen,

Lauren Child, Quentin Blake, Colin MacNaughton, Emma Chichester Clark and many, many more – apologies to those I've not mentioned.

17. There should be *Beano* annuals and football programmes open at the Junior Supporters pages. There should be books that tie in with TV shows and films.

18. Teachers could and should wrap up a meeting with parents with a read-aloud session, say, of a Julia Donaldson/Axel Scheffler masterpiece, with *compulsory* joining in!

19. Parents and grandparents should be encouraged to bring in and show off the books and magazines, no matter how humble, that they've kept since their childhoods.

20. Children's literature courses must be re-introduced to teacher- and assistant-teacher-training courses.
    I'll put this bluntly: if these twenty points aren't followed by the majority of schools, the picture book is in serious trouble. What's happened is that teachers and parents have become gobbled up by the schemes. Watch parents as they go into newsagents and bookshops. Many, many of them make their way to the Carol Vorderman *English Made Easy* booklet section, £1.99 'with Gold Reward Stars'. (How do I know? I bought one!) I don't blame parents for doing so. The environment in education, the atmosphere, the pedagogic air they breathe, has made them think that this is the route to achievement and success.
    Quietly and unobtrusively, the educated middle classes are buying books, taking their kids to the theatre, museums, guided history trails, filling their Anne Fine home-library markers, doing their Jacqueline Wilson reading aloud, and a big bloody hooray for all that. But this has to be what we should be aiming for for *all* children and, I repeat, it is only schools, inspired by all of us – but even more importantly – inspired by government and local authority – that can, in their word, 'deliver' it. And it can't just be a few sanctimonious words and a poster of Gordon Brown reading a book to his kids. It has to be a serious, thought-through programme that reaches into every single school and every single classroom.
    I see that there is a national year of reading coming up. Here's a chance to get serious. It really won't be enough to make nice noises. It really has to be a full-on effort to make every school become a place where the book-loving

culture can be put in place. If we don't do that, then we will simply go on discriminating against the children who don't have books at home, and in the process the picture book will stop being one of the best ever, most important examples produced in this country, in any art form, of mass-market, massively popular, top-quality artefacts – I repeat, mass-market, massively popular, top-quality artefacts! Put it this way: there isn't anything better than *The Gruffalo*, *Each Peach Pear Plum*, *Not Now Bernard*, *Amazing Grace*, *Where the Wild Things Are*, *The Tiger Who Came to Tea* – I could go on. There is only something different. *King Lear* and Goya's execution scene may be what I want and need at my age, in my place, but I'm not five years old. So, I have no hesitation in saying that these are examples of the human imagination at its best for the audience that reads them. I don't think this kind of brilliant invention will disappear. It is, however, in great danger of no longer being read by everyone.

That worries and offends me.

Children's Literature

I wrote this in 2008 as a contribution to the Oxford Companion to Children's Literature.

Children's literature is of course literature written for children. However, this poses certain problems: what should we say of the works which weren't written specifically for children but have ended up being read by many of them, or have been repeatedly adapted for a children's audience? It has been generally accepted by publishers and readers that these two kinds of literature (like folk tales and adaptations of such works as *Robinson Crusoe*) are part of the world of children's literature. Meanwhile, both the notions of childhood and its lived reality have changed radically in the time that a specifically juvenile literature has been produced. At the age of twelve, Charles Dickens, like hundreds of thousands of others of the same age or less, was working a ten-hour day. He would have been a daily witness to children dying from starvation and struggling to survive from begging, hard labour and prostitution. This was the world that he reflected in *Oliver Twist*, which itself has often been adapted for a child audience. In the twenty-first century, no twelve-year-old in the Western world is legally trying to eke out a living – though he or she may well be enjoying objects made in part by a twelve-year-old from somewhere else in the world. However, there is a literature directed specifically at children which does show ways in which children suffer the privations of the modern world, through war, poverty, discrimination, or abuse. Leaving this to one side, our idea of children's literature also has to encompass the fact that many of the works we regard as being for children have always been understood by writers, illustrators, publishers and audiences to be read by adults and children alongside each other – the books for the youngest children are a clear example of this.

Sociological, literary and historical approaches can all enrich our understanding of children's literature. Three key institutions have had a vital part to play: the publishing industry, education and, something more diffuse, the processes of child nurture. Adults create a set of activities around children, though it should be quickly added here that children have never been treated in the same way from one period to another nor from one child to another. There is no uniform child reader across the ages or across any given society. While it has usually been the task of adults to protect and nourish children, there has also been infanticide, abandonment and exploitation. Some children have been carefully educated to take the place of the adults, but there has also been widespread illiteracy and, until the 1960s, the production and distribution of printed material for children has been markedly differentiated from one kind of child to another. So, for example, a genre we might think of as one specific form, like the large full-colour picture book, has moved, thanks to publicly-owned pre-school institutions, schools and libraries, from being a luxury commodity consumed only by the well-off to something freely available to all. From the sociological standpoint, what distinguishes children's literature from other literatures is its unique position in relation to the three institutions of publishing, education and nurture. The publishing industry marks its productions as being child-specific, age-specific – and on occasion sex-specific. Education makes selections of appropriate children's literature and controls much of children's critical reading of books, though both the selection and the critical approaches may be laid down in guidelines and contested by teachers. The present discourse around child nurture (carried out most influentially by the mass media, including television, women's magazines and national newspapers) creates an environment where certain kinds of books and ways of reading are thought to be suitable for different kinds of child or home.

From a literary standpoint, it is possible to say that the literature itself has some common characteristics. There has long been an understanding that the spoken language of children develops in complexity with age, so one of the key markers of children's literature has been the linguistic registers of its texts – sometimes expressed as 'the use of simplified language'. Thematically, certain topics have, in different times, been thought to be more or less appropriate. Where once the subject of death was a central preoccupation of the stories and poems for children (especially in late seventeenth-century England), there have been whole periods when it was thought to be unsuitable. In the nineteenth century, the political aspirations of empire were made quite explicit in juvenile literature (especially in boys' magazines), while the mid-twentieth century marked a time when explicit political interventions were mostly, but not entirely, avoided. Throughout most of the history of children's literature, two important social taboos of the modern era, public talk in popular language about sex and bodily excretions, meant that these topics were off limits. However, since the 1970s, there have been mass-produced books, freely available to all children, which do not regard such subjects as out of bounds. Structurally speaking, one generalisation often thought to apply to children's literature is that the resolution of stories should involve some kind of redemption, reconciliation, hope or sense of homecoming. Whether in jest or seriousness, more and more books for a young audience have broken with this constraint too. Underlying children's literature has also been the notion that the books should improve the child, or at the very least not encourage behaviour that adults would regard as antisocial. Sometimes this idea of improvement has been explicit and didactic, whilst at other times the improvement has been thought to derive indirectly through the process of responding to fiction's call for empathy with others, or even from the very fact that the child is exposed in an accessible way to the complexities of written language. It should be said, though, that there has also been a powerful strain in children's literature that has mocked improvement, starting perhaps with Heinrich Hoffmann's satire of moralistic teaching, *Struwwelpeter* (Germany, 1845; England, 1848) and taken up in a different way (celebration of mischief, mostly) by comics such as *The Beano*, established in 1938. One strong current within the aspiration to improvement that we find throughout children's literature since the Romantic period has been the idea that it can develop or support the 'imagination' and that this has a key role to play in the development of personality.

Like its adult equivalent, children's literature has its novels, short stories, plays and poetry, but it also has forms which are more widely read than their equivalents in adult literature: picture books, pop-ups and 'movables', comics, magazines made up of comic strips and stories, annuals and illustrated story-book anthologies or miscellanies. In response to the demands of education, there has also been a specialist educational literature: many kinds of primers, 'readers', story books and collections aimed specifically at helping children learn how to read. The selection and editing of the written folk or fairy tale has played a crucial part in many of these areas, and their place in publishing and education has helped shape the tales themselves. Meanwhile, all these forms and the reading habits of children have been affected by changing technology. In the present time, it's quite possible for a child to relate to a book through any or all of the following: a film, a TV programme, a computer game, a website, a radio programme, a music CD or download, a magazine article, toy, duvet cover or any other piece of merchandising, along with some of the more traditional ways of mediating a book such as the classroom, library presentation or cultural club, as with *The Jungle Book* (Rudyard Kipling, 1894) and the junior division of the Boy Scouts – the Cubs – where the group leader is called Akela. Characters such as Winnie the Pooh (A. A. Milne, 1926 and 1928), which once existed only in specific, authored books, may now live in several different formats, and the original text may or may not be known to the child watching the TV programme or playing with the toy.

Children also create literature in their own right. The largely oral culture of their play produces jokes, stories, role play, verbal games, rhymes and songs every day, and at various times this has been recorded (as for instance by Iona and Peter Opie), anthologised or embedded in written poetry (as in W. H. Auden's and John Barrett's anthology *The Poet's Tongue*, 1938). Works that children have composed, often while they are at school, and mostly as poems, have also been published and are now appearing more and more frequently on the internet.

The beginnings of this complex world of literature are mysterious. We will never know exactly what kinds of stories, jokes and songs were made up specifically for or by children in the non-literate societies preceding our own. We can guess that adults sang lullabies and soothing rhythmic pieces to children, and it seems likely that they were included in storytelling and singing sessions. Once writing developed, some young children (usually the boys of the elite class) were taught to write and read, but clear examples of age-specific literature do not survive from the earliest literate societies. The first written forms aimed specifically at children are what we would now call lessons. For example, the *Colloquy* of Ælfric is a lively conversation in Latin between the teacher and his pupils, designed as an aid to teach boys Latin. Chaucer produced *A Treatise on the Astrolabe*, addressed to one 'Lyte Lowys' (Little Lewis), probably the poet's son. In the medieval period, there were also texts we can presume were for children, such as alphabet poems and etiquette poems addressed to children on, say, how to behave at table. Manuscripts of fables, exemplar tales (secular parables), legendary or miracle tales and bestiaries which circulated all over medieval Europe were read by or to some children, but were not specifically for them.

A key moment came with the production in 1658 of *Orbis Sensualum Pictus* (*The Visible World in Pictures*) by the Protestant Czech educator Jan Amos Kamenský, or Comenius. Each of its 151 little chapters (such as 'Aqua', 'Homo' or 'Mahometismus') is headed by a woodcut, whilst underneath a set of words in Latin and German names parts of the picture and relates what Comenius regards as the facts. Though *Orbis Pictus* marks a kind of beginning, for some hundred years prior to this a popular literature of scurrilous and miraculous tales, crimes, ancient tales, rhymes, legends and jokes circulated in the form of cheap sheets and booklets, known variously over the next two hundred years as blackletter ballads, broadsheet ballads, broadsides, street ballads and chapbooks. Autolycus in *The Winter's Tale* (1610) is a singer and pedlar who not only sells fabric, gloves, bracelets, perfume and such like, but also 'ballads'. If John Bunyan's account is to be believed, he read this kind of popular literature when he was a child. Once again, this is not an age-specific literature, but it could not have escaped the pedlars' notice that children were an audience for much of this literature. Interestingly, it was figures like Bunyan who in the seventeenth century produced didactic tales and poems for children as part of the Puritan tradition, in part as a reaction against the frivolities of the cheap ballads which were seen as devil's work. A particular focus of these Christian works was the notion of original sin, interpreted by Puritans as the fallen condition of every newborn baby. Baptism would save the child from hell, so there developed a graphic, or – as some might say today – horrific children's literature relating the fate of those who missed baptism. Others wrote verses (like Bunyan's *A Book for Boys and Girls, or Country Rhimes* [*sic*] *for Children*, 1686) that told children how to observe, interpret and love the world as God's creation, and how to perform the deeds of a good Christian. As the middle class grew during the sixteenth and seventeenth centuries, it found that it had sufficient wealth to produce many-roomed houses to live in (including rooms for children) and to endow schools and colleges to advance and perpetuate its status through the education of the younger generation. It also produced theories of how its children should be nursed and trained, and out of what we would now regard as the more liberal of these there appeared the first literature for children that looked to entertain the child. In 1744, in London, the printer Mary Cooper published *Tommy Thumb's Pretty Song Book* in two volumes, of which only volume one survives. It is the earliest surviving example of a collection of nursery rhymes, that is to say a set of verses mostly without known authors, made up of snatches from longer songs and ballads and songs culled from children's own singing. Over the years this body of popular verse has narrowed into a nursery rhyme canon. Crucially, *Tommy Thumb* is a children's book that has no didactic, instructional or religious intent. It includes versions of rhymes that have survived to this day ('London Bridge is falling down', 'Baa baa black sheep', 'Sing a song of sixpence') along with rhymes that would in the nineteenth and in most of the twentieth century have been regarded as unsuitably bawdy or scatological for children ('Piss a Bed,/Piss a Bed,/Barley Butt,/Your Bum is so heavy,/You can't get up.'). In the same year, the publisher John Newbery, influenced by John Locke's thoughts on education, produced *A Little Pretty Pocket-Book, intended for the Amusement of Little Master Tommy and Pretty Miss Polly with Two Letters from Jack the Giant*

Killer. Each letter of the alphabet has a rhyme and a moral and the book came with either a ball (for the boys) or a pincushion (for the girls). Meanwhile, the popular street literature of ballads, tales, legends, wonder-tales and jokes with a mostly working-class readership continued to flourish. In the same decade, Sarah Fielding produced what is thought of as the first full-length novel for children, *The Governess, or The Little Female Academy* (1749).

Over the following hundred years, the texts intended for children multiply and diversify. Each of the strands that were present by 1750 developed, often in reaction to each other. So, for example, in the hands of the Religious Tract Society (founded 1799), the didactic strain of Christian children's literature imitated the form and shape of the street literature to produce illustrated moral tales for the same price. Authored poetry for children continued to focus on morally uplifting themes, but also incorporated fantasy and nonsense, in part borrowed from the folk nursery-rhyme tradition (see in particular William Roscoe's *The Butterfly's Ball and the Grasshopper's Feast*, 1806). It is in this period that the traditions of oral storytelling and French aristocratic fairy-story writing combine to produce the child-specific, illustrated versions taken from such original collections as Perrault's *Les Contes de Ma Mère l'Oye* (*Tales of Mother Goose*, 1697), Antoine Galland's version of *Les Mille et une nuits, contes arabes traduits en français* (*The Thousand and One Nights*, 1704), the Grimms' *Kinder und Hausmärchen* (*Children's and Household Tales*, 1812), and the more authored tales of E.T.A Hoffmann (1816) and Hans Christian Andersen (1835). None of the tales in these original collections is a purely oral example of rural people's pre-literate culture. Both the original editions and the later child-friendly versions of these texts are complex hybrids of the oral and the written, marked with the social and political ideas of their day. For example, the Grimm brothers edited, altered and re-wrote the tales they had heard from their mostly middle-class female friends in order to fashion something that would help the much divided German-speaking world of that time find itself culturally, and would, they hoped, contribute to the creation of a modern, democratic state.

Much children's literature of the past two hundred years has been made up of retellings of these tales. As a result, their many versions have been examined in detail with a view to discerning the psychological make-up or needs of children, the political and social intent of the adults presenting the stories, and the prevailing moral values of countries that have promoted or altered them. It is interesting to note that there are motifs in these tales (including attempted infanticide by parents, unpunished robbery, cannibalism, violence, rape and deception, and bargaining around sexual favours) that writers of new children's literature throughout this period are told by their publishers to avoid. The distancing created by the convention of anonymously saying 'Once upon a time . . .' (and all the other non-real techniques of such tales) has allowed these usually impermissible themes and images to circulate.

Children's literature in Britain and North America has now become a diverse industry, flanked on one side by largely publicly-funded education and on the other by the massive multinational publishing, distribution, film, TV and merchandising companies. In the midst of it all sits the parent or prime carer who inevitably plays a key role in the selection and availability of books in the home. This produces two opposite pulls: the one towards mass production of bestsellers, and the other towards more locally or culturally specific books and readers. The child who is reading and consuming the *Harry Potter* or Disney products may well also be the child who is looking at a book with total sales of only a few thousand that ended up in her hands thanks to, say, the efforts of a small publisher, a book club, a librarian or teacher. In some circumstances, parents can and do play this role too, but for the mass of children, the route to the kind of book that may well cater for their more specific needs can only come through the central role of school or library.

In terms of theoretical availability, however, we are at a point where there has never been a greater diversity of books on offer. One reason for this is the internet. A great number of the children's books produced before 1900 are now available as downloads, while the internet book market of new and second-hand books has put small-scale productions of culturally specific books (as well as millions of out-of-print books) within the reach of millions. Another is the nature of business itself. For some twenty years or so, the mass marketing of children's books has deemed it more profitable to produce more titles with a shorter 'shelf life' in the book warehouses, than fewer titles with a long shelf life. Meanwhile, the technology of book production has meant that it has become very easy to produce copies of non-illustrated books on demand.

Is it possible to discern any patterns or tendencies in all this? Clearly, the multi-media blockbusters of recent years, J.K. Rowling's seven-volume *Harry Potter* sequence (1997-2007), Philip Pullman's trilogy (1995-2000), the revival of C.S. Lewis's seven-volume *Narnia* stories (1950-1956), and the work of J.R.R. Tolkien (1937-55) have tilted the reading habits of children (aged roughly between eight and fourteen) towards fantasy literature. Fantasy in the form of newly produced, child-specific novels starts in the nineteenth century. John Ruskin's *King of the Golden River* (1851) can be credited as one of the first self-conscious fantasies intended for child readers, and this is followed by

Charles Kingsley's *The Water-Babies* (1863), Lewis Carroll's *Alice's Adventures in Wonderland* (1865) and George Macdonald's *The Princess and the Goblin* (1872).

There are many ways of making cross-sections of the field of children's literature, each offering a different perspective. Issues of gender, class and race have been much discussed since the early 1970s, with predictably divided responses. To take these in turn, it has been pointed out that apart from some notable classics (including those by Louisa May Alcott and Laura Ingalls Wilder, and some works by Frances Hodgson Burnett [1849-1924], Edith Nesbit or Astrid Lindgren [1907-2002]), the role of girls and women in children's books of most kinds used to be largely domestic, and secondary to males. Meanwhile, others claimed that children's books helped to construct masculinity by repeatedly casting boys as adventurers. Scrutiny of the literature also showed a middle-class bias in children's literature, expressed in the kinds of schools, homes and spending habits of its protagonists. The corollary to this, it was claimed, was that working-class characters were again and again cast as a mix of fools, victims, servants or criminals. On the race front, there was an outpouring of books, comics and boys' magazines between 1880 and 1914 which represented almost anyone in the human race other than people of northern European origin in the same way as working-class people, but also as child-like, cruel and in need of chastisement or even, on occasions, summary execution. European white people were given, implicitly or explicitly, a mastering role at home and abroad.

The world of children's books has tried to change and a variety of books re-positioning these roles has appeared. Sometimes this has been done through historical fiction (like Mildred D. Taylor's *Roll of Thunder, Hear My Cry*, 1976); sometimes through modern realism (as in the work of Jacqueline Wilson or Benjamin Zephaniah); sometimes with picture books, like Mary Hoffmann's *Amazing Grace* (1991) or Allan Ahlberg's *Peepo* (1981). Meanwhile, attention has been increasingly focused on such matters as whether young people are becoming less exposed to mild but necessary risk, or are unduly exposed to danger from adults through abuse, motor vehicles and war, or through forms of cynical irony, explicit sex and violence. Should children's books try to address these problems or turn away from them, producing what is in effect an imaginative haven? In fact, both kinds of books are being produced. Libby Hathorne's *Way Home* (1994) is a stark, gritty large-format picture book about urban homelessness, whilst Nick Butterworth's *Percy the Park Keeper* stories, which began to appear in 1989, are Edenic adventures with talking animals, a paternal Percy and happy endings.

Another way of looking at this problem has been to focus on how books position readers through narrative technique. It has been claimed, for example, that some books over-explain and so patronise the child reader (a criticism levelled at Enid Blyton, for example), whilst others offer complex narrative techniques (unreliable, 'self-conscious' or multiple narrators, flashbacks and flash-forwards, deliberate gaps in narrative, inconclusive endings and so on). Most notable of such authors for older readers have been Robert Cormier and Aidan Chambers, and for younger readers, in a comic style, Janet and Allan Ahlberg and Jon Scieszka.

The age-ranking of children's books has been identified as a feature specific to children's literature, which raises the question of whether children's books reinforce the tendency of modern culture to hold children in a false sequence of development. At either end of this sequence there are books which are marketed, distributed and consumed as Baby Books and books for Young Adults or Teens. At one end you can find books you can play with or chew, and at the other end fiction which is largely adult in style but happens to focus on the lives of young people and children – rather in the way that J.D. Salinger's *Catcher in the Rye* (1951), William Golding's *Lord of the Flies* (1954) or Harper Lee's *To Kill a Mocking-Bird* (1960) have done. Incidentally, Judy Blume can be credited with having written the first novel produced by a children's publisher which had a girl and boy talking about their genitals and having sex (*Forever*, 1975).

There is reason to think of the picture book as one of children's literature's greatest inventions. Originating in cave paintings, two-dimensional storytelling was taken up in church murals, which give accounts of biblical scenes and medieval illuminated manuscripts of tales. Ballads and tales sold in the streets from the mid-sixteenth century onwards were nearly always accompanied by illustration. *Orbis Sensualum Pictus* and the works of John Bunyan followed the pattern. A splendid variety of illustrated books, often tinted by forced child labour, appeared in the nineteenth century. What has developed since is an art form, capable of telling stories with economy and complexity. It is a multiple approach, offering meanings through a variety of channels and in a variety of ways: print, sound (when read aloud), image and, on occasions, touch. So it is not simply a matter of a story with pictures. Several stories are told in a picture book, with all kinds of features being present in one thread but not in the other. However, this is not simply a matter of objects or characters; it also involves the sensual effects of the images working in conjunction with, or even in ironic contrast to, aspects of the words. The words often have a percussive or musical quality themselves, through alliteration, rhythm or rhyme. The images may well vary in size, intensity, focal spot or distance so that neither eye nor ear will rest as the pages turn. The books of Beatrix Potter opened the door for a long line of anthropomorphic, domestic and pastoral picture books, and her artwork in itself arises from the achievements of English Victorian water colourists. Far from being simple, easy-going tales, Potter's books are full of uneasy undercurrents of selfishness and danger. Mass production of cheap coloured children's books was pioneered in the Soviet Union in the 1930s and was taken up by publishers like Père Castor in France, Little Golden Books in the US and Puffin Books in England, who delivered brightly coloured books for the very young into anyone's home and school. Maurice Sendak single-handedly brought modern psychology into the picture book with *Where the Wild Things Are* (1969), where a naughty boy quite literally deals with his demons. The modern picture book now tackles such subjects as the Holocaust, sex or death alongside the happiest and lightest of themes.

Poetry for children has its own history, combining elements of the nursery rhyme, verse composed for children, poems not originally composed solely for children but later adopted by publishers and educationists in their anthologies, and children's own oral poetry. In this way, children have been exposed to a huge variety of poetry, from tiny musical rhymes to complex First World War poetry by Wilfred Owen. The nursery rhyme canon offers an abrupt, bold poetry: often surreal, violent and mocking, full of characters who don't follow traditional etiquette or behaviour, though sometimes traditional role models are reinforced. 'Sing a Song of Sixpence' describes a king counting money in 'his' counting house, while the queen eats bread and honey in 'the' parlour. Most of the canon is anonymous, but several rhymes embedded in the English-speaking world's culture to this day are authored: 'Twinkle Twinkle Little Star' was written by Jane and Ann Taylor (1806), 'Wee Willie Winkie' by William Miller (1841), 'Mary had a Little Lamb' by Sarah Josepha Hale (1830), and 'Old Mother Hubbard' by Sarah Catherine Martin (1768-1826), based on an older rhyme.

Etiquette, moral and religious poetry for children in English emerged in the medieval period and continues in many different forms to the present day. The chapbook tradition produced many rhyming sheets based on such characters as Tom Thumb, or told short traditional tales in verse form. In the late eighteenth century, perhaps inspired in part by Bunyan, nursery rhymes and chapbooks, a poetry for children emerges that takes pleasure in the observed world or creates absurd scenes, like 'Twinkle Twinkle Little Star'. A major shift occurred with Edward Lear, who applied all the skill of a great lyricist to create absurd, melancholic stories of loneliness and travel, or a gallery of oddballs in his limericks. Lewis Carroll was a highly accomplished writer of narrative verse and parodies, mocking, in particular, the kinds of verses being given to children in Sunday Schools. The four best known British writers of children's poetry prior to 1950 are Robert Louis Stevenson, Hilaire Belloc, A.A. Milne and Walter de la Mare, each contributing something very different. Stevenson is the first poet to celebrate his own childhood in poems intended for children. Hilaire Belloc built on the *Struwwelpeter* tradition with his *Cautionary Tales*, parodying moral verse. A.A. Milne took some of the themes from the poetry of adult humorous magazines and carried it over into children's books, while de la Mare created a dreamlike, mysterious, supernatural world. For older children in Britain from the late nineteenth century onwards there was a strand of patriotic and imperial poetry which celebrated Britain's role in battles defeating foreigners, most famously by Sir Henry Newbolt.

Just as complex in its production and mediation is the history of drama for children. The pantomimes of the early nineteenth century were seen by whole families, and a work often seen as the first children's play, J. M. Barrie's *Peter Pan* (1904) was also a family entertainment. Punch and Judy was always directed more specifically at children, while cut-out, paper and cardboard theatres came with plays attached, such as dramatisations of *Jack the Giant-Killer*. There are three strands to the modern world of theatre for children: the school- and museum-based touring companies; children's theatres; Christmas shows for children – pantomimes along with such modern classics as dramatisations of Raymond Briggs's *The Snowman*. School-based touring companies started to develop in the 1960s and adopted the radical techniques (and in some cases the politics) of agitprop and Brechtian theatre. In the present time, these educational companies tend to produce plays on such matters as dental hygiene or road safety. Children's theatres usually offer a mix of adaptations of old and new fiction, plays with totally new stories along with the occasional 'old' play such as Maurice Maeterlinck's *Blue Bird* (1908). Children themselves are involved in thousands of school- or club-based theatrical events, often writing them themselves. This too is a form of children's literature.

Clearly, the internet and the arrival of the electronic book are producing some major changes to what and how children read in the future. Writers have become increasingly accessible to their readers through websites and chatrooms, and children themselves can publish what they write from the moment they can use a keyboard. However, the physical object of the book fits into another strand of children's activity: playing with toys. The tactile holding of a small object that releases possibilities, fantasies, fun and speculation is perhaps not different in kind from a pile of building bricks. That said, the huge creative possibilities of texts and sounds delivered from hand-held screens have yet to be realised. New hybrids made up of moving photographic image, drawn image, computer-generated image, interactive game, linear text, music, sound effects and performance poetry or rap are likely to emerge over the next few years. Indications of this can be found anywhere from modern art installations to the children's pages of the BBC website. What follows from this is that the production of literature for children will be subject to two forces: one global, delivering mass-produced entertainment into every child's hand; the other, self-made and local. This is analogous to the production of the visual image for adults, where film is now widely available both as a mass-produced commodity and as part of a home-made process. Key to the creative power in this new era will be the role of education. Will those who control school curricula leave enough space and time for teachers and school students of all ages to make their own literatures? To do so will both benefit the development of new artists of all kinds, but will also help develop a critical readership amongst young people.

Preface to *Emil and the Detectives*

I wrote this preface to the Folio Society's 2008 edition of Erich Kästner's marvellous novel.

Emil and the Detectives was a ground-breaking book in many ways. It is probably the first of the child-detective books, a genre taken up and adapted so successfully by Enid Blyton and, more recently, by Anthony Horowitz and Charlie Higson. It is one of the first books for children that gives us a rounded, unpatronising picture of a child in a single-parent family of very little means. It is also one of the first books for children which treats the city as a place of excitement and worth. It supports the actions of children working together for a common purpose without the guidance of adults, and through its representation of dreams as a site of anxiety it draws on an awareness of Freud. Then, as if all this weren't enough, by way of innovation, the book tells its story in two different ways. A conventional stand-alone narrative is told to us in the third person by a knowing narrator, whilst interleaved amongst it are single-page commentaries on people appearing in the main story. They are written as if they are the narrator's soliloquies, who is thinking aloud for our benefit. In the original German, but not usually reproduced in translation, there is also an interesting sub-text running through the book in relation to language itself. Local urban speech, usually employed by writers to typify speakers as lower class and therefore stupid, incompetent or fatally flawed, is used in the book to support and strengthen the vigour and resourcefulness of the boys from Berlin who Emil meets. Though most, if not all, of these features of the book have been visited many times since in fiction for children, it's worth bearing in mind that in 1929 they were extremely rare or absent. To combine them all in one book is really quite remarkable.

So what kind of person could have produced such a piece of literature, and what sort of era did he live through? Erich Kästner was born in 1899 in Dresden, a sizeable city famous for its traditional porcelain works. His father was a saddler but Kästner didn't follow him into the milieu of skilled craftsmanship, but took the route to college, teacher-training and a PhD in German literature. This path into the arts was interrupted by an event that would affect Kästner's life and work from then on: the First World War. For those of us born into a time with no national conscription and no experience of huge battles or civilian casualties, it is not only difficult to imagine the intense training, the horror and devastation of the battles, but even harder to imagine the kind of intellectual effort and courage required to take a critical stance against the patriotic fervour and militaristic pride that supports the making of war. This is precisely what Kästner did; he became a pacifist and devoted his early years of writing to producing poetry and song lyrics that examined and mocked militarism.

The time between the end of the war and the writing of *Emil* was a period of massive upheaval in Germany. The experience of rapid industrialisation, extreme inequality and war produced a huge working-class movement that was deeply hostile to the status quo. A serious consequence of the First World War was a crippling reparations programme that Britain, France and the United States imposed on Germany, requiring huge amounts of money to be transferred from Germany to the allies for years ahead. Even so, in the political turmoil of those years, Germany created a society where there was universal suffrage for everyone over the age of twenty, proportional representation and strong regional government, and its provision of education, pensions and trade-union rights was unequalled. Meanwhile, Berlin was going through a mini-renaissance, becoming a place of cultural and artistic innovation. It was in this context that the young Kästner was approached by the head of a Berlin publishing house, Edith Jacobsen, with the suggestion that he might write a detective novel for children.

It's not immediately clear why people with Kästner's views should be interested in children – at this stage of his life he wasn't a father – but it should be remembered that one of the legacies of romanticism in particular is the notion that children are the carriers of hope and an uncorrupted wisdom. After all, it isn't them who have conducted the wars or created the poverty, it was argued. In England the young William Wordsworth put forth the now familiar idea that 'the child is father of the man', and in Germany the Brothers Grimm gave great strength to the complementary idea that there was, as they implied, some kind of pure and long-lasting wisdom to be found in those human beings who were closest to nature: children and those who worked the land. One of the reasons for the lasting popularity of *Emil* is that versions of these ideas have held sway, particularly in artistic circles, throughout the twentieth century.

So, there we have Kästner, brushing shoulders with the artistic community of cosmopolitan Berlin while all around them political argument raged. He is making a name for himself as a poet, song-writer and book reviewer and he sits down to write a novel for children. He tells the story of Emil Tischbein. Emil's surname translates literally as 'table-leg', which is a real German surname, but perhaps, in a Dickensian way, encapsulates the notion that Emil is no taller than a table. His father was a plumber but died, and his mother, as our narrator makes clear, has to work. She is a decidedly un-posh hairdresser, and she 'is glad that she can work and earn enough money'. In a touch of realism, we learn that 'Sometimes she is ill, and then Emil fries eggs for her and for himself.' This is a person Kästner wants us to believe in, so we are taken to yet one more level of realism: 'For he can fry them very well. He also knows how to fry a steak, chipped potatoes, onions and all.' For all our modernity and our attention to detail, there aren't many books for children that construct an image of a child who we are introduced to in a way that tells us exactly where he has pitched up in the social ladder, and what he has to do himself to support this place. In Emil's conversations with the boys in Berlin, this becomes even clearer.

Emil is set a task: take some money by train to his grandmother in Berlin. So, having been shown what money means to this family, we are able to enter into any anxieties about its fate through the eyes of Emil and his mother. One other crucial aspect of Emil's character is that he has committed a crime. As readers we may not feel it's a crime – the key point here is that Emil thinks that it is. In league with his friends he has drawn a moustache on the face of the town statue of the Grand Duke Charles – shades of Dada and the moustache on the Mona Lisa, perhaps! So, hovering over Emil and us, the sympathetic readers, is this crime against the state. Surely, in a children's book, this won't go unpunished?

On the train to Berlin, Emil sits in a carriage with Herr Grundeis (Mr Ground-ice, surely a name with menace), but against his best intentions, he falls asleep. When he wakes up, his money has gone and so has Herr Grundeis. This occurs not long after a quarter of the way through the book, so for the rest of the narrative we are dealing with Emil's emotions, encounters, plans and eventual capture of Grundeis. So far, I have accepted the notion that this is a detective novel, but to tell the truth it isn't, as strictly speaking it isn't a whodunnit and so doesn't involve the classic tropes of the form, the slow piecing together of evidence in order to entrap the villain. In a way this is a detective novel in reverse, as it requires Emil, and the boys he meets in Berlin, to ensnare the man they know has done it, and prove his guilt after the capture rather than before. There is also another level at which the book reverses the conventional detective narrative. The whole point of adult detective fiction is that it creates a form of super-human who will make the world safer for us ordinary mortals. He (and rarely, she) will be able to make that last brilliant link that will foil the threat to our orderly existence. It is, then, surely a contradiction in terms that a child (or children), who are the symbolic bearers of innocence, can commit the same deed as their adult fictional counterparts. They must therefore be super-super-human. But no, the whole point of Kästner's book is that these are real children, with flaws (they might fall asleep by the phone, fib to their parents, be prone to vanity), who manage this super-human deed.

Now, many adults reading the book to their children (as I have done on several delightful occasions) might be inclined at key moments in the story to stick their tongue firmly in their cheek and soldier on. We should remember, however, that children's fiction is particularly intent on appealing to a child's longing for omnipotence. As the smaller members of the human race, and the least powerful in very nearly all acts of decision-making going on around them, it's hardly surprising that the fiction that often appears to them the most delicious and the most tempting is precisely the one that implies that its heroes (and for that narrative moment, the readers) are capable of acts that go well beyond a child's usual capabilities. Again, Kästner's superb trick is to do this without the assistance of superguns, superpowers, magical assistants or a divinity. It is all done through the collective wisdom and energy of the all-too-human boys.

One last word. It is not only the boys, their families and the material of their lives that are drawn with painstaking care; there is also Berlin itself. Just as other great writers for children have lavished attention on landscape and house interiors, here for the first time are loving descriptions of what Kästner's contemporaries called 'street-noise' (*Strassenrausch*). With all the optimism of the milieu that Kästner belonged to, we meet a Berlin where even the passing buses are exciting. Here is one of my favourite pieces in all of literature, taking its place alongside the flowering of German expressionist painting of this time:

> It had already grown dark. Electric signs flared up everywhere. The elevated railway thundered past. The underground railway rumbled and the noise from the trams and buses and cycles joined together in a wild concert. Dance music was being played in the Café Woerz. The cinemas, in the Nollendorf Square, began their last performance of the evening. And crowds of people pushed their way into them.

The fact that this optimism was ill-founded for Kästner himself – something he came to realise only too well as he watched his own books being burnt – should be no reason to withhold or dampen that optimism as we share this book with children. Following Kästner, we can quite legitimately read with our children in the hope that the world may heal itself through the actions of its citizens acting in co-operation for each other.

Inaugural Lecture at Birkbeck

This is the lecture I gave as my Visiting Professorial inaugural lecture at Birkbeck, University of London on 12 May 2009.

Here's a poem I wrote, triggered by the NHS asking me to write something that would celebrate its sixtieth birthday. I thought that I was writing a poem for adults. It turns out that they thought I was writing a poem for children. It now turns out that it's going to go up on every surgery wall in England and Wales.

These are the Hands

These are the hands
That touch us first
Feel your head
Find the pulse
And make your bed.

These are the hands
That tap your back
Test the skin
Hold your arm
Wheel the bin
Change the bulb
Fix the drip
Pour the jug
Replace your hip.

These are the hands
That fill the bath
Mop the floor
Flick the switch
Soothe the sore
Burn the swabs
Give us a jab
Throw out sharps
Design the lab.

And these are the hands
That stop the leaks
Empty the pan
Wipe the pipes
Carry the can
Clamp the veins
Make the cast
Log the dose
And touch us last.

Quite often, the conversation about children's books focuses on questions of audience. Who's reading the books? Or who's the ideal reader? We hear about books being ideal for this or that age of child, or this book is a girls' book, or girls of 12 will like this. Again, it's quite usual to say of a picture book that it appears to be making nods to an adult reader, or that there are sly references in the text or pictures – as with a book by Anthony Browne, say, with his allusions to the painter Magritte. Another way of thinking of audience in these conversations is to notice that some kinds of books – famously the *Harry Potter* series and Philip Pullman's trilogy – are what are called 'crossovers'. Adults have been spotted reading them on the Tube. They've even been re-bound by the publishers in adult-friendly covers. This focus on audience is also the cause of a row in the publishing world; a campaign initiated by authors Anne Fine and Philip Pullman vigorously opposed the labelling of books with badges announcing what age of child was the ideal or intended reader of the book. Fine's and Pullman's argument was in essence about the way such labelling would, they claimed, restrict the audience for the books: books labelled for young children would scare off older children who wouldn't want to be sneered at for reading books that were supposedly too young, and books that were labelled for older children might frighten off younger children or, more likely, their parents, for fear of young ones getting into unsuitable stuff.

So, children's books are often surrounded with these discussions about audience. They are of course based on an assumption that children's books are for children. I would like to contest that idea, or at the very least modify it. I have two broad reasons for contesting it: one comes from why and how children's books are read and the other from why and how they are written.

There's a long and decent history of people trying to figure out what are the defining characteristics of children's literature. These are mostly attempts to find structural and/or generic elements in the books that can be said to exist only in literature for children, rather as biologists find the distinctions between sloths and apes. So Tony Watkins, for example, has examined how a large part of children's literature, very nearly all of it, for all ages (bar a few novels directed at young adults), involves some sense of restitution, a restoration, a redemption, a homecoming. Then we can all have fun looking for exceptions; Roald Dahl, who achieved a status for himself where he could overrule his editors, decided that the boy at the end of *The Witches* did not need to be restored to his human self but could go on being a mouse. Not very homecoming at all. Interestingly, the film of the book couldn't or wouldn't repeat this motif, and, just as the formula demands, it restored the boy to boyhood. So while I'm speaking now, you might want to consider children's books you've read and think of the endings. Have any or many of them left their main protagonist without hope, away from home, with matters unsolved, the self in a state of confusion or unremitting loss? Not many.

Another area of focus has been formal or generic: certain forms of book seem largely restricted to the arena of children's books – the picture book, the pop-up book, the lift-the-flap book or 'movables' as the antiquarian book world calls them; the heavily illustrated 'chapter book' for what are sometimes oddly called 'self-supporting readers' seems restricted to children's literature too. Then there are the classifications along thematic lines. These are harder to prove; take the Robinsonade, which developed out of *Robinson Crusoe* and became, within children's literature, the family or group of children who become stranded and isolated, starting of course with *Swiss Family Robinson*, the name being no coincidence. But as we know, some famous books like *Lord of the Flies* and Nobel Prize-winning Kenzaburō Ōe's *Nip the Buds, Shoot the Kids* are child-centred Robinsonades intended originally for adults. It's true that books which devote their whole story to a school seen through the eyes of a child – the school story – are largely a product of children's literature, though the first major novel in the genre – *Tom Brown's Schooldays* – was what we might now call a crossover book. The crime-busting child detective or secret agent is perhaps a children's-only genre – its origins lying most probably in Erich Kästner's *Emil and the Detectives* from 1928. It burgeoned in later years with the *Famous Five* and the *Secret Seven* and many others. But you could argue that these are parodies (not in the humorous sense) of the adult form – now most clearly stated with Charlie Higson's young James Bond novels.

Sex, murder, rape, incest, bloody violence and child abuse are almost entirely avoided in children's books, unless they are handled folklorically – as with the Grimms' so-called folk tales, or satirically and hyperbolically as with *Struwwelpeter* and Hilaire Belloc's 'cautionary' verse. Famous exceptions to the 'no sex and violence' rule tend to be clearly marked 'teen novels' or 'young adult' and the like. We may well find that whatever definitions and descriptions we come up with for children's literature, the teen novel escapes and refuses to be bound by the same descriptions and conventions. However, because of our tendency to live in mixed-age families – and children do insist on being born a few years apart – some books, like Judy Blume's *Forever*, escape from the corral and easily get into the hands of much younger children. For centuries, nudity, peeing and pooing were taboo, but there is a whole new genre of picture book that has opened its doors to this too.

There's an argument to be had at the level of language, perhaps. Children's books clearly work on the assumption that certain kinds of complex concepts, abstract argument, psychological and political reasoning (and the customary language these ideas come in) aren't suitable for a young audience. In fact, you could say that this is clearer now than it was in the past. If you compare the output of, say, Puffin novels from when I was a child and Puffin novels of today, it's clear that something has gone on here. The language of children's books has become much more informal, and the leisurely literary pace of novels from fifty years ago seems to have mostly disappeared. As the children's author Morris Gleitzman once told me, 'You have to start every scene as late on into the action as you can.' There is an assumption amongst editors and writers that children are informed by the timing of film-cutting, and novels should try to keep pace with that. And perhaps we could say that children's novels avoid the inner landscape, the interiority of the traditional novel, just as film and television have to, though even as I say that, children's fiction has recently been revelling in the 'diary' form, which is often a feast of interiority. The problem with this linguistic approach as a defining characteristic of children's literature is that there is of course plenty of literature for adults that is linguistically simple, fast-moving and low on interiority too.

So all these ways of trying to define children's literature leave us with a bit of a rag-bag, don't they? As people interested in literature, we might like to have something clearer than that. After all, if we go about calling something with a distinctive name – a dog, an elephant, 'children's literature' – we should be able to come up with a neat and tidy species description, based on either what the books are about, or on how they are written.

But I think we are looking in the wrong place. I've a feeling that the answer doesn't lie inside the books, an intrinsic definition, if you like, but outside – an extrinsic definition.

So, to my mind, children's literature is distinctive for sociological reasons. Unlike any other literature it sits within or in very close relation to two social institutions of massive importance: nurture and education, with the understanding in both institutions (and always made explicit) that an essential part of the audience will be children.

It is largely through these two institutions or processes (nurture and education) that adults relate to children. That's to say, the people who mostly deal with children are carers and educators. We have devised buildings and rooms for this – flats, semis, detached houses, bedrooms, dormitories, nurseries, schools, classrooms and the like. Millions of people work at it: parents, grandparents, playgroup leaders, teachers, teaching assistants, librarians, head teachers and many more. There are even ministers in government who are actually or theoretically in charge of it all, sending out directives and policy documents, creating taxation and benefit systems and the like to mould the processes as they see fit. The major media outlets – TV, magazines, newspapers and the internet – devote millions of words to both matters: how to have a happy baby, how to make your kids clever, how to deal with stroppy teenagers, and the like. A discourse around motherhood and fatherhood rages in the press, with examples of what is seen as bad parenting regularly making the headlines, and there are regular alarms sounded about the state of children and teenagers and what measures should be taken to restrict their movements. We can say here as a rough guide that the prevailing attitudes to children that emerge in mainstream discourse demand that children should be protected, punished and instructed: protected because they are innocent, punished because they are evil (don't worry about the contradiction here) and instructed because they know nothing.

Meanwhile, a cluster of capitalist enterprises delivers products and services into the institutions of nurture and education – formula milk, frame-steel structures for schools, kids' clothes, toys, school-friendly equipment and, of course, books.

When we get closer in to all this, we can see where books are. Carers are sitting with their children on their laps or alongside them at bedtime, reading books out loud, talking about books with their children. Some carers construct shelves for their children's bedrooms. Schools spend hours and hours a week teaching children how to read and historically varying amounts of time encouraging children to read whole books. But let's freeze frame here. Though it is clear that the books in these processes are being consumed by children, it is also clear that they are being handled and shared by adults too

– mostly the carers and educators. Yes, we might spot a child in a corner of a nursery looking at a book on her own, a child at home sitting in his bedroom reading alone – but the means by which the book got there, the context for the book itself, is nearly always one mediated and arranged by the adult carers and educators. Not every piece of children's cultural life is like that – the passing around of rude jokes and rhymes, for example, is usually carried out furtively and privately between children, with no adult intervention.

So I would suggest that what we call children's books are in fact shared books, books shared between children, carers and educators, and this sharing nearly always goes on in the context of nurture and education or as an immediate and direct consequence of nurture and education. In other words, built into the children's book is a multiple audience – adults not just as buyers, but very often as actual reading or listening partners. So I would say that one of the defining characteristics of the children's book is not simply or only that it is for children but that, unlike its adult counterparts, it is a book for a shared audience in the two contexts of nurture and education. When we say that this or that book is suitable for a six-year-old boy, what we are really saying is that it is suitable for a six-year-old boy when he is at home or in school near or with a carer or educator.

I'll put that another way: I think that children's books are literary interventions into two discourses – the one about nurture and the one about education. So, children's literature does what literature does: parades scenes and narratives and images predominantly with language, but does so in these two specific contexts, and either intentionally or as a consequence jumps straight into the ding-dong battles over how children are raised and how children are educated. In other words, the books frequently engage with those three broad themes that I mentioned earlier – the requirement that we protect, punish and instruct our children. And it does these things in the knowledge or with the awareness that much of what is written addresses the shared audience of those taking part in those two contexts – the adult carers and educators on one side and the children on the other.

To take one example: a book like Maurice Sendak's *Where the Wild things Are* shows us a boy who has said to his mother that he'll eat her up. The text tells us that he's done wild things. He's sent to his room from where he magically goes away to a place where he tames some very large wild things and returns to find that someone has put out his supper and it's still hot. This is a book which is about how children handle being brought up and which will nearly always be read in the context of either that bringing-up – at bedtime, on a carer's lap, or within education at playgroup, nursery, or early-years schooling. It speaks to both child and adult as it negotiates questions of what is an OK way of going on, either as a child or as a parent, raising questions around the issues of punishment and forgiveness. It pinpoints with painful accuracy the moment of emptiness when the child 'wanted to be where he was loved most of all', which at first glance appears to be about the child (it's about 'he wanted'), but in the context of an adult reading raises for that adult questions of whether that adult or any adult can or will or does deliver that kind of love, that intensity and totality. This is why the book will instantly create conversations in the contexts of its reading. Having read it many times with my then three-year-old, he suddenly said, as I read the line 'where he was loved most of all', 'Mummy!'. Just to remind you, we never see Mummy in this book, she is the off-stage presence who has sent the boy to his room, and presumably, though it's not said, she is the presence who has left the supper in the bedroom waiting for him after his trip to tame the wild things. What my three-year old decided was that she's also the agent in the passive construction 'where he was loved most of all'. What I'm saying here then is that *Where the Wild things Are* is children's literature because it is an intervention for both children and adults in the conversations we have about the processes of nurture and education. The book is not (as some would have it) simply or only about how a child should or could handle his anger, but is as much about how we as adults get to understand that anger and how we should or could negotiate with that angry child. It will of course do this partly by awakening memories in ourselves of how we were angry as children and how we felt when we were punished or forgiven or loved. And then as we read the words out loud and turn over the pages, children tell us what they think and what they want, so the book becomes a platform or springboard for talk within an ongoing relationship. With the active participation of adult and child the book helps modify that relationship, if you like. I think this is a different view of what children's literature is about or for than is usually described.

When it comes to looking at the history of children's literature, I'm suggesting that what we are really looking at is the history of a kind of literature that is written in intimate relation to prevailing attitudes and policies to nurture, and prevailing attitudes and policies in education. It is not simply or only a matter of a history of kinds of books. It is virtually always and inescapably tied up with questions for carers on how we raise children and for educators on how we teach and run schools.

What kind of exceptions might we think of? Perhaps the economically self-sufficient 11-year-old who goes shopping with her mates and buys up the latest Jacqueline Wilson or Meg Rosoff does at that moment appear to have broken free of nurture and education? Yes, but no. Most (not an absolute all, admittedly) of the books for pre-teens and even teens involve a key moment where the adult carers and educators have to be negotiated with. Take Robert Cormier and his two *Chocolate War* novels or *After the First Death*. They take place in the contexts of how the people designated as your educators or ultimate carers have political concerns that appear to run counter to humanistic values. This is the meat of the three novels. One of the most child-led book-buying phenomena of the present era – the very first *Harry Potter* book – is on almost every page about how a child or children collectively negotiate adult carers or educators. So, even when the buying and private reading habits (children avidly reading the books in their bedrooms with doors clearly marked 'keep out') would appear to counter my argument that this is about a shared audience, we find that the books themselves address the adult-child relationship, and in a matter of months are gobbled up by adults and turned into films for family viewing, for that shared audience.

What I want to do now is read you some poems and trace why and how I came to write them. This way, I hope to get a sense of how I grasped some understanding of who I wrote them for. I think it will be possible to see within the poems how I've incorporated a sense of the shared audience I've been talking about, and how these poems have been what I'm calling literary interventions in the discourses of nurture and education.

> I share my bedroom with my brother
> and I don't like it.
> His bed's by the window
> under my map of England's railways
> that has a hole in just above Leicester
> where Tony Sanders, he says,
> killed a Roman centurion
> with the Radio Times.
>
> My bed's in the corner
> and the paint on the skirting board
> wrinkles when I push it with my thumb
> which I do sometimes when I go to bed
> sometimes when I wake up

but mostly on Sundays
when we stay in bed all morning.

That's when he makes pillow dens
under the blankets
so that only his left eye shows
and when I go deep-bed mining
for Elastoplast spools
that I scatter with my feet
the night before,
and I jump onto his bed
shouting: eeyoueeyoueeyouee
heaping pillows on his head:
'Now breathe, now breathe'
and then there's quiet and silence
so I pull it away quick
and he's there laughing all over
sucking fresh air along his breathing-tube fingers.

Actually, sharing's all right.

*

Father says
Never
let
me
see
you
doing
that
again
father says
tell you once
tell you a thousand times
come hell or high water
his finger drills my shoulder
never let me see you doing that again

226

My brother knows all his phrases off by heart
so we practise them in bed at night.

I wrote these poems when I was about twenty. I think in my head was an idea that I could apply the principle James Joyce manifested in *A Portrait of the Artist as a Young Man*. That is, I could write about my childhood in the voice or imagined voice or simulated voice of the child at that stage of life. I remember very clearly thinking that reading Joyce gave me permission to try that way of writing myself. In passing, I would say that a good deal of my experience as a writer has been like that: coming across a kind of writing that I haven't encountered before and finding that that writing has, as it were, said to me, 'Now you have permission to write like that.' So I sat down and wrote what I thought was a kind of writing that people who read poetry would read. I knew people who read poetry. They were my parents, and friends of theirs who, incidentally, mostly seemed to be teachers.

As a consequence of writing that poem and a sequence of others, I discovered that the publisher who had published a play I had written and which had gone on at the Royal Court didn't think that they were worth publishing. The children's editor in the same publishing house didn't think they were suitable for children either, as they were, she said, written in the voice of a child. However, eventually they were published in a book clearly marked as being for children, with illustrations by Quentin Blake. This was 1974.

I should say that this process of being drawn into the world of children's literature wasn't quite as passive as I've made it sound. While I was playing with this kind of writing, both my parents were avidly engaged both theoretically and practically with the question of how to teach literature in primary and secondary schools. That's to say that they were teachers of literature; they were anthologisers and broadcasters of poetry for schools; they produced papers, talks and books on literature, including poetry in the classroom. Part of this involved my mother sitting at the kitchen table with piles of poetry books, looking for poems either for her class or for the next schools broadcast, while my father sat on the other side of the table writing a paper on, say, secondary students' language in the classroom. It did occur to me that if I shoved some of what I was writing my mother's way, she might think it was worth putting it in one of her radio programmes. When I heard her saying that she was doing a programme about 'looking closely' or about 'the child alone', I would look at the poems she had found by such people as Leonard Clark, James Reeves, Robert Louis Stevenson, James Stephens, and then nip back upstairs and have a go myself. I discovered that there was an overlap between my experiments with Joyce and what these poets seemed to be doing.

> In the daytime I am Rob Roy and a tiger
> In the daytime I am Marco Polo
> I chase bears in Bricket Wood
> In the daytime I am the Tower of London
> nothing gets past me
> when it's my turn
> in Harrybo's hedge
> In the daytime I am Henry the fifth and Ulysses
> and I tell stories
> that go on for a whole week
> if I want.
> At night in the dark
> when I've shut the front room door
> I try and
> get up the stairs across the landing
> into bed and under the pillow
> without breathing once.

Meanwhile, the wild figure of English teacher and poet Geoffrey Summerfield would appear in the house with bundles of proofs and samples of a brand-new kind of book under his arm: a poetry anthology which would be full of poems and songs and chants and proverbs and lists from all over the world interleaved with the most fantastic photos, paintings and drawings that could be collected. New kinds of poetic voices suddenly appeared in the house: American, Australian, African, Caribbean, Scots, cockney – names like Carl Sandburg, Vachel Lindsay, Langston Hughes.

> My brother is making a protest about bread.
> 'Why do we always have wholemeal bread?
> You can't spread butter on wholemeal bread
> You try and spread butter on
> and it just makes a whole right through the middle.'
>
> He marches out of the room and shouts
> across the landing and down the passage.

'It's always the same in this place.
Nothing works.
The volume knob's broken on the radio you know.
It's been broken for months and months you know.'

He stamps back into the kitchen
stares at the loaf of bread and says:
'Wholemeal bread – look at it, look at it.
You put the butter on
and it all rolls up.
You put the butter on
and it all rolls up.'

Clearly, this was all going on in the context of education, but in my own personal case, the educators happened to be my parents, they were the nurturers, if you like!

But to return to the book that was published and which included the poems I've just read: what happened to me in relation to that book? How and where was it read?

Well, anyone who writes a children's book soon finds that they are confronted with a choice: do you take up the invitations that immediately come in from the agencies of children's literature? Or do you ignore them? These invitations are about audience. Do you go and talk to or read to this or that group of children in a school, a nursery, a library, a book group? Do you talk to this or that group of educators or carers about your book, or about writing or perhaps about encouraging children to write? I chose to take up every invite that came.

This altered the reading process that surrounded the book. It set up oral situations where the poems were received by the audience as performance. The context for this was nearly always educational. I found myself in front of classes, sometimes – scarily to start off with – in front of whole schools of children. The performance of the poems was, then, an intervention in a pedagogy, or even a moment of pedagogy in itself. Apart from anything else, the poems started changing from quietly intoned readings into acted-out dramas, monologues, chants and songs. The implication here was that there was space in schools for this kind of thing. It said or implied, 'Whatever English studies or literacy or literature teaching is, it could include the performance of poetry.' What's more, as I quickly found out, it could be directly linked to children's and school students' own writing. Just as I had found a springboard with, say, James Joyce, I was being asked by teachers to use my poems as a springboard for children's own writing.

Gone

She sat in the back of the van
and we waved to her there

we ran towards her
but the van moved off

we ran faster
she reached out for us

the van moved faster
we reached for her hand

she stretched out of the back of the van
we ran, reaching

the van got away
we stopped running

we never reached her
before she was gone.

Pebble

I know a man who's got a pebble.

He found it and he sucked it
during the war.
He found it and he sucked it
when they ran out of water.
He found it and he sucked it
when they were dying for a drink.

And he sucked it and he sucked it
for days and days and days.

I know a man who's got a pebble
and he keeps it in his drawer.

It's small and brown – nothing much to look at
but I think of the things he thinks
when he sees it:
how hc found it
how he sucked it
how he nearly died for water to drink.

A small brown pebble
tucked under his tongue
and he keeps it in his drawer
to look at now and then.

So, let's put this into the ideas that I began this talk with. Poems that began their life as an intended exploration of childhood with an adult poetry-reading audience had ended up in the institution of education. On occasions, I would hear of people who had read the poems at home, within nurture, if you like. The life described in the poems seemed on occasions to have given some people fun on car journeys and on evenings when they were on holiday.

We sit down to eat and the potato's a bit hot
So I only put a bit on my fork
And I blow
Phooph phooph
Until it's cool
Just cool
Into the mouth
Choop
Lip-smack
Nice!

My brother's doing the same
Phooph phooph

Until it's cool
Just cool
Into the mouth
Cccchoop
Lip-smack
Nice!

And my mother's doing the same
Phooph phooph
Until it's cool
Just cool
Into the mouth
Cccchoop
Lip-smack
Nice!

But my dad.
My dad!
What does he do?
He stuffs a great big bit of potato
Into his mouth.
And that really does it.
His eyes pop out, he flaps his hands,
He blows, he puffs, he yells
He bobs his head up and down
He spits bits of potato onto the plate
And he turns to us and he goes,
'Watch out everyone.
The potato's really hot.'

I think the effect of all this was almost unavoidable. That's to say, the phrase 'sense of audience' was becoming tangible. In the performances and classroom conversations about the poems and in the sessions where children wrote poems themselves, I was becoming more and more aware of effects and responses from children, the business of what interested them, what interested me, what interested teachers and, as I say, on occasions what interested parents. This all sounds rather abstract.

Mart was my best friend.
I thought he was great,
but one day he tried to do for me.

I had a hat – a woolly one
and I loved that hat.
It was warm and tight.
My mum had knitted it
and I wore it everywhere.

One day me and Mart were out
and we were standing at a bus-stop
and suddenly
he goes and grabs my hat
and chucked it over the wall.
He thought I was going to go in there
and get it out.
He thought he'd make me do that
because he knew I liked that hat so much
I wouldn't be able to stand being without it.

He was right –
I could hardly bear it.
I was really scared I'd never get it back.
But I never let on.
I never showed it on my face.
I just waited.
'Aren't you going to get your hat?'
he says.
'Your hat's gone,' he says.
'Your hat's over the wall.'
I looked the other way.

But I could still feel on my head
how he had pulled it off.
'Your hat's over the wall,' he says.
I didn't say a thing.

Then the bus came round the corner
at the end of the road.

If I go home without my hat
I'm going to walk through the door
and mum's going to say,
'Where's your hat?'
and if I say,
'It's over the wall,'
she's going to say,
'What's it doing there?'
and I'm going to say,
'Mart chucked it over,'
and she's going to say,
'Why didn't you go for it?'
and what am I going to say then?
what am I going to say then?

The bus was coming up.
'Aren't you going over for your hat?
There won't be another bus for ages,'
Mart says.
The bus was coming closer.
'You've lost your hat now,'
Mart says.

The bus stopped.
I got on
Mart got on
The bus moved off.

'You've lost your hat,' Mart says.

'You've lost your hat,' Mart says.

Two stops ahead, was ours.
'Are you going indoors without it?' Mart says.
I didn't say a thing.

The bus stopped.

Mart got up
and dashed downstairs.
He'd got off one stop early.
I got off when we got to our stop.

I went home
walked through the door.
'Where's your hat?' Mum says.
'Over a wall,' I said.
'What's it doing there?' she says.
'Mart chucked it over there,' I said.
'But you haven't left it there, have you?' she says.
'Yes,' I said.
'Well don't you ever come asking me to make you
anything like that again.
You make me tired, you do.'

Later,
I was drinking some orange juice.
The front door-bell rang.
It was Mart.
He had the hat in his hand.
He handed it to me – and went.

I shut the front door –
put on the hat
and walked into the kitchen.
Mum looked up.
'You don't need to wear your hat indoors do you?'
she said.
'I will for a bit,' I said.
And I did.

I probably don't have to spell out that this piece of writing has a dual focus, how Mart reacted to the way I behaved and how my mother behaved. I've been fairly true to what actually happened there. In a sense, the dual address (child and parent) that I've mentioned is right at the heart of the writing. I have memories here that I was writing to the kinds of conflict that I would see around me in classrooms and playgrounds. I seem to remember that this was around the time when what were called 'beanies' came in, woollen hats, and hat-grabbing was big in Holloway Boys' School, where I was a writer in residence. In a way, I saw myself as a translator – translating experiences that I had had and making them understandable to people who lived in the present world, for children who had backgrounds very different from mine. You might be amused to know that this story in fact took place on a camping holiday and the Mart in question threw my hat over a gate into a field. I have then constructed a fiction based on what happened – 'transformed my sources' as the phrase goes. So you could argue that I've gone in for a bit of self-censorship, effacing what I think I may have feared was a context that wouldn't speak to the children I was meeting. They didn't do camping, but they did do buses. And with a bus, I could introduce a time element into the story, and give it a sense of urgency. Teachers, who were almost solely responsible for my poems being read, would, I thought, be able to get children talking about ripping hats off people's heads, toughing things out, mums' or dads' responses to lost and mutilated clothes, by way of getting their pupils writing from their own experience and in their own language. All notions I had imbibed at that kitchen table from my parents.

Another way to incorporate the audience was to listen to what that audience said and performed. At the time, the couple next door to me had three boys, Jason, Junior and Otis, three boys born in Hackney with a mother from Jamaica and a father from Saint Lucia. In the early eighties they were seriously into hip-hop and would regularly ask me to write them some hip-hop lyrics. At first I resisted, saying that it was for them to make them up so that I could watch them performing them. In the end, I wrote something that wasn't of any use at all to them, but was in a way a reply to them.

The Michael Rosen Rap

You may think I'm happy, you may think I'm sad,
You may think I'm crazy, you may think I'm mad,
But hang on to your seats and listen right here
I'm gonna tell you something that'll burn your ear.

A hip. Hop. A hip hop hap.
I'm givin' you all the Michael Rosen rap.

I was born on the seventh of May
I remember very well that awful day
I was in my mother, curled up tight
Though I have to say, it was dark as night.
Nothing to do, didn't have to breathe,
I was so happy, didn't want to leave.

Suddenly, I hear some people give a shout:
One push, Mrs Rosen, and he'll be out.
I'm tellin' you all, that was a puzzle to me,
I shouted out, 'How do you know I'm a "he"?'
The doctor shouted, 'Good Lord, he can talk.'
I popped out my head, said, 'Now watch me walk.'
I juked and jived around that room,
Balam bam boola, balam de ditty boom.

A hip. Hop. A hip hop hap.
I'm givin' you all the Michael Rosen rap.

When I was one, I swam the English Channel.
When I was two, I ate a soapy flannel,
When I was three, I started getting thinner,
When I was four, I ate the dog's dinner,
When I was five, I was in a band playing drums,
When I was six, I ate a bag of rotten plums.
When I was seven, I robbed a bank with my sister,
When I was eight, I became Prime Minister,
When I was nine, I closed all the schools,
When I was ten, they made me King of the Fools.

So that's what I am, that's what I be
With an M, with an I, with a K, with an E.
That's what I am, that's what I be
Mr Mike, Mr Michael, Mr Rosen, Mr Me.
A hip. Hop. A hip hop hap.
I'm givin' you all the Michael Rosen rap.

Most children's writers I know engage with the ideas of either or both of the institutions of nurture and education. Some, like me, go further and take an active part in political activity in these spheres. So, for example, my own children have been put through the so-called SATs, and have experienced the crude rehearsals for these tests that have become the substance of so much of the curriculum. What that description misses out, however, is that the very nature of the SATs focuses children and teachers on one very narrow set of concerns: the logic, chronology, sequencing and so-called facts of narratives. What follows from this is that schools then issue the children with worksheets that guy the SATs papers. The reading of literature is reduced to a logical positivist inquisition. Here's one that my daughter brought home:

Perseus and the Gorgons

This is part of a myth from ancient Greece.

At last Perseus found the Gorgons. They were asleep among the rocks, and Perseus was able to look at them safely.

Although they were asleep, the live serpents which formed their hair were writhing venomously. The sight filled Perseus with horror. How could he get near enough without being turned to stone?

Suddenly Perseus knew what to do. He now understood why Athena had given him the shining bronze shield. Looking into it he saw clearly the reflection of the Gorgons. Using the shield as a mirror, he crept forward. Then with a single blow he cut off the head of the nearest Gorgon. Her name was Medusa.

In one mighty swoop, Perseus grabbed the head of Medusa. He placed it safely in his bag and sprang into the air on his winged sandals.

Questions

1. What were the Gorgons doing when Perseus found them?
2. What was unusual about the Gorgons' hair?
3. What would happen to Perseus if the Gorgons looked into his eyes?
4. Why had Perseus brought a bag with him?
5. What happened to Medusa?
6. Look at the picture *[which was provided]*. Why do you think Perseus needed to have sandals with wings on?

1. Who had given Perseus his shield?
2. How did Perseus look at the Gorgons without looking at them?
3. Why do you think the Gorgons had snakes for hair?
4. Write down the word in the third paragraph that tells you Perseus moved very carefully towards the Gorgons.
5. Write down the word in the second paragraph that means wriggling.
6. Using two or three sentences write down what you think happens immediately after Perseus flies into the air on his winged sandals.

Myths are old stories that tell us amazing tales about the heroes and gods who walked the Earth in ancient times.

In *myths* people who do wrong are often punished by being turned into monsters.

The *Gorgons* were once three sisters. They were turned into the monsters you can see in the picture.

Write the story that explains why these three sisters were turned into such dreadful creatures. What had they done to be punished in this way? Why were they given snakes for hair and the power to turn people into stone?

This is a story that could take a group of children in all sorts of directions and explorations. We might like to ask a set of open-ended questions. What is brave and what is foolhardy? If you were a woman and wanted to be dangerous, what would you make yourself look like? Imagine if you could turn people into stone, and you began to wish you couldn't. What do the other Gorgons think when they lose their sister? Instead of which, my daughter, and hundreds of thousands of other children across England, are required to find 'correct' answers to footling and sometimes absurd questions. 'Why had Perseus brought a bag with him?' Perhaps that's where he keeps his winged sandals.

Because I engage in this sort of thing, I ponder a lot on the kind of education I had. I find myself relating the two. So, here's something I wrote that is in a way a bridge between two kinds of education, my own and children's today. It talks of the one and talks to the other.

The Bell

There are forty-eight children in my class.

We sit in four rows of twelve.
We sit in twos, one next to the other,
at desks, with two lids, side by side,
one each.

Miss Williams works out where we sit.
We do tests: Arithmetic and English.
She adds up the marks
and whoever's got the best mark
sits at the top of the class
in the desk at the end of the first row,
next to the window.
Whoever gets the worst mark
sits at the bottom of the fourth row,
furthest from the window.
And she works out everyone else's place
from the mark that they get.

She does this every week.
Every week, we do tests.
Every week, we change places.
We take everything out of our desks
and move (very quietly) to where
she tells us to go.
This way, we always know
who's better than you
and we always know
who's worse than you.
Unless you come top,
when there's no one better than you.
Unless you come bottom,
when there's no one worse than you.
The same people are always in the top row.
The same people are always in the bottom row.
The same people are always in the two rows
in between.

Miss Williams says that only the top two rows

will pass their Eleven Plus.
She stands next to the last person on the
end of the second row.
She holds up her hand as if
she is helping people cross the road.
This side will pass, she says.
This side will fail, she says.

This way we know who are the
Eleven Plus Failures
and who are the Eleven Plus Passes.
We know all that
before we've even taken
the Eleven Plus exam.
Next door, there's another class.
They are all
Eleven Plus Failures.

I want to be twelfth.
This is because the person who is twelfth
sits nearest to the bell that sits
on top of Miss Williams's cupboard.
When you're twelfth,
you take the bell,
you go out of the room,
you go downstairs
and you stand in the hallway
outside the head teacher's office
and shake the bell so loudly
that the gonging fills the classrooms
and all the spaces in between.

All the children and teachers hear the sound
and come out of their classes
and walk (very quietly) down the stairs
and out into the playground.

All because you rang the bell.

I never have come twelfth.

I have two young children, eight and four, and one of their demands is that I should tell them either true things that happened to me, or jokes. The true things should ideally be occasions where I've been naughty. I thought I had run out – surely not – when I remembered the episode I'm going to read to you. Having told the story several times, I went away and wrote it.

The Hole in the Wall

I loved sharing my bedroom with my brother
but one day my parents said that my brother
was going to move out of our room.
He was going to have:
A Room Of His Own.
We wouldn't share any more.

So he moved out the model cars he had made
and the model trains and the model planes.
They all went off to the room next door.
His room.
In there, he set up the model cars he had made
and the model trains and the model planes.

And soon he got to work making something new.
Something Really Big.

I wanted to be in there
while he was making it.
But I had to go to bed in my room.
The room that used to be our room.

So I had an idea.

I had a metal ruler, a hard steel ruler
with sharp edges and corners.
I got into bed with this metal ruler
and just where the bed meets the wall,

just out of sight of anyone looking,
I started to scratch the wall
with the hard corner of the metal ruler.
Scratch scratch scratch.
Scrape scrape scrape.
I was making a hole
through to my brother's bedroom.
I twisted the corner of the metal ruler
round and round and round.
Scratch scratch scratch.
Scrape scrape scrape.

After ages of scratching and scraping
all I had made was a tiny dent in the wall.
So I went to sleep.

The next night, I got working at it again.
Scratch scratch scratch.
Scrape scrape scrape.
The dent got a tiny bit deeper.

And the next night.
And the next.
Scratch scratch scratch.
Scrape scrape scrape.
After a few nights
I reached a bit of wood.
Should I try to scrape *through* the wood
or round it?
I decided to go over the top.
But this would make the hole wider
and maybe someone would see it . . .
 . . . but I didn't care. I had to go on.
I had to make the hole.
I had to get through to my brother's room.
Scratch scratch scratch.
Scrape scrape scrape.
It was now a little cave in the wall.

A secret tunnel.

I wet my fingers in my drink
and then dabbed the dry plaster with my fingers.
The plaster went dark.
The secret tunnel was wet.
What if I could shrink myself down
and crawl through it?
Be an explorer bravely climbing through
the dangerous cave.
Will I get through
or will I be trapped in here forever?
Just then my dad popped his head
round the door.
'Goodnight, Mick!' he said all cheerily.

I hadn't heard him coming.
Oh no, he mustn't see it.
So I sat up in the bed
and quickly twisted round
to cover up my hole in the wall.
He mustn't see the hole.

But he saw me do this sitting-up, twisty-round thing.

Oh no, he's seen me!
Instead of going back downstairs
he opened the door
and walked into the room.
Still cheery, he says,
'Hey, what's that you're doing?
What are you covering up there?'
'Nothing.'
'No, come on, Mick, look at you,
I can see from the way you're sitting
you're covering up something.'
'No.'
Still cheery, he says,
'Come on, come away from the wall.

244

Let me have a look.'

What could I do?
I had to let him see.

So I leaned forward.
He saw it straight away.
The Hole in the Wall.
Oh no.
It's the moment when the cheery stuff
stops.
It's the moment when the cheery stuff
stops.

He stood there staring at
The Hole in the Wall.
He pointed at it.
'What's that?' he says.
'It's a hole in the wall,' I said.
'I can see it's a hole in the wall,' he says,
'but how in heaven's name
did you make a hole in the bedroom wall?'
'With this,' I said, and I pulled the metal ruler out
from under the covers.
He slapped his hand on his forehead.
'You've wrecked the wall,' he says.

He shouted for my mum:
'Connie, Connie, come and look at this.'
And of course my brother comes running along
behind her.

All three of them stood by my bed,
staring at
The Hole in the Wall.
'Look what he's done,' says my dad.
'Look at it. Look at it.
He's wrecked the wall. It's wrecked.'

'Oh, Michael,' says my mum,
and my brother is giggling and giggling,
'Wa-ha-ha-ha, ho-hee-hee, ya-ha-ha-hee!
It must have taken him ages,' he says.
And Mum is saying,
'But, Michael . . . what did you think you were doing?
Why did you do it?'
And I said,
'I was trying to get through to Brian's room.'
And my brother says,
'But, Mick,
you could have just got up,
walked out the door,
walked across the landing
and in through my door.'

So, in a way, this was written for and to my children. Once again, it involves that bridging gesture, talking of a past bit of a child's thought and action; talking, to start off with, to some specific children. As it happens, as the writer of this, who also happens to be these children's parent, the piece does precisely what I suggested most children's literature does: it enters a relationship between adult and child, it talks of an example of that relationship, it enters the discourse about nurture, and when I read it or tell it, it serves as a kind of yardstick, for me and for them, of child and parent behaviours.

So across the poems I've read, I've explored some variations in where they spoke from and who they speak to.

However, this is not sufficient. What I've done here is describe, if you like, the processes going on around these poems as a way of trying to explain who they are for. But there is another way of looking at the matter. Every piece of writing uses forms of language that its author or authors have acquired. This goes on at every level of language and form – the combination of sounds, the kinds of words, the grammar, the structuring of phrases, clauses, sentences, paragraphs, verses; the narratological methods – first-person narration, omniscient narrator; the forms – poem, story, play and so on. A writer has acquired these prior to taking up a pen or hitting the keyboard. They are what has been called a 'repertoire' in the writer's head, or the 'already' the writer works with.

When we talk about who a writer writes for, perhaps the answer is to be found somewhere in this repertoire – or, more accurately, in the elements of that repertoire that the writer has used, transformed or embedded in his or her writing. When a writer starts to write, some of the choices being made (some would argue that it's all the choices being made) are to do with that repertoire. The point is that repertoires aren't neutral. Each and every text that a writer might be calling upon is loaded up with baggage that tells of where it's been, who it hangs out with, what kind of people like it, what kind of people despise it, what values and attitudes are attached to it and so on. To take an example: when I first started to write about personal experience, it seemed unexceptional or indeed necessary and logical that I should write in free verse: 'I share my bedroom with my brother and I don't like it'. I've already mentioned the 'already' of James Joyce here, but there are also a few hundred years of lyric poems beginning with the word 'I' and about a hundred years of free-verse poems mixing talk of a state of mind around a set of actions – think D.H. Lawrence. There's over a hundred years of the dramatic monologue, which traditionally is a monologue that reveals more about the speaker than the speaker appears to know himself or herself. Think Robert Browning. And there's also a tradition of poems in the first person, about childhood and about play, and addressed to children. It was a literature invented by Robert Louis Stevenson with *A Child's Garden of Verses*.

So, when we ask a question like, 'Who is a poem for?', yes, one route to go down is the one I've pursued for most of the time in this talk, but it's also true that in a way a poem like 'I share my bedroom with my brother' is 'for' or 'about' or 'in conversation with' its predecessors, its forbears, its shadowy ancestors. When the poem talks, the ancestors talk. I'm OK with that. More than OK, for a rather obvious reason. I'm very fond of these ancestors. Not simply because I like the things they said and how they said them, but because I mainly acquired them through the loving devotion of my parents. Their fingerprints are all over them – parents whose grappling with theories of the teaching of literature in schools was partly how they parented. But no matter who they were, can we say a poem is 'for' this or that audience because its audience is encoded in its language and forms? If I say to you,

He had a little sticker
and he had a little ticket
and he took the little sticker
and he stuck it to the ticket.

Now he hasn't got a sticker
and he hasn't got a ticket.
He's got a bit of both
which he calls a little sticket.

They won't let you on the bus with a sticket.

. . . doesn't it announce itself as a child's nonsense poem by the end of the second line? In a very tolerant way, you adults have perhaps smiled at it, but it won't be printed in the London Review of Books, will it? If we ask, 'Why not?' I don't think it's much to do with whether it's any good or not, and very much to do with how its audience is encoded in its language and form.

One last thought: even in the fifties, at the height of eleven-plus fever, and weekly tests, schools seemed to know that you had to give children space to listen to and enjoy and perform poems and stories. The imposing Mrs MacNab would rehearse us in the art of choral speaking, and in so doing we felt the shape and rhythm and music of poetry without anyone giving us the inquisition. '"Is there anybody there?" said the Traveller, knocking on the moonlit door' . . . we chanted. 'Yes, I remember Adlestrop, the name, because one afternoon of heat a train drew up unwontedly . . .'

These poems seemed to have been written out of a sense of unease or disembodied melancholy, and we chanted them in a world that seems to me now to have been anxiously trying to make everything secure after the six-year trauma of a second world war. That classroom I described in the poem about the school bell. So anxious about security. A few months ago, I worked with some children from London schools who looked at Robert Capa's photos of the refugees walking away from Barcelona during the Spanish Civil War. Some of the children in the classes were themselves refugees, most came from families where they or their parents were migrants. They wrote poems about what things and thoughts and memories they would or actually did bring with them if they left home in a hurry. I thought of my great-grandparents and grandparents who were migrants too. I thought of the young people I and my wife have met in a kind of reception centre in East Ham, who had arrived in London as asylum-seeking unaccompanied minors. I played around with a poem I had half-written before. I wanted to make something that would have shape and rhythm and music, would even invite an audience to join in – chorally if you like – as I had joined in chorally all those years earlier, but this time I wanted it to be without that sense of disembodied melancholy. I'm hoping that it will turn out to be a poem that will, like the NHS poem I began with, find quite a few different kinds of audience . . .

On the Move Again

You know
You gotta go.
No time to grieve
You just gotta leave.
Get away from the pain
On the move again.

You gotta move it
To prove it.
Prove it
To move it.

Take the train.
Catch a plane.

Make the trip
In a ship.

Take a hike.
Ride a bike.

Go by car.
Going far.

Use your feet
On the street.

Get stuck
In a truck.

You gotta move it
To prove it.
Prove it

To move it.

Then you arrive
And you're alive.
You arrive.
You're alive.

What you leave behind
Won't leave your mind
But home is where you find it.
Home is where you find it.
Home is where you find it.
Home is where you find it.

And to finish, a poem that I'm trying to find an audience for:

Car School

One day a car pulled up at our school
and said,
'I'm your new head teacher.'
The old head teacher was taken out the back
and put in a skip
and the car drove into her office.

The car changed the name of our school.
It was called Car School
and we got a new uniform that had
a picture of a car on the front pocket.

The mayor came to our school
and said how lucky we were
that the car had come
and was sharing with us all that it knew
about cars.

Car School was in the local newspaper.

Everyone wanted to go to Car School.
To get in you had to do a Car Test.
There were questions about cars.
The mayor said that cars had a lot
to offer to the community
so that we could all move forward.

Some of the old teachers left
and the new teachers were cars.
Blue, red, silver, dark green.

A boy in my class wrote a story
about a car that ran someone over.
He was asked to see the head teacher
and we never saw him again.

A woman came to the school
to talk about road safety
and she said how going by bus
was a good idea.
One of the cars stood up
and said that what she was saying
was unbalanced and unfair.

I go to Car School.
Brrrrrrrmmmm.
Brrrrrrrrmmmm.
That's our school song.

Why and how Children's Literature is for Adults too

No children's literature 'is an island, entire of itself'. This is a lunchtime lecture on how and why adults read, re-read and remember children's books. I gave it at Birkbeck, University of London on 11 November 2009.

I'm going to assemble a taxonomy of adult responses to children's literature. In other words, to look at the many different ways in which adults are part of the audience for children's books, whether that's in the same continuum as children or in terms of people's memory. This arcs back to how and why this literature is written: as part of the conversation going on about childhood. The customary tendency to deny, conceal or diminish these connections is ideological and serves dominant ideas about children and their subservient role. The more we can acknowledge it and change our practice accordingly, the more we can challenge those dominant ideas.

Last week, I spent my lunchtimes on BBC Radio 2's Jeremy Vine show talking with him about children's books. The context for this was a radio poll to find listeners' favourite bedtime read-aloud story. So a list of some 30 books was chosen as a short list. As a result of a first round of voting, this was whittled down to eight. Then, each day for a week, Vine and I looked at two books. The discussion involved hearing from someone who championed the book, there was a reading by Vine himself, and after I left the studio listeners rang in to talk about the books being discussed. By the end of the week, some twenty thousand votes had been received.

How might we describe what was going on here? I've used the phrase 'children's books'. In another context, I might have said 'children's literature'. These are of course the usual ways in which we talk about a genre of literature represented by thousands of stories, poems and illustrated books that have been appearing over the last 350 years or so. They have become part of how many people in the West view childhood itself. In other words, it's understood that there is an early stage in human life where certain kinds of books are 'suitable' or 'appropriate' for that age or stage. In fact, the suitability and appropriateness of the books will be part of how the older human beings supervising children will try to ensure that the children will do suitable and appropriate things: like avoiding going into houses where three bears might live; avoiding building houses out of straw or twigs which make them very susceptible to being blown down by wolves.

Another way of looking at this body of work is to look at what it says about adults' aspirations for children. So, not only do we hope that children *will do* suitable and appropriate things, and *will avoid doing* unsuitable and inappropriate things, but there are some assumptions we will make about what will be good for them in psycho-social ways. These are often expressed in terms of children's books offering children perspectives on ideas and worlds wider than their own; in terms of giving children an opportunity to learn compassion through the process of empathy; of allowing children to face dangerous, bewildering or difficult experiences in a safe, vicarious way; of giving children a chance to spectate or even give voice to their own anxieties as their own psycho-dramas are acted out by proxies in the stories they're reading. They show that ethical behaviour is the best way of going on; they give children a chance to see that change can and does take place – neither they nor the world is static; and, following from that, other kinds of existence are possible.

It's also possible to make some kind of case about the nature of writing itself. Experience is non-linear and multi-sensory. In this room each individual amongst you is feeling, hearing, seeing, smelling many things simultaneously even as you respond to those experiences and indeed even as you determine what and how you perceive and interpret them with your consciousness.

Writing, from a purely physical point of view, is sequenced, word by word, line by line, page by page. Though it looks like that, we don't really understand it in that way, because we can only follow what's going on if we gather up or harvest as we read, and indeed anticipate images, sounds, words, ideas, motifs of what's to come. The phrase 'I think it was the butler who did it' conceals a great deal. It means that the person saying the phrase knows that this is the kind of story where we will find out who did it, that butlers are possible perpetrators, that it was – within the rules of realism and the facts as given by the narrator – possible for the butler to have done it, and so on.

What's more, the written language is like a dialect of its own, very distinct from spoken dialects. Apart from when it comes inside quotation marks, it appears in complete sentences with certain structures of verbs, regularly conjugated in them. It assumes that you can't see the gestures or hear the tone of the voice of the narrator, so it has to tell you what things sound like. It is without hesitation or ellipsis. Its system of back referencing has to make clear who or what is being referred to: it, she, he, they and the rest are often not enough.

The point about this in relation to children is that very young children do not know the written dialect (as I'm calling it), but if they learn to read a good deal, they will learn it and be able to reproduce it themselves. It's possible to argue that this enables such children to take possession of certain kinds of abstract and complex ideas which are extremely difficult to get hold of through talk alone. This is almost an argument about democracy, or at least about entitlements in relation to the complex kinds of knowledge required to negotiate society.

Perhaps a more refined version of this argument is to suggest that literature works at finding expression for difficult feelings and ideas, and that the linguistic form it does this in is in some way transferable to the reader. So that when the reader faces difficult feelings and ideas, the language of literature will be there to assist him or her.

Because children are viewed as immature people, then much of what I'm talking about here is a matter of initiation. We see ourselves as introducers, inviting children to take part in this worthwhile activity.

Another way of looking at this is to say that children's literature is a form of discourse defined by its discursive limits. It *is* what it is allowed to say and how it is allowed to say it. As yet, there isn't a book for children that begins, 'Fuck off you wankers, if I want to have sex with my brother, I can.' And there isn't a children's book that has a passage in it like: 'Julian looked at George and said, "Don't be silly, George. It's not that consciousness determines our state of being. It's that our state of being determines our consciousness."' In a rather dull way, I could specify which particular limits are broken with these examples, but I don't think I need to.

You could all think of many others, I'm sure, and at Christmas there is usually a good number of jokey books that play with these discursive limits. If Roger Hargreaves would allow it, I'm sure you could all write some wonderfully lewd versions of the *Mr Men* books that would make the same point.

So one way or another we arrive at a body of literature with what seems to have some kind of satnav attached. It comes with a directional guide: this is good for a five-year-old; this is a good girls' book. And so on. In so doing, we will not only be describing the *book*, but we will also be *prescribing the child*; that's to say, we construct the child into what we want a five-year-old or a girl to be when we give them this or that kind of book. In less aware times, this was quite explicit. You only have to look at the pages of boys' and girls' magazines of the late nineteenth century to see how the stories were told as a way of offering model kinds of behaviour for particular ages, classes, for the

254

nationality and the sex of the child. Fantasy books are often described as 'pure escape' but are quite often constructed around model forms of behaviour.

In my inaugural lecture here, I suggested that all this literature is in fact not 'children's literature' but is shared literature. It is literature that children can understand and enjoy, but it crucially also involves adults, and it involves them in two key areas: nurture and education. That's to say, at the points of consumption and reception, adults as carers or adults in the process of education have a heavy if not determining presence. So, the classic way for a young child to consume and receive a picture book is for it to have been bought or borrowed for her by an adult, and for it to be read to that child on a parent's or carer's lap. The classic way for a slightly older child to come across a book is either through parents at home, or through teachers at school. There is no adult-free way of getting at children's books before you're free to walk out of your house and get to a library or bookshop on your own, or use a debit card online, by which time you're probably what the book market calls a young adult or a teen anyway.

I also suggested that there is not only this material fact of a shared literature, but that one of the purposes the literature serves is that it is an *intervention* in those discourses about nurture and education. Both the process of shared reading and the subject matter of the books invite us to think about how children are brought up, cared for and educated. So, to take an example of a kind of book often thought to be about children on their own – Enid Blyton's *Famous Five* – you can see that Blyton's work and Blyton herself are the subjects of massive amount of talk between adults; and that the content of a *Famous Five* is full of stuff to do with how adults and children negotiate each other.

Meanwhile, the argument goes on between adults about whether Blyton wrote well or badly, whether it's suitable today, whether it ever was, whether it's full of 'pure adventure' or snobbery and racism, should the books be in school or not, and so on.

I don't want to elaborate this much more. Instead I want to make a slightly different case: that not only would I like to reconfigure children's books as cross-age, shared books, but that within that sharing there is a range of adult positions in relation to children's literature. In fact, we could construct a taxonomy of adult response and use of children's books that furthers my claim that calling them children's books is misleading. However, I don't think this is some kind of oversight, or that it is innocent. I would like to make the case that calling them children's books and trying to sustain this position serves a purpose . . . but I'll come to that later.

My first observation is that children's books don't go away. In ways that are impossible to unravel, they last. So, if you were someone who read or heard children's books when you were a child, part of being human and being a reader is to embed texts and their feelings and meanings into your being. In other words the language of a book, the significance of a book (more accurately, what we make significant), and the range of emotions we have in relation to a book all make their way into our consciousness and into our actions.

Let's begin with an experiment and take these one by one. Text first. I can remember Kipling's 'great grey greasy Limpopo River'. Turn to the person next to you and talk to them first about any word, phrase or sentence that you remember from a children's book you read or heard as a child . . .

Now let's do that for feelings. I can remember a sense of yearning when I read Cynthia Harnett's *Wool Sack*: of wanting to live in that time in that place – fifteenth-century Suffolk, I think. And great fear of the puppet-master who captures Pinocchio. Talk to that person again about any feeling you had about a character or a moment in a children's book . . .

And now any sense that you derived a meaning or a significance from a children's book. Partly from *Hue and Cry* and from *Emil and the Detectives*, I derived some sense of masculine ganging togetherness and had a daydream fantasy that me and my friends would take over the school. Your turn! . . .

I think that no matter what you've said just now, there will also be texts, feelings and meanings that are part of your consciousness in ways that you can't grasp or have even repressed. Something that we would find almost impossible to unravel is the way in which the very idea of story, its methods and its motifs are laid down in our childhoods. We use the phrase 'learn to read' and this usually means something to do with sounding out letters or being able to recognise whole words or being able to reproduce the sound of a word according to adult norms. In fact, learning to read is also about discovering that opening a book and reading the words is about agreeing to play a certain kind of game, where you the reader will agree to abide by the conventions of the game, such as not trying to physically reach into the book to save the life of a drowning man, letting a narrator hop into the minds of one or more people in the book to tell you what they're thinking, letting that narrator go to all sorts of extraordinary places in order to tell you what the characters are doing. Learning to read is also learning that the events described in a story are not randomly assembled eruptions but that they are linked – characters do things and think things because they have motives and desires and fears; the beings in the book exist in the book's time and place and not your own;

if you hang on long enough, something you wanted to know will probably be revealed to you; if someone is identified as, say, fairy godmother or teacher or (as in a *Famous Five* book) fisher-boy, these words come full of significances.

All this is learned stuff and the chances are that if you are an adult reader it is because you've absorbed all these cognitive processes. There is no separation between you the adult reader and you who were a child reader.

Another key way in which children's books are part of us is in our role as a carer or an educator. So, in the last few weeks, I've both read to my children and worked with teachers in trying to encourage them to read whole books – and not extracts – with their classes. I've been reading to my own children *The Guardian*'s 'Fairy Tales' supplements, Catherine Storr's *Clever Polly and the Stupid Wolf*, taking part in conferences that looked at Michael Morpurgo's *Friend or Foe*, and announcing the winners of the Roald Dahl Funny Prize. How about you?

Then, there's a more hands-off kind of intervention which is to do with buying, borrowing and suggesting. I bought Geraldine McCaughrean's *Stories from History* for my eight-year-old recently, and she would like me to buy her some more Sally Gardner books. Why did I buy her the McCaughrean? I thought it made the past accessible and intriguing. It wasn't a sequence of tales about Britain's rulers, but covered a range of places and social circumstances. And we had noticed that she is someone who likes non-fiction as much as fiction. How about you? Have you intervened by suggesting, buying, borrowing?

What about revisiting? Has anyone here revisited a book they read as a child? I don't mean revisited by reading to children in your care, but revisiting it entirely by yourself.

What's going on here? In a sense all of this seems to me to be quite unremarkable. Most of us reflect on our past; we try to recapture moments from our past in a variety of ways. We look at photo albums, read old letters, we talk with contemporaries from our childhood, we revisit places we inhabited as children, and so on. One part of our past is what we could call 'our reading past': the texts, feelings and meanings we had at specific times in our past. I've found that if I re-read an old book I read as a child, I can remember in a very powerful way the sensation I had at that moment. I can turn the pages of, say, a *Babar* book and remember how I felt when Zephyr ended up in the custard. I think part of the way we support our ego, support our sense of self, is to revisit our past and acknowledge it and, if we're lucky, enjoy it.

Now something much more specific: study. Has anyone here studied a children's book? Have you sat as an adult and exposed a children's book to any kind of critical thought? If you did, what did you discover about the book? What did you discover about yourself?

I'll give one example: *Rose Blanche* is a book about the Holocaust as seen through the eyes of a young German girl living in a small German town. She befriends a boy who is living behind the fence of a concentration camp, and the book ends slightly mysteriously with the girl and the boy being gunned down (not seen in the illustration) and flowers growing in their place. The book has often been hailed as a remarkable introduction of the Holocaust to children. Why did I dislike it? I found myself looking again and again at the end, and first of all found something along the lines of the limits of discourse at work. The book is illustrated in a hyper-real way, almost as if we are looking at photographs, but the ending is almost a negation of that, primarily because it refuses to show death. But given the hyper-real approach, there is also a strange refusal of reality in relation to who did what to whom. And finally, the old motif of flowers replacing people seemed so freighted with notions of sacrifice and organised religion that I wasn't sure it had anything to do with the events that preceded it. In fact, I suspected that the authors had accepted that limitation on children's literature, that children's books should offer hope or restitution, but had done so in the least appropriate circumstance: in relation to the Holocaust. That's to say, the Holocaust to my mind doesn't represent any hope, any redemption, least of all through death and sacrifice. I wondered if the book was offering a Christian appropriation of the Holocaust.

As you can see, I wasn't really concerned here with second-guessing what children would make of this, or observing how they were reading it. I was just focusing on how I and the book interacted ideologically.

If you've done any kind of critical work on a children's book, share it with the person next to you for a moment . . .

Related to this is the matter of reviewing. Some of us review children's books. This is what I wrote about Carol Ann Duffy's most recent book for children:

> This is a highly peopled book. Among the multitude, we meet Peggy Guggenheim, Rabrindranath Tagore, Nippy Maclachlan, Johann Sebastian Baa (a very talented sheep), the Loch Ness Monster's husband, Miss Fog, Brave Dave and Elvis – a mix of the real, the invented, the folkloric and the skittish. But we don't only meet people: there's a host of insects, birds, dogs, skeletons, foxes, rats, monsters, scarecrows and Elvis.
>
> As a one-session read, this compendium of four collections plus

some new poems makes for a busy, let's say frenetic, experience. Of course poetry collections are for reading any which way and I reckon this one is for many, many bites. This way we can find the quieter, dreamier places like 'Don't Be Scared', a paean to the dark: 'The dark is the wooden hole/behind the strings of happy guitars', or the new nursery rhyme, 'Pestle and Mortar', where mother and daughter go to sea in a mortar and pestle, 'I'll sit in the bowl / and you can row / over the water. // Then I'll take a turn / and watch you sleep / for three hours and a quarter'. This lullaby encapsulates the Janus in poetry for children – the double perspective of the adult and child. So C.A.D. (can I call her that?) is never afraid of talking about having been a child, about being a parent, about being a teacher and about being a modern child now, all in the same breath, it seems.

To tell the truth, she gives the impression of not being afraid of talking about anything, whether that's monsters, ghosts, quicksand or the taboos which in the past have been told to stand outside the door of children's literature. C.A.D. welcomes in forbidden words, love and sex.

There are many signs here that she is also the teacher's friend. For one thing, her work for children is like a poetic Newnes Encyclopedia, gobbling up and regurgitating phenomena phenomenally – she casts schools as places where you will discover wonderful things. What's more, 'Your school knows your name – / Shirin, Abdul, Aysha, Rayhan, Lauren, Jack – / and who you are. / Your school knows the most important thing to know – / you are a star, / a star.' And even with the staff, in one touch she can turn the factual into the mythic. She begins one poem with: 'Mrs Leather's told you about quicksand' – there's nothing more topographical and plain than that, but we are soon drawn into the horror of 'Its moist suck / drinks the hem of a new blue dress / to the waist – / Your hands will panic over your head, / claw at space.' By the end, with the whole town 'searching, searching with blankets and lights', it's 'too late; only your satchel's found, at dawn, at the edge of the field / by this gate.' Poetry like this gathers ghastliness from other places, from other people: the missing, the molested, the lost.

Talking of other people, the collection is full of shadows and spirits. The anonymous creators of nursery rhymes and folk tales speak through C.A.D.: Christopher Smart, who 200 years ago rejoiced in the beauties of his cat in a biblical way, seems here to be talking about fruit and veg.; Wilfred Owen is half-rhyming all over the place; and, rooty tooty, there's Little Richard both in person and quoted. And there's Elvis. That's all right, Mama. Well, the truth is, C.A.D. is an 'All right Mama'.

And then there's the crossover text, as it's come to be known. Out of interest, how many here have read to yourself, by yourself, a book that has been marketed for children: a *Harry Potter*, a Philip Pullman; or indeed books that are much older: *Alice*, George Macdonald, *The Hobbit*, *The Wind in the Willows*?

And then, in this taxonomy I'm creating, is collecting. I collect children's books, comics, chapbooks – all sorts. Why? The impulse to collect anything must be something to do with security. My mother collected corned beef. In tins. The world is chaotic and dangerous. If you collect something then at the very least you've made order out of that tiny bit of the world. But why books for children? I suspect that this has something to do with trying to retrieve the irretrievable. I can't have my childhood back (assuming that it would be desirable to do so) so all I can do is assemble symbols of it, as represented by books.

So, there I've compiled a rough, preliminary taxonomy of adult use of children's books. I'm sure it could be expanded and refined and in so doing we would discover more and more ways in which childhood and adulthood are not quite such markedly different states as we are often led to believe.

In fact, this is where I would like to end. I want to make the claim that when or if we deny the shared nature of children's books, we sustain a division that is a crucial part of the status quo. Education and nurture are full of assumptions and practices to do with hierarchies and rankings. So, for example, children in schools are always ranked by age and often by so-called ability, often by behaviour norms. As young as five, six and seven, children are segregated into fast, medium and slow groups; into possessors of more or fewer smiley faces and good behaviour certificates. It's only possible to do this through power structures that exclude children. In fact, very nearly all of these practices are presented to children as *faits accomplis*. They are normal. They are how life is. They aren't up for negotiation. They aren't even discussed. Other possible ways of being aren't suggested. In other words they are deeply ideological.

I would like to suggest that one small part of the way in which we as adults sustain this kind of structure and these power relations is through a denial of our own childhoods. And part of that denial is to deny that we are readers or beneficiaries of children's books.

Humour in Children's Books

This was my professorial inaugural lecture at Goldsmiths, University of London, given in 2014.

First, may I thank Goldsmiths, and in particular Professor Carrie Paechter, the Department for Education Studies, and the Warden, Pat Loughrey, for appointing me as Professor of Children's Literature. Thanks also to the staff I've already met and worked with for being so welcoming and generous with what they've said to me.

Thank you all too for coming. The words 'professorial inaugural lecture' don't sound like the most inviting of reasons for coming out on a Monday night, so I can tell you from up here that it feels very good to see you all. Thanks.

When I was at school doing what were then called 'O-levels' – and, who knows – might one day soon be called that again, for, as we all we know, those times were the best of times, when me and my pals were much brainier, had much more knowledge in our heads, behaved ourselves much better, and were in all respects nicer, kinder and more moral than the wicked and stupid young people of today because we sat in rows in desks and our teachers wore suits . . .

Yes, when I was at school and doing what were then called 'O-levels', we were told many times never to start an essay with the words, 'There are many kinds of . . . '. 'If you are writing an essay on "Rain",' they said, 'never begin your essay with, "There are many kinds of rain . . . ".'

I've carried this message throughout my writing life, and you will never find anything written by me that begins with the words, 'There are many kinds of . . . '. However, today I'm going to begin with something nearly as awful. There was no escaping it. Here goes:

'There are very few . . . .' (that was it), there are very few books about children's humour, children's sense of humour, things children find humorous, and, in particular, about books that children find humorous. There are some, but very few.

As you might expect me to say, I think the reasons for this are political and ideological. Over the hundreds of years that we have created a literature for children, we have also created religious, educational, social and intellectual reasons for encouraging it and promoting it. Mostly, these have been to do with saving the child. Going through the whole period right from the beginning, what the child reader was going to be saved from has ranged across such things as hell (that is, eternal damnation after death), sin, sinful thoughts and sinful deeds, ignorance, stupidity and, more recently, something that has been called 'a lack of cultural capital'. It has been hoped by some that children's literature at different times could save children from any of these things. In the span of my lifetime, and much more so today than ever before, evidence and proof that a child *has* been saved can in the final analysis only be provided by doing exams. Loads and loads and loads of exams. The minority who do well in the exams are saved; the majority who don't do well are whatever you are if you're *not* saved – lost, presumably. If literature can be enlisted for this great project – alongside much more instrumental stuff to do with reading out loud nonsense words, naming the difference between the active and passive voices, and doing what has been called, without irony, 'retrieval' – then so much the better. Indeed, if by chance you are a Secretary of State for Education, you can make great play of how you are increasing the cultural capital of the nation by the compulsory input of great, classic texts, and you do this at the very same moment that you ensure that these great, classic texts are used in tests and exams to segregate the saved from the lost.

That's just the present-day context. I would say that for much of the time, over the last few hundred years, amid various religious, educational, social and intellectual justifications for children's literature, the funny book doesn't fit the bill. It is full of latent danger, full of the potential to be trivial, distracting, pointless, subversive, debasing and dirty. This I suspect is the reason for its neglect as something worth thinking about seriously; and so today I'm going to give it a go.

Now, there's no point in my saying all this if we don't get to look at the creature itself. So, though there are very few books ABOUT funny books for children, there ARE of course many books OF children's humour. And over the centuries, there have been many, many more. So the creature exists in bucket-loads.

To get an angle on this, we can think about 'funny books for children' in three dimensions:

The first: the thousands of funny books available now.

The second: the tens of thousands of funny books that may or may not have amused children in the past, stretching back hundreds of years.

The third: the handful of funny books that each of us can think of that we were personally amused by.

So, three dimensions: now, the history, and our own personal reading history.

In the time available today, I'd like to tackle this third one, partly because it's stuff going on in this dimension – that is, in our own personal reading histories –that explains why most of us are here today. I'm going to guess that we have each read and enjoyed books. Going back to each of our childhoods, I'm going to guess that at least one – probably some, or perhaps many, of these books, aimed at you as a child – has been funny.

So, why not turn to the person next to you, and tell her or him of the title of any book or piece of literature that you read, saw or heard when you were a child, let's say before you were 13, some part of which you found at least mildly funny, and tell the person next to you something about it and something to do with why you found it funny.

[Which they did . . .]

Now, I would dearly love to collect all that up. I think it would provide an instant cross-section, across the last 60 years or so, of what this particular milieu of people found funny in what they read or had read to them. Perhaps I can cull one or two of them quickly . . .

[Which I did . . .]

OK. Now, as this is a lecture and not a seminar, let me do a bit of personal delving into this dimension of myself and you can compare your personal history with mine. On the way, I want to identify some features of funny books for children for you to consider. Can I say, this talk will not be littered with references to books of theory, as in my experience they are very hard to take in, in a talk like this. However, I am quite happy to share with people the kinds of critical books I've looked at in thinking about this subject. Just email me. I will be mentioning today the titles of the books I read as a child, though.

So let me begin with my very first memories.

One is a book which says on the title page, *'Mischief the Squirrel* by LIDA, lithographs by Rojan, translated by Rose Fyleman. No 1 of Père Castor's Wild Animal Books, with that delicate gaiety which shows they come from the French'.

It was first published in England in 1939 but I must have been given it some time around 1950. It was published first in France in 1934 as *'Panache l'Écureuil'*.

I'm intrigued by that phrase 'with that delicate gaiety which shows they come from the French'. I suspect that it's a health warning. It sounds to me as if the publishers of the time wanted to warn buyers of the book that there might be something INdelicate going on, and so dressed it up as: uh-uh watch out, here's a book with some of that delicate gaiety stuff that those funny, unconventional French people do.

Two moments in the book tickled me: first with the baby squirrels. (By the way, I promise, I'm not reading this with the intention of making adult double-entendres):

> Mischief, Sprite, Elf and Flame grew so fast that you could almost see them getting bigger under your eyes. They all had glorious red coats. But Elf's was the finest. And wasn't he proud of it! He spent no end of time cleaning it with his paws and his little tongue. As for his tail, it looked as though it was blown out with air, almost like a balloon. Elf was always fluffing it up. His mother never had to say to him, as she did to Mischief, 'Fluff out your tail.'
> What a clown Mischief was! All day long he frisked about and played the fool, and didn't mind the least about his tail being dirty and sticky with resin from the pine-tree.

For me aged five, in the time and place I was, this seemed funny. The way Mischief was a fool was wrapped up with the idea that he was dirty and the way he was dirty was that his tail got sticky with the stuff on pine trees that I knew about from the pine trees in the park. So, like I got resin on my hands playing in the park, Mischief got resin on his tail. However, I should tell you that the moral code of the book suggests – it's not made explicit – that Mischief not cleaning his tail leads to him being shot by a hunter, injured in the leg and captured. Not that I picked up that sense of punishment at the time. I just had a sense of it being bad luck. No, the fact that Mischief 'didn't mind the least' suggested something much more powerful: that he was a free spirit, something brought out in the next passage:

> . . . a squirrel's tail, you must know, is the most wonderful thing imaginable. It is a sort of aeroplane. A squirrel can jump from the highest tree, a tree that seems to touch the sky, without doing himself the slightest harm, thanks to his tail . . . He lets it float out while he is falling, and comes to earth as though he had wings.

This sense of freedom is strongly represented in the illustrations, which showed me a paradise of lush green trees, everlasting woods stretching into the distance with avenues of lush, long grass, while high up the red squirrel family leaps and floats between the branches. This, I think, owes something to the Garden of Eden.

But there is also a second moment in the book which produces a different kind of humour – that exultant 'Yessss' laugh when your hero does something tricksy to overcome an obstacle.

As I said, Mischief is shot, but he is also captured and put in a cage. In the cage, Mischief thinks that his 'little swing' can't (I quote) 'compare with the living branches of a larch or pine-tree! That's the place to swing in. Mischief couldn't forget his great forest trees.'

In other words, Mischief's lost paradise calls to him . . . but

> One day, just as Mischief was thinking about all this, he noticed that little Jean had forgotten to fasten the door of the cage.
>
> Mischief put out his head, very, very quietly. He looked to the right, he looked to the left: not a soul about.
>
> Hop! He was out of the cage. Another hop, and he was at the open window. Hop, hop, hop – he was in the garden and hop . . . he was over the low wall.

This passage is illustrated by a picture of an open window with Mischief leaping out of it, his tail splayed out behind him.

So, though I might think today on re-reading this that there is a not-at-all-funny sub-text going on here, about, let's say, first being bad, followed by punishment, penance and incarceration – doing time, if you like – as a child, the passage told me something that was a funny and glorious victory. After all, it's a jail-bust, not a release.

So, looking back on this, I can see that the stuff I found funny in this book revolves around two things to do with the body: soiling it and enclosing it. Of themselves, these two things don't make for laughs. For soiling the body and enclosing it to be funny, they both have to be in the context of power. When it comes to the soiling in the book, it's the mother who has the power. It's her power he defies. When it comes to the incarceration and escape, it's the humans he defies.

So even though I can read this book today and see underlying themes of Mischief the squirrel in the Garden of Eden discovering sin, receiving his due punishment and finding redemption through being incarcerated, my memory of the books is of pleasure in his defiance. Today, I can find a theme in the book to do with the body being the location and focus for all this – the free flying, the sinful soiling, the bullet to the leg, the cage and the free flight – as if it's on the body itself that these moral issues are played out. So I ask, 'Why should that be? Why should the body be the site for this little drama?'

This connects Mischief to hundreds of years of struggle in the West over the idea that goodness rests in our minds and in its ability to control the bad, naughty and sinful things that our bodies might do. The joke at the core of the scene in *Twelfth Night* when the steward Malvolio reads the letter that he imagines has come from Olivia, the aristocratic lady he serves, is that he is a Puritan, supposedly in control of his body, complaining that Sir Toby Belch and his companions do uncontrolled things with theirs – like getting drunk. Yet, when the Puritan Malvolio reads the letter, he doesn't know – but we the audience do – that he is saying out loud stuff to do with women's anatomy. He is out of control.

As a four-year-old, this age-old struggle, dressed in the very different clothes of a squirrel's fur, was given to me, and in spite of itself gave me the giggles and drew me back again and again to it. It was a book I loved and I still have my copy of it.

A little later in my life, a page in a book called *The Building of London* by Margaret and Alexander Potter, published as a Puffin Picture Book in 1945, seemed to me very funny. The text alone was not a barrel of laughs:

Stopping Londons [*sic*] Growth

During the Reformation, the monasteries were closed and their grounds closed. Outside London the grounds were used for building. The Government was afraid that the city would be too big to control and passed laws against such building. It even ordered houses to be pulled down. More often the kings made money by selling permits to build. Thus, in James 1st's time, Red Lion Square was built and Covent Garden.

I have no memory of actually reading this. Looking at it today, I can see that what the passage describes is a complex sequence of events, confused and bumbled into empty or meaningless phrases like 'the monasteries were closed' or 'made money by selling permits to build'. Closed by whom? Selling permits to whom? In fact, they're rather like the weird, confusing sentences dished up in the tests and exams I was talking about earlier. They sound as if they're telling us important stuff even as they prevent us from knowing it.

This is partly why the picture next to this text was so funny. This shows three men looking a bit like Desperate Dan or men in a Viz cartoon heaving on a rope attached to one of the stilts under a half-timbered house. They are pulling the house down. They are under the direction of a bearded, high-hatted, Charles-the-first-looking gent in very fancy coloured breeches. Up above, looking from the windows, balcony and roof are people hurling down bricks or, even more importantly for me at the time, one of them tipping a potty onto the heads of the gent and the guys heaving on the rope. The stuff coming out of the potty is yellowy-green. My brother told me that this was wee.

For me at the age of around 7, this was unbearably funny. I should say that in the context of my own home, it didn't cross any taboos. My father was a great performer of ribald and scatological songs like:

> You ought to see Michael water
> It makes such a beautiful stream.
> It runs for a mile and a quarter
> and you can't see poor Michael for steam.

The gag in the book is a gag because of where it is, in the context of this particular book in this particular time: that alongside such a formal text there should be something so informal and incongruous as wee being tipped onto the heads of these men. Hand on heart I can say that I have never done this myself; however, I have lowered plastic spiders onto the heads of people walking into a youth hostel, and stuffed a twig into my brother's bed as revenge for him telling on me. All this is the humour of indignity, meted out through defiling. The reason for it in the book is that the posh developers have turned up and the house is in what we might call today a 'regeneration zone'. It's not that the wee itself is funny but that it is wee talking to power. So, when people say things like, 'O children love wee and poo jokes,' or something more disparaging like, 'O there's no need to sink to that level,' they miss the point. Context is all.

Wee itself has symbolic power. Our modern existence revolves around putting wee in the right place and if you put it in the wrong place this arouses condemnation and the consequence of condemnation is shame. So loose wee, wee on the run, wee escaping, wee leaking is a carrier of shame. At the heart of a good deal of comedy is anxiety. Will I receive condemnation, will I experience shame if I am found out, if I reveal what's worrying me, if I leak? If I am relieved of that anxiety, if the focus of my anxiety is taken out of the context of shame and put into, let's say, the context of defiling the powerful, then this seems to become funny. I am relieved of the anxiety. In this particular book, there is not only the power of the developer and his team of workers pulling down ordinary people's houses; there is also the power of that empty, abstract, educational text which too is in its own way defiled by the potty-emptying.

About this time, or perhaps a little later, a book given to me by a friend of my parents, and read to me by my mother, was called *The Amazing Pranks of Master Till Eulenspiegel*, retold by L. Gombrich, with figures, scenes and drawings by E. Katzer, photographed in colour by The Adprint Studios, published by Max Parrish in 1948.

This was a selection of stories that were first written down in the early 1500s about a German trickster figure who comes from a poor peasant background. When he's a boy, he plays tricks on the adults from his village; when he goes to the towns and cities, he plays tricks on shopkeepers; and when he goes to palaces and universities, he plays tricks on princes, kings, bishops and even university professors. His name appears to mean 'owl glass' or the mirror which Till holds up to society to show its follies. However, in dialect, as '*Ul'n speghel*', it means 'Wipe your arse'.

The book I had has 46 stories; the first complete collection from 1515 has 95.

I can't tell you how much I loved this book. I thought it was the funniest, cleverest book that existed. The tricks, the repartee, the outrageousness of Till were burstingly funny to me, and after my mother read it to me I read it and re-read it many times over. I still have my copy. I've often wondered why and how it gave me such pleasure.

Let it be said that if I had known some of the original stories I would have found it even funnier. So, for example, after Till is caught trying to trick a wine-seller by secretly swapping a jug of water with the jug of wine, he is sentenced to be hanged and stands on the gallows ready for his sentence. He points out that there is a custom in this town – it's called Lübeck – that a convicted man can 'crave a last boon'. He's granted that wish, and in my book (that is, in the 1948 edition) Till Eulenspiegel's wish is that:

> You, the magistrates and aldermen of this noble city, together with my friends here, the hangman and his mate, shall hold vigil here with my dead body for three nights in succession from sunset to dawn.

And it turns out, says the text, that 'not one of the city worthies felt inclined to spend three nights in the open, under the gallows, in company with the hangman, to keep vigil for a felon and a thief.'

The magistrate tries to reason with Till and break the deal. But Till sticks to his guns, he demands that the favour is given. As they won't, and each gives his excuse – 'One was far too delicate to face a night in the open without running a grave risk to his health; one admitted that he was scared to death by the mere thought of it' – Till takes the noose off his neck, his hands are freed, he makes (I quote) a 'magnificent bow to the crowd', thanks them 'for having turned out in such great numbers' and off he goes.

As a child, once phrases like 'crave a boon' and 'hold vigil' were explained to me, I thought that this was a wonderful, clever, funny trick and I would read and re-read it with delight. Along with the other 45 or so tricks and snares in the book, this particular episode was of course a fine example of the little guy escaping the clutches of the powerful. One moment his life was in their hands. They had the power to hoist his living body up on a rope in front of the people of Lübeck till he was dead, and the next he was a free man. One moment his body was theirs, the next it was his again. And they were rendered undignified. They were humiliated in public. Looking back on it, it was as near to political humour as an eight-year-old might expect to understand. It had all the politics of the pay-off in Browning's *The Pied Piper* but with humour rather than pathos.

In the Oxford World's Classics translation of the 1515 earliest known complete edition of the tales, the equivalent passage reads thus:

> . . . Till said, 'You honourable gentlemen of Lübeck, as you've pledged your honour, I'll make my request of you. And this is it, that after I've been hanged, the wine-tapster [whom Till had tricked] come here every morning for three days – the bartender first and the skinner, who'll dig my grave, second – and that before they eat, they kiss me with their mouths on my arse.'
>
> Well, they vomited and said this was hardly a civilized request.
>
> Eulenspiegel said, 'I consider the esteemed Council of Lübeck honest enough to keep its word with me – that it has pledged me by their hands and sworn oaths.'
>
> They all went off to consult about this – with the result that, by permission and for other appropriate reasons, it was decided that they would let him go. Well, Eulenspiegel went on from there to Helmstädt, and was never again seen in Lübeck.

In another scene from the book that I read when I was a boy, Till pretends to a prince that he is a great painter, but when he comes to show his painting to the prince, we see that he has left the canvas empty. He tells the Prince that *fools* won't be able to see it, so of course the prince, not wanting to admit that he's a fool, pretends that he *can* see it. In the original, from 1515, the joke is that Till tells the prince that *illegitimate* people can't see the painting – a painting, Till says, that shows the Prince's glorious, royal past. Again, the Prince and everyone else wants to avoid being known, as the text puts it, as the 'son of a whore', so they pretend they *can* see it.

So, intriguingly, the book that I found so unbearably funny had done some cunning juggling, on the one hand snipping and clipping what at the time would have been thought inappropriate for children to read – the stuff to do with illegitimacy – in order to keep some elements of the subversive power-play humour going, with 'fool' being substituted for 'illegitimate'.

The whole history of what children's literature does with the re-tellings of anything from the Bible, the Greek myths and Shakespeare to the whole world of folk and fairy tales is represented by these two texts. And of course it's not a constant story, with the books children read changing even as society changes. In the version of the Till stories, known as *The Wicked Tricks of Till Owlyglass* by Michael Rosen, the ending of the hanging scene goes:

> I would like every judge, the Lord Mayor and all his aldermen to come every morning for three days to where I am lying dead and one by one, I would like each of them to kiss my bum three times before breakfast.

And again, they refuse and have to let him go.

In the painting story, my version has the prince boasting about his royal blood, but it isn't true. So I've made it that it's *liars* who can't see the picture, and of course the prince pretends that he isn't a liar and can see the picture displaying his royal forbears. This time, though, it is in a way true. The picture is blank because the royal forbears don't exist anyway.

In all three versions, the humour lies in the exposure of the hypocrisy and vanity of the rich and powerful. And Till, from a humble background, is the one who benefits: he makes off with a handsome fee for having supposedly done a great painting. It's only afterwards that the court admits that Till left the canvas bare and that they have been done.

In 1933, Norman Hunter wrote a book called *The Incredible Adventures of Professor Branestawm*, illustrated by W. Heath Robinson. Puffin Books published it in 1946 and *how* I read it was as important as the book itself.

I shared a bedroom with my brother who is four years older than me, and something in his personality meant that he felt that it was his duty and his pleasure to educate and entertain me. On the one hand this meant teaching me to read and, when I was older, teaching me such things as calculus and modulation in Beethoven's symphonies. On the other hand, it meant putting on shows, doing imitations of our father and reading out loud anything and everything he found funny. So Professor Branestawm came to me as a piece of shared fun, something that made me and him tick. I'll say in passing that traditional criticism – and, in the context of exams, the kind of criticism often used to judge children by – starts and finishes with the book or the text. The meaning of books is supposedly in the text and the job of the critic or the exam candidate is to extract that meaning. It's not the meaning for that candidate or critic in that moment, in that situation, in that time, in that place. Magically, we critics and exam candidates are supposed to be able to leave our moments and places and situations behind and find an absolute or essential meaning that is outside and beyond the specific moments or our specific selves. It's not the 'meaning for me', it's The Meaning, the One True Meaning. One of the reasons why I'm standing here today, I confess, is that I got to be quite good at saying that I knew what this One True Meaning is, especially in exams. I suspect the same also goes for anyone who has ever set an exam, marked one, or perhaps sat in the Department for Education and sent out a directive requiring children and students to do more of the same.

Now the meaning I make in my situation may well overlap with the meaning you make in yours – that's why exams and a lot of criticism can get away with saying that the meaning in my situation is the One True Meaning. I want to talk about Professor Branestawm in the particular context of my situation.

So, with Professor Branestawm, yes, there may well be all kinds of fun and meaning that I share with *some* or even *many* other people, but in truth the starting point for me has to be a bedroom upstairs in a flat in Pinner, Middlesex, with two parents who are teachers, who have no idea why they are living in Pinner, Middlesex, because, apart from anything else, they are probably the only Communists, probably the only Jews and definitely the only Jewish Communists living in Pinner, Middlesex in 1950. One of their refrains was, 'Why are we here?' As a child, you can't answer that question.

Our flat was my home but to anyone from Pinner, Middlesex who came into it, it was a bit suspect: it was mysteriously full of books, the walls were strangely covered in reproductions of the paintings of Pieter Brueghel the Elder, the tables were littered with dangerous newspapers and magazines.

Something was going on in that home to do with knowledge. It was important, very important, but also up for questioning. It appeared as if anything that anyone said, broadcast or wrote could be challenged. My parents shouted at the radio, using Yiddish, French or German words. '*Kvatch*,' my father would say, 'What about Oswald Mosley?' my mother would say. At the same time, they breathed a reverence for knowing stuff, for figuring things out, for getting to the bottom of things. Their explicit maxim was, 'Be curious.' The non-explicit message that they passed on was, 'Feel entitled to go anywhere, find out anything. Never think that you are someone who is not entitled to know that, see this, watch that, read this, get to understand that; whether it be *Hamlet*, the origin of the species, a folk song or a joke, it's yours if you want it.'

So, around 1954, my brother is reading to me chapter 4 of *The Incredible Adventures of Professor Branestawm* – 'Burglars!'

Branestawm has a housekeeper. At the time I had no idea what a housekeeper was; I had no idea what class and gendered information is wrapped up in that one word.

> 'Mrs Flittersnoop,' says Branestawm, looking at her through his near-sighted glasses and holding the other four pairs two in each hand, 'put your things on and come to the pictures with me. There is a very instructive film on this evening; all about the home life of the Brussels sprout.'

On the one hand this was nothing like our family set-up; on the other hand in that sentence, 'There is a very instructive film on this evening; all about the home life of the Brussels sprout', there *was* something of all of us. My mother taking us for walks, telling us that she was collecting specimens for the nature table at school, my brother teaching me Boyle's Law while I was still at primary school, and my father looking up from a book he's reading to tell us that the naturalist Konrad Lorenz hovering over a nest full of hatching goose eggs led to the goslings following him for ever more.

The joke of the cranky, obsessed, life-ignoring professor was in part a joke on us.

While Branestawm and Mrs Flittersnoop are at the pictures, they are burgled. So Branestawm says that he's going to invent a burglar-catcher. Mrs Flittersnoop thinks they should tell a policeman. While she talks to the copper, Branestawm goes to his shed.

> [The burglars] couldn't . . . take any of the Professor's inventing tools, because the door was fastened with a special Professor lock that

didn't open with a key at all but only when you squeezed some tooth-paste into it and then blew through the keyhole.

Again this was instantly recognisable. My parents thought that one of their duties was to take us on long, cold, rainy camping holidays with gear that was improvised and lashed up with rope, tape and something called 'webbing'. Actually these camping holidays were more than a duty. There was something ideological about it; part of being Communists was that we should go camping. I don't remember the bit in *Das Kapital* where Marx says that families should go camping, but it must be there somewhere.

Anyway, 'toothpaste in a lock to make it work' sounded in its own way like a mickey-take of our parents.

Branestawm invents a 'burglar-catching machine' and Heath Robinson drew it with all the bits of piping, brackets, knotted string, re-cycled bellows, brollies and hooks that he is famous for. We loved following the logic of these pictures, absurdly right and wrong at the same time. The 1950s were full of people who bodged and diddled and impro'd with junk. When an old thing broke, like a teapot or a table lamp, my father would sigh with a regret that floated up from an impoverished childhood in the East End or from the *shtetls* of Poland. Heath Robinson speaks to many people in different ways.

Having tested the burglar-catching machine with a pillow, Branestawm goes to the pictures again, because 'he'd missed bits of it before'. Strangely, Mrs Flittersnoop finds that he doesn't come home.

'Forgotten where he lives, I'll be bound,' she said.

She's just about to fetch a policeman when

'Brrrrring' went the Professor's burglar-catching machine.
'There now,' cried Mrs Flittersnoop. 'A burglar and all. And just when the professor isn't here to see his machine thing catch him. Tut, tut.'
She picked up the rolling-pin and ran down into the cellar. Yes, it was a burglar all right.

Now, it turns out that the burglar is so trussed up with 'straps and tapes' that it's not possible to see any of him.

'Ha,' cried the Housekeeper, 'I'll teach you to burgle that I will,' but she didn't teach him that at all. She hit him on the head with the rolling-pin, just to make quite sure he shouldn't get away.

Then she goes to fetch the police. The policeman puts the burglar head first into a wheelbarrow, still trussed up.

And, mysteriously for Mrs Flittersnoop, the professor still didn't come home.

Meanwhile, the burglar, still trussed up, is taken to court.

The court usher called out 'Ush,' and everybody 'ushed.

[I read the rest of the scene, which is in copyright.]

As I said, I was surrounded at home by people who knew loads, wanted to know more, challenged everything, took the mickey out of a lot of things including each other, and regarded authority as something which at the very most had to justify itself, but which for most of the time was not legitimate.

That's where, if you like, that scene landed when it turned up in our bedroom. That was its 'reading situation'. And the result was an explosion. A repeated explosion. It became one of my brother's turns, along with many, many, many readings of a book not usually thought of as children's literature, *Down with Skool* by Geoffrey Willans, with pictures by Ronald Searle.

So, what should we make of Branestawm in my personal history of children's literature?

I think Branestawm is a kind of anti-matter. He is on the one hand an inheritor of the spirit of Loki, the Norse God of fire, who is capable of making and destroying. He can create something in order to safeguard life but what he makes can take life away – even his own. After all, that trussed-up figure, described at one point as a 'mummy', is an image of death. Then, the court, because it has to follow its procedures, is unable to interpret the very thing we as readers *can* comprehend, so the procedures, which are supposed to secure justice and light, turn out to be self-destructive. They give and they take away.

At one level, this ought to be troubling. It's a scene which in the first half implies the destruction of self and in the second the destruction of society. And yet my brother and I found it hysterically funny. I think that's because it's about authority. We read that book before the 1960s. The '60s probably mark a time of many changes but one of the most important of those changes concerns authority. Again and again in the 1960s, somebody or some event questioned whether the way things were set up was right and correct simply because that's the way things were. To take one example that may seem trivial but which also joins up in a way with children's literature: to my mind the Beatles' act in itself was not particularly subversive or questioning. If anything, Elvis or Little Richard some eight years earlier had stirred the waters more than the Beatles did in terms of how and what they performed and to whom. No, it was the Beatles' interviews on TV that were out of the ordinary. They didn't obey the rules of waiting for questioners to finish their questions, they interrupted each other, they answered things in ways that made the question seem banal. Rather than looking as if they were being questioned, they looked and sounded as if they were having a laugh and someone rather dull – the interviewer – was trying to interrupt them. Sometimes they glanced at each other as if to say, 'Who is this plonker?'

Apart from Spike Milligan going off on one on his own, I don't think anyone had ever done this sort of thing before.

This watershed – and all the other authority-challenging moments and events of the '60s – came after us reading Branestawm. So, Branestawm in that pre-'60s moment, in that pre-'60s place, felt risky, breath-catching, dangerously absurd. Perhaps I had a sense that it created cracks in the edifice of order. It wasn't as naughty or as mischievous as the Beatles' interviews felt a few years later. But in the first half of this Branestawm chapter it felt ridiculous that a clever man – like our father perhaps, like teachers at school, or someone like A.J.P. Taylor on the TV, say – could be so wrong; and the second half of the scene said that the people above that, the judges, MPs, prime ministers, could talk complete rubbish even as they thought they made sense to themselves.

Perhaps there was something Oedipal about all this, knocking down the patriarchal figures who, according to this theory, sat in our minds, policing and governing our thoughts and feelings. So, to erode the power of these figures, represented by a professor and a judge, to destroy it even, gave us a great release. And in turn, we might say, that sense of release can be traced back to the old rivalry for the love and affection of Mrs Flittersnoop, who we might think of, perhaps, as the displaced figure of our mother, who, thankfully, we may have thought, regards Branestawm as a bit of a dead loss, especially as he symbolically emasculates himself.

But the origin of that patriarchal power lies where? Purely or only in the tiny network of mums, dads and sons? I don't buy that. Or does that kind of power derive its energy from structures of ownership and control in society as a whole? Which, by the time I was eight or nine and my brother was twelve or thirteen, we were getting more than an inkling of who had it and what they did with it. So, were Branestawm and the judge perhaps not only transformations of the father-figures we knew, but also of the versions of people paraded in front of us in the 1950s as infallible saviours, like Winston Churchill? Or the people they called 'captains of industry'?

So, I've looked at *Mischief the Squirrel*, *The Building of London*, *Till Eulenspiegel* and *Professor Branestawm*. One way to look at all this is to think of funny moments and funny books as being quite serious. It's not so much that they raise serious matters, but that the underlying causes of the laughter are serious.

Because not an enormous amount of attention has been paid to it, a good deal of this is unexplored territory. As I mentioned at the beginning, there are the other two dimensions to look at: the history of funny books for children as a whole, stretching from now all the way back to the popular street literature of the seventeenth century; and what's going on in the world of funny books for children today. I'll leave these two dimensions for another time.

I'll finish with an irony.

Millions of pounds have been spent by the government on subsidising schools to buy what they say are the right kinds of reading schemes. Schools have spent millions of pounds buying these schemes. Millions more pounds have been spent creating and running what they call the Phonics Screening Check, given to children towards the end of Year 1. Millions more are spent testing children with the Spelling, Punctuation and Grammar Test at the end of Year 6. There is no evidence in existence anywhere to suggest that any of this helps children to understand what they're reading or to help children write in more interesting or informative ways.

Many, many people, myself included, have been to see ministers and advisers, mostly because we've been summoned – and we have said that for children to understand what they're reading and for them to be interested in writing, they need to be surrounded with books and writing which they want to read, are given the chance to choose what they want to read, and are given time to talk about what they're reading. While we have been saying this, libraries have been closing, there is no statutory requirement for schools to have a library, and it is not easy for many schools, struggling to keep up with the requirements of the curriculum, the requirements of the testing regime and the anxiety about league tables and Ofsted inspections, to link literacy to the pleasurable activity of 'reading what you want to read'. It is much easier, and more obvious for some schools, to link literacy to worksheets, online imitations of worksheets and exercises made up of imitations of whatever the tests ask for. This is what I would call 'literacy-in-doing-tests', not literacy.

I'm inclined to put this situation into the context of a mix of Puritanism (or Calvinism if you prefer) and the morphing of the concept of education into a servant of business. A form of Puritanism or Calvinism delivers suspicion of pleasure, it delivers work as a virtue in itself – no matter how pointless or mind-numbing it might be – and it delivers the idea that we should accept our lot in life no matter how hard-up, bored, oppressed and exploited we might be. An exam-driven curriculum does this kind of Calvinism very well. If you are part of the majority who don't get the top marks, but you are told that everyone can succeed, then surely you have only your self to blame. You've no right to complain. Job done.

Meanwhile, education has become tied to ideas about international economic competitiveness or, more simply, tied to what employers ask for. But hang on, international competitiveness relies mostly on paying employees as little as they can whilst making sure that those employers can avoid paying taxes as much as they can. And employers may well say that school leavers aren't good enough. But then they've been saying that school leavers aren't good enough for a hundred years. If Pfizer takes over Astra Zeneca and thousands of people are laid off, or when Barclays announces that they are laying off thousands, it won't be because the employees aren't good enough. What business needs at the moment of lay-offs is not what they *say* they need: that every school leaver should be highly skilled. What business needs at that moment is that people should leave quietly. What business needs at that moment is for people to blame themselves for not being good enough.

A school system that turned out a whole population (and not just a minority) who read 'widely and often' would be informed and critical. One of the great spurs to reading widely and often is amusement and entertainment. As I've tried to show, amusement and entertainment are serious matters. As I hope I've shown, humour is often critical of power.

Call me paranoid, but I suspect that the ultimate reason why reading for pleasure is kept at arm's length by the authorities, and why comics and comedy in children's books are treated by the authorities as trivial, is because quite often they are a threat to those authorities.

Reader and Response: a Classroom View

I wrote this as a chapter for The Bloomsbury Handbook of Reading Perspectives and Practices (2020), *edited by Bethan Marshall, Jackie Manuel and Donna L. Pasternak.*

I came across a booklet that had been produced by some hard-working and conscientious teachers. It was intended for KS3 students working on *Oliver Twist*. It had the heading, 'Assessment Preparation Booklet', for students writing an essay with the title: 'How does Dickens create tension and a sense of horror in the scenes showing the death of Nancy?'

We might ask ourselves at this point, 'Why is this a question to put in front of KS3 students?' I think it would be fair to say that we ask students these questions because the study of English literature is in theory about helping students understand that literature has structure, methods and approaches which, we say, produce 'effects'. In fact, there is no agreed matrix as to how literature does this. The last people to produce a matrix were the ancient Greeks, who worked off a system of 'rhetoric' or 'rhetorical devices' which were learned by writers and politicians in order to achieve these effects. More pragmatically or empirically, we might ask, 'How do we know that a given approach in a piece of literature does produce a given effect?' Ultimately, the only way we know that is to investigate how readers read. However, readers themselves know something of how they read, and if they speak or write honestly they can record this in a variety of ways. Alternatively they can offer 'interpretations' of literature using other art forms: painting, music, dance, film, video and the like. This 'interpretive' mode of responding to literature once had high status. We only have to visit a Great House or Palace, stuffed full of grand paintings of classical scenes, to see how high that status once was. In education, it has very low status. Within secondary-school English studies, there are no marks for writing a piece of music, performing a dance or painting a painting in response to a Wilfred Owen poem.

In other words, this question is based on a rather narrow assumption that certain ways of writing produce 'tension' or 'horror'. All we can say is that they may or may not, depending on the person reading, the social situation of their reading, the background of that reader and the time that reader is living through.

We might possibly deduce that an author used certain structures or devices in the hope that they would produce these effects. That is a reasonable suggestion because writing is of course 'conventional' in the sense that it is full of conventions that writers borrow from each other. In that sense, we are back with the ancient Greeks and the study of rhetoric. However, as I've said, no matter what examiners say, we shouldn't really fool ourselves with their equations: 'this piece of rhetoric produces such-and-such an effect'.

The booklet is divided into sections:

'Assessment Objectives (what you will be assessed on)' – this tells the student to, e.g., 'write in formal, academic style', 'select and interpret evidence', 'analyse how language and structure are used by writers to create meaning', 'use specific terminology (e.g. adjectives, powerful verbs, metaphor, symbolism, short utterances, etc.)'.

The next section, 'Submission and Presentation Information', has some 'Dos and Don'ts', e.g. 'Do use a detached, impersonal and formal voice' or 'Don't comma splice', 'Do use connectives'.

The following section is: 'Reviewing Language Features' and these include 'adverb', 'symbol', 'lexical field' and 'listing'.

The section 'Annotating Nancy's Death' asks the students to annotate the chapter (which is given in the booklet) by 'identify[ing] any language features/techniques being used', and directs the student to use words like 'implies', 'indicates', 'suggests', 'reflects', 'emphasises' and 'signifies'.

Finally, there are two sections on how to write the essay itself: 'Essay Introduction' and 'The Body of Your Essay, PEC Paragraphs'. The author of the booklet has given the student here four points which are in effect summaries of what was Dickens's intention in writing the scene, and the student will rank them in order of what the student most agrees with. This will help the student write a 'thesis statement' for the final sentence(s) of the introduction. The 'Body of Your Essay' section gives advice on how to write PEC paragraphs and final tips like 'try to meet all the success criteria'.

All this is great on organisation. It helps the KS3 student, I would say, in the strange new world of the academic essay. If the questions in a student's mind are 'What do I write about?' and 'How do I write about this stuff?', this booklet provides answers. That, I guess, could be the end of the matter. We might say that the booklet leads the students to learn how to present 'knowledge about' the text.

However, if we come back to the matter of 'effects', we meet a problem. I'll put it this way. 'What is the purpose of literature?' It is indeed to create 'effects'. Using a related word, writers use literature in order to 'affect' readers. I summarise this by saying that literature has at its core 'ideas and feelings intertwined with each other and attached to beings (human or otherwise) that we come to care about'.

This raises questions like: what ideas? what feelings? how do we come to care about the 'beings'? Following from these, we might ask, 'How do these feelings and ideas change as we read the piece of literature? Why or how do we think these changes came about?'

These questions are nothing like the questions in this booklet. This leaves me asking why or how it comes about that we can create a system of work about literature which to my mind doesn't engage the reader with what I am claiming to be its prime purpose: how the reader is affected by the text.

The text in question is the death of Nancy. If you're not familiar with it, do please take a moment away from reading this article and look at it on-line. It's chapter 47: 'Fatal Consequences'.

I can't speak for others, but the big moment in the scene for me is the exact moment of the murder. At the moment she realises that Bill is going to threaten her, we see her 'clinging to him'. Then, when Nancy conjures up a scene of Bill and her going away together to lead better lives in 'solitude and peace', we see her 'striving to lay her head upon his breast'. Horrifically, we see Bill turning his pistol round and starting to 'beat it with all the force he could summon on the upturned face that almost touched his own'.

I have no idea what Dickens's 'intention' is here, though with excavation into some historical context on the contemporary presentation of prostitutes, London, the 'criminal class', I might hazard some informed guesses. But, according to the booklet, this would seem to be more like KS4 or A-level work. What I can do, then, is investigate how I feel about this scene. I can ask of myself not so much, 'How is the horror created?' but rather, 'What horrifies me? Why am I horrified? What other analogous things horrify me whether in real life or in other stories, films, or any other art form?'

If we want a name for this, we can call it the 'primary response'. I am asking for an investigation of what it is that affects me and why. When I ask these questions of what I have already selected from the chapter as a whole, I come up with a horror of the fact that Nancy is 'clinging' to Bill even as he is killing her. She isn't protecting herself or trying to run away. There is, then, for me, a terrible contradiction, or lethal mix, of close, intimate contact of bodies in what we think of as love or sex for one partner in this moment at the very second the other partner is beating her with the pistol and murdering her. What does it remind me of? The death of Desdemona in *Othello*. Note: I'm not claiming that this is where Dickens got it from! This is an 'intertextual' point in my mind, released by asking myself, 'What does this remind me of?' I also have a vague sense of something religious, some kind of inverted *Pietà* with Mary holding the body of Christ. Perhaps it's the air of love at the moment of death. Again, that is just in my mind . . .

My point then is that on letting in my primary response to this chapter I find my attention drawn to something that the whole apparatus of the booklet doesn't reach: the horror of that moment, the love-in-death grapple. Again, we might perhaps surmise that Dickens is 'implying' that amongst such depraved people there are good, kind, loving moments; or that it's the conditions of their existence that have created such bestiality. Perhaps? Nancy is used as a narrator within the main narration (through her speech) to conjure up a better world somewhere else. This tells us perhaps that Dickens is telling us that people in these conditions do have hope, do wish things could be better.

I would suggest, though, that it's very difficult to come to this conclusion in any kind of authentic way that matters to me as a reader. The only authentic way, for me, is through investigating how it is I am affected by the scene.

What I am not suggesting, though, is that the organised and detailed work that is in the booklet is pointless or useless – far from it. My main view is that whatever its virtues, these should come after the investigation of readers' primary responses. It is through these primary responses that we come to see how we are really 'affected' by the structures, language and techniques in the writing. Or not. I think this primary response engages more authentically with writers' purposes than the apparatus of the booklet does when carried out without engagement with that primary response.

My 'Secret Strings' Game to Unlock 'Texts' (Stories, Poems, Plays, Non-fiction, etc.)

I wrote this on my blog on 28 April 2021.

You tell the children/students that they are going to be poem or story 'detectives' and their job is to find the 'secret strings' in a poem or story – or play or any 'text'.

Secret strings run within texts linking words, phrases, sentences and pictures or 'images'. The students' job is to find them.

Sometimes the link is to do with sound – e.g. alliteration, assonance, rhythm, rhyme, repetition, long phrases, short phrases.

Sometimes the link is to do with images – similar, contrasting.

Sometimes the links are to do with repeated actions or 'motifs' or themes.

Sometimes it's different words with a similar theme – 'lexical field', as it's called.

Anything links to anything else if you can prove it.

Authors quite often don't know the secret strings that they themselves have created.

The longer you play the game, the more you find out about how a text is put together.

The longer you play the game, the more you start to come up with thoughts about what the text means and why it's been put together in a particular way.

Here's one example of 'motif'. In *Where the Wild Things Are* Max says he'll eat his mother up. His mother sends him to bed without having anything to eat. The Wild Things say they'll eat him up. When Max gets home, there's something for him to eat. Secret strings. If we ask what is the symbolic meaning of 'eating', we might say, 'Gratification? Pleasure?' Then the secret strings tell us a little story about forbidden, withheld and granted pleasure . . .

Then there are the secret strings between texts – called 'intertextuality'. You can apply the same method – echoes, allusions, shared themes, shared imagery, shared archetypes, shared plot lines, shared genres . . . these are all the play of secret strings between texts. Looking for them, finding them, talking about them is a great way to discover how texts are structured, helping us to find out how themes and ideas are given to us.

You can play these games by actually drawing on texts (if that's allowed!).

I've seen children sitting on the floor with a poem copied in large format onto a sheet of sugar paper with huge margins all round. The children had different coloured felt-tips and drew loops round the items they were linking and lines for the 'secret strings'. Using different colours for different reasons for the link is fun.

How We Read: Reading Processes

I put this piece on my blog on 7 September 2021.

There have been many attempts to describe the things we do as we read. See for example the 'matrix' on pp. 360-361 in *Understanding Teenagers' Reading: Reading Processes and the Teaching of Literature* by Jack Thomson, published in 1987 by the Australian Association for the Teaching of English.

I've had several goes at it on this blog.

Here's my own quick summary of these processes, in particular for reference for teachers attending courses that I've been speaking on. I expand on this in the talks.

1. We use our life's experience in order to understand what the language, images, characters, scenes mean. This will always be full of matters to do with our identity, self-image, social position, our sexuality, our sense of self, our sense of what cultures we are part of.

2. We use our experience of other texts ('intertextuality') to understand the text we are reading: its language, themes, plot lines etc. ('Texts' = anything written but also can include e.g. songs, films, musicals etc.)

3. We use our empathy, sympathy, antipathy as regards characters, their actions and thoughts, i.e. how our emotions 'flow' towards or against characters and scenes.

4. We identify with characters, we think about what we would do in those situations. We 'go with' them on their journeys, adventures, with their problems. We might want to 'be' them. Or very much not want to 'be' them.

5. We make judgements about what's going on – whether things are fair, or unfair, right/wrong, OK/not OK ('evaluation').

6. We figure out 'causation' – why or how things are happening in a particular way. The key word is 'because'.

7. We are affected by the 'music' of the language ('prosody').

8. We experience 'emotional flow' – feelings of tension, release, anger towards characters, envy, hopes etc.

9. We have a sense that the text expresses ideas, messages, 'ideology'.

10. We have contextual thoughts about e.g. the period or place of the story from our knowledge from e.g. history or real life.

11. We become aware of the text's structure, e.g. that it's like another text in the way that it unfolds, or the 'genre' of the text, e.g. sci-fi, biography etc. Or a text's 'motifs', e.g. sibling rivalry, or 'loss'.

12. We become aware of how the text's language is structured, e.g. what kind of sentences it has, whether it's figurative or not, whether it uses some or a lot of dialogue, what its grammar is like, how the grammar changes.

13. We notice how the story is narrated (e.g. first person/third person?), reliable/unreliable narrator.

14. We become aware of the text's 'time frames' (e.g. flashbacks, flash-forwards?).

15. We become aware of whose 'point of view' we view through. This will change as the text unfolds.

16. We become aware of how the tension is being created – often through 'reveal-conceal'.

17. We speculate about what might happen next.

18. We make predictions about what might happen next or later.

19. We are surprised if our predictions are wrong or not quite right.

20. We 'harvest' what we have read. This is 'intratextual' reference.

21. We puzzle. Why is this happening? What does this mean?

22. We speculate about 'authorship' – why did the writer write this or that?

23. If we think that we have an 'unconscious' (see psychoanalysis), it will come to play in how we read. E.g. feelings and thoughts we have repressed might be 'given voice' by our reading of the text. Similarly, our wishes, fantasies, e.g. yearnings, desires, wishes for domination etc., might be 'realised' by our reading of the text. As might the classic Freudian processes of transference, displacement, condensation, cathexis (i.e. obsessive preoccupation) and projection.

The thinking here is that the reader can behave when reading as if they are encountering people in real life. To take each of these in turn:

Transference: this involves transferring feelings that one has for e.g. your father to a character in a book. So we might 'read' e.g. a male, patriarchal figure as if he is 'my' father.

Displacement: perhaps a story might confront us with a person or situation which we can't tolerate or which makes us feel uncomfortable. We might 'displace' our discomfort onto another scene or character.

Condensation: we might discover that the reason why we have feelings for a character or a scene is because we pour feelings from other situations into or onto this one. (A good deal of popular music works this way.)

Cathexis: an obsessive reaction towards a character based (according to Freud) on one's libido.

Projection: where we project feelings we have onto a character. We might say, for example, 'I know what she wants to do now . . . ' when in fact that's what 'I' would do. Arguably, this is one of the main 'motors' of response through 'identification'.

(There's also a view in psychoanalysis that texts – stories and myths in particular – can 'contain' our feelings, in particular ones that give us suffering or uncontrollable anger. Stories give us a safe space in which we can experiment with our feelings in situations which we don't have to live or re-live. We might have some sense of this as we read, along the lines of 'this is like me'.)

24. Awareness of the way the text has symbols, how what we're reading 'represents' something else outside of the text, 'bigger' than the text, bigger than a particular image, motif etc.

25. Awareness of how there are patterns, repetitions in the text in terms of language, repeated images, repeated plot lines, motifs, characters' actions.

26. Fiona Maine suggests adding 'immersion in story-worlds'. As we read, we go into the whole world of a story, which we can inhabit by building on the given details adding in e.g. sensations that are not there – smells, tastes, sights etc. Another way of talking about this is that every text invites us to 'play the game' in a particular way, e.g. rom-com or tragedy, fairy tale or epic. Or again, it might be what Bill Corcoran calls 'picturing'. That is, where the reader can translate what they read into images. Many readers can or will say what a character or scene 'looks like' even if the writer hasn't described that person or place.

27. So, 26 is in part about genre. We become aware that what we are reading belongs to a genre. We might implicitly or explicitly say to ourselves, 'I am reading a fairy story,' or 'I am reading a narrative poem,' or 'This is a rap,' and so on. We are positioning the text in relation to texts it is 'like' or 'unlike'. M.A.K. Halliday says that language-choice is in part determined by genre. It flows from this that our reading of language would be similarly affected by a sense of genre.

28. Fiona Maine also adds 'dialogic interaction'. There's a way in which as we read we are in effect having a conversation with the text: asking it questions, trying to answer questions that are often posed by texts, as in e.g. 'I didn't know what to do next . . . ' The reader might (in their mind) start thinking up possible scenarios of what the character could do or should do.

29. Texts work hard to make us feel we are there. We could call it the writer's 'being-there work'. The texts often run through some or all of the senses when describing scenes, people etc. They tell us what things look, sound, smell, taste or feel like to touch. As we read we might just absorb these. (Which is part of the reading process itself.) We might also 'notice' these more consciously, and think to ourselves, 'He had curly hair,' or some such.

30. Resistant reading, i.e. refusing to accept what appears to be the bias/message/ideology of the text. This may well be very important when thinking about old texts in relation to modern ideas (e.g. Shylock, Othello etc.). Also resistance in the Freudian sense of resisting empathy or recognition of tropes for reasons of repression. Or indeed to refuse to read the text! (I can remember my three-year-old throwing a book away because it was too scary.)

31. What about wish-fulfilment? Stories are full of living out what we might want to happen to us. A fantasy in which we are given a part, through reading? Perhaps we read with this kind of hope and/or satisfaction . . . 'This could be me . . . with this kind of power to . . . e.g. attract others, beat others, overcome others, achieve this or that, etc.'

32. What about the opposite of wish-fulfilment? Fear-fulfilment or shame-fulfilment? We read with a fear for the characters that they will behave as we feel we are, or are ashamed we are? A kind of negative fantasy about ourselves. Or, 'I don't know what I would do in that situation.'

33. Reading 'motive' and 'intention': as we read, we are sometimes told what people (characters, protagonists) want to do and sometimes we are told why they want to do something. (This can be done with 'tags', e.g. 'she thought', 'he wondered' etc., or by versions of 'indirect discourse', e.g. 'what should she do next?', without the 'tag'.) And other ways. Sometimes, we aren't told and we have to guess, infer, interpret what people's motives are. We do this based on our experience of life (see above) and/or on our experience of texts ('intertextual' – see above) and our experience of 'genre' (see 26 and 27).

34. Dramatic irony: many texts create situations where the reader knows more than the character. (Famous one: *Romeo and Juliet,* e.g. where Juliet's father says that Juliet will marry Paris but we know that she is already married to Romeo and that she has spent the night with him.) We read this through 'harvesting' (see 20 above), i.e. 'intratextual' awareness. When people talk about 'heart-in-mouth' moments in fiction or films, these are sometimes caused by dramatic irony. Can also of course be created by 'jeopardy'/'peril' where we share the fear (usually) of the protagonist based on 'what would I do?/how would I feel?' in that situation of danger.

35. At this point, it's interesting to talk about 'distancing' and/or 'alienation effect'. This raises the question of who does the work, when reading. Author? Reader? Both? Distancing is the idea that writers can use various techniques which ask the reader or viewer to be more dispassionate about what's going on in the story – the opposite of 'identification', 'immersion', 'escapism', 'lost in the story' and Aristotle's idea of catharsis through immersion. Brecht tried to create dramas where the viewer 'came out' of the emotional involvement and considered the whys and wherefores of what the drama had just shown.

Methods he (and Brechtians since) used were e.g. an on-stage narrator, sudden juxtapositions, use of slogans and light boards with information, mixing of media, deliberate use of sets or lighting to make the drama 'non-realist'. Fiction can do similar things, e.g. multiple narration, mixing of fiction with use of headlines, non-realistic artwork, mixing of genres and so on. So some (e.g. John Stephens) have argued that this requires or creates 'sophisticated' reading, but Stephens sees the work being done here is by the text doing the distancing, i.e. distancing the reader. Another view would be that the reader perceives the text as e.g. being non-realistic through their intertextual awareness. If the alienation methods are accessible (e.g. a light board with information about how many soldiers were being killed during WWI in Joan Littlewood's production of *Oh What a Lovely War*) then it's the reader/viewer who does the work of relating the light-board information to the dramatic scene unfolding in front of it. Again, in the book *Dance on my Grave* by Aidan Chambers, there is the distancing effect of multiple narration where the main character both observes and is observed. The reader has to weigh up questions like 'What is real?', 'What is really going on?', 'Who is telling the truth?' If the reader does this work, then they are not immersed in the usual sense of the word. They are immersed in their minds in a debate about what is the truth here.

36. Reading picture books, comics, graphic novels: this clearly involves other ways of thinking and interpreting not mentioned so far. One thing that happens with this kind of reading is a 'relay' between picture and text. Our minds can synthesise the two in order to perform the processes above. Perhaps talking about 'the text' or 'the story' is wrong with graphic books. Perhaps we should say 'texts' and 'stories' going on simultaneously, intertwined with each other, commenting on each other. Even the word 'illustration' may be wrong. After all, the pictures don't really 'illustrate' the text. The reader is doing a lot of work to interpret the pictures and make them work with the text that they're reading (or, in the case of a young child, hearing). Does the one refer to the other, tell something different, if so how? The classic scholarly work on this 'two stories' view is Margaret Meek's *How Texts Teach What Readers Learn*. It's a masterpiece of exploration of how a child interprets *Rosie's Walk*, a fine example of two stories being told that the child will synthesise. I'll draw attention to another. Look at Max's bedroom in *Where the Wild Things Are*. What 'story' does it tell? Is it busy, friendly, full of loving care from adults? Or is it bare and lonesome? Or what? Does Max find the place 'where someone loved him best of all'? If so, where? If not, how do we know not? If maybe, why the doubt?

Who do Children's Authors Write for?

I wrote this article, about what a children's author needs to take into account when writing, for the Children's Writers' and Artists' Yearbook 2022.

People who can write for children don't come with a same-format personality or a made-to-measure range of skills. We aren't people who can be easily categorised or lumped together. In part, this is because the world of children's books is constantly changing, starting out from a very diverse base in the first place. This derives from the fact that the world children inhabit is changing, and indeed that there is a recognition within the children's books milieu that books are for everyone, not just one small section of the population.

In a way, this means that this is a great time to be writing or illustrating children's books. But that comes with a warning: diverse and changing, yes, but within a set of conventions (I won't say 'rules') and formats. Quite often, people who have written some stories or poems for children ask if I would take a look at them. Sometimes, the first problem that I can see with what they've written is that it doesn't 'fit in'. Or, another way of putting it, the writer hasn't taken a look at what's out there in the bookshops and schools and thought, 'How can I write something that could go alongside that book, or fit the same niche that that particular book occupies?'

But what about artistic freedom? What about the rights of the writer to write about anything? Two things in response to that: nothing can stop you writing about anything you want to, however you want to. But there's no point in kidding ourselves that writing is really 'free'. We all write with our 'reading heads' on. That's to say, we write with the words, sentences, pages, chapters, plots, characters, scenes of the books we've read. If you say to yourself, 'I want to write a novel,' or 'I want to write a picture-book text,' you're only doing so because your mind is full of novels or picture-book texts. They are the 'already written' or the 'already read' material we write with. This affects everything we write, right down to the shape and structure of what we write, the tone we hit in the passages we write, the kinds of dialogue and thoughts we put into the writing. A crude analogy here is cooking. We cook with the ingredients that we are given. But more: if we say we are going to make a cake, there is an understood outcome of what that will be (the cake), and an agreed set of ingredients that can arrive at that understood outcome. So, in a way, we not only cook with appropriate and given ingredients, we also cook with an understood outcome in mind. It has a shape, a smell and a taste that we expect the moment someone says, 'Here is a cake.' Our memory of past cakes prepares our mind and taste for what is to come. This set of memories of past writing and reading is what is in our mind as we write, and indeed in the minds of the child readers as they sit down to something they can see is a book. These are what are known as the 'intertexts' we read and write with – memories of past texts.

Secondly, I would say that if you're interested in being published, then you have to look very, very closely at what publishers publish. This means looking at books not only from the point of view of what they say and how they say it. It also means looking at what kind of book you have and inquiring whether there are other books like it. How would you categorise it? This line of questioning puts into your mind a sense of format, of shape, of outcome to guide you as you write. Another analogy: an architect who is asked to design a house knows that he or she has to create rooms that are high enough and large enough for people to live in, that there is a basic minimum of kitchen and bathroom, there is a door to get in and out of, and so on. If it fulfils these conditions, we will call it a house – and not a factory or a warehouse, say. It's a great help sometimes to look at books from an architect's point of view: what is particular to a book that makes it work? Ask yourself, 'How did the writer reveal what was coming next?' Or, 'How did the writer hold back and conceal what was coming next?' (Writing is a matter of revealing and concealing!) How did the writer arouse your interest? Was it an invitation to care about the people or creatures in the story? Or was it more to do with events or happenings? Or both? Did the book announce itself as being of a particular genre: thriller, historical fiction, comedy, etc.? How did it do that? What are the requirements of that genre? Or is it a hybrid?

If all this sounds too technical, let me introduce you to someone: the child. If you say to yourself, 'I'm going to write for children,' then even as you say this, you're putting an imagined child (or children) into your mind. This is what literary theorists call 'the implied reader'. We do this in several ways. There might be a real child we know. Robert Louis Stevenson wrote *Treasure Island* largely as part of his relationship with his stepson, Lloyd. But even though we might say, 'RLS wrote it for Lloyd,' this doesn't really explain things. What Stevenson was doing, possibly without knowing it, was keeping a mental map of Lloyd's speech and personality in his mind, so as he wrote he had his version of Lloyd in his head monitoring, guiding and censoring what he was writing.

There is no single way of importing the implied child reader into your head.

Some writers do it from memory, connecting with the child they once were and using that version of themselves to guide them in what they write and how they write it. They use memories of what they liked to read, how they themselves spoke and thought, and perhaps wrote, when they were a child. Others immerse themselves in the company of children – their own, their grandchildren, nephews and nieces or children in playgroups, nurseries or schools. And some do it by immersing themselves so thoroughly in children's books that they pick up the implied child reader from the actual books. And of course, it's possible to work in a combination of all of these ways. What I don't think you can do is ignore them all.

In fact, what you write can't avoid an implied reader. That may seem odd, because you might say that you had no one in mind when you wrote this or that. The reason you can't avoid it is because the language we use comes already loaded up with its audience. So, if I write, 'Capitalism is in crisis,' this is a phrase that implies an audience that first of all understands English, then understands the words 'capitalism', 'crisis' and the phrase 'in crisis'. But more than that, it's an audience that wants to read something like that and is, in a sense, hungry or prepared and sufficiently 'read' to want to read such a sentence – or, more importantly, to go on wanting to read what comes next. If I write, 'My dad was attacked by a banana . . . ' then I'm already positioning the reader to think about someone who is a child and that child is telling something a bit absurd or possibly funny, perhaps the beginning of a family anecdote or family saga. It's also a 'tease', in that a reader who 'gets it' will know that bananas don't attack anyone. It implies a reader who knows that. In other words, the 'implied reader' is 'inscribed' into what we write. In a way, these implied readers are stuck to the words, phrases, sentences, plots and characters we write.

This means that as we write – and when we go back over what we've written – we need to think about the implied reader we've put there. Who is the child who is going to 'get it'? Who is the child who won't? What kind of children are we talking to? What aspects of those implied children's minds and childhoods are we talking to? The fearful person in the child? The envious one? The yearning one? The lonely one? The greedy one? And so on.

A last thought: we talk of 'writing for children'. To tell the truth, I don't think we do just write for children. I think we write as a way for adults to join the conversations that adults have with adults, adults have with children, children have with children – on the subject of what it means to be a child and live your life as a child. Because it's literature, this conversation often comes in code, with ideas and feelings embodied in symbols (teddy bears, giants, etc.), it arouses expectations and hopes (what's coming next?), and because it's literature that children can and will read, it often comes along according to predictable outcomes (getting home, getting redeemed, being saved) that remove the obstacles to unhappiness and imperfection that the story began with, and so on. Nevertheless, children's literature has a magnificent history of saying important things to many people, often in a context where adults are caring for children. I think that's a good thing to attempt.

POETRY

How to Write a Poem and What Makes a Good Poem

In case you don't know, the Polka Theatre is a brilliant theatre for children in Wimbledon in south London, and (puff, puff) I'm a patron. As a result they asked me to write something for their brochure about poetry. Here it is.

People often ask me how to write a poem and what makes a good poem. The first way I answer is usually by not answering at all. Like this:

The best thing for anyone who wants to write poetry to do is to read a lot of it. What you need to do is get the hang of the way poetry works, the way it sounds, the way poets put thoughts, ideas and events together. Treat yourself, get yourself one anthology full of poems by different authors, and one collection of poems by a poet you like. Read these two books over and over again.

The second thing to do is get yourself a notebook. In this notebook, write down any words, phrases, sentences, snatches of language, notices, jokes, odd thoughts and sayings that strike you as interesting. Just keep collecting. Sometimes you may want to copy out part or all of a poem. Sometimes it might be something that your grandmother said, or that you overheard on the bus. Keep all of it. Sometimes you might think it's interesting how this or that word rhymes or nearly rhymes with another. Jot it down. Sometimes you might have a really odd thought, or you discover that if you re-arrange a well-known phrase something odd comes out. Jot it down. Other times you might discover that if you put two words or two phrases together that usually don't go together, something interesting happens – like 'scary' and 'tomato' or 'sleepy' and 'pencil'. Jot them down.

Other things to remember are:

It's a great idea to write when you feel like writing. Don't delay it. Don't put it off.

It's a good idea to show what you've written to people whose views you respect. Some people will be able to help you, others won't. You'll find out who these people are by yourself.

Poetry is a very wide-ranging field, full of many, many different ways of writing, full of very many different things that people have chosen to write about. Don't ever get yourself into the trap of thinking that poetry can only be one way of writing, or about one kind of subject. That simply isn't true. Let yourself be open to all kinds. Let yourself be surprised. Always be ready to try out different ways of writing, different subjects.

When you read poetry, see if you can spot how the poet has got you interested. Is that something you can do?

Here's the subject for a poem:

'What you see, isn't me.'

The Poetry-friendly Classroom

I regularly update this piece on my blog.

Now it so happens that teachers sometimes ask me, 'What's the best way to get children writing?' and one of the ways I answer is to suggest that the first thing to do is to create a 'poetry-friendly classroom'. In other words, you can't really talk about writing poems that matter unless you make a classroom a place where poems are welcome. I usually suggest in my workshops that there are many ways of doing this and I can suggest some, but it's usually a good idea if teachers and the whole school think of ways this can be done. Here are some I suggest:

1. Without any explanation or questions being asked of the children, just try writing out a poem that interests you onto a very large piece of paper and sticking it up on the wall. You could also put some post-its next to it, telling the children that they could write anything that they want to do with the poem on a post-it. This could be questions that they would like to ask anyone or anything that appears in the poem, or it could be a question that they would like to ask the poet. At a later stage, you could all sit round and look at these slips of paper and see whether people have answers to any of the questions, have anything to say in reply to anything on any of the post-its. They could pretend to be the poet in order to answer the questions directed at the poet. If there were questions that were factual, they could come up with ways of finding these out: e.g. when did the poet live?

2. If you read a poem to the children and start looking at it in class, see if you can restrict yourself to only asking the children questions that you, the teacher, don't know answers to. So, instead of saying, 'Count the adjectives,' or 'What kind of poem is this?' and the like, how about asking, 'Does this poem remind you of anything you've ever read before (or anything you've ever seen on TV or in a film)? Does anything in the poem remind you of anything that's ever happened to you? What kinds of things going on are similar and what kinds of things are different? As with the post-its, what kinds of questions would you like to ask of anyone or anything in the poem and/or of the poet? Is there anyone in the room who would like to have a go at answering these?' (It might help to act out an interview here as if, say, you were interviewing Humpty

Dumpty about how he felt about no one being able to put him together.) You could ask if anyone can see what I call 'secret strings'.

A secret string is anything that links one word or phrase to any other. As we know, the most common of these is rhyme, but there's also rhythm, sentence length, repetitions of sound, phrase, image, patterns of various kinds. Quite often, the more you look, the more you find.

3. Poetry Swap. This is a deal you can strike with children where you take it in turns to read poems: i.e. teacher reads one, a child reads one. That way you don't simply keep repeating the same kinds of poem. You could encourage anyone who reads to say why they chose the poem.

4. The Poetry Show. You divide the class up into threes and fours and each group chooses a book of poems and a poem from inside the book. Then in twenty minutes they choose a poem to present to the rest of the class. They can do this in any way they like so it could be reading the whole poem together, or it could be doing a mime and reading all or some of the poem. It could be taking a line or two and making up a song or a dance to it. It could be dividing the poem up into different voices, solo and chorus. It could be using musical instruments and percussion of some kind.

5. Poem Posters. The children could make poem posters, taking a poem and working out a way of turning it into a poster that could go up on the wall in the school for a while. The more often these change, children in the school get the idea that there are hundreds of poems and you don't have to stick with just a few.

6. Using other art forms. Poems are great ways to start work on other art forms: pottery, painting, dance, drama, music and film. They're great platforms for starting creative work in many different kinds of ways.

7. Notebooks. Encourage the children to keep a poetry notebook. Suggest that they can write down any words or phrases that strike them as odd, interesting, difficult, amazing, puzzling, scary, etc. If they have an idea for any interesting ways of saying things, jot them down. If they come across a phrase, a verse, a line from anything they've read anywhere – poetry, the newspaper, street sign, anything – jot it down. Write out poems or parts of poems in the notebook too. To help them, you can make a 'public' notebook that is up on

the wall in the classroom, where you can write things that you've noticed.

8. I'm sure anyone reading this could think of plenty of other ways of making poetry-friendly classrooms and schools. In this context, to talk about 'writing a poem' is completely different from the context of a non-poetry-friendly classroom where, let's say, you hope that by reading a single poem, or by using a 'trick' from one of the How To Write A Poem books, you can get children to write great poems. If you create a poetry-friendly atmosphere, what you do is build up a repertoire of poems in the children's heads. It's a resource they'll use without even knowing why or how.

Writing Poems

When it comes to writing poems, I suggest that one way to think of it is to ask how can we create a time in which the children can gather some thoughts and ideas that we can use to make poems. One way is to think that the resources we have at hand are the things we say or that other people say to us, the things we can see going on, the things we hear, the things we think, the things we feel, the things we are doing ourselves. There are many routes to tap into this: using photos, other poems, a title, a situation, a feeling, a memory, a story that I've been told, a moment or a scene in a play or a novel, a piece of music and so on. If we ask a question for each of these 'resources', as I've called them, then we can pool the answers. So, let's say we started from a situation like 'Breakfast Time at Home', and we ask: 'What can you see going on?' You can pool the answers on a big piece of paper and pin that up. Same again for each of the other 'resources': what are you and others saying, thinking, feeling, seeing going on, doing? So you end up with a series of big posters of all the things that people have come up with. This is a resource you can use to make poems, either class poems or individual ones.

You can show, either by doing it yourself, or by comparing what you're doing with poems that have already been written and published, that you can make poems out of each or several of these different 'resources'. So you could write a 'seeing' poem about breakfast. Or a 'saying' poem about breakfast. Or you could write a 'thinking and feeling' poem interrupted by 'hearing'. And so on.

There are also ways in which you can introduce patterns to what you're writing, through rhythm, repetition and chorus. If you've got a poetry-friendly classroom going then these are the 'secret strings' I've talked about that you've probably started to notice.

You can also talk about what I've called 'Impossible Writing'. You can show that you can write things that don't make sense but in a funny way they do. Take 'Hey diddle diddle'. A cow jumps over a moon. A dish runs away with the spoon. That's quite odd and is meant to be a bit funny, perhaps. But you can also do impossible writing about sad, scary or mysterious things. Like 'the bed started to eat me'. Or 'the sky bent down' or 'the lemon drove off'. This gives us another resource, another way of thinking that we can introduce into 'real' situations like breakfast, or as a way of writing in itself, say, about autumn, or the market or whatever. In a workshop I did with children where we looked at photos of the Lodz Ghetto, one child wrote ' . . . and the leaves called out my name.' Yes!

Using this range of words to describe writing – saying, seeing, hearing, thinking, feeling, and impossible writing – actually gives you very accessible ways of talking about poems that you read. You can spot how poets switch between these different senses.

What is a Bong Tree?

This is a lecture I gave at the Centre for Language in Primary Education in September 2007.

'Narrative poetry is poetry that tells a story. The most popular form of narrative poetry is probably the ballad, which you'll remember we looked at last week when we read "Lord Randal". Some narrative poems are long, some are short. Some very long narrative poems are made up of many shorter ones. Here is a narrative poem:

The Listeners
by Walter De La Mare

'Is there anybody there?' said the Traveller,
 Knocking on the moonlit door;
And his horse in the silence champed the grasses
 Of the forest's ferny floor:
And a bird flew up out of the turret,
 Above the Traveller's head:
And he smote upon the door again a second time;
 'Is there anybody there?' he said.
But no one descended to the Traveller;
 No head from the leaf-fringed sill
Leaned over and looked into his grey eyes,
 Where he stood perplexed and still.
But only a host of phantom listeners
 That dwelt in the lone house then
Stood listening in the quiet of the moonlight
 To that voice from the world of men:
Stood thronging the faint moonbeams on the dark stair,
 That goes down to the empty hall,
Hearkening in an air stirred and shaken
 By the lonely Traveller's call.
And he felt in his heart their strangeness,
 Their stillness answering his cry,
While his horse moved, cropping the dark turf,

'Neath the starred and leafy sky;
For he suddenly smote on the door, even
  Louder, and lifted his head:-
'Tell them I came, and no one answered,
  That I kept my word,' he said.
Never the least stir made the listeners,
  Though every word he spake
Fell echoing through the shadowiness of the still house
  From the one man left awake:
Ay, they heard his foot upon the stirrup,
  And the sound of iron on stone,
And how the silence surged softly backward,
  When the plunging hoofs were gone.

The first things I'd like you to do are:

1. Identify the poetic techniques in the poem

2. Do a syllabic count

3. Answer this question: Are there any similarities with the ballad poem we read last week?

Next I've got a couple of comprehension questions for you:

1. Who is the traveller?

2. Who are the listeners?

Then I want you to look at the structure of the poem – and answer these questions:

1. What happens in the poem?

2. Where does one section end and the next begin?

And finally I want you to:

1. Look at the words in the poem which describe sounds

2. Write down in which sections of the poem there are noises and in which there is silence.'

I'm sure that thinking about what I've just said has been particularly exciting and stimulating, so let's just take a step back and ask ourselves a different kind of question:

What have I just been doing? What's it for?

I began by telling you something about what is often called 'genre' – I'll come back to that in a moment; I've read you a poem that has been read in schools from at least as early as 1954, which is when it was first read to me in a state primary school in Pinner, Middlesex; and I've asked you a set of questions and cues for activity that have focused on:

what are called 'poetic techniques';
comparisons with another poem;
identifying who the protagonists are;
what is called the 'structure' of the poem;
words that describe what I presume are regarded by the anonymous questioner as essential or fundamentally important about the poem, namely 'noises' and 'silence'.

I used that phrase 'what are called' or 'what is called' several times just then, because I'd like to challenge some of the ideas that lie behind what's going on here.

First, the idea of 'genre' in poetry.

I'm not clear why anyone thinks that it's a good way to spend time and energy telling children that this or that poem could or should be clumped with another poem on the basis of some arbitrary category or other. Another way of raising this matter with children is, as some of you will be well aware, the one that goes:

'What type of text is it; how do we know?'

As that's a question that has been puzzling literary critics for several thousand years, I'm not sure why or how primary-school children are supposed to know, unless they come up with the answers that have been so over-simplified by the official education documents that they are probably fibs. You know the sort of thing: 'It's got rhythm and rhyme so it must be a poem.' Well, the explanations of rhyming slang have rhythm and rhyme: 'Your plates are your feet, plates of meat, feet.' But even a slack definer like me would probably say that isn't really a poem.

There are of course many problems with allotting categories or indeed with wanting to do it in the first place.

When we say that dogs are a different breed or species from cats, we have an important piece of material reality to back us up: neither in their behaviour nor in their chemistry are they able to combine sexually. They are, in part, defined by what they're not.

When it comes to literary or, more specifically, poetic genres, we have two kinds of chaos going on: the one that plucks a set of characteristics out of the world of poetry and deems these particular characteristics significant enough to become a category; and the one that says that once this category has been chosen, a poem that fits this set of characteristics belongs to this category and not another.

So, someone a long time ago thought that it was significant that a distinction be made between, say, narrative and lyric poetry, the one 'telling a story' and the other, supposedly, more 'personal'. However, take a quick glance across articles and books that like doing this sort of thing, and we find the business of genre expanded into a wonderfully disorderly, un-systematic range of categories. One moment the word is used to describe something to do with the form of a poem, as with the supposed 'genre' of 'prose poetry', the next with a poetic effect, such as 'satirical poetry'. It doesn't take long to figure out that a poem could be, say, a personal, satirical, narrative prose poem combining all these so-called genres in one. In fact, I've been trying to write such things for years. Where does one genre end and another begin? And if they really are categories, then just as you can't have in real life (though you can in stories, poems and jokes) a catty dog or a doggy cat, surely you shouldn't be able to have a mix of genres? Or is that OK in the world of literary genres that we keep trying to teach children about?

So, to make my position clear, I have nothing against people hanging on to their jobs, and if coming up with poetic genres and defending them against barbarians like me who say that it's a nonsense keeps them in work – fair enough. But telling children that it's important or useful to know that 'The Listeners' is a 'narrative poem' because . . . er . . . it's a 'narrative', then I say, no, I don't think so.

Of course, telling children this is very handy for the purposes of testing because, in the event of the question being asked in an exam, 'What genre of poem is this?' or 'What type of text is it; how do we know?', the examiner will have a check list, and the answer, 'A narrative poem', will be the only one to score. It's a markable factoid. This process enlists the reading of poetry into the power game of education which alludes to a mystical authority which lies outside, beyond and above the confines of classrooms and schools: an authority that knows that the category of 'narrative poetry' simply exists and must be learnt. Teachers become the janitors and schools the storehouses for this mystical, mostly unauthored knowledge, and they are required to pass it on in a mystical way, that is by stating things as definite and certain when they're not, by saying that processes or literary happenings are facts rather than leaving them open to investigation and discovery.

So, 'The Listeners' is a narrative poem and that's that.

Now to 'poetic techniques'.

Two processes are at work here: a false dualism and fetishism.

This is the problem: whatsoever we would like to express in poetry is expressed in words, or, if you prefer, in 'signifiers'. It is the selection and arrangement in a poem of these signifiers (or 'form' if you prefer) that readers will negotiate in order to make meaning. A reader reading a poem (or listening to it) cannot get at some kind of content outside of or beyond the poem in any way other than doing it through the signifiers. The way Yeats expressed it was to say that you cannot see the dance without the dancer. Yes, as Terry Eagleton points out, you can refer in an abstract way to a dance (the foxtrot, the jive) but you can't actually see it or do it without a body doing it. Yes, you can read or know material outside of a poem, and this material may or may not tell you, say, that the 'I' in 'Daffodils' refers to a person and that this person is William Wordsworth. (Though, of course, even this may not be true, as an alternative story tells us that the 'I' of 'Daffodils' refers to the consciousness of both William and his sister Dorothy, and it was she who gave him the idea that it was a 'cloud' that he might be 'wandering lonely as'. Things aren't always what they seem in poetry. The word 'I' can be as big an invention as the jabberwock.)

But I don't want to be overly dogmatic here. Just as we can talk about kinds of dance without seeing the dancer, we can talk about poetic techniques, because as humans we are quite capable of creating abstractions out of concrete situations. The question, though, is: does creating abstractions out of concrete situations do young children reading poems any favours, or is it, yet again, a means by which poems can be reduced to markable factoids, that get you gold stars or smiley faces for on the end of your worksheets?

But we do know that there's another agenda behind the 'poetic techniques' game, don't we? It's the one exercise that has dominated the teaching of literature for at least fifty years. This is the one that not only identifies the poetic techniques but also asks why they are 'effective'. Oh, what a big deal is wrapped up in this little word 'effective'. How many millions of children and students have sat in lessons and exams trying to figure out what is in a teacher's or an examiner's head as they write their paragraph on why this or that bit of alliteration or this or that metaphor is effective. Once again, the great mystical authority who stands in a land beyond the classroom is invoked: the authority who has at some point determined that this simile or that verse structure has been effective, and evermore shall be. And it has of course also determined that the very process of saying that it is effective is an important and useful activity too. There is an alternative notion: that to debate and discuss and re-enact how a piece of writing has affected you is perhaps a more significant activity. More of that anon.

Pause a moment, and let's hear it for 'the forest's ferny floor'.

Using my 1950s education, I can tell you that that is alliteration. Using my training in guessing what is in examiners' minds, I might suggest that it's effective because the letter 'f' is a soft sound and contributes mood and quiet to the moment of 'silence' that comes after the Traveller has just shouted. But of course we don't really know that it contributes to that mood, because we haven't got anything to compare it with. This isn't a science experiment with a control group of poems about other travellers knocking on moonlit doors and shouting, followed by a line of poetry with no ferny forest floors in it, whereby we could prove that alliterative 'f's are genuinely and definitely and provably effective in doing softness. No matter. I reckon I'd get my mark for saying my bit just there. I have reunited the form (alliteration) with the content (feelings of softness). The idiocy that I've just expressed, however, comes about because, as I've said, the only way I could get to the softness feeling or the softness meaning is through the words that have expressed it. If, say, someone else reads those three words and connoted the letter 'f' with a kind of hissing, and read it as, let's say, the contempt of the forest for the traveller who has arrived and disrupted the peace – there is no one who can argue with it. In spite of the strenuous efforts of generations of critics, buttressed by generations of examiners, no one can ever quite succeed in deducing definitive meanings from form. All they can do is pretend that they can as part of a curriculum method.

And so to the most intriguing questions of all:

'Who is the Traveller?' and 'Who are the Listeners?'

Now, I have to say, of all the questions so far, these are the ones that have me stumped. In all honesty, I don't know who the Traveller and the Listeners are. In all the many times I've read the poem – I even spent a few weeks learning how to perform it as part of an inter-school choral verse-speaking competition in 1955 – I have never known who the Traveller and the Listeners are, and I suspect I never will. And do you know, I'm actually quite happy with that. It's quite possible for me to enjoy something about the poem without needing to know or even wanting to know who they are.

And here we might have landed on something important about poetry. In most but not all stories, our expectations derived from thousands of years of storytelling give us a need or a desire. It goes like this: in the event of us being told that the main protagonist is a traveller who arrives somewhere and knocks on a door, and then in the event of us being told that there some phantom listeners doing some listening, we have a desire to be told who they are within the story and a legitimate expectation that we will be told. That's what most stories do. They give us whys and wherefores and recognisable outcomes. Yes, I know Virginia Woolf and Marguerite Duras don't, but that's why I said 'most stories' and not 'all'. One of the distinctive features of poetry is that we, as experienced readers, will often read poems from start to finish and, without even being aware of it, suspend our desire to know exactly who is talking, who the protagonist is, where we are, or even why people do things. I cannot stress how important this is. I would even go so far as to say that one of the reasons we read poetry for pleasure is precisely because many poems have this quality of withholding many of the specifics we have come to expect in stories.

Back to 'Daffodils' – which, as you'll know, wasn't called that by Wordsworth. He gave it no title, but we have written that part of the poem for him. Another example of a gap in a poem that readers fill, perhaps. He might have wanted to call it 'Inner Eye' or 'My Couch' or 'A Day Out with Dorothy'. No matter.

For experienced readers, the poem comes attached to Wordsworth and the Lake District. But that's only because we've been told it is. There is nothing intrinsic in the poem that tells us that the 'I' is a man from two hundred years ago, living in a particular place and time, walking and thinking in a particular place and time. In other words, poetry offers us the possibility, should we so choose, to read a poem without knowing or needing to know this sort of thing. It's as if this kind of poem says to us, 'You don't need to know all that stuff about what I had for breakfast before I went for the walk, or who I was with, or anything else that happened that day. I don't need to tell you what happened to the daffodils. I'm drawing your attention to what I'm drawing your attention to, which is that when I got home I thought about the daffodils.'

This is at the heart of why poetry is a kind of writing that refuses to be tied down. It keeps slipping out of a critic's grasp. Very often, there just isn't enough stuff there for us to make the definitive statement. What's more, the very act of trying to wring this statement out of the poem – or worse – out of children, is anti-poem. It runs against the grain of the poetic impulse, which more often than not is an impulse to suggest, imply, hint, infer, and to withhold even as it reveals.

With de la Mare's poem, I can of course do that exam thing of culling info from it. This will tell me for example that the traveller is male, he's on a horse, he's travelled at night, he can smite, he is capable of being perplexed, he has grey eyes, either he or his call (or both) are lonely, he can 'feel in his heart' the 'strangeness' of something he can't see or hear, and yet he also feels he can address this strangeness; he has some kind of undefined relationship with a 'them' which refers to a plural entity he has come to see; he has some sense that he wants this entity to know that he's a man of his word. We also know that his horse's hooves are shod.

Who is the Traveller? I have no idea beyond saying that he appears to be someone that someone called Walter de la Mare wrote some words about in a poem called 'The Listeners'. At this point in my thinking, the Traveller is all text.

Who are the Listeners? Well, they're 'phantom'. And that doesn't mean much more than that they're made up, which, as it's a poem, we kind of knew anyway.

So, quite why I'm being asked the questions, 'Who is the Traveller and who are the Listeners?' is not clear. In fact, I'm quite cross I've been asked these questions. I feel that I'm being asked something that I shouldn't have to answer. What's more, because I don't know the answers, I feel embarrassed and uncomfortable because I've got quite a good idea that other people in the room do know who they are. And the teacher or examiner knows. And I don't. I am not good enough to know. I'm not good enough to understand this poem. In fact, it's now turned into quite a horrible poem . . .

And as we all know, one of the first and most important lessons many of us learn from reading poetry in school is that quite often and for a large number of children it's a mildly humiliating experience. It's a means by which we learn that we aren't quite good enough. Just beyond reach, there is a right answer out there, an answer that someone knows, and that someone for sure ain't me.

Now, I think there might be interesting ways of asking questions about the Traveller and the Listeners – note that I've conceded that they're worth asking questions about.

I'll give it a go:

Who might the Traveller be? (And I might add here, that I don't know who he is. Honestly I don't. Really.)

Who might he have been coming to see? (Same again, I really don't know.) But who do you think it could be?

Why do you think he came?

If you could talk to the Traveller, is there anything you'd like to ask him, or tell him? Is there anyone here who would like to be the Traveller?

Now, who would like to ask him anything?

Do you think there are some Listeners of some kind, or has the Traveller imagined them?

Let's all pretend to be a Traveller who's just arrived at an empty house in the middle of the night in the middle of the forest . . .

How do we feel?

Let's all pretend to be Listeners watching someone arrive at the empty house where we hang out . . .

How does that feel?

Does anyone want to ask one of the Listeners what's going on?

Now I'm going to make a suggestion here. I don't really know what 'The Listeners' is about; or more accurately, I don't really know what the poem means for me.

I might surmise some things about its role in our national life, though. I could perhaps describe its iconic status in the teaching of poetry over the last fifty years. I could even offer up some answers as to why that is, like . . . perhaps we like giving children literature that has some kind of respectable mystery at the heart of it. By 'respectable mystery', I mean a mystery that doesn't appear to be about sex, drugs or rock'n'roll, or indeed anything nasty to do with how children get on with each other or with the adults in their lives. Literature, through a poem like this, can serve its time not only as a means of test-led instruction, but also as a means by which we can lead children into the land of unexplained mystery. In fact, I could suggest that by asking the very questions that avoid the active engagement of the reader, we sustain the status of a poem like this in the land of respectable mystery. It can exist sealed off from us, unexplored.

But that said, before engaging with the poem, I don't know what 'The Listeners' is for. However, I not only don't think this matters – that is, I don't have to know what it's for – but I also think that its unknowability might be what's important or interesting about it. In other words, there is a strange contrast between the purposefulness of the Traveller, smiting on the door, and the complete lack of revealed matter about who he is or what he's doing or what he's doing it for. We know he's got a purpose but we don't know what it is.

So this leaves us with another kind of prospect. We can ask of the poem, not the kind of question we might ask of a play or a novel – like, say, 'What are the protagonists' motives?' or 'What do you think of the outcome of the poem? In this case, what do you think about what happened to the Traveller at the end?'. Instead, we can ask ourselves, 'Is there anything about the feeling of the poem and the feeling of its scenes that we might say are in some way or another representative, or transferable?' That's too abstract a question to ask in most classrooms, so in terms of asking questions of you or a class, it could be phrased thus:

'Is there anything about the poem, or characters in the poem or scenes in the poem, or the sounds of the poem, that remind you of anything that's ever happened to you, or anything that you've ever read?'

Now that's a simple question that conceals a whole load of theory.

If I ask you, 'Does this poem remind you of anything you've ever read?' I'm asking you a question about intertextuality – that process by which every text we ever read is, through the minds and acts of readers, joined to other texts. In fact, it's impossible to conceive of a text that isn't joined to other texts. It's the nature of texts that they are in a sense constructed out of the shapes, colours, molecules of other texts, and that in some way or another (unpredictable at the time of writing) contribute to other texts that come after it. Accessing a poem's intertextuality through a class's intertextual investigations and questions might be a way by which we can get to know more about who someone like the Traveller or the Listeners are. After all, these characters are in part, perhaps mostly, perhaps entirely (I won't get into that) textual entities.

As a way of inviting students to enter into this sea of texts, we can keep it simple and open by asking them the 'reminding' question. And there's no need to get hung up about chronology here. If 'The Listeners' reminds a reader of something that was composed years after the composition of 'The Listeners', then that can serve to remind us that motifs and themes and phrases and sounds travel about in the world of literature gathering or losing significance, becoming stereotypes and archetypes, gaining or losing their power as the epochs pass.

And if I ask you, 'Does it remind you of something that you've experienced in your life?' you'll note I'm not saying that this poem is about that experience – I'm saying that the best route by which we might access what we could call the 'symbolic psychology' or 'symbolic sociology' of the poem is through a dialogue with the kinds of experiences that we the readers have had.

So, pause a moment. Back to 'The Listeners'. Turn to the person next to you. Try these two questions:

were there any moments in the poem
any words
any phrases
or any sounds of the poem
that reminded you of, first, something else you've read
or, second, anything that has happened in your life?

Perhaps you have at some time or other been like the Traveller, or like the Listeners, or alternatively perhaps you know someone who has been like the Traveller or like the Listeners. You can treat the questions (that is, reminding you of a text or reminding you of an experience) as separate or together, as you wish, because in truth the way we describe our experiences is itself a text that is informed by other texts.

It may help you to restate what you think is the bare essence of the poem . . . or it may not.

[People talked to each other . . .]

I'm going to think aloud . . .

The idea of opening a piece of writing with a question reminds me of several things: the writer Morris Gleitzman once told me that the key to grabbing a reader's attention is, 'Start writing as late on in the action as you can. You can always go back and fill in details if you need to.' In other words, you don't have to start a poem, a play, or a novel by describing where we are, or why we are where we are. You can dive straight in with a statement or a question that will intrigue a reader or listener.

So, what pieces of writing do I know that begin with a question?

Hamlet begins with 'Who's there?'; there's a nursery rhyme that begins with 'How many miles to Babylon?'; a folk song begins with 'Who will shoe your pretty little feet?'; a French folk song begins, '*Qu'est-ce qui passe ici si tard?*' – Who's that coming here so late?' In other words, it's a piece of literary rhetoric, the question as opening gambit, going back hundreds of years, borrowed by de la Mare.

What poems or stories do I know with a man on horse arriving somewhere? There are many, aren't there? A knight arrives at a castle or a tower to free a lover, or slay a dragon, or meet his fate in a fight with an enemy.

And what poems or stories do I know about listeners? *The Borrowers* perhaps, with those little beings under the floorboards; and literature, particularly Shakespeare, is full of people who overhear or eavesdrop: Polonius in *Hamlet*; Toby Belch, Feste and Fabian spying on Malvolio in *Twelfth Night*; Oberon and Puck listening to the lovers in *A Midsummer Night's Dream*; there's the overhearing of Rumplestiltskin revealing his name. And then, of course, there's a way of thinking of all literature as a means by which we eavesdrop on what people think, say and do. We, the readers, are invited to be eavesdroppers and listeners.

And I could go on like this, thinking about empty houses, forests, knocking on doors and so on, and I can build up what I'd call a map of awareness about the themes, motifs and feelings that are in the poem. Any or some of these may well help me find a point of contact with the poem, an entry point that makes whatever is proving difficult or odd about the poem feel more familiar or more accessible. After all, poems are almost by definition strange ways of using language, one moment appearing to say too much, next appearing to say too little – full of ornament, inversion, compression and comparison, making ordinary things seem extraordinary and extraordinary things seem ordinary. To get at them or into them, I'm grateful for any bridge, any link, any way in which the poem's charge can leap across to me.

So let me try this (it's actually one of the questions that the beastly test-type questions asked us at the beginning of this talk!): 'How would I describe what happens in the poem . . . [but I'll humanise it by adding] . . . if it's me who's the Traveller?'

I arrive with something important to say, but there is no one there to hear. I am not heard. I plead that I have been honourable. I've kept my side of the bargain. I have a sense of a hidden world that hears, but it is unresponsive. It witnesses but says nothing. The people I wanted to hear me weren't there. Instead, I'm surrounded by a landscape that has a life of its own that is indifferent to me.

So, now I'm thinking of those moments when, say, one of my children has asked me a question and I've tried to answer it. Then, the moment I start talking, I've become aware that they are instantly bored. They walk off, or suddenly start to find that the grains in the wood on the table are incredibly interesting or that they've left a sandwich in their lunch box. And I'm thinking, I'm keeping my side of the bargain, I'm answering your question, but you're not listening. The rest of the room is listening but it's inanimate. OK, the cat's there but even the cat isn't listening. The frying pan isn't listening. Or is it? And you, you're there while I'm explaining that thing you asked me to explain . . . I think it was about clouds or was it about Henry VIII . . . anyway, you're not listening. You exist in your own ecology, and anyway then you scamper off and watch *Kim Possible* on the Disney Channel. So you're not there. Fine. And I'm here. On my own. In fact, I could do that thing I call 'recruitment', where people like me say to themselves or to our children, 'Well you may not want to do x or y, but there are lots of other children out there who would!' In a lot of our moments of stress we try to recruit invisible assistants, don't we? As my mother used to say when looking at me at the end of the day, 'I'm sure the other children in your class didn't go to school in shoes they hadn't polished!' And when we're lonely, we can often imagine how much better it would be if only we could get this or that person over for a chat . . .

(Yes, I know I've conflated the absent 'them' whom I came to see with the listening 'them' – but so be it.)

Anyhow, through reading the poem, I've accessed something about me. A quirk, a trait. Through my reading, I've helped myself become aware of something about me and the way I behave. In some peculiar way, it's helped me extract something inside me that feels very individual and full of self-importance, and this process has helped me to put these feelings outside of me to contemplate them alongside the poem. It has, as the jargon has it, helped me objectify my experience.

But wait a minute, hasn't it also thrown me back on what I called the symbolic psychology or symbolic sociology of the poem? And won't I now need to revise my rather glib account of 'The Listeners' as standing as some kind of convenient icon for respectable mystery?

In ways that are difficult to unravel, this poem seems to chime with a sense that I've had that there are times when I haven't been heard. And this is a lonely place to be. And there might be an awareness that there is some kind of 'other' out there, who, if they could only be 'recruited', would make me feel better, less lonely.

Again, I've got a feeling that only by accessing all this can I get a sense of why or how what I called this poem's respectable mystery becomes much more problematic, much less comfortable.

Now, it's my view that any set of questions, any curriculum plan or strategy in connection to poetry implies a view as to what poetry is for.

The questions that I began this talk with seem to me to imply an idea that what poetry is for is that it should stand as a kind of assault course, a training-ground in answering closed-ended questions with an end result that has very little to do with feelings or meaning. The poem and the contact it might or could make with readers through the intermingling of its intertextuality and its reference to experience is secondary or, worse, invisible.

The questions I've asked so far are intended precisely to engage with this potential for contact. I'm trying to avoid constructing artificial points of contact – that's how I would typify all those questions about 'effectiveness'. Instead, I'm trying to set up little platforms for readers of all kinds to establish those points of contact for themselves. Even all those questions about alliteration and metaphor don't need to be phrased in such a way that they appear like the questions in a pub quiz, with the question-master holding the answers in his hand, and these are the only right ones. Anything else, you don't get your point.

If you want to refine that question, 'Is there anything that reminds you . . . ?', you can say, 'Are there any sounds, any pictures, any words, any phrases, any way of saying things that remind you of something you've seen, heard, or read somewhere else? What are they? Where are they? How did they remind you?' The questions we ask about poetry don't have to be ones that we know the answers to. That's my undogmatic way of putting it. My dogmatic way is to say, 'The questions we ask about poetry should always be ones that we the questioner don't know the answers to.'

This opens up the possibility of asking a question that invites questions – I've mentioned some already in relation to the characters of the poem. But we can also expand that into things like, 'Is there anything we would like to ask the writer? Who would like to be the writer, and try to answer those questions? Is there anything we would like to find out about the writer? Or the time and place the writer lived through? There are 211,000 entries for Walter de la Mare on Google. I wonder if any of them is interesting. Will any of them give me a point of contact with the poem?' Maybe, maybe not.

So, back to our title: what is a Bong Tree?

Well, as we know, Edward Lear created a kind of poetry that lays a false trail. He tells us that something is a spoon, or a tree, or that there is some kind of creature that uses a sieve for a boat, but then he obscures the whole thing by calling the thing or the person by a name we have never heard of: 'runcible', 'Bong', 'Jumblies' and the like. In so doing, he created worlds that had a logic that you can figure out – and yet they do not correspond to the world we know. A sieve is a receptacle but it wouldn't work as a boat unless you're a . . . Jumbly. Quite why it would work for the Jumblies isn't clear. In other words, this is a world where motives and empirical explanations will work only up to a point. There is no legitimate 'yes' outside of the poem to the question, 'Is it possible for an owl and a pussycat to marry?' In fact, why am I asking such a silly question of myself?

So Lear in a way crystallises the problem at the heart of all poetry and all literature: we create these beings and creatures, these scenes, these dramas, but we readers do not really know who the characters are or why they are. Like the phrase 'Bong Tree', the words signify something, but the only way I can access this meaning is to find out how they chime with what I've read and what I know and what I've felt and what I've done.

For poetry in schools to be both a significant and enjoyable way to spend time, I suggest that we have to go back to the reader's place in the poem in order to find out the poem's place in the reader, and that we put this process at the heart of our activities.

Today I've just suggested one or two ways. There are many others – through painting, dance, drama, mime, photography, film, wall displays, yes, even choral speaking; in other words, ways that don't ask any questions at all.

Very soon, we'll have a place on the Book Trust's website where teachers and poets can share ideas of how we can all create poetry-friendly classrooms. I see that the most recent documents to emerge from one of the acronym-laden authorities that speak to schools and teachers are making noises that are, I'd say, more poetry-friendly, with an emphasis on children making their own anthologies, doing poetry performances and the like. Perhaps they've suddenly remembered what literature is for . . . I hope so.

In the meantime, in case anyone was still wondering . . .

For me, though perhaps not for you,

A Bong Tree is
A Bong Tree is
A Bong Tree is
a tree that goes bonggggggggggggggg!

Not so Much a Lesson, More a Song and Dance

In The Guardian *on 2 October 2007, to mark National Poetry Day, I wrote this piece, suggesting fifteen ways to make a classroom poetry-friendly.*

One of the oddities that has emerged out of years of government-inspired curriculum development is the notion that there are perfect lesson plans which you follow and that these will deliver perfect results. I think the best learning takes place when you create an atmosphere of curiosity and excitement. So, I ask myself, how can we handle poems so that a whole class will be curious and excited enough to want to read, write, perform and think about poems? Poetry has never been written with the intention of making young people irritated, bored, anxious or humiliated, and yet the consequence of the test and exam system often does just that. So, rather than begin with lessons, we can talk about structures with a view to making your classroom poetry-friendly.

1. Find any poem that you think is interesting. Copy it out in your own handwriting onto as big a piece of paper as you can. Pin it up on the wall. Don't ask any questions about it, don't set any homework in relation to it. You could try leaving some post-its next to it, so that the class could write things on the post its and stick them to the poem. If anyone asks you questions about the poem, see if you can ask back a question about how we might find out the answer. Looking in a book? On the internet? Writing a letter to someone? Or how? After a week, take the poem down and put up another one.

2. Read poems to the class when they know that you can't set them work – that is, just before breaks or at the end of the day.

3. Bring in a pile of poetry books, divide the class into twos or threes and ask them to go away and prepare a poem to perform to the rest of the class in twenty minutes' time because that's when you're going to have a poetry concert.

4. Discuss with the children all the different ways you could perform poems: mime, dance, song, using instruments, cutting bits, adding in repetitions that aren't in the original poem, turning some of the scenes of the poem into tableaux, and so on.

5. Look at a poem together. Ask questions that you don't know the answers to. Is there any part of the poem that reminds you of anything that has ever happened to you, or that you've heard of happening to someone else? Why and how did it remind you? Is there any part of the poem or sound of the poem that reminds you of anything that you've ever read before? Why? How? Have you got any questions that you would like to ask about the poem?

Ask if any of your students could have a go at answering these questions. Is there anywhere we could go to find answers? Books? Internet? What if you could ask anyone or anything in the poem a question, what question would it be? Would any of your students like to pretend to be that person or thing and answer that question? What if you could ask the poet or the publisher of the poem a question? What question? Does anyone want to pretend to be the poet or the publisher and answer it? Is there anywhere we could find out more about the author or the time and place that author lived through? Are there any patterns or shapes in the poem that anyone wants to talk about? Do you like these? Or not?

6. Choose a book of poems by one poet. What if we turned that book of poems into a show? We could use any poem or part of a poem, we could make up our own, we can use music, photography, costume . . .

7. Choose an anthology of poems around a theme. Let's look at this theme. Can we make up some poems on this theme? Make a show of some of the poems in the book mixing it with your students' poems.

8. Have a poetry cabaret night with your students' parents. Everyone is going to bring either a poem they've written or a poem they like and perform it. Turn out all the lights, use a microphone and stage lights. The audience will sit round tables and then poets and performers get up out of the audience to perform their poem. Two sets of twenty minutes each with music in between. Interval – juice and cakes made by the parents.

9. Poetry swap time! Have a session where the teacher and the class swap poems they've chosen and read them out.

10. Turn the poems that the children write into poem posters, poetry booklets and books.

11. Writing poems can start from many, many different places. Use photographs, moments in stories, dreams, music, dance. Use the soliloquy principle, i.e. stop the action in any art form, any moment, any scene in your own life and ask the protagonist (or yourself), 'What are you thinking? What can you see? What are you going to do?' The answers can make a poem.

12. Write poems for your class or about your class and with your class. Often!

13. Invite a poet to your school and ask her questions.

14. Go to a poetry reading at the local book festival.

15. If an Ofsted inspector comes into your room, ask her or him to read a poem to the class.

Poetry in Primary Schools: Stuck in a Thorn Bush

I wrote this article for the May 2008 edition of Junior Education.

At present, poetry in many primary-school classrooms is, to my mind, stuck in a thorn bush. The National Literacy Strategy laid down when and how poetry should be taught and, following from that, materials and anthologies of poems have been published to fit in with this programme. I think this was the wrong approach. Reading and writing poetry shouldn't be confined to systems of work that slot neatly into boxes with learning outcomes attached. Reading and writing poetry shouldn't be a matter of following a nationally fixed progression from this or that kind of poem in Year 1 to this or that kind of poem in Year 2 and so on up through the school. Reading and writing poetry shouldn't be something that is paralysed by the kinds of questions that have only one answer. You know the kind of thing: how many adjectives? can you see the metaphor? where is the personification?

Poetry itself is a way of using language in exciting, musical and surprising ways in order to ask questions of the world inside our heads and around us in the world. It often suggests and probes things, without coming up with fixed conclusions, happy endings and neat resolutions. It's not a neat and tidy way of writing. Poems often start right in the middle of a scene or a feeling, without explaining where we are. Sometimes they never tell us and we have to guess. Sometimes one part of a poem is attached to another part without the writer explaining why. This makes them very different from stories, which nearly always do explain such things. And across the world of poetry, poems are very different from each other. They come out in different shapes, different lengths and they talk of any subject. Sometimes they seem to tell stories, sometimes they just seem to be about looking, or hearing, or thinking. Quite often they don't appear to ask any more of their readers than they should just sit down and have a bit of a think. Sometimes, we re-read poems without knowing why. Perhaps it's the sound, perhaps it's the pictures in our heads, perhaps it's because of a feeling that echoes with a feeling in our own lives.

This is why, to my mind, the approach in the National Literacy Strategy is so inappropriate. Instead, I think we should value and cherish the way poetry has of giving readers suggestions, and leaving them time to think and wonder. And this needs a different way of working. We need to make our schools and classrooms poetry-friendly. This means inventing ways in which whole schools can possess poetry and make it belong to them. In my experience, the moment a group of teachers is freed up from having to follow the Strategy and invited to come up with ways of enjoying poetry, there's no shortage of ideas. Here are some I've come across as I visit schools:

If we ask, 'Where shall we put poems?' then we can say that they're great for reading and performing in assembly – but only if everyone can hear them. Use handheld microphones. Think carefully how the performances can be improved – many poems benefit from repeating lines in chorus. Some are great with pictures projected behind them or accompanied by rhythms on blocks. Some are great with the children taking up the positions as if they're in a freeze frame or photo, as the poem unfolds.

The corridors and walls of a school are great places to put up poem posters. Get the children to make them, or make them yourselves. No need to restrict the poems you put up to the size of an exercise-book page. Make them massive. Project them on to walls. If you put a poem up in a classroom, why not suggest that the children can pin post-its to the poem with their questions and thoughts about it?

When it comes to reading poems in class, try to find as many ways as you can for these to be just read and enjoyed, without asking questions. This might mean getting the children to record and perform the poems. Bring in a box of poetry books. Invite the children to go off in threes, each group with a book, and come back in twenty minutes with the performance of one poem. Make it an event and say it's a poetry show with ten acts. Take a collection of poems (anthology or a book by a single author) and work out a way of turning it into a show for the whole school, using the poems to make monologues, dialogues, choruses, mimes, live-music interludes, masks and dance. Don't be afraid to change and adapt the poems to fit the overall show. Add in poems and lines written by the children inspired by the collection.

When it comes to asking questions about poems, see if you can restrict the questions to ones that you don't know the answers to. Put the children into groups with a poem, with the job of asking, 'Does this poem remind you of anything you've seen, read, heard before? What? Why?' Bring them back together and write up the questions and answers as they give them to you. Talk about these answers. Value them. Encourage everyone to ask or answer something. Ask, 'Is there anything you'd like to ask anyone or anything in the poem?' Write up the questions where everyone can see them and see if there's anyone who would like to have a go at being the person or object in the poem to answer the questions. Or is there anything the children would like to ask the poet? Who would like to be the poet and have a go at answering the questions? Use the internet and books to help. Show that you take every question and answer seriously. Add in your own questions in a way that doesn't inhibit the children asking theirs.

This way, poems become focal points for discussion and debate, where ideas and feelings flow. When someone notices something strange or significant about a poem, foreground it. I promise you, if you trust this whole process, and if you trust the poem and the poet, the older children will take you to the processes of poetry too – the alliteration, the rhyme, the metaphors and similes. They will start to notice the patterns of poetry – how one poem is like or unlike another. And indeed, how they can write like this poet or unlike another.

A Special Way of Talking and Writing

I wrote this piece for the July 2008 issue of Lovereading.

Poetry is a special way of talking and writing. Poems are often musical, playing with the sounds of language while they tell stories, reveal feelings, make pictures and give us ideas. We all find this pleasurable, but children especially do. I guess that's because for very young children, language often comes at them as something they hear without necessarily understanding it. Then poems come along and hit the same channel, sound, rhythm, rhyme, repetition and all the other tricks in the poet's bag.

Poems can be snapshots: small pictures of a moment, an object, a scene, a feeling. They can be like photos in the family album: a moment frozen which we can look at over and over again and wonder why it matters to us.

Poems are also places where you don't have to say it all; they don't have to tie it up in a neat knot in the way that stories usually do. Poems can end with questions. Poems can end with no answers. Poems can pose problems. And that's fine, because life doesn't usually finish with neat little endings. Life itself is full of questions and problems. Particularly for children.

Poems are great for exploring those fascinating questions once posed by the painter Paul Gauguin: where do we come from? where are we now? where are we going? These are questions about what kind of background we have, what kinds of things we believe in and care about, what do we want our lives to look like in the future. Poems often explore these themes. And they do it in personal, direct ways, saying, in a thousand different ways, 'This is me, this is us, I wonder what kind of person I am, I wonder what's going to happen,' and so on. And aren't these questions that children ask over and over again?

Poetry is great for what is almost the opposite of this: pretending we aren't who we say we are. Poets write poems where they pretend to be goddesses, houses, worms, graves, long-dead ancestors, aliens. This allows poets to explore feelings they didn't know they had, and in so doing they invite children to wonder about other lives, other states of existence, other possibilities.

Poetry can be impossible. As we proceed along our logical, sensible lines, relying on gravity to keep our plates on the table, days to follow nights, our blood to flow round our bodies, poems don't have to obey these rules. Whether it's through nonsense (remember the dish who ran way with the spoon?) or through making one thing like another (perhaps our plates aren't sitting on the table; rather, the table is tired of carrying the plates), poetry can get us to see the world in strange, new ways and from strange points of view.

Poems are often full of echoes, gathering together hints and memories of other poems, other stories, films, signs, speeches. They gather up and change words. It's as if poems like this point us at the very language we see and hear around us and invite us to stop, think and wonder if the words we are used to are right, honest or worthwhile. For children, this is especially important. If you think for a moment, very nearly all children enter school using a language that is theirs, only to find that school is full of language that seems to belong to other people. If poetry plays with language and, through its music, invites children to remember and imitate it, this becomes a language that they can possess.

Theory, Texts and Contexts: A Reading and Writing Memoir

This is a lecture I gave on 20 April 2009 at Poetry and Childhood, a conference at the British Library.

The Hole in the Wall

I loved sharing my bedroom with my brother
but one day my parents said that my brother
was going to move out of our room.
He was going to have:
A Room Of His Own.
We wouldn't share any more.

So he moved out the model cars he had made
and the model trains and the model planes.
They all went off to the room next door.
His room.
In there, he set up the model cars he had made
and the model trains and the model planes.

And soon he got to work making something new.
Something Really Big.

I wanted to be in there
while he was making it.
But I had to go to bed in my room.
The room that used to be our room.

So I had an idea.

I had a metal ruler, a hard steel ruler
with sharp edges and corners.
I got into bed with this metal ruler
and just where the bed meets the wall,
just out of sight of anyone looking,

I started to scratch the wall
with the hard corner of the metal ruler.
Scratch scratch scratch.
Scrape scrape scrape.
I was making a hole
through to my brother's bedroom.
I twisted the corner of the metal ruler
round and round and round.
Scratch scratch scratch.
Scrape scrape scrape.

After ages of scratching and scraping
all I had made was a tiny dent in the wall.
So I went to sleep.

The next night, I got working at it again.
Scratch scratch scratch.
Scrape scrape scrape.
The dent got a tiny bit deeper.

And the next night.
And the next.
Scratch scratch scratch.
Scrape scrape scrape.
After a few nights
I reached a bit of wood.
Should I try to scrape *through* the wood
or round it?
I decided to go over the top.
But this would make the hole wider
and maybe someone would see it . . .
. . . but I didn't care. I had to go on.
I had to make the hole.
I had to get through to my brother's room.
Scratch scratch scratch.
Scrape scrape scrape.
It was now a little cave in the wall.
A secret tunnel.

I wet my fingers in my drink
and then dabbed the dry plaster with my fingers.
The plaster went dark.
The secret tunnel was wet.
What if I could shrink myself down
and crawl through it?
Be an explorer bravely climbing through
the dangerous cave.
Will I get through
or will I be trapped in here forever?
Just then my dad popped his head
round the door.
'Goodnight, Mick!' he said all cheerily.

I hadn't heard him coming.
Oh no, he mustn't see it.
So I sat up in the bed
and quickly twisted round
to cover up my hole in the wall.
He mustn't see the hole.

But he saw me do this sitting-up, twisty-round thing.

Oh no, he's seen me!
Instead of going back downstairs
he opened the door
and walked into the room.
Still cheery, he says,
'Hey, what's that you're doing?
What are you covering up there?'
'Nothing.'
'No, come on, Mick, look at you,
I can see from the way you're sitting
you're covering up something.'
'No.'
Still cheery, he says,
'Come on, come away from the wall.
Let me have a look.'

What could I do?
I had to let him see.

So I leaned forward.
He saw it straight away.
The Hole in the Wall.
Oh no.
It's the moment when the cheery stuff
stops.
It's the moment when the cheery stuff
stops.

He stood there staring at
The Hole in the Wall.
He pointed at it.
'What's that?' he says.
'It's a hole in the wall,' I said.
'I can see it's a hole in the wall,' he says,
'but how in heaven's name
did you make a hole in the bedroom wall?'
'With this,' I said, and I pulled the metal ruler out
from under the covers.
He slapped his hand on his forehead.
'You've wrecked the wall,' he says.

He shouted for my mum:
'Connie, Connie, come and look at this.'
And of course my brother comes running along
behind her.

All three of them stood by my bed,
staring at
The Hole in the Wall.
'Look what he's done,' says my dad.
'Look at it. Look at it.
He's wrecked the wall. It's wrecked.'
'Oh, Michael,' says my mum,
and my brother is giggling and giggling,

'Wa-ha-ha-ha, ho-hee-hee, ya-ha-ha-hee!
It must have taken him ages,' he says.
And Mum is saying,
'But, Michael . . . what did you think you were doing?
Why did you do it?'
And I said,
'I was trying to get through to Brian's room.'
And my brother says,
'But, Mick,
you could have just got up,
walked out the door,
walked across the landing
and in through my door.'

Every artistic endeavour has a theory hovering around it. What I mean by this is that when human beings do things, we are not only capable of having ideas about what we're doing, but that the very *act of doing* and the product of *that doing* springs from a world of talk, ideas and, yes, theory. There are several routes to unravelling this world: let's take Shakespeare as an obvious example. Textual scholars are able to reveal, from the intrinsic evidence of the texts themselves, the likely sources and secondary texts that Shakespeare was grappling with: the Bible, Ovid, Aristotle and so on. Meanwhile, a more historical approach looks at extrinsic evidence asking such questions as, 'What was in the school curriculum of Shakespeare's time? What were the debates circulating in the Court, the Church, Parliament and the Privy Council?'

In more recent times, with developments in the kinds of criticism that draw on interviews with writers and what writers themselves say about joining movements in their manifestos, it's been possible to engage with this matter in yet another way. So, where a school of criticism of the past tried to unpick author intention from analysis of texts (the so-called New Criticism of Brooks, Wilmsatt and Warren), there is now a body of material where critics can engage with the stated intentions of authors.

So any piece of literature, group of texts, a single author's oeuvre and the like, not only sits amongst the kinds of secondary texts and conversations that I described in relation to Shakespeare, but it also sits amongst the many statements by and conversations with fellow writers. All of this context has an impact on when, how, why, where and what a writer writes. It's as if a writer sits in a bath of ideas about texts.

Now we're missing something here. Texts aren't just produced in a world made up of texts. They are part of a real world going through its convulsions, struggles, moments of calm and the like. No matter how hard writers might try to keep that world out, the truth remains that they have to feed, clothe and house themselves and they experience a range of desires. The combination of all these needs and desires is that writers, along with everyone else, have to engage with whatever arrangements the society around them has for satisfying these needs and desires: flats to live in where you have to pay rents; breakfast to eat, so somewhere to buy bread; love and sex, so monogamy or polygamy or whatever for that; having children, so families or care homes for that. So, sticking with the bath of ideas, we also have to think of what heated the water, what kind of bath it was, or indeed who might or might not be there when you get out of the bath.

To summarise, we have a complex web of intertexts surrounding a work and these interact with the complex real world.

So who's going to look at all this?

Usually, there's a division of labour. The writer writes primary texts or 'literature' as it's usually called. The critic writes secondary texts or 'criticism'. But there are no lines of demarcation here. There is nothing to stop a writer being a critic. And, to go further along this line, though it might be thought to be narcissistic, there's no law to stop a writer being the kind of critic who is concerned with analysing what's inside their bath of ideas about texts and their own material contexts. That is, the ones surrounding their own work.

Let's see what that looks like.

A lot, but not all, of my writing for children has been about where I lived, who I lived with, how I lived with them and then what happened when I went to school, who I played with, and so on.

> My brother is making a protest about bread.
> 'Why do we always have wholemeal bread?
> You can't spread butter on wholemeal bread
> You try and spread butter on
> and it just makes a whole right through the middle.'
>
> He marches out of the room and shouts
> across the landing and down the passage.
> 'It's always the same in this place.
> Nothing works.
> The volume knob's broken on the radio you know.

It's been broken for months and months you know.'

He stamps back into the kitchen
stares at the loaf of bread and says:
'Wholemeal bread – look at it, look at it.
You put the butter on
and it all rolls up.
You put the butter on
and it all rolls up.'

Harrybo

Once my friend Harrybo
came to school crying.

We said:
What's the matter?
What's the matter?
And he said
his granddad had died.

So we didn't know what to say.

Then I said:
How did he die?
And he said:
He was standing on St Pancras station
waiting for the train
and he just fell over and died.

Then he started crying again.

He was a nice man
Harrybo's granddad.
He had a shed with tins full of screws in it.

Mind you,

my gran was nice too
she gave me and my brother
a red shoe horn each.

Maybe Harrybo's granddad gave
Harrybo a red shoe horn.

Dave said:
My hamster died as well.
So everyone said:
Shhhh.
And Dave said:
I was only saying.
And I said:
My gran gave me a red shoe horn.

Rodge said:
I got a pair of trainers for Christmas.
And Harrybo said:
You can get ones without laces.
And we all said:
Yeah, that's right, Harrybo, you can.

Any other day,
we'd've said:
Of course you can, *we* know that, you fool.
But that day
we said:
Yeah, that's right, Harrybo, yeah, you can.

These people are nearly all of a kind (or I have written about them in such a way) for them to appear familiar to enough people I meet or live near for me to have an audience. I and the people in the poems appear to be doing things that come within the range that might be called 'typical'. But of course they were also of a specific time and place, social position, and the people were on their own real journeys through society.

I was brought up in a home environment where both my parents were on a journey transforming themselves. They came from immigrant families who had arrived very poor, in my father's case almost destitute, into the East End of London in very overcrowded difficult conditions. When I joined them, they had had two children, one had died, the other was four and my father had professionalised himself by becoming a teacher, and very soon my mother was doing the same. We were living in north-west London in a rented flat over a shop (not theirs) in a place that had once been a village but was now embedded within a suburbia that followed the building of the Metropolitan Line.

Though this time is often depicted as rather static, in fact there were serious changes going on – changes which my parents' own lives mirrored. A whole layer of the urban working class had done just what my parents had done: leave the old traditional areas of what we now call the inner city, and started to live in areas around the city or even in new satellite towns, and in so doing started to acquire non-manual skills.

A lot of what I have written and go on writing is about describing the world I found myself in and exploring odd fragments of what remained of the past my parents came from: their parents and the phrases and language they brought with them.

Don't Tell your Mother

When my mum goes to evening classes
my dad says,
'Don't tell your mother – let's have *matzo bray*.
She always says:
"Don't give the boys that greasy stuff.
It's bad for them."
So don't tell her, all right?'

So he breaks up the *matzos*
puts them into water to soften them up.
Then he fries them
till they're glazed and crisp.

'It tastes best like this,
fried in *hinner schmaltz*,
skimmed off the top of the chicken soup,'
he says,
'but olive oil will do.'

Then he beats up three eggs
and pours it on over the frying *matzos*
till it's all cooked.

It tastes brilliant.
We love it.
Then we wash everything up
absolutely everything
and we go to bed.

Next day,
Mum says to us,
'What did you father cook you last night?'

Silence.

'What did you father cook you last night?'

'Oh you know . . . stuff . . .
. . . egg on toast, I think.'

(*Matzo bray* is the Yiddish name of a dish made of *matzos* and egg. *Matzo* is unleavened bread that tastes like water biscuits. *Hinner schmaltz* means chicken fat.)

One other change we were all part of, and this is what I want to examine more closely, was in the world of education, which itself is always interleaved and folded into the wider world. I didn't know at the time that my brother and I were part of what was in effect an experiment: the mass education of everyone beyond the age of thirteen in new types of school: primary schools which now all finished their job at 11, and all, bar the private ones, under the umbrella of the state – even the religious ones. Then – another interesting new idea – everyone went to a secondary school. There were different types – single-sex, mixed, church, non-denominational, local-authority run or run directly from government, and – most famous of all – some selective grammar schools and technical schools, with the majority (yes, a majority of some 80%) for children who had failed the selection exam at eleven.

All this required a great new positioning for people in this country. In families where no one had ever received an education beyond the age of thirteen, all children were now staying on in some kind of school till they were fifteen. Some from this kind of background were choosing to stay on till sixteen and some till eighteen and beyond before going to various kinds of college and university.

But this wasn't some kind of smooth roll-out. It was riven with division, conflict, snobbery and tension. The last years of primary school, in my memory, were wracked with anxiety, horse-trading and fiddles. The curriculum was obsessed with getting the children up to the level required of the exam.

The Homework Book

Miss Williams said that from now on
we would have homework
and that we were to bring
a homework exercise book to school.

This was serious stuff:
all about passing The Exam,
The Exam called 'the Eleven Plus'.
Everyone was worried about
The Eleven Plus.
Would I pass?
Would I fail?
Everyone was worried.
Teachers, parents, us.
I couldn't get to sleep.
Mum brought me hot milk.

On Mondays
Miss Williams went through
the homework in our homework books.
While she was talking, I got bored.
I drew a picture in my homework book
of a man with a big beard
right in the middle of my maths homework.
He was carrying a bag.
He put things he picked up off the pavement
into his bag.

I called him Trev the Tramp.

Miss Williams went on going through
the homework with the whole class.
This was really important.
We had to listen or we wouldn't pass

The Eleven Plus.
Everyone was listening.
Everyone was concentrating
so that they could pass
The Eleven Plus.

I bent down behind the boy
sitting in front of me.
I looked across at my friend Harrybo
and held up my picture of Trev the Tramp.
I pointed at Trev the Tramp.
I whispered, 'Trev the Tramp'
Miss Williams saw me
holding up the homework book.

She was on to it in a flash.
'What's that, boy? What is it?!'
I quickly shut the homework book.
'Nothing, Miss Williams.'
She rushed over.
(She was brilliant at rushing over.)
She grabbed the homework book.
She flicked through the pages.
She found the picture of Trev the Tramp.
Right there in the middle of 23 x 12.

'This is it, isn't it?' she said.
'In your homework book!
I'll tell you what's going to happen
now, boy,' she said.

'You're going to take your homework book
home to your parents along with a
letter from me.'
She pointed at herself when she said, 'me'.
'My goodness, you're in trouble, boy.
Serious trouble.'

For the rest of the day
I was very quiet. I put my feet down
on the ground, carefully and I made
sure I didn't bump into anything.
At going-home time, she handed me
a big, white envelope.
'The letter to your parents is in there,
along with the homework book.'

But when I got home
I couldn't face giving it to my mum.
I couldn't face giving it to my dad.
I nipped upstairs and slipped it
under my bed.
All evening I was thinking
about the big white envelope
with the letter from Miss Williams,
the homework book and the
picture of Trev the Tramp.
I didn't want to give it to them.
I didn't want to see their faces
as they read the letter and looked at
Trev the Tramp.

What I did was put the big white envelope
on their bed when I went to bed.

In the morning, my dad said,
'Oh dear, you poor old thing,
you must have been so worried
about that letter, eh? I'll write one back.

I'll say some things in the letter
that will make sure you won't have
to worry about this stuff anymore.
And I'll get you a new homework book.'

At school, my friends said,
'Did you get in trouble?
Did you get the whacks?
What happened?'
And I said,
'My dad said I wasn't to worry.'
They didn't believe me.
And I don't know what my dad wrote
but Miss Williams never said
anything about it ever again;
the head never said anything about it again.

My dad was a teacher
and maybe he wrote in some kind of
special teacher language
that meant Miss Williams wouldn't
ever say anything again.
Some kind of teacher code . . .
that's what must have done it.

The grammar school had parallel anxieties about status, form and hierarchy.

These were the places where I learned how to read, where I found my
level and place in society, where I acquired the kinds of knowledge that society
at that point thought was suitable for a boy who was going to pass and did pass
the exam at 11.

Because this is part of the way the middle class of my era defined itself, many
of these processes have been what has been called 'naturalised'. That's to say,
the processes I went through have acquired a sense of being 'natural', right,
appropriate, usual, legitimate, normal, correct not just for then, but for all time.
So, for example, there was something called geography. This was the study of
places. It was separate from something called history. When years later people
suggested that places are the way they are because of history, and history always
takes place in a place, this threatened this sense of normality and legitimacy.

However – and this is the big 'however' – I lived in a very particular bath of ideas in this new experimental and changing world. The years of my parents' teenage and young married life together had been infused with some major political events arising out of what were their own particular real-life situations. Not only was it a time of poverty for them, it was also a time when one of the solutions being offered to society was to imprison, exile or exterminate them. So, along with action against that poverty (through rent strikes and industrial strikes) they were participants in actions locally, nationally and internationally against those people who wanted to impose the new world order which would involve their extermination. At the time, they thought that the way to fight all this was to join the Communist Party and though they would leave it in 1957, when they were 38, when I was ten, this was the formation and memory they brought with them into the suburbs, into our flat above the shop there and into their new profession – teaching.

Just to get a perspective on this, within ten years of them leaving the Communist Party, I had become a keen writer of poems which focused on who I was, where and how I lived, who I lived with, and where I and they had come from.

I can now see that writing poems wasn't just a literary practice. It was an educational one too. Perhaps all of us who write for children sit in some relation or another to education. After all, schools are largely the place where children learn how to read. And by that I don't mean simply it's where they learn *to* read. Schools are where children learn about what kind of behaviour reading is. Are books things that you get questioned about? Or things you read to yourself? Are books things that sit on shelves that you never read, because you only read worksheets? Do you hear books read to you? Are you expected to just read silently to yourself? Is it a private or a social behavioural act? And so on.

In my case, though, I can see clearly that it was an acutely *educational* practice. I'll explain.

My parents were teachers but they were also theoreticians. In the period covered by the time I was thinking about whether I would write up till when I decided I would, my parents were deeply involved in these various kinds of work: my father had moved from teaching in a suburban grammar school where he was blacklisted and prevented from becoming a head of department to one of the new comprehensive schools, this one situated just off the Old Kent Road. From there, he moved to Borough Road Training College where he started teaching on a variety of courses for trainee teachers, and then from there to becoming a lecturer at the University of London Institute of Education. My mother meanwhile was teaching in a primary school in Croxley Green and began a life-changing course (a diploma in primary education) with the eminent and *éminence grise* Christian Schiller, doyen of progressive education. She became a deputy head and then started to train teachers at Goldsmiths College. However, during this time, my father and mother were also involved separately or together in presenting poetry programmes for BBC Schools radio, helping first James Britton and then Geoffrey Summerfield in producing ground-breaking anthologies for schools: the *Oxford Junior Poetry* collection with Britton, and *Voices* and *Junior Voices* with Summerfield. My father had prepared many documents, papers, essays and talks on a variety of topics around the secondary English curriculum, including a policy document for Walworth School, that comprehensive I mentioned. Here's an extract:

> Whatever language the pupils possess, it is this which must be built on rather than driven underground. However narrow the experience of our pupils may be (and it is often wider than we think), it is this experience alone which has given their language meaning. The starting point for English work must be the ability to handle effectively their own experience. Oral work, written work and the discussion of literature must create an atmosphere in which the pupils become confident of the full acceptability of the material of their own experience. Only in this way can they advance to the next stage.

Later, he was doing a PhD (done mostly at the kitchen table, we would claim) in which he critiqued a crude mechanistic system of classifying children's sentences that had taken off in the USA. Then, together, my mother and father wrote a book called *The Language of Primary Schoolchildren*, which was similarly discussed through teatimes, holidays and the like as it was being assembled and written. These are the opening words of chapter 1:

> Language is for living with. Children's language emerges from the lives they lead and we cannot hope to make sense of it without understanding their lives.

Why am I telling you this? I find it quite difficult to describe and explain, but I'll try. My parents were of course my mother and father who mothered and fathered my brother and me in their own idiosyncratic ways and with all that baggage they brought with them from the East End into the suburbs. They were also educationists who mothered and fathered with their knowledge and ideas. Education is a very octopus-like creature. Its tentacles reach out into real life, up into theory, back into anecdotes about classrooms, about individual children, along with stories about colleagues, struggles with authorities, off into the resources that can be brought into the classroom. What I'm trying to say is that these kinds of conversations took place around my brother and me. Now, in my head, I can see my mother and father crawling along the floor, looking at Geoffrey Summerfield's handwritten notes and copies of the poems he had found for *Voices*; going for a walk in a bit of suburban woodland with my mother while she gathered up what she called 'bits' (holly or beech masts) which she said she would take back to her class; my father reading out why he thought that this or that statement by this American professor talking about T-units was nonsense; my mother reading out poems that the children she taught had written; my father reading out a talk that my mother would type for him, the pair of them bashing out a bit of linguistic theory, and so on. It was going on around us and as I happened to be a child who for whatever complicated reasons wanted to listen to this stuff, then it was in me as well.

So that's the form of what was going on, but was actually being said? And this is where we get to the nitty-gritty. I think my parents left the Communist Party in order that their lives could accommodate the kinds of ideas that they were developing around the teaching of literature and language to school-age children. At the time, the CP's education policy-makers had a very reductive idea about the education of working-class children, which followed a determinist model: so if the ruling class deprived the working class of its true deserts it also deprived it of language and culture. My parents were developing a counter-theory that if you wanted children to get hold of education (knowledge, skills, processes or whatever) you had to start with the languages and cultures of the children in front of you. The starting point for children – say – responding to a poem, shouldn't have to be a prescribed language, but it should be from the language-base of the child itself. Here they are in the preamble to a long transcript of three children discussing 'Old Florist' by Theodore Roethke.

We can hear their talk developing and absorbing the poem as they surround it with their experience of language and of life and their readiness to project *outwards* from it into their own imaginings in order to penetrate *inwards* to its meaning for them. Collaboration it is, but at the same time they demonstrate how active a process reading has to be for the individual reader; every story and poem has to be placed in the reader's world, made part of his patterning of life; every story and poem must be actively worked upon so that its design can be added to a larger design.

Part of this approach also involved the championing of particular kinds of literature – a literature that embraced and enjoyed the everyday, that worked with and not against contemporary vernaculars. I should insist here that this wasn't a matter of excluding other kinds, but was meant to spread the net wider than was traditionally the case. My mother, for example, was very fond of W.B. Yeats, who doesn't fit this pattern of writing at all, and yet she was always on the hunt for poems about objects around the house to slip into her radio programmes. She sometimes enlisted my help in trying to find poems for her in her collection of anthologies: *Come Hither, Iron, Honey, Gold* and so on. This was one of the most direct triggers for me to start writing. I wrote a poem for my mother's schools radio programme. It's not hard to see that this is both filial (and all that that involves) and theoretical. I wrote something that fitted a particular educational philosophy that was being developed that valued children's own experiences as part of education and not as something to be left at the school door.

Stop!

Every few weeks someone looks at me and says:
my you've grown
and then every few weeks someone says:
they've grown too long

and silver scissors come out of the drawer
and chip at my toes and run through my hair.

Now I don't like this one little bit.
I won't grow if I'm going to be chopped.
What's me is mine and I want to keep it
so either me or the scissors or my nails had better stop.

It was written to my mother, to the theory, to the practice of schools radio broadcasting, to the practice of making books out of poems and giving them to children in classrooms so that they might write poems themselves.

This was a theory that was developing the idea that children could be writing readers and reading writers and I was writing to it.

My first book of poems appeared in 1974. I was 28, my parents were 55. My mother was now at Trent Park, running the kind of diploma course that Christian Schiller had run. My father was at the Institute of Education, and (as I seem to remember) falling with a mix of delight and cynicism on post-structuralist theories of narratology, reader-response, interpretation and language. He and his colleagues were beginning to teach a Diploma in the Role of Language in Education.

As anyone who writes a children's book knows, there follows the immediate possibility that you will be taken into a place called 'Children's Literature': a network of libraries, schools, colleges, book clubs, bookshops and magazines. You are embraced and then pushed in front of the audience.

For some writers and illustrators this is not a happy experience. For me, it was at first curious, a bit embarrassing, a bit awkward, but very soon became the most important thing I found that I could have done. I had written the poems in what I'll call a mix of cool or warm contexts. The cool context was the passing of books between adults. Reading poems to yourself. The warm contexts were the broadcasts and readings on disc and tape that my parents played to us in our front room: Robert Graves, Dylan Thomas, Richard Burton reading Dylan Thomas, poets reading their own poems on BBC Radio's Third Programme, actors reading the poems my mother had chosen for her schools radio broadcasts. There were hot moments for literature – this, I thought, was theatre, Shakespeare, Pinter, my acting class at Questors Theatre, Osborne, Wesker, Shaw, Arden, Brecht, sketches in revues at university, the two plays I had written myself. With my first poetry book in my hand, standing in front of a class of children or a whole school of children, my first inclination was to go warm: to read the poems as if it was a schools radio broadcast. Thanks to a teacher at Princess Frederika School in Kensal Rise, one Sean McErlaine, I was shown that poetry for children could be hot. You can perform poems. Suddenly, a world that had been building up behind the dam burst out: the mix of the theories about working with everyday experience, the kinds of performance methods I had learnt at Questors, or for that matter watching my parents tell stories about their day at work, the theories about writing readers and reading writers, all came together in this act of performance.

But where was I at this moment? Was I in that north-west London primary school in 1955? Was I even with the offspring of children who had been to that kind of school? Not very often. Mostly, I found myself in and amongst the children who had themselves arrived in this country in their own short lifetimes, or were the children of arrivants.

At this point, I see that another mechanism came into play. In biology, showbiz and focus groups it's called 'feedback'. The problem with the word is that it doesn't indicate just how complicated it is. If you write something and perform it, or work with it in a classroom, you discover all sorts of things about the poem, about the child, about yourself. Then, it's not necessarily a matter of consciously calling this feedback, it's there in your consciousness anyway. Next time you write anything approximating to that field or structure of writing, you cannot escape the sensation and feel and understandings that you experienced on that occasion when you read the poem. In one sense, you now write with that sensibility added in to everything else you are. Then, in turn, you take the next piece of writing out into performance in front of an audience and, in turn, that goes through the same process. You and the writing are changing all the while, often in ways that you're hardly aware of yourself: an inflection, a phrasing, a topic you've chosen to write about.

The Rhythm of Life

Hand on the bridge
feel the rhythm of the train.

Hand on the window
feel the rhythm of the rain.

Hand on your throat
feel the rhythm of your talk.

Hand on your leg
feel the rhythm of your walk.

Hand in the sea
feel the rhythm of the tide.

Hand on your heart

feel the rhythm inside.

Hand on the rhythm
feel the rhythm of the rhyme.

Hand on your life
feel the rhythm of time
hand on your life
feel the rhythm of time
hand on your life
feel the rhythm of time.

But something else was going on. Education has always been of particular interest to politicians. Throughout the whole period I've been publishing books, education has been a battleground for competing ideas. If people wanted me in the midst of their classrooms and schools, then coming from the kind of background I came from, I could hardly stay aloof from these debates. Or, put another way, these debates would themselves be part of what and how I write.

The Project

At school
we were doing a
project.

You know the kind of thing:
THE VIKINGS –
TRANSPORT –
WOOD –

My son Joe
has done THE VIKINGS three times.
He did
STREETS
last term,
and the teacher didn't even take them into
a street.

He did
A VIEW OUT OF THE WINDOW
without even looking out of the window.

Our project was
HOLLAND.

There we were
reading:
'My friend Hans from Holland'
and we made windmills
and stuck blue strips of paper
onto white strips of paper.
They were canals.
And we kept talking about tulips
and cheese.
In the end
I thought they grew cheese
and ate tulips.

Then suddenly one day
our teacher
Miss Goodall
said that there was an inspector coming in.
She said he wasn't going to inspect us.
He was going to inspect her
and we were all to help her
by being really good
and answering all the questions that he asked us.

Later that day he came in.
He had a moustache.
We behaved.
Miss Goodall behaved.
There we all were
sitting in our rows
behind our desks
breathing very very quietly

and he looked at our windmills
and our canals
and he said:
What do they eat in Holland?
And I didn't put my hand up
in case I said tulips
but Sheena Maclean said cheese
and he said:
What do they grow in Holland?
and I didn't put my hand up for that one either
but Margot Vane said tulips.

And he asked some more questions
and we were doing really well.
Miss Goodall was trying very hard
not to look proud
and then he asked:
Who is the queen of Holland?

There was silence.

No one knew who was the queen of Holland.

Miss Goodall frowned
and started looking all round the class
with her eyes looking all hoping.
Then suddenly I remembered this funny little rhyme
that Harrybo used to say.

I put up my hand.

Yes, said the inspector.

Queen Juliana
is a fat banana, I said.

Miss Goodall looked awful.
Harrybo was sitting in front of me

and I saw him snort and start giggling.

What did you say? said the inspector.
Queen Juliana, I said.
Good, he said.
You're right, quite right.
Miss Goodall was delighted.
I was delighted.
The inspector was delighted
and Harrybo was still snorting away like mad.

I think we have reached a key moment for literature in schools. At present, it's no exaggeration to say that for children between the school years of Year 4 and Year 9 inclusive, books are an optional extra. It's literacy without literature. Literature can be reduced to an extract on a worksheet where the questions asked are about facts, chronology and logic. When poems are put in front of children, teachers are required to ask children (it's been modelled in the government's own magazine, *Teacher*) what form the poem is. I got an email the other day from a girl who asked me what form my poems 'Something Drastic' and 'Conversation' are. I wrote back saying that neither of these forms has a name. The first is a short rhyming poem with a repeated refrain or chorus, and the second is a dialogue or what we would call in the theatre a 'sketch'. She said thank you very much, but she had some maths homework too, was I any good at long division?

The education theory that has taken over the teaching of literature is logical positivism. That's to say, it is the notion that every process can be reduced to its component facts, chronology and logic. This is a lie. When we engage with reading or writing, we become involved in patterns of feeling. Our feelings about people, scenes and outcomes ebb and flow and change as the drama unfolds. This is how we grapple with the ethics inside ourselves and which we perceive as immanent in what we read. We do it with our feelings. Feelings and ethics. This is the stuff of reading and writing. The tyranny of the last fifteen years has been to exile this, stick it outside the classroom. And part and parcel of this has been the rise of hundreds of different kinds of selection processes, inside classrooms, inside schools, between schools: the regime of the SATs, the smiley-faces chart, the quick and slow tables, and the non-selective school that selects. Children who come from homes with no books may well never encounter whole books as part of their education. In so doing, they are discriminated against, because it's through the reading of whole books that we most pleasurably and most easily access complex and abstract ideas. Only the other night, while reading a Greek myth with my eight-year-old, we discussed what the word 'pity' meant.

Under this polity, poetry has become a bit of elastoplast that is slotted into the curriculum after tests, at the end of term as part of a ludicrous process of working through poetic forms. Once again, logical positivism wins out over humanism. You can name poetic forms because this is markable, testable knowledge, but you can't mark what people feel. Anthologies have been produced that fit this particular bill – spot the poetic forms – so that the idea of engaging with a poet (we're the people who write the stuff) has in many places been squeezed out. Teachers have to fight the pressure of SATs and Ofsted to develop humanistic approaches to literature.

The other day I wrote this:

Car School

One day a car pulled up at our school
and said,
'I'm your new head teacher.'
The old head teacher was taken out the back
and put in a skip
and the car drove into her office.

The car changed the name of our school.
It was called Car School
and we got a new uniform that had
a picture of a car on the front pocket.

The mayor came to our school
and said how lucky we were
that the car had come
and was sharing with us all that it knew
about cars.

Car School was in the local newspaper.
Everyone wanted to go to Car School.

To get in you had to do a Car Test.
There were questions about cars.
The mayor said that cars had a lot
to offer to the community
so that we could all move forward.

Some of the old teachers left
and the new teachers were cars.
Blue, red, silver, dark green.

A boy in my class wrote a story
about a car that ran someone over.
He was asked to see the head teacher
and we never saw him again.

A woman came to the school
to talk about road safety
and she said how going by bus
was a good idea.
One of the cars stood up
and said that what she was saying
was unbalanced and unfair.

I go to Car School.
Brrrrrrrmmmm.
Brrrrrrrrmmmm.
That's our school song.

But I also wrote this:

The Bell

There are forty-eight children in my class.
We sit in four rows of twelve.
We sit in twos, one next to the other,
as desks, with two lids, side by side,
one each.

Miss Williams works out where we sit.
We do tests: Arithmetic and English.
She adds up the marks
and whoever's got the best mark
sits at the top of the class
in the desk at the end of the first row,
next to the window.
Whoever gets the worst mark
sits at the bottom of the fourth row,
furthest from the window.
And she works out everyone else's place
from the mark that they get.

She does this every week.
Every week, we do tests.
Every week, we change places.
We take everything out of our desks
and move (very quietly) to where
she tells us to go.
This way, we always know
who's better than you
and we always know
who's worse than you.
Unless you come top,
when there's no one better than you.
Unless you come bottom,
when there's no one worse than you.
The same people are always in the top row.
The same people are always in the bottom row.
The same people are always in the two rows
in between.

Miss Williams says that only the top two rows
will pass their Eleven Plus.
She stands next to the last person on the
end of the second row.
She holds up her hand as if
she is helping people cross the road.

This side will pass, she says.
This side will fail, she says.

This way we know who are the
Eleven Plus Failures
and who are the Eleven Plus Passes.
We know all that
before we've even taken
the Eleven Plus exam.
Next door, there's another class.
They are all
Eleven Plus Failures.

I want to be twelfth.
This is because the person who is twelfth
sits nearest to the bell that sits
on top of Miss Williams's cupboard.
When you're twelfth,
you take the bell,
you go out of the room,
you go downstairs
and you stand in the hallway
outside the head teacher's office
and shake the bell so loudly
that the gonging fills the classrooms
and all the spaces in between.

All the children and teachers hear the sound
and come out of their classes
and walk (very quietly) down the stairs
and out into the playground.

All because you rang the bell.

I never have come twelfth.

And this:

The Two Poems

Once there were two poems.
One day they went to school.
The first poem went into class
and the teacher had been given some questions to ask:
Ask the children what kind of poem it is.
Ask the children why it is an effective poem.
Ask the children to underline the adjectives in the poem.
Ask the children what kind of green is pea-green.
Ask the children to tell you where was the ring before it was bought.
The second poem went into class
but this teacher had left the list at home.
The poem sat down and one child said,
'You remind me of when my auntie died.'
Another child said,
'I like the way you say things
over and over again in a sing-song sort of a way.'
Another child said, 'I'm going to write a poem
about being in a crowd of people.'
And another child said,
'I'm going to find some more poems like you.'
Soon the room was full of poems.
That night,
when the poems got home,
the first poem said,
'Today I had a strange day.'
The second poem said,
'Today I made lots of friends.'

What is Children's Poetry for? Towards a New, Child-specific *Apologie for Poetrie* (Philip Sidney, 1579)

This is the text of the Philippa Pearce Memorial Lecture which I gave at Homerton College, Cambridge on 10 September 2009.

First, many thanks to Homerton College and to the Philippa Pearce Memorial steering group for inviting me to give this lecture, and thanks too to all of you who've made the effort to come today. I knew Philippa a little, and always had the sense about her that she was part of the reason why I and all of us writing for children have the good fortune and pleasure of having an audience. She created scenes of such powerful feelings – anxiety, loss, mystery, danger, fun and the like, full of meaning and significance – that she created readers, and readers create other readers.

My job today is to talk about poetry, and I should clear up something right at the outset. The word 'apology' does of course mean some kind of statement to do with being sorry, but there is an older meaning of the word which signifies a defence of a position, coming from the Greek word we know today as 'apologia'. So, I won't be saying sorry for anything today. I will be putting up an argument in defence of poetry. You might well ask, but who's attacking it? And this takes us back to Philip Sidney, who wrote a paper which was named – not by him – but by his first publishers, one as *An Apology for Poetry*, and the other as *The Defence of Poesy*. It was probably written in the winter of 1579-80.

Philip Sidney grew up at the heart of the ruling elite's political and religious struggles.

He was given a full formal education from the age of 7, first with tutors from whom he learnt Latin, Italian and French. Then, at the age of 10, he was sent away to Shrewsbury Grammar School, a move that allied the family with the English Protestant hierarchy but also entailed a rigorous, nine-and-a-half-hour day working through Cicero, Terence, Cato, Tully, Caesar, Livy, Ovid, Horace, Virgil, Xenophon as well as the French romances of Belleforest, amidst a good deal of worship along Calvinist lines.

Next stop was Christ Church, Oxford with yet more Cicero, Horace and Virgil, along now with Aristotle's works on rhetoric – or what we would now call literary theory. It was at this point that he caught the eye of the Tudors' top man – Sir William Cecil. To spell this out, this meant that Philip Sidney was going to be groomed for high office in Protestant England. One of the consequences of this was that he was sent by Queen Elizabeth on a kind of three-year prototype Grand Tour of Europe, taking in Poland, Prague, Hungary and Italy as well as places nearer to home, intermingled with diplomacy and scouting for possible suitors for Elizabeth – or playing the game of scouting for suitors. This amazing period also drew him into the circle of the Tudors' spymaster, Sir Francis Walsingham, and many of Europe's major power players.

When he gets back in England, he is clearly one of Elizabeth's boys, with his life, career and marriage circumscribed by the nuanced requirements of the Elizabethan experiment with nationalist, unreformed Protestantism. So what is someone of this background doing writing a defence of poetry?

Well, the year he wrote it, Edmund Spenser had dedicated his poem 'The Shepheardes Calender' to Sidney. But there was another event. You'll remember that the Elizabethan experiment didn't simply involve a struggle between Catholic and Protestant but also involved what would turn out to be a deeper and more long-lasting struggle – signs of it are all about us today: Protestantism's conflict with the various strands of Calvinism which we've come to call Puritanism.

In 1579, one Stephen Gosson dedicated a pamphlet to Sidney called:

THE
Schoole of Abuse,
Conteining a plesaunt inuective
against Poets, Pipers,
Plaiers, Iesters and such like
Caterpillers of a commonwealth;
Setting vp the Flagge of Defiance to their
mischieuous exercise, and ouerthrowing
 their Bulwarkes, by Prophane
Writers, Naturall reason, and
common experience:
A discourse as pleasaunt for
Gentlemen that fauour learning,
as profitable for all that wyll
follow vertue.

This title in itself lays out very well the Puritan position: it is militant with its 'flag of defiance'; it is, in spite of the Puritans' seeming hostility to unfettered imagination and sensual imagery, happy to introduce a visceral poetic image: 'Caterpillers of a commonwealth'; and it lumps together a set of people whose activities in the name of verbal and bodily pleasure he deems to be 'mischieuous': 'Poets, Pipers, Plaiers, Iesters and such like'. More surprisingly, perhaps, the writer claims that these people can be overthrown not by religious argument but by 'common experience', 'Naturall reason' and the words of 'Prophane [i.e. non-religious] Writers'. The result will be 'profitable for all that wyll follow vertue'. 'Vertue' is a key word here. Puritans are virtuous people, who if they work, study and are industrious will achieve 'vertue', a godly state of being here on earth. Poets, pipers, players and jesters don't have virtue. They are mischievous. Here is Gosson in full flow (and I should interject that part of this talk today is about us enjoying the vigour, self-confidence and inventiveness of sixteenth-century poetic prose as a form of poetry in itself).

> The deceitfull Phisition giueth sweete Syrropes to make his poyson goe downe the smoother: The Iuggler casteth a myst to worke the closer: The *Syrens* song is the Saylers wrack: The Fowlers whistle, the birdes death: The wholesome bayte, the fishes bane: The Harpies haue Virgins faces, and vultures Talentes: *Hyena* speakes like a friend, and deuoures like a Foe: The calmest Seas hide dangerous Rockes: the Woolf iettes in Weathers felles: Many good sentences are spoken by *Danus,* to shadowe his knauery: and written by Poets, as ornaments to beautifye their woorkes, and sette theyr trumperie too sale without suspect.

NB 'iettes' is 'jets' and in this context means 'struts about'; 'Weathers felles' means sheep's skins. In other words, the wolf struts about in sheep's clothing.

> No marueyle though *Plato* shut them out of his schoole, and banished them quite from his common wealth, as effeminate writers, vnprofitable members, and vtter enimies to vertue.

If you enter the school of Poetry, as Gosson calls it, you will pass on to

> . . . Pyping, from Pyping to playing, from play to pleasure, from pleasure to slouth, from slouth to sleepe, from sleepe to sinne, from sinne to death, from death to the deuill.

In other words, through disguising its knavery and trumpery, poetry leads you downwards – via music, laziness and sin – to Hell.

So Sidney decided to defend poetry against this. Firstly, we should be clear that Sidney uses the word 'poetry' to sometimes mean what we would also call 'poetry' but at other times he means literary writing – verse, fiction and drama. This poetry has to be defended because it is, he says, always derived from 'nature', a word which we can take today to mean more like the whole of existence and experience. However, the poet isn't tied into representing nature as it is – as mathematicians, lawyers, grammarians and philosophers have to do.

> Only the poet, disdaining to be tied to any such subjection, lifted up with the vigour of his own invention doth grow in effect into another nature, in making things either better than Nature bringeth forth, or quite anew, forms such as never were in Nature, as the Heroes, Demigods, Cyclops, Chimeras, Furies and such like.

So literature has a Promethean quality of *creating* nature. When it imitates by means of Aristotle's 'mimesis', Sidney argues, it is:

> a representing, counterfeiting, or figuring forth to speake Metaphorically. A speaking Picture, with this end to teach and delight . . .

– quite the opposite model of Gosson's syrup and poison, where the problem is the pleasure. This image of the 'speaking Picture' has rightly become famous. Poetry as a speaking picture is an idea we can take with us into the present with its purpose to 'teach and delight'.

But this poesy has other functions. People sing the Psalms 'when they are merry', 'and I knowe,' Sidney says,

> [poesy] is used with the frute of comfort by some, when in sorrowfull panges of their death bringing sinnes, they finde the consolation of the never leaving goodnes.

Comfort and consolation then, even at death. Again, the opposite view to Gosson's, who saw poetry as taking you to the devil. What's more, says Sidney,

> This purifying of wit, this enriching of memorie, enabling of judgement,

and enlarging of conceit, which commonly we cal learning . . . the finall end is, to lead and draw us to as high a perfection, as our degenerate soules made worse by their clay-lodgings, can be capable of.

Enriching of memory, enabling of judgement, enlarging of our conceptual abilities (that's 'conceit'), pleasure, consolation, perfection and salvation. This is what you can get from poetry, Sidney is saying. Then, in a remarkable passage, he explains that whereas other disciplines explain and argue, poetry can show us emotion manifest in action.

Let us but hear old Anchices, speaking in the middest of Troies flames, or see Ulisses in the fulnesse of all Calipsoes delightes, bewaile his absence from barraine and beggarly Itheca . . .

We gain what he calls 'insight into anger' when we see Sophocles's Ajax 'whipping sheep and oxen', and further insights into feelings such as 'remorse of conscience in Oedipus', 'soon repenting pride in Agamemnon', 'self-devouring cruelty in Atreus', 'the violence of ambition in the two Theban brothers', and 'the sour sweetness of revenge in Medea'.

And how do we, as readers and listeners receive these? Sidney says, '. . . we seeme not to heare of them, but clearly to see through them.' So that's to say, I think, that through absorbing these moments in literature we come to understand their true purpose and essence; their meaning becomes transparent or clear without our consciously hearing how. And the result of all this is that when we read, say, of 'Dives burning in hell, and Lazarus in Abrahams bosome', these 'inhabit both the memorie and judgement'. So he is saying that by showing us these emotions in action, poetry ends up being 'memorable' but is also absorbed into our 'judgement' – or, as we might call it, our value-system.

The poet, Sidney concludes, is a 'popular philosopher'. But this isn't boring taught philosophy – and he mocks dry dusty academic philosophy teaching. This kind of teaching – through poetry – happens in another way:

For who will be taught, if he be not mooved with desire to be taught?

– a notion that flew in the face of the caners, beaters, drillers and bores of Sidney's own time and goes on flying down through the centuries since.

The poet – and he really does intend our meaning of 'poet' here – can do this because:

hee commeth to you with words set in delightfull proportion, either accompanied with, or prepared for the well enchanting skill of musicke . . .

And as an aside, he adds, it's not just the great classic writers who do this:

Certainly I must confesse mine owne barbarousnesse, I never heard the old Song of Percy and Duglas, that I founde not my heart mooved more than with a Trumpet; and yet is it sung but by some blinde Crowder . . .

He is referring here to the old folk ballad now known as 'Chevy Chase'. But how does poetry work? Sidney says:

Verse far exceedeth Prose, in the knitting up of the memorie, the reason is manifest, the words (besides their delight, which hath a great affinitie to memorie) being so set as one cannot be lost, but the whole woorke failes . . . Besides one word, so as it were begetting an other, as be it in rime or measured verse, by the former a man shall have a neare gesse to the follower.

There is in poetry a way in which a formal poem is measured out in such a way that dropping a word spoils the whole, and this in turn gives it a predictive quality: the pattern enables us to sense what is coming next.

I think all this constitutes a fascinating defence. There's a good deal we can take straight into now to help us understand what poetry offers us and what poetry can do.

But surely, in the present context, poetry doesn't need to be defended. And I should say my job today is not to talk about poetry in general – as Sidney did – but to defend it as an art for children. And yet, surely no one's attacking it? Well, I'm going to suggest that there *has* been an attack, and the attack has gone on by default, even as publicly, and in official policy, poetry has been defended. The process will be familiar to many of you, if only because I've talked about it before – perhaps too often – so excuse me going over old ground.

I'll put it this way. I was speaking at a joint meeting of head teachers from the NAHT and teachers from the NUT to discuss the forthcoming campaign against SATs. One head teacher was quite explicit. He said that he taught in a school made up almost entirely of children whose first language is not English. By comparing results in the SATs from year to year, he now knows (or is it 'thinks'?) that he can inch his school's position up the local league tables if he drops all reading of poetry and stories and spends most of Year 6 drilling the children in exercises geared to matching the tests. He hates doing it, he says. He can see the effect it has on the children emotionally, behaviourally and intellectually, but the league tables rule. He would love to be reading stories and poetry but he can't take the risk, he said.

So, we don't have a Stephen Gosson, as Philip Sidney had; we have a process, or a set of practices that quietly and insidiously has taken over in many schools. Not all schools by any means. Where teachers and parents have had the confidence to carry on reading and enjoying books, poetry included, this attack has been resisted. What's more, where parents have the knowledge and experience of what books and poetry can do for children, they too have carried on borrowing, buying, reading books and poetry with their children . . . which leaves a percentage – how big? perhaps we'll never know – of children of whom we can say that if they don't come across books and poetry when they're at school, they will probably never come across it. And somewhere, deeply embedded in what I've called a quiet and insidious practice, is a notion that says, in effect, 'So be it. It doesn't matter. If those children don't get books and poetry, tough.' Instead of Sidney's account of 'insight into anger', the soon repenting pride in Agamemnon, the self-devouring cruelty in Atreus, the violence of ambition in the two Theban brothers and the sour sweetness of revenge in Medea, those children will have this (I quote verbatim from a worksheet and in its entirety; it's not me cutting anything here; and again excuse me, those who've heard me read this before):

Perseus and the Gorgons

This is part of a myth from ancient Greece.

At last Perseus found the Gorgons. They were asleep among the rocks, and Perseus was able to look at them safely.

Although they were asleep, the live serpents which formed their hair were writhing venomously. The sight filled Perseus with horror. How could he get near enough without being turned to stone?

Suddenly Perseus knew what to do. He now understood why Athena had given him the shining bronze shield. Looking into it he saw clearly the reflection of the Gorgons. Using the shield as a mirror, he crept forward. Then with a single swift blow he cut off the head of the nearest Gorgon. Her name was Medusa.

In one mighty swoop, Perseus grabbed the head of Medusa. He placed it safely in his bag and sprang into the air on his winged sandals.

To my mind this is utterly insufficient. It's an act of deliberate deprivation to deliver this up to children, as it denies them the context and motive for action, and in so doing drains the story of fear and tension. Or to put it another way, as we don't know why Perseus is going to see the Gorgons, we don't feel with him the danger. If we don't feel the danger, we don't enjoy the ingenuity of his success or the pleasure in his ultimate victory. The engine at the heart of literature has been taken out of this piece, purely in order that the writing can be used as a pretext for asking a set of comprehension questions as printed on the other side of the story:

Why had Perseus brought a bag with him?
Who had given Perseus his shield?

And so on for ten more questions like it, each with specifically right answers. Empricism has seized power. Sidney is overthrown. So, I say, in the face of this kind of mental cruelty, I think we need as stout a defence of poetry for children (and perhaps I'll leak over into Sidney's broader use of the word poetry than our contemporary usage) as Sidney offered. Where he was speaking with all the confidence of a rising class of Tudor Protestant nationalists and humanists, I'll borrow some of that humanism and marry it to some ideas to do with the rights of individuals to explore their identities – including and especially language; along with what is in effect a form of *inter*nationalism which work in classrooms affords us.

I've spoken too long on this subject without reading a poem. This is by Paul Lyalls.

My Mate Darren

When I was a kid, my best mate Darren had
a great way of getting his toy soldiers to have a war.
He'd line them up on the kitchen floor,
close the kitchen door, draw the kitchen window blind,
set an alarm clock to ring in one minute's time,
switch off the kitchen light, making the kitchen dark as night.

Then he'd take his tennis racquet
and swing it from left to right with all his might
knocking his soldiers everywhere,
sending them flying through the air.
Making them spin – even his dog joined in,
scampering about with a mouthful of toy soldiers sticking out.
Then when the alarm clock would ring, whichever side
had the most soldiers still standing would win.
Years later, Darren now a man, strong and big,
was helping his mum bring in a brand new fridge.
When he moved the old one,
he found underneath, in the dirt and the grease,
3 toy soldiers who were still fighting the war,
waiting for an enemy that wasn't there anymore.
He dusted them down, stood them gently on the ground
and with as much love as he could,
he told them.
'It's over. You no longer need to be a toy soldier.
You can go back to your wives,
your families and friends you used to know,
lead your former lives. The fighting finished 10 years ago.'
As gently as he could he told them 'there is no more war'.
But no one told his dog,
who ran back in and chewed them up once more.

My first point will be to say that poetry like this does a lot of things at the same time. Here are some of them:

It tells a story.

It offers us Sidney's 'speaking picture'.

Which, in turn, teaches and delights us . . . and delights us in many different ways, one of which is that it is derived from nature – or as we would say now, from experience and existence.

But part of this is that it 'counterfeits' and 'represents', as Sidney put it – that's to say there is something symbolic going on in the poem that is more than what it appears to be talking about. There is also emotion manifest in action – some of which we can give names to – delight in play, something to do with the absurdity of war or destruction, and something to do with the difference between humans and animals, perhaps . . . and a whole lot more besides.

We've also got something here of Sidney's 'well enchanting skill of musicke'. The unfolding of the poem with its rhythm and rhyme (and the expectations that go with these) gives us the sense that this story will roll along through to a conclusion, but also perhaps in the rhyme there is some kind of gentle self-mockery, that undermines the seriousness of the protagonists. And what of the Promethean aspect? Well, the construction of the whole piece – its crescendo, Darren's supposed speech – are precisely this. 'A form that was never in nature,' as Sidney says.

And the poem enters Sidney's 'memory and judgement'. We are aided in the memory by the rhyme – when I see Paul Lyalls I've started saying to him:

> there is no more war
> but no one told his dog,
> who ran back in and chewed them up once more.

And what about the judgement, that value-system inside us? By some process – that, Sidney says, taught us by *moving* us to be taught', the values of the poem find their way in, find their place – 'inhabit', Sidney says, perhaps snugly, perhaps by challenging it, perhaps by co-operating with it – whatever value system we call our own. So, at one level perhaps it does say, with the poem, 'no more war' but at another, doesn't the poem have a laugh at the simplicity (or is it the simplistic nature?) of saying 'no more war'? Is there a conversation here being had with the end of 'Dulce et Decorum est', when Wilfred Owen says:

> If you could hear, at every jolt, the blood
> Come gargling from the froth-corrupted lungs
> Bitter as the cud
> Of vile, incurable sores on innocent tongues, –
> My friend, you would not tell with such high zest
> To children ardent for some desperate glory,
> The old Lie: *Dulce et decorum est*
> *Pro patria mori.*

Then again, the poem seems also to be inhabiting similar territory – but in a comic, ironic way – to the end of *The House at Pooh Corner.*

> Christopher Robin was going away. Nobody knew why he was going;

> nobody knew where he was going: indeed, nobody even knew why
> he knew that Christopher Robin *was* going away.

In Milne's words, there is something ineffable and mysterious about 'the going away' of growing up. But then in place of 'that enchanted place on the top of the Forest' where 'a little boy and his Bear will always be playing', we've got the gritty naturalism of Paul Lyalls' soldiers stuck under an old fridge, followed by the dog eating them again.

So I think this constitutes something like Sidney's 'popular philosophy'. In the place of A.A. Milne's time-fighting suggestion that either childhood goes on forever, or that it survives because of his own book, we have Lyalls's bluntness that leaves us with Darren not as a child but as a man and the soldiers gone – apart, once again, from their presence on the page in Lyalls's poem. The poem plays with time, change and continuity. It sends us as adult readers back to our childhoods. With children, I suspect it breaks them out of their synchronic continuum – the state of permanent childhood, which I can never sort out clearly in my mind as something we foist on children or something they fight to preserve – and it brings them sharply into the diachronic continuum so brilliantly and amazingly presented to us, of course, by Philippa herself with *Tom's Midnight Garden*.

So, yes, popular philosophy too.

Something I like about Sidney's defence is that it appears to be talking about wisdom encapsulated in poetry. He talks of 'insights' and 'judgement' and 'learning'. I see literature as being, in effect, three thousand years of wisdom about human behaviour put in a form that we can understand and take pleasure in. And yet, for some incredible reason, we have created an environment in some schools, in some classrooms (not all, please note), where the writing of summarisers, extract-hacks and writer-substitutes has been promoted above the level of those who've spent their whole lives trying to perfect ways of encapsulating wisdom and feeling into literary form. So not only do we get the banal re-writing of 'part of a myth' but we also get – and I'll hesitate to give the exact example – people who produce school textbooks on say, personal development, which include sessions on bereavement, anger, jealousy and the like, but the writer of the lesson plans, knowing that poetry often deals with this sort of thing, chooses not to find great poetry to stimulate talk about such things. Instead, she sticks in a bunch of poems of her own, saying thereby, 'All that stuff written in the previous three thousand years won't be able to do its job better than me.'

363

So, I'm going to say that what poetry and all fictions do is encapsulate wisdom about human behaviour, and they do this, as Sidney implies, by marrying ideas with feeling and putting them into sequences derived originally from experience and existence but which may also involve creatures and beings that have never been seen or heard of before. And in the process of reading this, we will find out what it feels like to be someone facing danger or love or disaster or fun and the like. The poem or the story will do some experimenting for us.

Now, I would like to add some more defences. This poem is by Jackie Kay.

The Angler's Song

Down where I am, my love, there is no love.
There is no light, no break of day, no rising sun.
Where I am, I call you in; I open my large mouth.
The only light down here comes from my body.

Down where I am is deeper than you imagine.
There is no food, no easy prey, and it is freezing cold.
I sing to make you say my name. My big eyes weep.
This is the world of never-ending darkness, like pain.

Come down. I have been waiting for you a long time.
I wait without appearing to wait.
I see without being seen to see. You know me.
I am big-headed. I am hideous. I am ugly.

Come down. When I find you, I will bite into your belly.
What you see is what you get with me.
There is no other way. I will become you, let us say.
All that will be left of me will be my breathing.

Come down where I am. In and out, out and in.
Down at the very bottom of the deep dark sea.
When I become you, my mouth will stay open.
My open mouth like the river mouth down at the bottom.

Come down where I am. I will flash my lights for you.
My large eyes will take you in, contain you.
I make no promises. I offer nothing. Not even light.
Down, deep down in the dark, at the bottom, is my bed.

My sea bed, love, where there are no promises of love.
Dark – where there are no promises of light.
Where there is little hope of food.
Where day and night are night and day.

My sea bed. I tell no lies so your heart
will not be broken. I offer nothing.
All you will have is my breathing.
But I will give myself up to you.

I will give myself up for you.

Much of children's lives is circumscribed by explicit and implicit rules. These come ultimately from all the adults around them. No matter how hard we as adults try, we find it very difficult to grant children autonomy over parts of their own lives – even when there is no justification in an argument for health and safety, or psychological danger or whatever. I look at our new kitchen and realise that at present we've put a lot of things out of reach of the children. Is there any reason why children shouldn't be able to get a bowl or a cup by themselves? Why have we built dependence even into our kitchen?

I think poetry, when handled well, offers autonomy. It does this, I would argue, through several channels:

Suggestion
Reflection
Juxtaposition
Physicality of language
Mutability of language
And interculturalism.

Jackie Kay writes in her poem:

My sea bed. I tell no lies so your heart
will not be broken. I offer nothing.

This is elliptical. We have no means to judge or determine exactly why the angler fish will tell no lies, why it will offer nothing. All we can do is infer and guess and wonder. We will occupy a space that is unfamiliar for many children, and yet it's one which is terribly important – a space where vague and indeterminate sensations are all we have to go on. Very often, for life to carry on, we can't assume that there are right and wrong answers. We have to figure out what other people's behaviour is about and for. And this sort of thing needs reflection.

And yet it seems that for some children, some schools are forced into saying, in effect, 'There isn't time for reflection.' And I mean here the kind of reflection that looks at something, wonders about it, and hears a variety of voices alongside you that also wonder about it. I'm not such a poetry chauvinist that I think this can only come about through poetry. It can come about from a group of children looking at how a dandelion has grown between two cracks in the pavement. But poetry, nevertheless, does offer this potential.

My sea bed. I tell no lies so your heart
will not be broken. I offer nothing.
All you will have is my breathing.
But I will give myself up to you.

I will give myself up for you.

The meaning of poetry does indeed often come to us musically – repetition being one of the musical cadences available to poets, but it also comes to us through the sideways process of juxtaposition. Here, Jackie Kay has juxtaposed the idea of a sea bed with 'no lies' with 'no heart broken', and then with nothingness being on offer. Then on to all that's being offered is breathing. Then on to the idea that the 'I' of the poem will give itself up to the 'you' of the poem. These six or so images aren't necessarily or easily linked. There are only two 'connectives', as the National Literacy Strategy called them – a 'so' and a 'but' – but they don't really seem to help us in making a logical connection between things. But please note, extract-writers, comprehension-question-setters, SATs-testers, logic is not what's going on here. The poem is forcing us to make connections simply by placing images side by side. I can't speak for people here, but by reading, re-reading, reading and thinking, I start to get a feeling about the angler fish, perhaps a feeling about me. A feeling about saying things, through breathing and not talking. A feeling about trust, I think. In some kind of bed.

I'm going to make the claim that to go through this process in an open-ended way, in a co-operative way with people you trust – or entirely on your own – gives children – and all of us – a chance to investigate how and why, in daily life as lived, feelings and ideas are inseparable.

Moving on, Sidney also talked of poetry's music and proportion. And following that, I think that in one respect, one side of poetry has a particular part to play in children's lives. It's in its physicality.

> He had a little sticker
> And he had a little ticket
> And he took the little sticker
> And he stuck it to the ticket.
>
> Now he hasn't got a sticker
> And he hasn't got a ticket
> He's got a bit of both
> Which he calls a little 'sticket'.
>
> They won't let you on the bus with a sticket.

Whatever else this poem does, it draws attention to something about the similarity of the words 'sticker', 'ticket', 'stuck' and 'sticket'. This runs across what language is thought to do, which is that it's there to convey meaning, as if words only exist to give you facts. It turns out that the poem conveys very little factual meaning apart from making a connection between words, as they say, at the level of the signifier. For children, this has a special role. One of the important parts of being a child is hearing words, whether spoken directly to you, or spoken in the air, without knowing what they mean. Instead, all you hear is the word's physicality, its material existence, if you like – its sound, its tone, its pitch, its volume, its rhythm, its place in a cadence of words, and the like. In this environment, such words exist as signifiers without signifying, through what's been called the process of denoting. Instead, it conveys feeling through connoting – gathering up and delivering the words' associations. And, as people like Julie Kristeva and Jacques Derrida have suggested, a lot of what's being connoted will be because of how one word sounds in relation to the similar sounding words around it. Apart from poetry and song, there are very few, if any, outlets for children in schools to explore this area of being, much of which must be tinged with anxiety. Think of how we feel when we travel to countries where we can't speak the language. Physical poetry like my sticker-ticket poem allows, I would suggest, a release through play from some of that anxiety. It plays with words. Instead of treating words as sacrosanct little parcels of meaning, it offers relief from the relentless signifying of history, geography, maths, school rules, home rules and comprehension exercises about the Gorgons. It gives us all, but children in particular, a space in which to acknowledge the fact that language exists in its own right as a puzzling, peculiar set of phenomena just as rocks, birds and houses exist in their own right. Poetry is then also about language itself.

But there's more to this. When we show children words being physical, we also show them that language is mutable. It can be played with, according to patterns of sound, in order sometimes to see what signifiers might spring up. And this is one of the bases of nonsense poetry which creates new worlds, just as Sidney described, often held together by recurring sounds, peopled by beings whose names, like Jumblies, Jabberwocks and Snarks, half-echo previously heard places, people and creatures. Most of education travels in the opposite direction: it teaches correct usage, as handed down from those of us who know what correctness is. It teaches apposite and appropriate usage – *le mot juste* – whether that's in French, maths, history, school rules or wherever. A lot of poetry, in particular poetry for children, suggests that that correctness or appropriateness can be subverted, and you, children, can – if you want – subvert it too.

> Ladles and jellyspoons,
> I come before you, to stand behind you,
> To tell you something I know nothing about.
> Next Thursday, which is Good Friday,
> There will be a mothers' meeting for fathers only.
> Admission is free, pay at the door,
> Pull up a seat and sit on the floor.

> We will be discussing the four corners of the round table.

Apart from anything else, this suggests that you can play not only with language, but also with the world.

And so to interculturalism.

Now, it's been argued that Sidney's *Apology* was in part a defence of something specifically English – there hasn't been time to explore this. Instead, I would want to propose a process that is rarely celebrated in relation to poetry. I would argue that no matter how we write, or even how we read, we do so with the culture we own, live with and live through. We cannot escape the processes of acculturation that we have lived – food, language, gesture, frame of mind, habits – all of it and much more. Poetry can't escape it either. However, there is a theory around in education that knowledge and skills are value-free, that they aren't cultural – or if they are, there are some that are so absolute and universal we shouldn't waste our time describing them as being cultural.

Poetry doesn't waste much time doing this either. It just gets on and 'does' culture. It expresses the way we are, the way we live, the way we think. It offers this up in what are now (less so in Sidney's time) a huge range of forms – some very short, others long and expository. It can be imagistic or full of dialogue. It can be interior monologue, it can be narrative, or it can fight narrative and explore states of being and existence. It can draw attention to its writerliness by playing with words, or it can appear (though this will be an illusion) to be seamless with reality by being bald, concise and simple. All this makes it hugely various, open to choice by readers to find the shapes and forms that they want and like and indeed might want to adopt or adapt themselves.

More mutability.

The Difference

In Glasgow
the hotel gave us something called
'Soap'.
In Edinburgh
the hotel gave us the same stuff
and it was called:
'Skincare Bar'.

So, by scavenging around in the displayed words and detritus of human existence – itself an important process to show children – poetry can express how people define themselves or how others choose to define them. If we put that into an open-ended context of several or many people sharing ideas like this, poetry becomes intercultural. It shares.

I would suggest (just as Sidney did in claiming a seriousness for poetry at the level of salvation) that in a way interculturalism possesses the ingredients for a kind of salvation. Not heavenly, but earthly. I've seen children looking at pictures of refugees escaping the bombing of Barcelona in 1936 and then writing poems based on the idea that right now, they've got to leave and take with them important things, important memories, important wishes and desires. And then I've seen these children, some of them refugees themselves – from a wide range of faith and national backgrounds: Bangladesh, Nigeria, the Caribbean, Eastern Europe and the UK – share these around in a circle, talking of such intimate details as a hug from a grandmother or a look in someone's eyes. Whatever else we do to make the world safer and better, we will have to do quite a lot of this kind of sharing of feeling and understanding.

Many thanks to Paul Lyalls and to Jackie Kay for allowing me to read their poems in the talk, and to reprint them here. Jackie's poem originally appeared in her Red Cherry Red, *published by Bloomsbury.*

Poetry for Children

I wrote this as a chapter for Modern Children's Literature: an Introduction, *edited by Catherine Butler and Kimberley Reynolds, published by Macmillan in 2014.*

The most common approaches to literature for children attempt to define the field in terms of intention, style, content or audience – or all four. Poetry written for and read by children poses at least one extra problem: a good deal of what has been traditionally served to children   particularly in the context of education – only becomes poetry for children by virtue of it being in an anthology clearly marked for and framed by its intended audience. So, poems which might start out life (or live for many years) as poems circulating between adults may well be found, and approved of, by a group of adults (anthologisers, editors, education advisers), who put them in, say, a school anthology, a child's Christmas annual or a commercial out-of-school anthology. Where this differs from the rest of children's literature is that the process happens for all ages of children, including the very youngest. Adult books like *Robinson Crusoe* (1719) and *Oliver Twist* (1838) have of course been published for children, but with these there is a tradition of editing and abridging the texts, while the anthologised adult poems – Shakespeare's songs, for example – have often been offered in their entirety. This means that such poems become a form of children's literature by virtue of their 'framing' and the 'reading situation'.

Within the English-speaking world, poetry for children has tended to develop a distinctive national – sometimes explicitly nationalist – tradition. This has mainly revolved around the choice of poets put before children in their respective countries. The exceptions are what come to be called 'classic' poems, a tiny few of which travel around the English-speaking world, or where a particular effort is made to publish collections by individual poets from other countries or specifically international collections with the aim of representing poets from many cultures and countries. An essay could be written about how nation and nationalism have been yoked to poetry for young people in a way that is not done with, say, music. The consequence is that the development and progress of poetry for children in anglophone countries tends to unfold in the countries' respective bubbles. I make this point partly to make clear that this essay is in its own way 'national', as it largely charts the development of children's poetry in Britain. This follows the pattern laid down by the two most important critical books in this field, *From the Garden to the Street:*

Three Hundred Years of Poetry for Children, Morag Styles (1998) and *Poetry's Playground: the Culture of Contemporary American Children's Poetry*, Joseph T. Thomas Jr. (2007).

So, given that there is a distinctive quality to the category of 'poetry for children' (in this case within the UK), one approach that may help us corral and examine the species is to ask, 'Where is poetry for children?' Here is an outline answer to this question.

Anthologies made up of many poets' work, often graded or selected in terms of age, kind of school, sex of child, a particular examination, published in ways that clearly mark them out to be 'school books'

So long as we consider the reading habits and tastes of all children, and not a highly specific group of children, it cannot be emphasised enough that education plays the pre-eminent role in the history of the reading of poetry by children. No matter how popular individual poems or poets have been, e.g. Robert Louis Stevenson or Shel Silverstein, the means by which most children become acquainted with what we might call 'literary poetry' has been as a direct consequence of what teachers in schools have done with it. That said, we shouldn't forget that the consumption of the school anthology has had to match the extent of mass full-time education, i.e. for very few in 1800, say, but for almost everyone under the age of 11 by 1900.

I suspect that anyone reading this essay will be familiar with at least one anthology from their time at school, though there seems to be some mystery about when these books first started appearing. An argument could be made that from as early as the mid-sixteenth century, middle- and upper-class boys were taught poetry through special editions of Latin and Greek poets (see Mack, 2002: 17-19). It seems as if it was harder for editors to prove to teachers (or teachers to editors?) that poetry in English (unless it was specifically for initial literacy teaching – see below) had a fit place in the school curriculum. Vicesimus Knox (1752-1821), the editor of *Elegant Extracts: or useful and entertaining PIECES OF POETRY, Selected for the Improvement of Young Persons* (London and Dublin, 1789) sets out his stall in the Preface:

> . . . if I should be asked what are its [the book's] pretensions, I must freely answer, that it professes nothing more than (what is evident at first sight) to be a larger Collection of English Verse, FOR THE USE OF SCHOOLS, than has ever yet been published IN ONE

VOLUME. The original intention was to comprise in it a great number and variety of such pieces as were already in use in school, or which seemed proper for the use of them; such a number and variety as might furnish something satisfactory to every taste, and serve as a little Poetical Library for school-boys, precluding the inconvenience and expence [*sic*] of a multitude of volumes. [p.vi. Apart from square brackets, brackets and upper case as in original.]

Interestingly, according to Susan Allan Ford (2007) one of Knox's collections is mentioned in Jane Austen, and

...when Thomas James, headmaster of Rugby, in 1798 advised Samuel Butler, new headmaster at Shrewsbury, on developing a library of English books, he thriftily emphasized anthologies.

This collection lays down something of a blueprint for the category of both the school and home anthology (see the next section). Its two volumes are arranged into 'Books'. In Book I, 'Sacred and Moral', the editor offers readers a selection of the Psalms; hymns including some by the then-living 'Mrs Barbauld' (Anna Laetitia Barbauld, 1743-1825); verses from Isaac Watts's (1674-1748) *Divine Songs* (first published 1715), including 'Against Idleness and Mischief' which begins, 'How doth the little busy bee . . . ' (p. 61, Vol. I) and which would be parodied sixty years later by Lewis Carroll; verse fables from 'the late Mr GAY' (John Gay, 1685-1732, best known for *The Beggar's Opera*); 'FABLES for the FEMALE SEX, by Mr. MOORE' (Edward Moore, 1712-1757); and several poems by Robert Burns (1759-1796) and Alexander Pope (1688-1744). One clear survivor from this part of the anthology is 'An Elegy, written in a Country Church-Yard' (p.22, Vol. I) by Thomas Gray (1716-1771).

Book II is devoted to the 'Didactic, Descriptive, Narrative and Pathetic'. In this section, names familiar to us now are Oliver Goldsmith (1730-1774), Alexander Pope (1688-1744), John Dryden (1631-1700), Thomas Gray (1716-1771), William Cowper (1731-1800) and George Crabbe (1754-1832), the selection of last two poets putting down a clear marker of the editor's sympathies with the rural poor.

Book III is titled, 'Dramatic &c.' and includes 35 extracts from Shakespeare, including (from *The Tempest*) Ariel's songs, 'Full fathom five' and 'Where the bee sucks . . . ' and Caliban's anti-colonial speech, 'This island's mine . . . '.

In Book IV, 'Sentimental, Lyrical, and Ludicrous', we find Milton's 'L'Allegro',

'Il Penseroso' and 'Lycidas' (staples of upper-school literature courses in British grammar and public schools), a good deal from Edmund Spenser (c.1552-1599), Jonathan Swift (1667-1745), Cowper, Dr Johnson (1709-1784) and long-serving anthologists' favourites, Robert Burns's 'To a Mouse' and Oliver Goldsmith's 'An Elegy on the Death of a mad Dog'. Indeed, this 'Book' is full of animals and includes anonymous and comical epitaphs and epigrams (including Rochester's subversive epitaph for Charles II), Cowper's 'The Negro's Complaint' – suggesting that Knox was an abolitionist, followed by a last section, 'Songs, Ballads, &c. &c.' Survivors from this section include Henry Carey's (1687-1743) 'Sally in our Alley' – clearly thought to be not too risqué, Christopher Marlowe's 'Come live with me, and be my love . . . ', the subversive 'The Vicar of Bray' (anon.), and some more Shakespeare songs ('Under the green-wood tree', 'Come follow, follow me'). Number 86 (p. 908, Vol. II) seems to be taken from a popular broadside, telling the story of a 'maid in Bedlam' whose lover was sent to sea by his cruel parents. Number 101 (p. 912) is 'The Children in the Wood; or, The Norfolk Gentleman's last Will and Testament', probably taken from a chapbook; Number 102 is 'The Hunting in Chevy Chase' and so on through a strong selection of classic folk ballads (the kind classified by Francis Child) and which Knox could have found in Bishop Percy's *Reliques* (1765) or *A Collection of Old Ballads* (1723) or from even earlier: *Wit and Mirth: Or Pills to Purge Melancholy* (edited by Thomas d'Urfey, 1698-1720). There's even room for a comical broadside 'trade' ballad telling how a barber woos and wins a woman who runs a fish stall at the end of Fleet-market. The fee for the wedding is paid by the barber by shaving the parson's chin, while the bride 'entertain'd him with pilchards and gin' (pp. 952-953, Vol. II). The book ends with a selection of prologues and epilogues.

(The 1805 edition comes in at 1016 pages in the two volumes.)

Knox espoused some of the 'progressive' or 'liberal' causes of his day, including feminism and pacifism. In contrast to the school anthologies of the Victorian and Edwardian eras, there is hardly any representation in the book of poems celebrating war, and where later anthologies would overlook women completely, Knox gives a presence to the strongly anti-establishment writers Anna Laetitia Barbauld and Charlotte Turner Smith (1749-1806).

The modern school anthology – that's to say published within an educational market, selling books aimed at every single child – bears the marks of having had to take note of many of the cultural streams of thought hovering in and around the educational world. These, like Knox's beliefs, are 'liberal' ideas to do with class, gender, race, environment and social action. This means that general school anthologies of the last fifty years have tried to represent poets from a wide range of social and cultural backgrounds. The breakthrough moment in Britain for the modern school anthology came with the collections *Voices* (1968) and *Junior Voices* (1970), edited by Geoffrey Summerfield (1931-1991) and published by Penguin Education. In the *Handbook* (1968) for *Voices,* Summerfield laid out a programme that has served to inform many since:

> I have not attempted in my selection to provide a bird's eye view of English poetry. I wanted to provide a diverse range of voices that can and will speak to pupils and to their condition. Modern and contemporary poetry dominate: this is due to my own pupils' enthusiasms . . . Poems serve to sharpen our sense of life and to present others' sense of life. To the poems we bring our own lives; in sharing the poems with our pupils, we also to some degree share our lives. (p. 7)

This child-centred view of the anthologist's job reverses the note that many anthologists hit when claiming that a poem will of itself uplift and enlighten. In a short chapter, 'Poetry in the classroom' (pp. 9-11) and in some footnotes on the poems, Summerfield outlines what might appear to some as strange: the guidelines offer a 13-point way 'in which poem, pupils and teacher can meet', but these don't involve the usual closed-ended interrogation that has dominated poetry within education for decades. Instead, the emphasis is on developing interest and taste through choice, discussion, imitation, performance and thought. Through these methods (not instruction), Summerfield claims that the pupils will attend to 'such matters as tone, rhythm, intention, emphasis, form and so on'. At the time this method was revolutionary; it moved to centre stage in the decades following and in the present era has become revolutionary again – or should I say, in exile? To appreciate what a departure from the previous era this was, we should also factor in the wide range of cultures and poetic types that were represented in these seven volumes.

Themed school anthologies have appeared over the last thirty years focussing on, for example, the environment, the supernatural, women poets, 'scary' poems, 'world' poetry and Caribbean poetry, while another tug on the anthologist has come from specific curriculum requirements. So, for example, when England and Wales laid down what was in effect a graded (by year and by term within a year) poetry curriculum as part of a National Literacy Strategy, some anthologists stepped in to provide the books to suit the strategy.

It is within the school anthology, particularly since the 1960s, that poems from all over the English-speaking world have reached children in the UK. The presence of poems from Seamus Heaney, Ogden Nash, Rabindranath Tagore, Carl Sandburg, Eve Merriam, Dennis Lee, Mary Ann Hoberman, Nikki Giovanni, Shel Silverstein, Jack Prelutsky, John Ciardi, Langston Hughes, William Carlos Williams, Banjo Paterson, Louise Bennett and many others has been as a consequence of anthologists seeking them out and teachers reading them with children. In addition, a sub-canon of translated poems has been established with strong favourites reappearing from, e.g., Arthur Waley's translations of ancient Chinese poetry, Basho's haiku, Miroslav Holub and Christian Morgenstern.

Anthologies made up of many poets' work, clearly marked for an intended child audience at home

As Susan Allan Ford has shown, *Elegant Extracts* not only appears in *Emma* but also had a place on the Austen family's shelves, so we may take it that for some middle-class people, the idea of reading poetry at home and not as a specifically religious practice had already taken root by the late eighteenth century. Another early anthology for children was put together by Lucy Aiken in her collection *Poetry for Children, Consisting of Short Pieces to be Committed to Memory* (1801), which by its title tells us what one of the purposes and practices of reading poetry was. By virtue of its prosody, reading poetry carefully selected by adults for children may well enable us to commit it to memory, but bundled up with that came notions about why this is a virtuous or worthwhile or enlightening activity. This may include any of the following: showing children a correct way to follow religious observations; to open the eyes of children to the nature of God's creation and/or of 'Nature'; stirring children to be patriotic; awakening children to the iniquities, absurdities and mysteries of humanity; showing children that they can meditate or reflect on anything from the smallest to the largest phenomena, and/or their incredible diversity; passing on wisdom; revealing the possibilities and beauty of what can be done with words. In Aiken's words:

By the aid of verse, a store of beautiful imagery and glowing sentiment may be gathered up as the amusement of childhood, which, in riper years, may soothe the heavy hours of languor, solitude, and sorrow, may strengthen feelings of piety, humanity, and tenderness, may soothe the soul to calmness, rouse it to honourable exertion, or fire it with virtuous indignation. (p. 3)

We may note that this last intention to do with firing up 'virtuous indignation' was a political statement linked to Aiken's selection of such poems as 'The Vanity of Greatness' (Shirley), 'The Orphan Boy' (Thelwall), 'Against Slavery' (Cowper) and 'The Dying Negro' (anon.).

In the modern era, sometimes the power of full-colour artwork has been brought to bear on poetry in these home anthologies, while others have produced cheap paperbacks accompanied by black and-white drawings or cartoons. This divergence expresses a split between on the one hand those who have a sense that poetry is, or should be, edifying and uplifting, and on the other those who want to revel in its potential for populism – vulgarity, even. At the heart of this discussion is the question of the 'classic' poem and its sub-category, the classic poem for children. A canon is culturally constructed, but the exact instruments of the construction are not always visible. In the case of poetry for children, the canon has been effected largely through co-operation between those at some level of power within education and those who make school and home anthologies. It's a kind of double-sieving process involving recommendations, quotations and presentations.

This raises some questions. What ideological outlook is represented by the canon? What ideological outlooks lie outside of the canon? Does the canon change? *The Puffin Book of Classic Verse*, edited by Raymond Wilson (1995), is divided up into sections: 'Come! Come Away!', 'All in a Day', 'Creatures', 'Very Remarkable Beasts', 'Ghosts, Ghouls and Witches', 'The Sea', 'Mystery, Dreams and Enchantments', 'Love's Moods', 'Song and Dance', 'People', 'Figures of Fun', 'School', 'The City', 'War', 'Reflections', 'Seasons' and 'Journey's End'. Most of the poets are English, male and dead. Non-English poets here include the Americans Robert Frost, Walt Whitman, Don Marquis, Bret Harte, Vachel Lindsay, Ogden Nash, Jack Prelutsky, the Scots Robert Louis Stevenson, the Irish James Stephens and the Welsh Dylan Thomas. There are 19 female poets (out of 146 poets in all, excluding a handful by anon.), including Christina Rossetti, Emily Dickinson, Elizabeth Jennings, Stevie Smith, Dorothy Parker and Amy Lowell. There are 18 poets in the anthology who were living at the time Wilson was editing the book.

To be absolutely clear: I am not pillorying Raymond Wilson. Far from it. I've edited a collection of 'classic' poetry myself with a not dissimilar distribution of poets! What I'm raising here concerns the composition of the category 'classic' and the question of why we want or need poetry to be packaged up in this way. It should be said that Wilson, in a collection as large as this, has diverged from some aspects of the classic children's poetry mould by adding on what I suspect are personal favourites, whilst laying to rest some of the more tub-thumping poems of the British Empire that were compulsory fare in British schools until the 1960s. However, there is hardly any room in the collection for poems by anyone of colour – the notable exception being the African-American poet Margaret Walker. It also goes without saying (though perhaps we should question this) that 'classic' poems do not include anything in translation unless it's from the Bible, or from Anglo-Saxon or Chaucer. So we can say that Wilson and I find ourselves constructed by the category. This raises the question of whether the term 'classic' suggests to people (adult buyers, probably) that it offers young readers all that's worth reading by way of poetry; it offers a sufficiency. Or, to reverse that, does the term 'classic' suggest that simply by being given that designation the poem will reach and touch all children? In both cases, I would hope not.

Themed anthologies for home consumption have been published in the present era but they find it difficult to make headway in the market unless they come clearly marked as being comic.

Verse narratives or verse texts in chapbooks, comics, comic annuals; as the verse narratives or verse texts in stand-alone books

From at least as early as 1630, a Londoner could buy from a ballad-seller in the street a printed ballad version of the Tom Thumb story, presented as: 'Tom Thumbe, his life and death: wherein is declared many maruailous [sic] acts of manhood, full of wonder, and strange merriments . . . ' (reprinted in Ritson, *Ancient Popular Poetry from Authentic Manuscripts and Old Printed Copies,* 1884). Earlier still, the printer Wynkyn de Worde (in around 1512, according to M.O. Grenby [2008, p. 26]) published the verse narrative 'The Friar and the boy', a tale of a boy who enchants his stepmother to fart in public. This tradition of popular verse flourished as 'street literature' until the mid-nineteenth century, when it became absorbed by comics. In the present era, there are very few rhyming texts to be found in comics, though the style flourishes in the picture-book tradition, most successfully with Julia Donaldson. There is a revival of this genre, with many authors and illustrators telling stories in picture books in verse, most often (apart from Donaldson) in the four-line verse ('quatrain') ballad form that 'Tom Thumbe' was told in.

As a clearly defined and named category, 'nursery rhymes', to be found in collections of a range of literature for the youngest children, or as stand-alone books of nursery rhymes

The story of the 'nursery rhyme' has to be told with caution and fortunately we have the stern hands of Iona and Peter Opie to warn us off speculation and fantasy. Their approach in *The Oxford Dictionary of Nursery Rhymes* (1951, 1997) was to chart the first appearance or reference of each rhyme. In their 'Introduction' (1997, pp. 1-51) they make clear that the rhymes are mostly not composed by children; they were often fragments of folk songs, theatre songs or ballads. The great majority of the rhymes are more than 250 years old, some much older than that.

Though they appear in popular miscellanies earlier, the first known printed collection is the remarkable little two-volume book, *Tommy Thumb's Pretty Song Book*, published in London in 1744. Survivors from Volume I (as reconstructed by Andrea Immel and Brian Alderson, 2013) include, probably appearing for the first time: 'See-saw Margery Daw', a version of 'Oranges and Lemons', 'Who Killed Cock Robin?', a version of 'Hey Diddle Diddle', part of 'Sing a Song of Sixpence' and 'Mary, Mary, Quite Contrary', alongside 'Little Jack Horner' (not first appearance); and from Volume II (which survives), the first appearance of: 'Ladybird, ladybird', 'Hickory Dickory Dock' and 'Baa Baa Black Sheep' alongside 'London Bridge' (not first appearance), and others.

So, we can see here a clear laying out of a tradition which survives to this day. What doesn't survive are the bawdy, scatological and what we would now describe as racist rhymes. In the present day, nursery rhymes are not as widely shared as they were, say, fifty years ago. They are missing from modern reading schemes where once they were staple fare, e.g. in *The Merry Readers* (Beeny, 1915), which is made up of 38 nursery rhymes. Publishers keep trying to revitalise the tradition with many kinds of illustration. Perhaps advertising jingles, snatches of songs from singers seen on TV or circulating as i-tunes fulfil the nursery rhymes' role.

Rhymes that pass between children, mostly orally, mostly without adult intervention, known mostly as 'playground rhymes' or 'street rhymes'

In spite of their obituary having been written many times, these continue to flourish in several forms: clap-rhymes, counting-out rhymes, parodies of carols and modern songs, rude rhymes, nicknames, skipping rhymes. What seems to have almost died out are the rhymes chanted with ball games.

Iona and Peter Opie, with their *The Lore and Language of Schoolchildren* (1959), showed how one rhyme started out its printed life as a poem by Henry Carey (see Carey also for 'Sally in our Alley' above in *Elegant Extracts*) from his 'Namby Pamby' of 1725, and was being recreated orally by children in 1954 in York (Opie and Opie, 1959, pp. 10-11). Over and beyond that, we might assume that children created, parodied and shared rhymes long before then.

Poetry produced by children, mostly as encouraged by teachers and poets working with children in schools, libraries and poetry clubs. The ultimate location of this poetry may be the classroom or library in question, or it may be anthologised into locally produced anthologies, websites, blogs or commercial anthologies where it may appear alongside poems by adults or may be clearly marked as collections of poetry written by children

In the old 'public' (i.e. private) schools there is a long tradition of pupils composing new verse in Latin, often for a competition of some kind. Interest in the idea that children in state schools could write poetry in English seems to have begun before the First World War. By the 1920s and '30s it was possible for a local authority like Tottenham in London to publish *Children's Verse* (1937), an anthology of poems written by pupils of elementary schools in Tottenham. Again, this tradition survives, sometimes cramped by formulaic methods, other times following the Geoffrey Summerfield or Barry Maybury tradition, putting the child at the centre of the poem and the writing. Key exponents of this way of working now in print are such people as Michael Lockwood, James Carter and Jean Sprackland.

Poetry produced by adults in stand-alone collections of single poets, clearly marked by the publishing industry as poetry for children. In the last fifty or so years, these have occasionally been produced by educational publishers but mostly they are produced by the commercial publishers of children's books

This part of the tradition starts most famously – as a name-on-the-frontispiece and stand-alone author – with John Bunyan and his *A Book for Boys and Girls: or, Country Rhimes* [*sic*] *for Children* (1686), though Abraham Chear was in the late 1670s a known and much-read poet for children and had his poems collected posthumously in 1673 in *A Looking-glass for Children*. These were both 'Puritan' poets who believed that their poetry could take children along a path of righteousness. The idea of adults writing and producing volumes of poetry for children has ebbed and flowed since then, sometimes with a foot in one or other of the Christian churches and Sunday Schools, at other times with a clear view to being 'used' in schools; at other times, particularly since the publication of Spike Milligan's (1918-2002) work in the 1960s and '70s (e.g. *Silly Verse for Kids* [1968]), with a view to being unofficial, subversive even. My own contribution to this aspect of poetry for children was to write poems (first in *Mind Your Own Business*, 1974) from the child's point of view (indeed as A. A. Milne [1882-1956] and Robert Louis Stevenson [1850-1894] had done) but about the world I had known in the 1950s and knew through my own children from the 1970s onwards.

At times, these stand-alone collections by single authors have done very well in the open market, at others they have all but died out. My own theory is that the fate of this part of the tradition rests largely on how the school curriculum is devised and dictated. When teachers, advisers and publishers are given the scope and freedom to explore the world of poetry for themselves, many flowers bloom. When it is dictated from central government, the choice narrows and the numbers of books sold and published dwindles. It's an example of how education policy affects the commercial part of book distribution.

That said, there is a wide range of poets in Britain writing for children, trying many different kinds of poetry. One particularly strong strand has been Caribbean (or Caribbean in origin), with poets like John Agard, Grace Nichols, James Berry, Valerie Bloom, Benjamin Zephaniah and others. Poetry for children by women in stand-alone collections has always been strong, and it still is with Carol Ann Duffy, Mandy Coe, Lindsay MacRae, Jackie Kay, Julia Donaldson, Judith Nicholls and many others, while male poets in the modern era who have excited and interested children include Ted Hughes, Spike Milligan, Adrian Henri, Vernon Scannell, Roger McGough, Brian Patten, Charles Causley, Adrian Mitchell, Kit Wright, Roald Dahl, Allan Ahlberg, Gareth Owen, Spike Milligan, Philip Gross, John Hegley, Wes McGee, Brian Moses, Tony Mitton, Colin McNaughton and John Mole. New poets writing for children tend to find it hard to get single stand-alone collections published, which is why I put them together along with more established writers in Rosen (ed.) (2009). The two US poets who have travelled best to the UK in single-poet collections are Shel Silverstein and 'Dr Seuss'. At the heart of most of this writing is a strong commitment to the idea that poems can do something special with language in order to talk about the world in ways that children can enjoy or even imitate. Each of these poets interprets the world and their place in it with a distinct tone and approach, drawing on many different traditions, landscapes and inner worlds. It might have been possible in the past to distinguish clear divisions between the few poets working in this field, but the key characteristic of the present era is the opposite: a diversity which is hard to grasp in a short but wide-ranging essay like this one.

More informally, there is a variety of verse for children which exists 'below the radar', not often referred to directly as 'poetry', but which in terms of affecting the 'repertoire' of poetry known by children, parents and carers is quite often significant. So, in no particular order:

Since at least the early 18th century, published and unpublished poets have written occasional verse for a child or children known to the poet, like 'The Pied Piper of Hamelin' (Robert Browning, 1842), originally written for a boy whom Browning knew – the son of Browning's theatre producer. These may eventually end up in commercial circulation as books or anthologised poems, or they may stay within family groups.

On school walls, bedroom walls, samplers, in books intended for children, from the medieval period onwards, various kinds of instructions, guidance and etiquette for children have been put into verse.

There is a long tradition of mnemonics (going back at least to the Roman era), such as those to aid the memorising of the numbers of days in the months, or various kinds of alphabet poems.

Initial literacy verse found in primers and reading schemes.

Recreational books – chapbooks, parlour-games books, annuals, various kinds of puzzle-poems, rhyming riddles, 'riddle-me-rees', rhyming rebuses, and the like.

Dedication verse written on books when given as presents.

In family and social gatherings where a recitation tradition has been active.

In out-of-school youth groups, various kinds of chants and collectively performed rhymes.

On birthday, Easter and Christmas cards clearly intended for children.

In 'reciters', elocution books, collections for poetry-performance exams, poems (often with speeches, extracts etc.) either selected or written with the express purpose of being recited for public performance.

In specifically religious contexts like Sunday Schools, or other forms of religious instruction.

In stories, novels and plays intended for children, where characters have spoken newly created verses, parodies, riddles and the like from within the narrative, or occasionally as prologues and epilogues to novels and stories.

According to Shirley Brice Heath (1997), in 1986 a private collection of a 'nursery library' was discovered that had been created by Jane Johnson (1706-1759) for her own children as they were growing up and which includes many of Johnson's own rhymes:

> The Man with his Dogs
> went out to kill Game,
> His Gun it went off,
> and shot the Dogs
> lame.

Since the 18th century, children have received poems written by parents and carers, or jokey verses made up on car journeys, birthday wishes, Easter rhymes to aid the hunting of eggs, parodies of hymns, carols and songs and the like.

In *The Oxford Book of Children's Verse* (1973, p. 3), Iona and Peter Opie select as their first poem part of Chaucer's *'Manciple's Tale'*, where the manciple imitates an etiquette verse beginning (as translated), 'My son, keep well thy tongue . . . ' When religious institutions had great control over the nurture and education of young people, verse admonitions and guidances were extremely common; in particular within the dissenting traditions of Christianity, they mark out the duties of a Christian subject. In the present day, though much of this has disappeared, what survives in some quarters are rhyming and alliterative slogans put up in schools full of words like 'believe' and 'achieve', 'know' and 'grow'. Some of this seems to derive from marketing training where new recruits are told such things as 'retail is detail' or 'eye-level is buy level'.

Not all mnemonics rhyme as does 'Thirty days hath September . . . ', which seems to have started out life in the sixteenth century. Many people remember with poetic phrases such things as the order of the colours of the rainbow, ('Richard Of York Gave Battle In Vain'), planets revolving round the sun ('My Very Educated Mother Just Served Us Nachos'), the wives of Henry VIII ('Divorced, beheaded, died; divorced, beheaded, survived'), the order of the geological eras ('Pregnant Camels Ordinarily Sit Down Carefully; Perhaps Their Joints Creak') and the like. These circulate around schools and families and now on-line too.

One of the first ABC rhymes was 'A was an apple-pie', cited by the Opies (1997, p. 53) and known, they say, in the mid-seventeenth century. Since then, many alphabet poems have been composed anonymously, and most famously by Edward Lear (1812-1888). Of course, teaching children to read didn't have to be done with alphabet poems and from the early eighteenth century onwards authors and educators had the idea that learning to read was aided by rhymes and alliterative sentences. In 1651, *An English Monosyllabary* produced: 'Ah! wee see an ox dy by an ax', 'Oh God! his game is gon, as sure as a gun. He that did ly on his bum, and ban, was his bane.' (Michael, 1987, p. 18) From the 1830s onwards, children were reading:

> Go now to bed,
> For you are fed.
> If Jem can run,
> He has a bun.
> Now my new pen
> is fit for Ben. (Avery, 1995, p. 5)

In the modern era, with the rise of systematic synthetic phonics, rhyme has been given a special place in the teaching of reading. From the late 1950s onwards, 'Dr Seuss' (Theodore Geisel [1904-1991]), wrote early 'readers' based on a different system: simple words from a reduced vocabulary, the first being *The Cat in the Hat* (1957). An argument could be made that for most of us these early rhymes, banal as some of the most elementary might be, lay down in our minds some long-lasting connections between school, rhyme, reading and childhood.

Puzzle poems flourished in particular in the nineteenth century, with books like *Selections from the Masquerade, A collection of enigmas, logogriphs* [*sic*], *charades, rebuses, queries and transpositions*, published in London in 1826. Number XL in 'Rebusses, &c.' is 'A CONSONANT add to a dignify'd Jew/A wild little quadruped rises to view.' This kind of verbal, poetic fun is much harder to find these days and yet, in my experience, when you play these kinds of games with children, they enjoy them a great deal.

In the nineteenth and early twentieth centuries, books known as 'Reciters', such as Carpenter's *Penny Readings in Prose and Verse* (1866), created a strong tradition of anthologising. In the modern era, as an equivalent to music grades, there are verse-reading exams, 'by heart' competitions of various kinds, and anthologies are still made up by examiners or mainstream publishers with a view to satisfying this demand. When governments decide that this is desirable (as at present), there is an increase in the number of 'by heart' anthologies available. The presence of reciters and of popular traditions of recitation, as with 'The Lion and Albert' (1932), the dialect poems of the Lancashire cotton-workers, Burns Nights and the like, it's hard to know which traditions survive and where. On occasions, writers (e.g. Jackie Kay [2011]) or interviewees on radio and TV reveal that their parents used to recite a mix of poems learned at school, folk rhymes, limericks, made-up ballads about colleagues and the like.

Members of youth groups, particularly those with a camping tradition, are often inducted into chants. The chant I know and have adapted as *We're Going on a Bear Hunt* (1989) seems to have started life as either a chant worked out in American Summer Camps or in the Brownies, where the Brownies chant, 'We're going on a lion hunt'. Most of these are un-authored and are part of communal chanting, reciting or singing that is seen as an important element of companionship, or just a fun way of passing an evening.

The key religious text is Isaac Watts, *Divine Songs*, attempted in easy language for the use of children (1715). He writes in his preface:

> There is something so amusing and entertaining in Rhymes and Metre, that will incline Children to make this part of their Business a Diversion. And you may turn their very Duty into a Reward, by giving them the Privilege of learning one of these Songs every Week well . . . (Unnumbered second page of 'Preface')

Apart from anything else, Watts explains, the learning and knowing of poems will ensure that children will 'not be forced to seek relief for an Emptiness of Mind out of the loose and dangerous Sonnets of the Age'.

The Sunday School tradition lives on, in particular in the Evangelical churches, but it doesn't seem as if poetry has as large a role to play there as it did in the eighteenth, nineteenth and early twentieth centuries.

In one of the first novels written explicitly for children, Sarah Fielding's *The Governess* (1749), there are several examples of verse: from those in popular style – 'I am a Giant, and I can eat thee:/Thou art a Dwarf, and canst not eat me' (p. 52) – to a more homiletic verse about 'Patience'. Lewis Carroll and J.R.R. Tolkien were renowned users of verse within fiction, as was Beatrix Potter with her riddling use of nursery rhymes in *The Tale of Squirrel Nutkin* (1903) and *The Tailor of Gloucester* (1902), among others. The folk-tale tradition is rich with short verses: the Brothers Grimm either collected or wrote verses for *Hansel and Gretel*, for example, whilst African and Caribbean stories are full of verse prologues, epilogues, repeated couplets and the like. It's probably in the storytelling tradition that this idea of including verse in fiction has best survived, and it appears in storytellers' performances in schools, libraries and at festivals everywhere.

An Autobiographical Approach

With your indulgence, I would now like to invert the process of this essay from what has been a generalised survey to a highly personalised one. This is not purely an exercise in egotism, and I am hazarding a guess that it might be appropriate on account of the fact that a) my parents, Harold and Connie Rosen, were professionally active in presenting one particular strand of children's poetry in the 1950s and '60s; b) I started writing poetry at that time and have been writing it ever since; c) my own interests in poetry for children have brought me into contact with most of the locations (or written examples taken from those locations) listed above; and d) at various times in my writing these examples have been part of my writing intertext.

I represent, then, several different protagonists in the field of poetry for children, from the time I was born in 1946 to the present day. These are, of course, highly specific in relation to location (north-west London suburb), social-class origins (my parents were teachers of working-class east London origin), education (state schooling at nursery school, two primary schools and two grammar schools), ethnicity (in origin, secular Eastern European Jewish), political world view (socialist), family intellectual outlook (libertarian, 'progressive'), sex (male), family position (youngest; no specifically named disability; two-parent nuclear family throughout my childhood).

The protagonists I represent across fifty years are, variously: boy audience of poetry in state schools; son of progressive, intellectually committed and active parents; post-Second World War child; teenage writer of poems about childhood; audience of the process of anthologising and broadcasting poetry for children by my parents and their friends; anthologised poet for children, published poet in single collections of my own work, poet performing in schools, poet writing about poetry, poet running teachers' workshops on poetry.

Within this narrow social, educational and political layer, I can ask myself the question, 'What was poetry like in the locations identified earlier? And what conclusions can we draw?'

My first encounters with poetry were at home: in comics, often as the under-text in comic strips; in nursery rhyme and Beatrix Potter books that my mother read to me; in various 'rude rhymes' or colloquial and familiar rhymes that my father either made up or recalled, some of which were partly in Yiddish. Alongside this, both my parents recited the whole or parts of poems and snatches of Shakespeare, many of which appeared in school anthologies of the time. Sometimes these home recitations were in French, German or Latin – memories mostly from my father's own schooling.

At school, we met poetry in school anthologies, never in collections by individual poets. They were in effect a form of the graded reader. My first memory of poetry, aged 7 in 'first year juniors', is of the teacher reading us poems. One boy had learned a poem and recited it to the rest of the class – 'Autumn Fires' by Robert Louis Stevenson. By the age of 10, I had been selected to be in the choral speaking group and was learning and reciting poems, like 'Adlestrop' by Edward Thomas, selected for inter-school competitions.

In the playground, I was with a group of boys who shared a good few rude rhymes and parodies, some of which we thought we had made up. I witnessed girls saying, chanting or singing skipping rhymes, ball-game rhymes, clap-game rhymes. A friend and I read the *Winnie-the-Pooh* books and we enjoyed reciting 'My nose is cold, tiddly-pom' together.

As we went up through the primary school, the poetry focused most heavily on Walter de la Mare, Robert Louis Stevenson and John Masefield. In the second year at secondary school, we 'did' dramatic monologues by Robert Browning. Homework was to write one. In the second year, in French, we had to learn off by heart a La Fontaine fable, *'Maître Corbeau sur un arbre perché tenait en son bec un fromage . . . '* When I was twelve, I joined a young persons' theatre group and we learned poems to recite in choral competitions, like Louis MacNeice's 'Prayer Before Birth'.

In my teens, I became aware of the poetry of D. H. Lawrence alongside American poetry either written or selected for children to read, in particular poems by Carl Sandburg. As Geoffrey Summerfield was a friend of my parents, he brought many of the poems he was trying out with *Voices* and *Junior Voices* into our house.

When I first started writing the poems that eventually appeared in collections for children, I thought that I was writing a D. H. Lawrence/Sandburg style of poetry about childhood, primarily for an adult audience. In fact, this didn't happen. By adopting the Sandburg voice, I didn't realise at the time that I was breaking with an English tradition of poetry for children which was up till then almost entirely formal verse. As my parents were actively involved in encouraging children to write poetry through their teaching, publications and radio work, I have a sense that I imagined that my poems were in a shape that

387

children could adopt and use to write poetry for themselves.

Another discovery for me was performance poetry, and I joined other writers of fiction and poetry in schools, libraries and at festivals performing to children. As a group of poets, we reach hundreds of thousands through our publications, performances and on-line presence. It's a diverse group of people drawing on a wide variety of cultural traditions, some of it overlapping with rap, storytelling, folk and rock music, some of it more traditional, drawing on the traditions of poets like Edward Lear, Lewis Carroll and Walter de la Mare.

Geoffrey Summerfield, much inspired by Carl Sandburg's own work of assemblages of oral utterances, tried to widen the range of what is entitled to be called poetry, incorporating riddles, free-verse translations, modernist poets' fragments and jokes, folk songs, children's playground rhymes, charms, chants, prose poems, poems and written monologues by children, Humpty Dumpty's prose explanation of 'Jabberwocky' from *Through the Looking-Glass*, graveyard inscriptions and so on. It's as if he was saying that on the one hand, 'All this is poetry,' and that on the other hand formal poetry of the canon (as understood by critics and publishers) is itself made up of this huge miscellany of utterances which carry many of the characteristics of formal poetry – metaphor, poetic prosody, compression and so on.

My view is that he succeeded, but it has to be said that it was part of a split in the small world of children's poetry: some favouring the clear demarcation of the genres 'poetry' and 'poetry for children', as exemplified by, say, Robert Louis Stevenson, but also by the layout on the page of the 'poem', by the poetry collection in a book, situated on a shelf; others finding poetry and poetic utterances everywhere – in those same books, but also on bus-shelter walls, in everyday speech, in sports commentaries, in the comments of three-year-olds, in puns, montages of song titles and so on. At times, central government has intervened in this discussion and expressed a wish or even a directive that a particular kind of poetry should be taught and learned in schools. My own view is that this is an attempt to tame poetry and confine it to approved shapes, sounds and meanings.

Works Cited and Further Reading

PRIMARY TEXTS

Aiken, Lucy, *Poetry for Children, Consisting of Short Pieces to be Committed to Memory* (London: R. Phillips, 1801)

Anon. (ed.), *A Collection of Old Ballads &c.* (London: J. Roberts, 1723)

Anon. (ed.), *Selections from the Masquerade, A collection of enigmas, logogriphs,* [*sic*] *charades, rebuses, queries and transpositions* (London: Baker and Fletcher, 1826)

Anon. (ed.), *Children's Verse, an anthology of poems, written by pupils of elementary schools of Tottenham* (Tottenham, London: The Borough of Tottenham Education Committee, 1937)

Beeny, Ada H. (ed.), *The Merry Readers, a whole-word method of learning to read* (London and Edinburgh: T.C. & E.C. Jack, 1915)

Bunyan, John, *A Book for Boys and Girls: or, Country Rhimes* [*sic*] *for Children* (London: N.P., 1686)

Carpenter, J. E., *Penny Readings in Prose and Verse* (London: Frederick Warne and Co., 1866)

Chear, Abraham, *A Looking-glass for Children* (London: Robert Boulter, 1673)

Fielding, Sarah, *The Governess or, Little Female Academy. Being the History of Mrs. Teachum, and her Nine Girls. With their nine Days Amusement. Calculated for the Entertainment and Instruction of Young Ladies in their Education* (London: 'The Author', 1749)

Geisel, Theodore ('Dr. Seuss'), *The Cat in the Hat* (Boston: Houghton Mifflin and New York: Random House, 1957)

Hall, Donald (ed.), *The Oxford Book of Children's Verse in America* (New York and Oxford: Oxford University Press, 1985)

Immel, Andrea and Alderson, Brian (eds.), *Tommy Thumb's Pretty Song-Book, The First Collection of Nursery Rhymes, A Facsimile Edition with a History and Annotations* (Los Angeles: Cotsen Occasional Press, 2013)

Kay, Jackie, *Red Dust Road* (London: Picador, 2011)

Knox, Vicesimus (ed.), *Elegant Extracts: or useful and entertaining PIECES OF POETRY, Selected for the Improvement of Young Persons* (London and Dublin: J. Johnson et al., 1789)

Milligan, Spike, *Silly Verse for Kids* (Harmondsworth: Puffin, Penguin, 1968)

Mitchell, Adrian (ed.), *A Poem a Day Helps you Stop Work, and Play* (London: Orchard Books, 2001)

Opie, Iona and Opie, Peter (eds), *The Oxford Dictionary of Nursery Rhymes* (Oxford: Oxford University Press, 1951, 1997)

Opie, Iona and Opie, Peter, *The Lore and Language of Schoolchildren* (Oxford: Oxford University Press, 1959)

Opie, Iona and Opie Peter (eds), *The Oxford Book of Children's Verse* (Oxford: Oxford University Press, 1973)

Percy, Thomas, *Reliques of Ancient English Poetry* (London: J. Dodsley, 1765)

Potter, Beatrix, *The Tailor of Gloucester* (London: Privately Printed, 1902; Frederick Warne and Co., 1903)

Potter, Beatrix, *The Tale of Squirrel Nutkin* (London: Frederick Warne and Co., 1903)

Ritson, Joseph (ed.) (revised by Goldsmid, Edmund), *Ancient Popular Poetry from Authentic Manuscripts and Old Printed Copies* (Edinburgh: Privately Printed, 1884)

Rosen, Michael, *Mind Your Own Business* (London: Andre Deutsch, 1974)

Rosen, Michael (illus. Helen Oxenbury), *We're Going on a Bear Hunt* (London: Walker Books, 1989)

Rosen, Michael (ed.), *Michael Rosen's A-Z, The Best Children's Poetry from Agard to Zephaniah* (London: Puffin, Penguin, 2009)

Summerfield, Geoffrey (ed.), *Voices, an Anthology of Poetry and Pictures* (Harmondsworth: Penguin Education for Penguin, 1968)

Summerfield, Geoffrey, *Voices, an Anthology of Poetry and Pictures, Teachers' Handbook* (Harmondsworth: Penguin Education for Penguin, 1968)

Summerfield, Geoffrey (ed.), *Junior Voices, an Anthology of Poetry and Pictures* (Harmondsworth: Penguin Education for Penguin, 1970)

Summerfield, Geoffrey, *Junior Voices, an Anthology of Poetry and Pictures, Teachers' Handbook* (Harmondsworth: Penguin Education for Penguin, 1970)

d'Urfey, Thomas (ed.), *Wit and Mirth: Or Pills to Purge Melancholy* (London: Henry Playford, 1698-1720)

Watts, Isaac, *Divine Songs, Attempted in Easy Language for the Use of Children* (London: M. Lawrence, 1715)

Wilson, Raymond (ed.), *The Puffin Book of Classic Verse* (London: Penguin, 1995)

CRITICAL TEXTS

Avery, Gillian, 'The Beginnings of Children's Reading to c. 1700', in Hunt, Peter (ed.), *Children's Literature, an Illustrated History* (Oxford and New York: Oxford University Press, 1995), pp. 1-25

Ford, Susan Allen, 'Reading Elegant Extracts in *Emma*. Very Entertaining!' Vol. 28, No. 1 (Winter 2007), *Persuasions On-line*, (Jane Austen Society of America) http://www.jasna.org/persuasions/on-line/vol28no1/ford.htm, accessed 6 January 2014

Grenby, M.O., 'Before Children's Literature: Children, Chapbooks and Popular Culture in Early Modern Britain', in *Popular Children's Literature in Britain*, eds Julia Briggs, Dennis Butts and M.O. Grenby (Aldershot: Ashgate, 2008), pp. 25-46

Heath, S., 'Child's Play or Finding the Ephemera of Home', in Hilton, Mary,

Styles, Morag and Watson, Victor (eds), *Opening the Nursery Door: Reading, Writing and Childhood 1600-1900* (London and New York: Routledge, 1997), p.26

Hunt, Peter (ed.), *Children's Literature: an Illustrated History* (Oxford: Oxford University Press, 1995)

Mack, Peter, *Elizabethan Rhetoric, Theory and Practice* (Cambridge: Cambridge University Press, 2002)

Michael, Ian, *The Teaching of English, from the Sixteenth Century to 1870* (Cambridge: Cambridge University Press, 1987)

Styles, Morag, *From the Garden to the Street: Three Hundred Years of Poetry for Children* (London: Cassell, 1998)

Styles, Morag, Joy, Louise and Whitley, David (eds), *Poetry and Childhood* (Stoke-on-Trent and Sterling, USA: Trentham Books, 2010)

Thomas, Joseph T. Jr., *Poetry's Playground: The Culture of Contemporary American Children's Poetry* (Detroit: Wayne State University Press, 2007)

An Introduction to 'The Hunting of the Snark'

I wrote this introduction for the Folio Society's 2014 edition of Charles Lutwidge Dodgson's wonderful nonsensical poem.

Nonsense is an odd word. We use it every day to mean something like 'no good', 'wrong', 'illogical', 'silly'. 'You're talking nonsense,' we say. It's an irritating put-down but not a description that retains the root of the word: non-sense, no sense. When we use the word in the literary field, we stray even further from the root. That's to say, whatever Nonsense literature is, there's no way we can say that it has no sense. What's amazing about a good deal of Nonsense literature is that we seem to be able to make sense of its poems and stories in quite unpromising circumstances.

Writers of Nonsense literature have at their disposal a knowledge that out there in the world are hundreds of thousands of readers and listeners with a glorious set of expectations in their heads. To write Nonsense literature, what you have to do is leave some of these expectations perfectly intact, but turn others into impossible, utterly surprising alternatives.

If we take 'The Hunting of the Snark''s sister poem, 'Jabberwocky', we can hear from the structure and sequence of the first verse that we're being given a setting for a story:

> Twas brillig, and the slithy toves
> Did gyre and gimble in the wabe:
> All mimsy were the borogoves,
> And the mome raths outgrabe.

The problem is that each of the elements of that setting is given to us with words that aren't immediately meaningful to us, but mysteriously could be. That's because the sounds of the words are within the phonology of English ('br' and 'sl' and 'out'), the words are formed in English-like ways with endings like 'y' and plurals using 's', and the sentences are structured like English sentences with obvious 'thing' words (nouns) like 'toves', 'borogoves' and 'mome raths', each preceded by a 'the'. There are words describing the nouns (adjectives) like 'slithy' and 'mimsy', and in between we can magically tell that there are words that inform us what these nouns are doing (verbs): 'gyre', 'gimble' and 'outgrabe'. Part of how we can tell this is that the phrase 'gyre and gimble' is preceded by 'did', and the last line of the verse is preceded by a line with a non-invented verb, 'were'.

In a way, this kind of nonsense is mimicking or parodying another kind of poetry by swapping invented words for the kind of words you might expect to be there. The other territory that nonsense can occupy is that of what we might call alternative or impossible action. What Nonsense literature does not do is break all the rules. Rather it uses the 'rules' we have absorbed and learnt in order to create new language and new worlds. And it's incorrect to say nonsense means nothing. Words like 'brillig' and 'toves' are heavy with suggestion. Perhaps 'nonsense' should be called 'new-sense' – but that would be a 'nuisance'.

A good deal of what Charles Lutwidge Dodgson ('Lewis Carroll') wrote involved a play on language and sense. In the *Alice* books, there is a quasi-logical justification for it all: Alice has gone through the portals either of falling asleep or of passing through a mirror. Perhaps fully fledged nonsense is at its best when there is no justification, no dream-world explanation, no portal, and that's what we have with 'The Hunting of the Snark'. It was written in 1874 and published in 1876, after the two *Alice* books.

The paradox at the heart of Dodgson's life is that on the one hand he lived and worked in a highly ritualised, hierarchical and rule-bound world, but on the other he produced a literature that constantly mocks, parodies and subverts that world. His world was that of Christ Church, Oxford – an institution full of prestige and a sense of its own very real importance in British and world politics. It was (and to a certain extent still is) a place full of rules, conventions, habits, traditions – rituals that go way beyond, say, a matter of timetables. A great deal of every day's actions was embedded in preordained structures: how and where to eat, worship, lodge. Conversation was structured and regulated: how to talk to each other, who to talk to, and so on. Dress was regulated according to status and occasion. In a way, this was an extreme form of Victorian life, in which the layers of society were ordered, where it wasn't just that people knowing their place mattered, but that, within the layers, tiny differences of accent, clothing, house arrangement, behaviour at times of marriage and death were all seen to be important. Meanwhile, the business at the heart of British Victorian life was in the massive, hugely energetic processes of manufacture, trade and imperial rule. While middle-class life created highly ordered, quiet, small-scale rooms for people to live and grow up in, working life for millions of people was loud, filthy and dangerous, and for many involved a huge amount of movement, transport, travel, exploration and, yes, hunting.

So when Edward Lear and Lewis Carroll created poems that travel, peopled by beings recognisably English, there is a way in which we can see these – no matter how nonsensical – as parodies or refractions of this moving, travelling, exploring aspect of Victorian life. According to the conventions of nonsense, the travelling is 'real' while the characters and many of the actions are nonsensical. These conventions are at work with names and expressions – and indeed in the core concept of the story: the 'Boojum'.

Dodgson was asked several times in his life about the meaning of the poem, to which he replied, 'I don't know.' This is a perfectly reasonable statement. Part of the wonder of Nonsense literature is that its ability to suggest, imply and provoke a wide range of meanings is greater than that of literature that appears to be describing believable, realistic and naturalistic events. Your Snark or Jabberwock or Pobble is unlikely to look like mine. This utterly human divergence of interpretation goes on at all levels of the poem. While it is great fun to come up with interpretations and explanations for the poem, it is, to my mind, quite absurd to imagine that any of them could be the 'right' one. Part of the method of nonsense is to parody the kind of story that usually does have a solution or resolution but, through creating invented beings whose actions are unpredictable, to leave matters open. Even the supposed solution of the poem, 'For the Snark was a Boojum, you see', is of course a mock solution because in the final analysis we don't know what a Snark is and we don't know what a Boojum is! Carroll was only too aware, through his work in the field of abstract logic and in his writing of the *Alice* books, that you can retain the outward form of a logical utterance while substituting impossible or fanciful or puzzling alternatives in their place. In school you learn 'reeling and writhing', roses change colour because someone paints them, 'mean what you say' doesn't necessarily mean the same as 'say what you mean', and so on. In other words, from the heart of the highly fixed, ritual world of Christ Church, Carroll produced highly unstable worlds.

'The Hunting of the Snark' is divided into eight 'fits', which is a little literary gag, a 'fitte' being a medieval word to describe the part of a larger work, while a 'fit' means some kind of pathological outburst or convulsion. It is, mysteriously, an 'agony', signposting perhaps that this isn't going to be a jolly romp. Harking back to the very origins of literature, the poem is a journey, an expedition (think of the *Odyssey*), but with ten heroes – a mix of human and non-human beings. This crew we can take in a sociological or psychological way – they are a parody of Victorian beings (a mock cross-section of the social classes) while also being the symbolic parts of Carroll's own psyche. In that unquestioning Victorian way, the travellers arrive somewhere that is shown to us as strange. Only very rarely before the mid-twentieth century do we ever hear in literature what the natives of strange lands thought of incoming Europeans. Even in nonsense, fantasy and science fiction, this basic motif remains intact. In the foreign land, the characters' relationships change, they clash, and even though the Snark is apparently found, the very finding itself is problematic: we've heard that Boojums can make people disappear, so when it turns out (apparently, allegedly!) that 'the Snark was a Boojum', destruction is the result. This is the entirely appropriate, mysterious, unsatisfying, contradictory, endlessly debatable, absurd ending that a good Nonsense poem deserves. It is laden with all the danger and wonder of the classic travel narrative – the mystery of the disappearance of Captain This or Colonel That on his trip up the Amazon or the expedition to the centre of Australia – but in this case involves beings we know to be pure inventions. So, while someone like Daniel Defoe used every trick known to have his readers believe that Robinson Crusoe was real and the book of the expedition was a true and fair account of real events, Lewis Carroll does all he can to tell us right from the start (well, by the time we read the fifth word of the title, to be accurate) that his story is untrue. And yet, because of the suggestive power of his setting, his naming and sketching of the characters, the seeming logic of the acts, deeds and speeches, the poem has the ability to evoke feelings of sadness, horror, dissolution, occasional fun and mystery.

As with the *Alice* books, Dodgson challenges any sense that a book is definitively for this or that particular audience. It's true that the poem was dedicated to a child, Gertrude Chataway (1866–1951), and Dodgson's relationships with children have been the subject of a good deal of debate and speculation in recent years. Whatever the case, he was clearly very interested in both listening to and entertaining clever children, especially girls. As many writers of children's literature testify, an encounter with a child can indeed often trigger the telling of stories and the writing of poems. However, it's not entirely logical to extrapolate from this the idea that a story created at such a juncture is necessarily and exclusively 'for children'. My own view is that the genre we call 'children's literature' has always been a shared literature, heard, read and absorbed in homes, schools and libraries with a mix of children and adults. What's more, there are many ways adults read this literature away from children: as a way of re-experiencing their childhood reading lives; as a way of understanding or enjoying the world through the kind of emblematic, symbolic storytelling we find in children's literature, and so on.

It seems to me that 'The Hunting of the Snark' is ideal for these kinds of readings: home, school, library, as a child with adults, as an adult with children, as a child alone, as an adult alone. Because Dodgson was a master of finely honed metrical verse, the poem makes for great recitation. He was, after all, part of that Victorian tradition of the parlour-game, home-performance experience that was one of the important ways in which middle-class literacy escaped from the constraints put on it by dull, repetitive, learning-by-rote, punishing schooling. The poem offers those anticipatory moments I described earlier with its rhyme and rhythm, even to the point where one key rhyme – 'true' and 'Boo' – is part of the poem's climax. There is scope for funny voices, noises, significant pauses, crazily expressive faces, a good deal of creeping about, looking into the far distance and terrifying glares. Better still, it makes for a great performance piece for many voices. Part of the thrill of literature is that it has the potential to inhabit our minds after it has been read or heard. One of the ways to realise this potential is for people to perform it and for others to attend the performance. And, if the experience is fulfilling for all, to repeat that experience. This is how the cadence of the language goes into our heads, how the scenes and images invented by culture come to sit in our heads, doing their work as and when we encounter similar moments in real life.

This is a book to read, perform, hear, enjoy and think about – over and over again. What nonsense!

POLITICS, EDUCATION AND CULTURE

Writer-in-Residence

I had a fantastic year as writer-in-residence at Vauxhall Manor School in 1976-1977. After that, I was a part-time member of the English department there. I contributed three papers to the collection of studies of language and learning which a group of teachers of a variety of subjects made at the school between 1974 and 1979. The collection was eventually published in 1982 as Becoming our own Experts[1].

Writer-in-Inner-City-Residence

Lorraine – fourth year [that's Year 10 in today's terms] – says she's fed up. School's a prison, home's a prison, she gets half an hour of freedom a day, a quarter of an hour on the way to school and a quarter of an hour on the way back. Why? What's the matter with home? Mum won't let her out. Why not? She makes too much noise in the streets. What – with friends? Boys? No – ball games. Two-balls up against the wall. 'I sing.' 'What do you sing, Lorraine?'

> Over the garden wall
> I let me baby fall
> My mother came out
> she gave me a clout
> She gave me another
> to match the other
> over the garden wall.

We made a tape of this and a few more she knew. Then I wrote Lorraine a letter. I wrote down all she'd said to me about home being a prison and all that. I wrote down all that I had asked her and then I wrote her a 'please'. 'Please will you write down all the songs you sing when you play two-balls?' All this was in large brown felt-tip, printed on unlined paper. She wrote out the rhymes, borrowed a polaroid camera and someone took a photo of her playing two-balls up against a wall. Is a writer-in-residence someone who resides and writes? Is a writer-in-residence someone who resides and reads what other people write?

My image of my job-to-be was me in a little room, jokes and pictures on the wall, and two things on a table in front of me: a tape recorder and a typewriter.

Somehow or another in the first week or two I was at the school, anyone or everyone would be happy to 'come up and see me some time' and I would simply switch on the tape recorder, or type out a story as I was told it, or receive across the table poems, stories and plays. It would then simply be my job to get these duplicated and put them into circulation round the school. But somehow things didn't quite work out like that – maybe for the better.

For a start off I'd forgotten that some schools don't have cosy little rooms hanging about waiting for lonely writers to come along and reside in. I'd forgotten that some schools aren't even really simple single-building places, but exist in separate chunks, outhouses, wings, huts and annexes. And of course the kind of school where all this is most likely to happen is in those places where the area, the schools or the people get called 'difficult', 'deprived', 'disadvantaged' and all that. (The less money you have, the more words you get to describe you.)

Also, I didn't know girls' schools. I didn't know any recent immigrants to Britain. I knew very few black British people. (For those of you who don't know who or what I am, in these terms, I am male, white, British third-generation immigrant Jewish of the 'Jewish-whatever-that-means' kind.)

So in fact I arrived at Vauxhall Manor as a stranger in probably all the ways possible, with my qualification for being there a book I had written (*Mind Your Own Business*), that is about me, my childhood and family culture that relies very much on readers finding likenesses with themselves in it.

It came as a complete delight to me to find that the idea, and the actual practice, of circulating the girls' own stories, poems and plays, the transcribing of tape recordings, was an integral part of the English department's job without any 'writer' (with or without a residence qualification) coming and telling them about this. So for a start off, I could do more of the same. I did. Here's one of many taped, transcribed stories made up into 50 or more booklets and circulated. A first-year [Year 7] girl told me the story; Jim Payne (head of English) listened through a tape of jokes, recitations and picked it out. Read it out loud to yourself as you read it.

Are You Difficult?

I'm going to tell you something now that's really rude, right? No, it is though. It's about this bloke.

It happened on Saturday. I'd gone to the launderette and I put the washing in the machine, then I went for some sweets. I went in the shop, got some sweets, came out and stood looking in the shop window, right?

While I was standing there this Italian or Spanish man came up to me and he – er – touched my bottom. And I thought he didn't mean to do it and I turned round. I looked at him and he went, 'Oh, I'm sorry.'

And you could see his teeth at the front and they were all bent in and they wasn't even his real teeth. They were false teeth because you could see the gums at the top where they joined up.

I was walking down a bit and I was getting scared and I tried to shake him off, only he started following me.

I was going to cross Lambeth Road and I was waiting for the traffic. But my friend was in the dry cleaners and I had to wait for her. And this bloke comes up again and starts asking me all these questions. How old was I? What country did I come from? Was I English or Jamaican? Where did I live? And I wouldn't tell him none of these things. And I was still waiting for my friend.

Then he asked me would I like to go to his house for a drink? And I said NO! I didn't know what else to say. I just kept saying NO!

And then my friend came out and I said to her, 'Why didn't you stay with me, you silly cow?'

You see he was asking me all these sorts of questions and making me go scared.

And then she went back in and the bloke comes up again and says, 'Are you sure you wouldn't like to come for a little drink – whisky, Martini, gin?' Then he goes, 'Cheeky, cheeky,' and touches my bottom again.

I says, 'Who do you think I am?'

He says, 'I'll give you £10. I'll give you £12.' And I was just going to say, 'Who do you think I am – a prostitute?' and I said to him, 'Who do you think I am – a p . . . ' and I very nearly said 'prostitute'.

And he said to me, 'Are you difficult? It would only take 15 or 10 minutes.'

And I was getting really angry with him, but I didn't say anything. And he could be one of these rapists or something like that.

And my friend was watching through the window. And I was asking her to come out – begging her to come out but she wouldn't come out. She just laughed at me through the window.

Then he puts his arm round me and I just *moved*! I was still holding onto my bike. Then he puts his hand on mine on the handlebars and I took it off and he touched the other hand and I started sort of backing away from him.

Sharon was still in the shop looking at me and I was trying to give her signs. I couldn't make her understand but she was still looking at me.

Then he says again, 'Are you difficult?' and he takes out his wallet and starts showing me his money! I was getting really angry! I was mad – but I didn't say nothing.

Thank God my friend came out of the shop then and we got away from him.

I didn't tell my Mum, though. She wouldn't understand. She'd just jump to conclusions. She'd just think the worst.

So – to come back to me . . . If I'm not sitting in the cosy little room of your dreams, what am I doing? I'm going round from classroom to library to staffroom and back again just meeting people, talking to them and thinking as quickly as possible, Is there anything useful I've got in my head, in my very heavy black bag, sitting on a shelf at home? Is there anyone I know in rooms, studios or workshops I've passed through who could add anything to what's going on here? At a Staff Association meeting I offered myself up for sale to anyone who thought they could use me.

History and Art did.

Over the year, on and off, I've seen a third-year [Year 9] history group doing the History of London. With them I have half-read, half-told various stories that might help the girls get inside the minds of the people they were studying – Beowulf, Hereward the Wake, the beheading of Anne Boleyn, how the Duchess of Nithisdale got her husband out of the Tower of London, the *Wife of Bath's Tale*, and some street ballads from the broadside sellers of London. To be quite honest, I'm not sure whether I made much contact here

– or more important – whether the stories and ideas did. Probably 'history' is never very exciting unless it's something people *discover* – no matter how you tell it, programme it or textbook it.

Art: here, just as an experiment, first-year art took me on as a 'stimulus'. I read the classes some animal and beast poems and we talked a little about some of the kinds of animals I had written about. Some of them are silly:

> Have you seen the Hidebehind?
> I don't think you have, mind you,
> cos every time you look for it,
> the Hidebehind's behind you.

Some are myths (the Phoenix, the Giant Red Dog Ankotarinjo from Australia) and some are fantasy like a half-cat half-dog, or Jojo who eats the sun and sucks the moon, and so on.

Some nice work came out of this. We photocopied the poems so they could each have a copy of the one they were working on. We'll do more of this and other things next year. We have planned a joint English and Art project which would involve a mixture of writing, mural painting, photography, taping of playground rhymes, street games, clapping games – an exploration of the girls' own culture.

I've mentioned that 'I circulate'. This is very important, because in my position as a roamer I can carry the news from 3X to 2M. That is, what someone writes in one class I can put in my black bag and take to another. The most dramatic effect I can remember was when Stephen Eyers passed on to me a play; a third-year girl had written it and it went downstairs to a second-year group who immediately read it and acted it out. At the time it made me think several things that I've thought could happen in an ideal world.

(i) The writing that staff or pupils do in a secondary school could circulate as freely as library books, comics, photos or records.

(ii) Sometimes, what we read and think is 'great', 'dead-on', 'exciting' is as 'great' as it is, not because it has stood the Great Test of Time as mediated by literary critics or university exam systems, but because at a given moment we needed an answer to a question we were asking, or a reinforcement and support to an answer we have just found. Maybe we needed some nostalgic reminiscing to echo our own nostalgic reminiscing or we needed to see a few tigers turned to paper etc. etc., and as it happens – just at the moment we needed it – something came our way that could do just the job. Denise came to me and very passionately said, 'I want a love story, I need to have a love story.' I gave her *In the Melting Pot* by Chelsea Herbert, a story about and by a black girl living in London. Within a minute there were eight other girls demanding, nagging, crying out for copies and more of the same.

(iii) To put this another way – sometimes it is very important for The Moment to be right, because everything about the situation is right. A very casual story or anecdote can be very powerful if we know the person telling it, why they're telling it, now, and to you.

(iv) Traditionally in schools, the seal of approval on any piece of writing either by an 'author' or a 'pupil' comes from one source only – that expert the teacher. In fact, most of us can open a school exercise book of a child's writing and approve or disapprove our way through it, even though our age, social position, hopes, experience, expectations in life are miles away from the writers. And of course it's very easy to read children's writing with a headful of a set of university or college criteria ('good imagery', etc.) rather than with a bellyful of our own feelings.

(v) To carry this one step further, let's ask: what does this mean for the writers, i.e. the children, concerned? No one writes into a vacuum. Every one of us, as we write or tell each other stories, has a 'sense of an audience' in our heads, helping us cross something out here, change this for that, emphasise this, mention that. Every one of us has a different built-in audience to deal with or please; a different sense of what this audience is like; a different ability to reach the audience we would like to reach. We all have different ideas and experiences to tell our audiences. What we do to children who only write for a teacher is draw children towards pleasing (or, as the case may be, infuriating) that taste, the teacher's taste. But of course the world is both bigger and smaller than us, the teachers. I would say it is more important to anyone who writes to try to please someone you choose to please; to learn to choose your audience, learn how to build it in your work. In other words, perhaps the most important audience for someone writing in a school is an audience of friends and fellow pupils. That's not to say it should be the only audience, or to deny that there are very important things that can be said between a child and a liked teacher.

(vi) Finally, on this point, is the question of the various statuses of the spoken word, the handwritten word, the typed word and the printed word.

To be a story*teller* in the secondary school sounds a bit like a rebuke – a liar, a boaster, a rabble-rouse, back-of-the-coach entertainer. To produce a totally legible handwritten account or story has normally had to involve quite a few hours logged up of spelling, punctuation, letter-formation and comprehension exercises to reach a time when the gap between what you *want* to say and what you have the *mechanical ability* to say becomes bearably narrow, i.e. when to say something in writing isn't just one hell of a grind.

Typewritten and printed words are for upper orders of school management or books. But it's a trick, isn't it? I mean, we who've won through on the writing front also have in our hands tape recorders with rewind buttons, typewriters, offset litho printing machines, paper and staple guns. With a bit of a nudge here and a cupboard cleared there, there isn't any real reason why Talk, Writing, Printing and Reading cannot become a very much less hierarchical business. A told story can become a booklet in a matter of days, circulating freely amongst any group in a school.

But never mind, for the moment, the hierarchy, present or absent, good or bad. We 'language people' – writers, teachers, experts or whatever – we think that confident sight-readers, fluent writers, fluent talkers have power. (How, why or to what effect, let's leave on one side for the moment.) At the moment the confident sight-reading and fluent writing people amongst us take up the positions of middle-ranking or high-ranking power in our society. Fluent *talkers* without much of the other abilities may or may not lead very full, very happy, very contented lives. More than likely the confident sight-readers and fluent writers amongst us will go so far as to despise such people – even to the point that makes them so unfluent at talking to *us* that we say they are 'linguistically deprived', 'have bad language problems', 'have no culture'. It makes us crusaders against infidels. I think what is going on at Vauxhall is the beginning of something that can challenge this bit of educational sociological rubbish. By the way, in a primary school in Tunbridge Wells, the school secretary doesn't sit all day typing the head teacher's memos – I think he's abandoned memos and uses his mouth now – she sits all day typing the children's writing . . .

Finally, some events. For many of the girls at Vauxhall, life is a bi-lingual or bi-dialectal business. They don't ask or need sympathy for this state of affairs. (I always think, by the way, that it's rather ironic that many 'educated' British-born people who spend many years of life slaving away at 'O' and 'A' level language exams in order to become teachers or experts, quite often find it very easy to dismiss these bi-lingual bi-dialectal people called pupils as 'slow learners', 'low reading age', etc. etc. Anyone watching Cockney Greek children in their parents' cafes doing simultaneous translations of Greek newspapers for their grandparents, anyone listening to West Indian children hopping from Cockney to patois knows that these children might do all sorts of things that nice people like us don't like, but one thing they are not is slow.)

At Vauxhall there are many, many languages and dialects the girls can speak. On the English side many of us care about the expression of opinions and feelings, think that to encourage self-esteem and self-confidence is a Good Thing, think that children walking about schools tongue-tied, humiliated and despised is a Bad Thing.

Having made that mildly humane step, it becomes a problem to decide what we think about, what we 'do with' all these dialects and languages. (I'm assuming the 'we' is the 'we' that accepts rather than resents our mixed cultural society – perhaps even enjoys the mixed culture as much as we enjoy the cheap tea, high-quality nursing, and clean public places that come with the cultures.)

Vauxhall has started producing books and booklets in West Indian dialects. That is to say the girls either know – or very quickly learn – how to write down their dialect so that it can be read off the page with the right tone, accent and phrases. What this means is that areas of life, talk and experience that would otherwise be left outside the school gates can now be a part of discussion and enjoyment inside school.

I spend quite a bit of my time in the corners of classrooms or libraries having a chat with one or more girls, in the hope that I can find a point of contact with a bit of this outside-school-gate culture.

Flora – fourth year – says she'll be OK with French and Spanish CSE, it's her English she's worried about. She's got to get that to become an air hostess. How come she's doing Spanish? She is Spanish, she tells me. I'd never have known. She sounds East End to me. 'Do your mum and dad speak English?' Mum, yes; Dad, he can't be bothered. Maria here is from Spain too. Andalusia. 'I'm proud I'm Spanish – Maria isn't.' I say, 'Spain's been quite a lot in the news just now.' 'It'll never be the same again,' she says. 'No more Franco.' She tells me the Civil War started in her village – her grandfather was in a Franco concentration camp. I find her Laurie Lee's memories of Andalusia, lend her a book of Spanish Civil War songs and fail to find the school's copy of *For Whom the Bell Tolls*. Maybe she'll tape her mother's stories about the Civil War, she says.

Colette – sixth form [Year 12] from country Jamaica – tells me a story, a ghost story her mother told her about a woman who gets up every night, leaves her husband's side, takes her skin off, goes off, sucks the blood out of a few babies, comes back, says, 'Kin a me, kin a me' (that means skin come back on to me, Colette explains to me) and climbs back into bed. The husband sees his wife doing this one night so the next night he pretends to be asleep and after she's gone, he puts salt and pepper on his wife's skin so when she comes back and says, 'Kin a me, kin a me' the skin does not jump back on to her and so she dies.

'That's not very scary,' says Agatha. 'My grandmother knows one about a boy who gets turned into a frog with big green eyes, and she knows a woman who can turn herself into a crab.' I ask her to take my tape recorder and tape her grandmother's stories. No, she says, she's scared. What of? Her grandmother? No – the stories. Agatha shares her bedroom with her grandmother and her grandmother tells her the stories in bed at night. Anyway I wouldn't understand them, she says. Why not? They're in French. Agatha's family comes from Saint Lucia. Instead she writes one of the stories out for me, translating it in her head as she goes.

Jane – first year [Year 7] – says that her dad is on social security ever since he was laid off work and he says he can't understand why we have to pay for the jubilee. She could afford to pay for it herself, couldn't she? Jane explains to me that her father has paid for his social security out of the taxes he's paid all his life. What he says is that the queen's probably got enough money, what with one thing and another, to put some of her money into the social security fund too, so people like her dad could get some. She writes this down.

In Their Own Voice

Multi-cultural . . . a lot of people know how to say it – not many have figured out how to do it. Part of the problem is that not many people had worked out how to do it before classrooms were full of Afro-Caribbean children, Asians and 'obvious' immigrants. Let's get to the point: do kids have culture? Does the working class have culture? Do schools work with it or against it?

During my time at Vauxhall Manor, I worked on the assumptions that – yes – kids have culture, yes – the working class has culture, so I must find ways of working *with* it. How? Two instruments are fundamental: a tape recorder, simple enough for *anyone* to handle, and a typewriter. A lot of the culture of both the kids and the working class is oral, i.e. song, story, proverbs, rhymes, repartee, anecdotes. Working-class people demand of schools that they make their children literate because many of them think they don't have the time, the ability or the patience to do it themselves. Using a tape recorder and a typewriter we teachers can help children find literacy in their own voice with their own culture.

Let me describe some incidents: with the first years, on entry to the school last year, we did a project on their rhymes, sayings, proverbs and skipping songs. The girls produced a scrapbook of the rhymes and written work describing the games; they drew each other playing the games; we made a tape of the rhymes; in the summer term some of the girls did an outdoor mural. The scrapbook is their collective knowledge. No one could teach them, or tell them what to write. So, their arrival in the 'big' secondary school was not an induction into 'higher' culture, but rather a collecting of their own expertise. Lorraine, white, Cockney, contributed this on the tape in strong Manchester dialect:

> I went into a treacle shop to buy half a pound of treacle. And who do you think I met? Mickey Thumb. He asked me if I'd go to the fair, and I thought a bit and I thought a bit and I said I didn't mind. And it were a fair. So I come home and took me bonnet off and a knock come at the door, and who do you think that was? Mickey Thumb's uncle to say that he were ill and would I go and visit him. So I thought a bit and I thought a bit, and I said I didn't mind. And he were ill. I came in, took me bonnet off and a knock come at the door and who do you think that was? Mickey Thumb's father to say that he were dead and would I go to the funeral. So I thought a bit and I thought a bit and I said I didn't mind. And it were a funeral. Some laughed over his grave, some cried over his grave, but I spat over his grave in the memory of Mickey Thumb. My mum told me that.

Three fourth-year girls who like each other and stick together seemed stumped for something to do one afternoon. Mandy had told me that her dad is Irish and he's told her he's proud of it. I had lent her various books of Irish traditional stories, and some translated Irish (not Anglo-Irish) poetry. She said that her dad sometimes tells stories – just silly things about Tarzan. I asked her if she would like to tell Gillian some of these stories on tape. She did. Here is the third one:

This was supposed to have happened on a dark, stormy night. Well anyway, this horse, it supposedly got free so my grandad went looking for it. But anyway it was so dark that he fell down this well. Well, he hit his head and he was out cold for about 10 minutes.

When he woke up he heard fiddling so he sees this hole in the well and he crawled through it. When he opened his eyes he found all these Little People.

My grandad it was, all right? He saw all these Little People and a Little Man said how he couldn't go. So my grandad said that he'd have a drinking contest because he had heard how good the Little People were at drinking. So the Little Man said, 'It's no good, I'll easily beat you.' So they had a drinking contest and my grandad won.

Well my grandad, well he still had his wits about him so he nicked the Little Man and put him in the bag and he got out the well and when he got up to the pub they were arguing how he'd caught a Little Man and when he opened the bag in the pub all that jumped out was a little white rabbit.

My dad just makes up them things.

We typed that up and produced 20 or 30 duplicated booklets of that story for other girls to read.

I overheard Monica in the first year say, 'Poor George and his Jackass.' 'What's that mean?' I said. 'It's a bit like – he bit off more than he could chew – he got more than he bargained for,' she said. 'Who was George?' I asked. She told me – but I didn't have a tape recorder handy, so I asked her to write it down for me. Her mother comes from Jamaica:

Sometimes my mum, she doesn't usually tell stories but say old proverbs like this one called Poor George and his Jackass. One day George was returning by night on his jackass when all of a sudden a duppy [a ghost] stopped him and got on the jackass with him and rode all the way home with him. That night the jackass died of shock, and George was sick for a while and that is the way we get the saying of Poor George and his Jackass.

Monica now knows she has taught me something that her mother taught her and I have told her I am very grateful. This is not an educationist's trick on her. It's fair's fair. I tell her jokes and stories.

Monica is friendly with Elaine who I happen to know hears Anansi stories at home from her mother, her sister and her neighbour. As I had asked Monica to write something for me (not something I often did at Vauxhall) I asked Elaine to write me 'something like Monica was doing'. She figured out that I was talking about 'something to do with the things that mothers say', so she wrote:

Greedy Anansy

One day as Anansy was going down de road him call pan breda tiga. Him se dat him no have no food fi him family and bredda tiger was de only good friend him have. So breda tiger give him some food. So him go a breda bears house him se to breda bear, bredda bear mi no have no food fi mi family and you is de only good friend mi have.

So bredda bear give him some food. So dat time him end up with lots of food so he went home and stof up his full frige.

(Spellings as written.)

Given time and care, any school could build up a library of its own oral cultures, on cassette and in booklets. It could use either the cassette or the booklet to trigger off more, or simply as good entertainment. They could be used as cross-cultural entertainment, education. Some children of Caribbean origin are not too happy about Africans, and have various unrepeatable words of abuse for them. Yet Anansi has his origins in West Africa. The tradition is alive and well there, and in the Caribbean, as well as in south London.

Many teachers are afraid of parents. They express this, not by saying they are afraid of the parents, but by saying the parents are afraid of the teachers. 'The parents don't want to come and munch twiglets and sip bad sherry with us.' I have no tips on how to solve socialising problems, but on a purely individual basis a couple of very exciting things happened while I was at Vauxhall.

Elaine's sister, Judith, had told something like eight or nine Anansi stories on tape – some of which we made into booklets – before it occurred to me that we could lend her a tape recorder and ask her to record her mother. This she did. Her mother, an 'ordinary' working-class woman, is as fine a story teller as anyone anywhere. You don't have to go to the Brothers Grimm, or to this or that Book of Beautiful Tales. Great storytellers are amongst us. Sometimes we call them parents. If you have some of those stories on tape and play them in school, what happens? The parents' culture becomes part of the school curriculum – even if it's only for five minutes at a time. And there was Farrah too, who speaks Punjabi at home and told me she didn't like stories, who told me she only really liked books about magnetism, but who finally let on that her grandmother tells her stories. The result of that is a tape of an old lady telling an epic in Punjabi which Farrah translated for us.

To my mind the educational possibilities are limitless here in the working-up of pupil-based materials. The emotional encouragement in the process of doing work like this is immeasurable. But more than that: it means that we teachers, educated away from vernacular, oral and working class cultures, have a unique chance to make up for this deprivation in our lives. I mean, just who *is* culturally deprived?

Our Culture – A Definition by Description of its Parts

Under the following headings is an attempt to define culture as it exists between young people in schools. The list is not in any order.

1. Proverbs
2. Rhymes
3. Riddles
4. Games
5. Laws
6. Rules
7. Punishments
8. Sayings
9. Stories
   a. Stories I've been told
   b. Stories my parents know
   c. Stories my grandparents know
10. Happenings and events in the history of our people
   a. Recent in my life
   b. In my parents' lives
   c. In my grandparents' lives
11. Jokes
12. Special Days – e.g. 'What we do on . . . day.'
13. Songs

14. Places we go
  a. Private, secret
  b. Public and social
  c. 'hanging-about' places
15. Celebrations and feasts
16. Foods – favourite dishes and recipes
17. 'The way we do it' e.g. the garden, dressing, hair, decorating our rooms
18. Hobbies, pastimes, pursuits, 'activities', 'crazes'
19. Musics
20. Sports
  a. Participatory
  b. Spectator
21. Kinds of work done by our people
  a. Me
  b. Parents
  c. Grandparents
  d. Brothers and sisters
  e. Interviewed people e.g. workers in the news
  f. Housework – who does what? Is this fair?
  g. Losing work/looking for work/living without work
22. Courtship, marriage, weddings and alternatives
23. Holidays, favourite places
24. Outings
  a. Organised
  b. Unorganised
25. Slangs, dialects, in-group jargons and new words
26. Family sagas
27. Street spectacles
28. 'Don't tell anyone'
  a. Superstitions and charms
  b. Oaths, secrets e.g. about hidden illicit deeds
29. Street cries, market traders, bus conductors, pub calls, etc.
30. True or false: local legends or myths, historic and contemporary
31. 'It's not fair!' – morals: who are the wrongdoers (cheats, con-men, cruel people)? who are the right-doers (friends in need)?
32. Heroes, heroines, anti-heroes, anti-heroines: local, showbiz, national, international, historic

33. Victims and scapegoats
   a. you as a victim or scapegoat
   b. you victimising or scapegoating others
34. Loyalties: taking sides (brother v brother v sister, mother v father, girls v boys), the gang, the football team, the 'nation', the community, styles (Rude Boys, Punk), trade union, school, political party, church, class, ethnic group
35. Divided loyalties: between two cultures, where do I belong?
36. Battlegrounds
   a. Places – street, estate, playground, park
   b. Types – fights, campaigns, marches, petitions, strikes
   c. In both a. and b. – yours, your parents' or grandparents'
37. Clubs and organisations
38. Girls and boys
   a. What do boys do (according to boys, girls)?
   b. What do girls do (according to boys, girls)?
   c. Will it always be like this?
39. The future, real and imagined
40. Death – deaths I have known, seen, heard about; bereavement

Note 1: Becoming our own Experts, *edited by Stephen Eyers and John Richmond, is available at www.becomingourownexperts.org.*

What's Politics Got to Do with it?

This is a lecture I gave at King's College, London on 6 June 2006.

I'm thinking of putting myself up for the leadership of one of the three main political parties. I'm not sure which one at the moment, but then I'm not sure that it matters very much. I've figured out that one thing I've really got to get right is what I'm going to say about education. Well, actually, one thing I will be getting right is the fact that it's education that I'll be mentioning. After all, how absurd would it be for me to be putting myself up for this job, and not mention education?

OK, let's take a step back here. What do I mean by the phrase 'mention education'? Do I mean some kind of general stuff about how important it is for us to 'enlarge the skills base'? Or that it's necessary to give our youngsters the best possible start in life? Or perhaps talk about how it's only when schools start teaching the difference between right and wrong again, that we'll be able to sleep soundly in our beds? Should I be a little more specific and talk about how it's only by returning schools to local control that we will lever up standards? Or should I be even more specific? Highly particular, in fact, and start talking about how the chanting method is the best way in which children should be taught their times tables, or that downwards rather than horizontally is the best way of learning the periodic table?

Judging by the records of people wanting to be party leaders, or indeed who have become one, all these ways of 'mentioning education' seem to be fairly well road-tested. Now, why should this be? What is it about education that makes it such a must-pack in the present-day party leader's suitcase?

Look at how David Cameron addressed the Conservative Party conference on 4 October 2005. In a speech that covered the European Union, world poverty . . .

> We don't just stand up for Gibraltar and Zimbabwe, but for the people of Darfur and sub-Saharan Africa who are living on less than a dollar a day and getting poorer while we are getting richer.

. . . and inner-city poverty . . .

> I want to be able to say to the people living in our inner cities, of

all races and religions, grappling with the problems caused by family breakdown, poor housing, and low aspirations: 'We know we have a shared responsibility, that we're all in this together, that there is such a thing as society; it's just not the same thing as the state.'

. . . it was, let's say, curious that in this speech, David Cameron's very first concrete policy initiative – I think that's what they're called – should have been synthetic phonics, which he got to via patriotism, freedom and aspiration.

Aspiration is enabled by education; how cruelly it is disabled by Labour today, when one fifth of children leave primary school unable to write properly, when one million schoolchildren play truant each year and when the very essence of aspiration – social mobility – is going backward in this country.

There are far fewer children from state schools going to our best universities. And it's getting worse.

What have Labour done? Created an exam system where 16% means a pass, where parents of children in failing schools have no redress and no way out.

And we're now a country where failure is called 'deferred success'. The government introduced the National Literacy Strategy. It's a good idea. In fact, it was Gillian Shephard's idea.

But why can't children be taught to read with synthetic phonics, a method that works?

Treating every child as if they are the same fails the child who is struggling and the child who is not. So why can't we have streaming and setting, to help all children reach their potential?

Yes, he hit synthetic phonics just 360 words into the speech; his second policy initiative being to bring in streaming and setting; and his third, you may remember, was to save special schools. Even more curious is that these were the only three policy initiatives in the whole speech. Presumably world poverty, inner-city poverty and Europe will come later.

Now, for all I know, this will prove to have been an incredibly successful strategy. As David Cameron walks into number 10, Andrew Marr and Nick Robinson and the rest will remind us of this speech and how it marked a turning point in (let's say they'll say) the history of the twenty-first century, or something as equally non-hyperbolic.

But let's look back at what Cameron was actually saying. The Labour Party is responsible for one fifth of primary-school children not being able to write properly. It's significant, isn't it, that no matter whether we agree with this statement or not, the proposition itself is not impossible. And that's only because we've reached a point where it's governments who sort out primary-school writing. Let's just hold that in our heads. This means that when I'm in a classroom working with some children on a poem, wondering if we're going to talk about getting lost in the supermarket, I'm part of government policy. This is the status quo, the state we're in.

Moving on, Cameron then says that there's a problem with social mobility in this country and links this directly to the matter of state-school children not going to what he calls the 'best universities'. Presumably one is the consequence and not the cause of the other. That's to say, the lack of social mobility, in Cameron's book, is preventing state-school students from going to, let's say, Oxbridge, though saying 'best' is full of resonant vagueness. As it happens, the lack of social mobility has many consequences, but you know, I wouldn't have thought that the low number of people going to Balliol from the comprehensives in Hackney was suitable meat and potatoes for a major political speech. But it is. I would have been wrong.

Next stop is the '16% is a pass' statistic. I'm not sure where this comes from. One of my kids is 19, so he's just gone through the whole system and I seem to remember that all the pass levels he came home with were the usual hoverings between 40 and 50. I've just marked some MA essays for one of the universities that is never called 'our best', and the pass was 50. Well, let's say Cameron is right – he wouldn't be fibbing; the implication of what he's saying is that we desperately need more kids to fail exams. Only then will schools succeed. Perhaps someone will tell me that I've misunderstood something here.

And then, under the stewardship of David Cameron, with failure rates running at acceptably high levels, with schools that used to fail now succeeding, (presumably with the consequence that we're back to that silly old Labour thing of too many kids passing too many exams), we're going to have synthetic phonics. Well, as we now know, we are going to have synthetic phonics. This is because of the Blunkett principle. Hold on, you're thinking, Blunkett's gone to his lair to lick his wounds, it wasn't him who introduced synthetic phonics. It was Ruth Kelly. Who's also gone somewhere to lick her wounds. So it'll be Alan Johnson. Unless he's going to be the next John Prescott. In which case it'll be someone else. No, the Blunkett principle is the one by which a Labour think-tank scans Tory Party think-tank statements and *Daily Mail* editorials and adopts these as Labour policy.

So let's pause awhile and contemplate what's happened here. The two major political parties are unanimous in implementing a policy that directs Year 1 and Year 2 teachers in what they do and how they do it every working day of their lives. I know analogies are dangerous, but let's see if we can find one. Doctors do medicine. As we know, the structure of their existence is directed from government, as are their budgets. But take, say, the case of MMR. You'll remember that Cameron and Kelly and the rest say that synthetic phonics works (we'll come back to that in a moment) which of course is what the NHS says about MMR. But whereas synthetic phonics will be compulsorily delivered to every five-year-old – yes, that's all forty-four phonemes, not ten, not twenty, not thirty-five, but forty-four – MMR is only delivered to the willing. So what is it about education that makes it so suitable for this kind of diktat while the nation's health is less so?

I'll leave that hanging in the air for the moment and come back to phonics. It's notoriously hard to get a grip on literacy levels. Every year, national newspapers make hay with attainment levels, thereby proving in an annual flash of statistical brilliance that some people are below average and some people are above it. A visit to the National Literacy Trust's website will show you a wildly fluctuating needle on the literacy dial, where experts struggle to tie down concepts like 'functionally illiterate', 'inadequate literacy' and the like. One test showed with a stunning lack of cultural bias that ten per cent of people couldn't understand the instructions on a packet of seeds, while in 2003 16% failed their GCSE English. (Ah perhaps that's where David Cameron got his 16 % from?) Meanwhile, 12 % say they have problems with reading, writing and spelling, but it's less than 1% who, it's claimed, I quote, 'can be described as illiterate'.

Well, we all know how to juggle with these figures in ways that might show on the one hand that the UK is now jam-packed full of people who can't read and write, and on the other that we're not doing too badly. But let's get this clear: a system that manages to teach most people how to read is going to be changed because of the failure of the minority. So, if policy A mostly works but not entirely so, you replace it with policy B. But what if policy B succeeds with those who fail under A but creates another set of problems? Well, that wouldn't matter, you might say, if policy B is shown to cut the number of problems and failures.

And so we come to how governments use educational research.

Sue Ellis, a lecturer at the University of Strathclyde, made the following observation in her study of the so-called Clackmannan research project:

> The Clackmannan phonics research reported by Watson and Johnston (2004, 2005) was an experimental trial to compare different methods of teaching phonics. It wasn't designed (despite media reports) to investigate whether phonics instruction provides a more effective 'gateway' to reading than a mixed-methods approach. The researchers did not collect the range of data nor conduct the sorts of fidelity checks that would be required to address such a question.
>
> *The Wider Context for Synthetic Phonics in Clackmannanshire: Evidence to the Rose Committee of Inquiry into Methods of Teaching Reading.* Susan Ellis, University of Strathclyde, September 2005

Let's think about that. So, what went on in this research project wasn't a test to find out whether synthetic phonics is the method that works better than methods currently in place. Well, well, well. So, we are about to switch a whole education policy affecting every single child in state education on the basis of research that cannot prove that this is desirable, necessary or, indeed, will succeed. This is extraordinary, isn't it?

But there's more. When we look at what actually happened when the synthetic phonics programme was introduced in Clackmannan schools, we discover that there was in fact a whole range of interventions going on. This was a local-authority initiative (oh, not one of those beastly LEAs, we're going to abolish them, aren't we?) and involved, of course, a whole set of new resources and teacher-training. But there was also staff development on general lesson planning, interactive teaching, importance of building on success, teaching of reading-writing links, developing literacy through play, and extra help with language-enrichment activities. Home-school link teachers were appointed to work with parents on literacy issues in four of the six pilot schools.

> These staff carried out home visits, ran story clubs and after-school homework clubs, worked with parent groups, set up library visits and borrowing schemes as well as working in classrooms.

Sue Ellis was 'told that parents particularly welcomed the emphasis on encouraging early writing and developmental spelling in the home.'

Schools were involved in a separate and concurrent initiative, the New

Community Schools Initiative, which introduced personal learning planning. This included some, but not all, of the early intervention schools.

It won't surprise anyone here that the project also received some extra funding from the Scottish education office, and of course it's not clear if this kind of extra funding would be available to everyone when universal synthetic phonics drops from on high.

Meanwhile, yet more things were going on in the Clackmannan schools:

The supported voluntary introduction of:

A thinking skills programme for older children, developed from Matthew Lipman's *Philosophy for Children* programme. This was introduced (and explained to the schools) as a specific initiative to bolster reading comprehension. In this programme, philosophical discussions arise from joint reading of a common text. Children are invited to suggest and then discuss questions or things that puzzle them about the story events, themes or characters.

At some point, additional staff development on teaching comprehension and developing reasoning in P2 and up was introduced, and additional reading comprehension lessons for children in P2 and P3 were inserted into the programme. This seems to have been in response to teacher feedback.

A spelling scheme was introduced.

Now all this is extraordinary. We have absolute agreement within the country's political establishment that there will be a major policy shift and that this policy shift is based on solid research, and yet when one researcher takes a closer look at what actually happened, she finds that the conclusions drawn by the politicians are not ones that can be drawn from that particular project. And where are the eagle-eyed journalists rushing off to Clackmannan to unearth this? And how interesting that though synthetic phonics was introduced as the core method of teaching to read, the children were involved in a whole other set of procedures to do with learning how to read. How would we know if some of these didn't perhaps contribute something terribly important to the children's success in reading?

I can just see it now. The next election will see Tory and Labour saying that they will implement synthetic phonics, and what's more they'll appoint home-school link teachers for every school and these staff will carry out home visits, run story clubs and after-school homework clubs, work with parent groups and set up library visits and borrowing schemes. Perhaps not.

But there's an obvious truth underlying all this, and it's one that suits our politicians to ignore: learning how to read is a complex and varied process and not all children do it in the same way. It's a basic truth that David Cameron has grasped. Look again at what he said:

> But why can't children be taught to read with synthetic phonics, a method that works?
>
> Treating every child as if they are the same fails the child who is struggling and the child who is not.

Have I got something wrong here? He says that every child will be treated as if they are the same when it comes to teaching them how to read, but then treating every child as if they are the same fails the child who is struggling and the child who is not. Actually, it's me who's struggling here. But then you'll remember it's because in the next sentence he says:

> So why can't we have streaming and setting, to help all children reach their potential?

This sort of thing gets the blood coursing and the feet stamping, but of course secondary education is already jam-packed full of thousands of systems of selection, grading, streaming and setting. Cunningly, Cameron didn't indicate whether he thought that now is the time to stream and set *primary* schools. Actually, I was streamed and set in primary school. I remember it well. At the end of what is now called Year 5, our teacher told us that we were all very able and clever children but next year we wouldn't be in the same classes. There was going to be one class for people who were good with their heads and one class that was good for people who were good with their hands. Miss Williams would teach the first class and Mr Baggs would teach the second. I was in Miss Williams's class, the one for people with heads. It soon became clear what the difference between the two classes was: we spent every morning doing maths. Half of this was mental arithmetic where Miss Williams would bark out sums at individual kids and you had to bark the answers back at her. She had a way of moving round the class to catch anyone who was glancing out of the window or down at his shoelace. 'Twenty four divided by three!' I think she was inspired by this:

Besides being possessed by my sister's idea that a mortifying and penitential character ought to be imparted to my diet – besides giving me as much crumb as possible in combination with as little butter, and putting such a quantity of warm water into my milk that it would have been more candid to have left the milk out altogether – my uncle Pumblechook's conversation consisted of nothing but arithmetic. On my politely bidding him Good morning, he said, pompously, 'Seven times nine, boy?' And how should I be able to answer, dodged in that way, in a strange place, on an empty stomach! I was hungry, but before I had swallowed a morsel, he began a running sum that lasted all through the breakfast. 'Seven?' 'And four?' 'And eight?' 'And six?' 'And two?' 'And ten?' And so on. And after each figure was disposed of, it was as much as I could do to get a bite or a sup, before the next came; while he sat at his ease guessing nothing, and eating bacon and hot roll, in (if I may be allowed the expression) a gorging and gormandising manner.

For such reasons I was very glad when ten o'clock came and we started for Miss Havisham's; though I was not at all at my ease regarding the manner in which I should acquit myself under that lady's roof. Within a quarter of an hour we came to Miss Havisham's house, which was of old brick, and dismal, and had a great many iron bars to it. Some of the windows had been walled up; of those that remained, all the lower were rustily barred. There was a court-yard in front, and that was barred; so, we had to wait, after ringing the bell, until some one should come to open it. While we waited at the gate, I peeped in (even then Mr. Pumblechook said 'And fourteen?' but I pretended not to hear him) . . .

from Chapter 8 of *Great Expectations* by Charles Dickens

When we had finished with mental arithmetic, we did 'practical arithmetic' and then we had tests. Every day we had tests and at the end of the week the test scores were averaged out and we were given positions or placings in the class and we all changed round. This way we could see which kids were brilliant, which kids were average and which kids were rubbish, in our class that was already selected. So there was a special built-in class-streaming going on because you only ever worked with someone who was about the same placing as you in the week's tests. Then we all sat down and did the eleven-plus exam which about half of us passed. This left the other half in our class and all the rest of the other class who were failures. Whenever I meet any of this majority, they can always tell me that they always knew that they were failures. And then an exam came along that told them they were failures. And then they went to a school for failures. It's an alluring prospect. Tell me I'm wrong, but I have a general feeling that it's something like this that's on its way back. Oh yes, it'll be called all sorts of different things; the way the particular segregation, selection, streaming and setting will take place will all have user-friendly well-spun names, but in essence, the system will be the same.

But I've strayed somewhat from David Cameron's little masterpiece. I had a few more thoughts about phonics. The original Clackmannan research by Watson and Johnston concluded this:

Is synthetic phonics teaching the way forward?

Synthetic phonics is not an exclusive approach – teachers may include synthetic phonics alongside their own programmes to boost the teaching of reading. Our purpose in carrying out these studies was to discover which aspects of phonics teaching are the most effective to ensure that as many children as possible become competent readers, but we recognise that this is only one aspect of effective teaching.

Accelerating Reading Attainment: The Effectiveness Of Synthetic Phonics Joyce E. Watson and Rhona S. Johnston, School of Psychology, University of St. Andrews

Which is what you might expect from a cautious researcher. After all, there are limits with all phonic methods of teaching reading. Just to be technical for a moment, a phoneme is the unit of sound that some linguists think our language can be broken down into and a grapheme is the letter or group of letters plus twiddles (accents and the like) that we use to represent a phoneme. English is often thought to have forty-four main phonemes. However, some of these phonemes can be represented in two, three, four or even more ways. Consider 'ow'. There's o,w in 'cow', there's o,u in 'sound' and there's o,u,g,h in 'bough'. No worries, says synthetic phonics, these are our building blocks. Bung the building blocks together (and already the wagons of educational suppliers are circling the schools offering jolly little phonic blocks to buy), and you make words. The snag with this is that we don't have exact grapheme-phoneme correspondence. That o,w of 'cow' can also give us the o,w of 'row' (as in a row of dots, not a row between people) or even the o,w of the poet Cowper (pronounced 'Cooper'). The o,u of 'sound' can also give us the o,u of 'you', and o,u,g,h can be found in 'tough', 'cough', 'through' and 'thorough'. Whatever glories and successes synthetic phonics will bring us, it will never bring us total reading. As Watson and Johnston make clear, other methods will be needed. But the complexity involved in saying all this won't fit a party leader's speech, a policy overhaul or a manifesto statement. In other words, education takes the back seat while politics takes over.

So how come we've got to a point in history where the day-by-day, minute-by-minute concerns of a Year 1 or Year 2 teacher are the building blocks (!) of a major political speech? I'm not sure there can have been many other times in the past when this has been the case. If we were living in 1902, then we would perhaps be having a heated conversation today about what Bonar Law had to say about elected school boards versus local education authorities. In 1918, we might be arguing about why Lloyd George had not made the raising of the school leaving age to 14 compulsory. However, between 1921, when it did become compulsory, and 1944 (educational historians please correct me if I'm wrong), I don't think you'll find many party leaders talking big about education in schools – a bit about training and apprenticeships, as far as I can make out, but no headline-grabbing stuff about reading schemes or the need for rigour in nursery schools. Then, the whole debate surrounding comprehensive education reached party HQs in the sixties and seventies, but at party leadership level this was about structure and the consequence of this or that kind of structure on the social fabric. For decades, what was taught and how it was taught was given a steer by groups of people who were chaired by the people whose names adorn the famous 'reports' – Plowden of 1967, Bullock of 1975 and before that people like Hadow and his reports of 1926 and 1931. That was how political all this stuff got.

So what was wrong with that? How did we get from Plowden, Bullock and Hadow to David Cameron? And why?

It's not a mystery, but we got there via the phenomenon we call Thatcherism. The group of people who brought about that political upheaval and transformation was, and still is, absolutely certain that education has a political outcome in two senses: one, in that there is a social and economic outcome to whatever structures and processes education policy puts in place; and two, if you make certain political noises in public about education, there will be a favourable election outcome. Some people will remember Margaret

Thatcher saying in her address to the Conservative Party Conference in October 1987:

> Children who need to be able to count and multiply are learning anti-racist mathematics, whatever that is.

Clever, wasn't it? Whoever wrote that could have spent two minutes finding out that some people thought that learning that algebra and the zero weren't all part of the seamless brilliance of Western civilisation might be something worth discovering about the world. What am I saying, 'could have spent two minutes finding out that . . . '? They probably did. But that's not the point. The whole point was to pretend you didn't know in order to suggest that there was some kind of conspiracy going on. Education had been taken over by fanatics who were preventing children from learning. Education had to be saved from people in education. There was, it was said over and over again, an 'education establishment', which was so powerful, so menacing, so entrenched in these kinds of ideas, that it would have to be seized and taken over by . . . er . . . an educational establishment. This wouldn't be powerful, menacing and entrenched. It would be on the side of the people, delivering stuff that works, like synthetic phonics and streaming. And academies.

Yes, take academies. I live in Hackney. Thanks to this on-the-side-of-the-people educational policy-making, London's education body, the old ILEA, was abolished and education was devolved to the boroughs. This meant in Hackney that one of the world's most incompetent and corrupt local authorities was suddenly in charge of a stack of schools. Partly because of the way the old boroughs' map was drawn and partly because of this incompetence, it was only a matter of months before Hackney was chronically short of secondary-school places and thousands of children were being bussed out of the borough. As time went by, and various audits discovered that Hackney had lost tens of millions of pounds no one knows where or how, its powers of running education were taken from it by central government and handed to a quango called the Learning Trust which it turns out can't be trusted and learns nothing. With no local accountability and minimal consultation procedures, the Learning Trust closes and opens schools as if they were tins of cat food. Then, the great solution to the lack of secondary-school places appeared from heaven. The political harmony between Tory and Labour over the establishment of academies has handed Hackney the mandate to invite in any old millionaire to help provide us with the kinds of schools none of us asked for. Stand by for forthcoming photo ops.

So where does this leave us in the political process? I was travelling on the train back from Birmingham the other day with an old friend and colleague, John Richmond. We worked together in the 1970s in a girls' comprehensive school in south London called Vauxhall Manor. An interesting time, an interesting place. I was a writer-in-residence and, looking back on it now, I can see that there was an immense amount of self-generated staff activity, producing policies, research documents, teaching materials and teaching methods. Some of it appeared in a book called appropriately *Becoming Our Own Experts*[1]. What a dangerous and subversive title that sounds today! I think, naively, we thought that it could be a model for every group of teachers everywhere: becoming their own experts and sharing that with others. Indeed, wasn't there a moment in the late eighties when something called LINC appeared? Language in the National Curriculum. Here was a structure whereby teachers researched their own practice, shared with others what seemed to work, which in turn was shared with advisers and inspectors and academics and bit by bit the whole profession would both be developing itself professionally and learning what seemed to be best. Well, that didn't last, did it? Someone somewhere saw it for what it was: a dangerous, autonomous, self-driven kind of an outfit that could well end up with something that most certainly would not make good election fodder for party-conference speeches. So it was dropped and twenty million quid vanished into thin air.

But back to my train journey with John Richmond. We had just been filming a programme for Teachers TV. I present a show called *Reading Aloud*. A simple concept: I talk to teachers about how they make books enjoyable for the children they teach and then we have a chat about some books that they enjoy reading themselves. On the train, I got to asking John about how it is that decisions are now made in education. How is policy made and implemented? I realised that I didn't know. How interesting. Here am I, someone with more than a passing interest in the subject. I come from a background steeped in education biz. Since 1979, every year has seen at least one of my children or stepchildren going through the state system, one more has just joined a reception class and there's one more about to go to a Sure Start Nursery in six months' time. Assuming that he stays on at school till he's eighteen, and I stay alive, I figure that I will by then have been a school parent non-stop for forty-four years. Even so, I stand before you as someone, prior to my conversation with John Richmond, with no real idea of how it is that education today is run.

Perhaps at this point you're looking at me with faintly supercilious smirks on your faces. You mean you didn't know the relationship between the QCA, SIPs, the TDA, the GTC and the PM's unit in Number 10? Are you really saying that you had no idea that SIPs are private? That they're run by Capita, the same people who run the congestion charge? And you didn't even know what SIPs stand for? School Improvement Partners, which are making sure that standards are being achieved. And there was me thinking that I knew what's what because I thought that that was the sort of thing done by the QCA because doesn't the Q stand for quality? No? Well it seems that it might just as well stand for Quidditch now, because they're feeling a bit sore about Capita muscling in on their patch. But hold on, wasn't Ofsted supposed to be rushing about doing what SIPs are doing? No, they've been pared down, while the GTC are getting a bit muscly themselves and wondering if they can get in on the whole curriculum-development thingy. But if that's all true, what goes on in a room in Number 10?

The bit of it that concerns you here in tertiary education is apparently called the Prime Minister's Strategy Unit.

Here's the explanation of what it is:

> The Strategy Unit (SU) was created in June 2002 as the result of a merger between the Performance and Innovation Unit (PIU), the Prime Minister's Forward Strategy Unit (PMFSU) and part of the Centre for Management and Policy Studies (CMPS). The Strategy Unit hosts the Government Chief Social Researcher's Office (GCSRO).

But apart from that I'll admit I'm floundering. After about half an hour on the internet, I've managed to glean that various people have floated through Number 10, making policy and apparently delivering it, people like Michael Barber who, it seems, has passed straight from there to McKinsey plc via a knighthood. I think people like Lord Macdonald and Lord Birt have been involved, but to tell the truth I couldn't figure out who it is or how it is that someone who is called the Secretary of State for Education will now learn what policy he will bring to the House of Commons next month. I am quite serious. Will we ever know how it was decided that synthetic phonics was made government policy? Are there minutes somewhere that will reveal how the Clackmannan project was evaluated?

So, yes, clearly education is highly politicised, but that word 'political' is a complicated creature. When, in the sixties, some of us walked about saying things like, 'The personal is political,' or 'Everything's political, man', I don't think we had in mind that this meant that everything I do or think should have a Number 10 policy unit considering it. So when educational sociologists like Pierre Bourdieu, Michael Apple and Henry Giroux started looking at what they called the politics or sociology of education I thought this was about things such as the political significance of how a school is structured, or the politics of how the curriculum is divided into subjects, or how it is that the social structure of a society reproduces itself through the education system. So, in a way, I'll admit it. I feel that we've been hoist with our own petard. When we said that politics had a lot to do with it, there was what might you call a 'professionalist' approach that said, 'No, education is just education,' – which some people took to mean that education is a way of imparting skills and knowledge and others said, 'Yes, it is all that, but you should add on some stuff about turning out decent human beings too.' The Thatcher-Blair-Cameron consensus seems to say over and over again that politics has everything to do with it, and we'll control what goes on through a set of committees, think tanks, quangos, exams, testing, inspections, selection procedures, compulsory curricula and prescribed teaching methods.

This, we are assured over and over again, will deliver anything from social mobility to freedom, via achievement for all, leading to greater competitiveness in the world market and therefore more prosperity for all in the UK. Of course much political banter of the politicking kind can go on over whether this or that test or method will deliver more, but in essence these are struggles over who looks more like they're on the side of parents who want the best for their kids – as if there are any parents out there who don't want the best for their kids.

The rhetoric around education as delivered by politicians has become a shorthand way to talk to people at their most vulnerable. It talks to those people who are parents and who are therefore anxious about the small human beings in their charge. The politician who talks caringly about education and critiques the status quo is the politician who's on my side. He or she will be making a contribution towards lifting one of my many anxieties about my children off my shoulders. It also talks to those people older than parents who feel in any way that things are getting worse. At several removes from schools, the political rhetoric can confirm that these older people came from a golden age before things went to the dogs. For younger people without children, politico-educational talk can sound buzzy and techno. It can be all enterprisey and Bluetoothy. In other words it's become a bottomless pit of connotation, a resonant signifier without a signified, a glory hole and a catch-all. What a gift we are to the people who rule us.

But I'm not by nature a pessimist. Teaching is done by human beings. The past twenty years have seen a steady rise in the ways in which teachers have been controlled. It's the only model that politicians seem to have for getting things done. Command and control. In its origins it's a military model which brings to mind that poem by Bertolt Brecht:

General, your Tank is a Powerful Vehicle

It smashes down forests and crushes a hundred men.
But it has one defect:
It needs a driver.

General, your bomber is powerful.
It flies faster than a storm and carries more than an elephant.
But it has one defect:
It needs a mechanic.

General, man is very useful.
He can fly and he can kill.
But he has one defect:
He can think.

(from *A German War Primer;* see *www.public-domain-poetry.com/ bertolt-brecht/from-a-german-war-primer-1502*)

I have always thought that teachers can think. In the particular segment of education where I mostly work, with literature and language for primary-age children, I've come to the conclusion that literature and reading have become so reduced, dissected, cross-examined, abridged, chopped-up and tested that the most subversive, exciting and political thing to do now is to rush about creating moments in schools where the children will know for certain that all that they'll have to do with a book, a poem, a story or a play is enjoy it. No questions, no tests, no learning outcomes.

Yesterday, five poets – myself, Francesca Beard who's Chinese Malaysian in origin, Jared Louche from New York City, John Agard from Guyana and Valerie Bloom from Jamaica – read, performed, danced and sang to nearly two thousand primary-school children at the Barbican Centre accompanied by a band with art and photos playing on a huge screen behind us. The children themselves joined in the poems, sang and danced; they heard about Windrush, Singapore, New York cabs, Chinese names, Yiddish rhymes, migrations, birth, lullabies; they heard raps, free verse, chants, couplets, street cries, calypso and quatrains, boogy woogy and *klezmer*. Next term at the London Metropolitan University a pair of us are hoping to set up the first of many conferences that will be devoted to nothing more nor less than making literature fun. Anyone anywhere who's ever found a way of introducing the stuff we call literature to children and students in such a way that means that they have a good time and want more of it will be welcome. I could spell out the politics of this. I could go in for some whole disquisition on let's say the *jouissance* of the text, the politics of ambiguity, the utopian imperative, the cultural significance of heteroglossia, subversive laughter, the art of the possible and the possible of art, rendering the unfamiliar familiar and the familiar unfamiliar, the raised status of the implied reader raising the status of the real reader, and the intertext in all of us. But do you know? I won't. To my mind, the premium in this time, in this moment, is literature is fun, eh? Which I think makes the acronym L, I, F, E. Which is something I'm rather in favour of.

Note 1: Becoming our own Experts, *edited by Stephen Eyers and John Richmond, is available at www.becomingourownexperts.org.*

On Multiculturalism

I gave this talk in 2011 at NewVic, Newham Sixth-Form College.

Let's begin with David Cameron.

I'd rather not but what he said (and got away with saying) deserves a reply.

I say 'begin with David Cameron' but it's not as easy that.

What every politician knows is that his or her speech is really two speeches.

The first is the full-length one, heard by those present in the room or hall at the time and printed out in full in three or four newspapers at the most. The second is the sound bite, the cut and pasted slogan that is broadcast and blogged and tweeted and emailed and headlined all round the world.

So, David Cameron in a recent speech said that 'state multiculturalism has failed'.

I'm going to begin by suggesting that this speech on multiculturalism may or may not have been a lengthy or thoughtful analysis of the subject; it may or may not have been an analysis of how or why the state supports this or that group of people's cultural activities, but it's my view that neither he nor his party office care very much whether it is or it isn't a thoughtful analysis. What counts to them much more is the sound bite and the headline. And the headlines and tweets and international newspaper paragraphs that he won for himself read quite simply: 'Multiculturalism has failed'. What's more, this very same phrase chimed exactly with speeches given by the President of France, Nicolas Sarkozy, and the Chancellor of Germany, Angela Merkel, who in some kind of orchestrated way were talking about the same group of co-religionists: Muslims.

Now I don't know how you in this room tonight read and interpret that phrase, that salty little clip, but when I saw it, I took it in one way only: he and his party and government were saying something about our society, how we live. Actually, he was saying several things: that, yes, we live in a multicultural society, it isn't working, there's something wrong with it, it's broken down *and* – behind that lay the hint, the whisper that if it's broken – a word he's used elsewhere about our society – then surely he and his government should be given permission to do something about it. What that something might be, we could only guess at. And, if you're as keen on conspiracy theory as I am, you might think that such a headline would guarantee him a few votes from people who might otherwise not vote, or vote for parties or support groups that think

POLITICS, EDUCATION AND CULTURE

and say that not only has multiculturalism failed but that we're going to do all we can to make society less multicultural, whether that's through attacking mosques, or claiming over and over again that white people are this society's victims or that multiculturalism has gone too far – whatever that means.

Now, as I said, David Cameron didn't really say 'multiculturalism has failed'. He said that 'state multiculturalism has failed' and he said this because his full speech was an argument about whether previous governments had encouraged people to live segregated lives.

This is what he said:

> Under the doctrine of state multiculturalism we have encouraged different cultures to live separate lives, apart from each other and the mainstream. We have failed to provide a vision of society to which they feel they want to belong. We have even tolerated these segregated communities behaving in ways that run counter to our values.

Now I want to hold that up for examination for a moment.

As we travel about Britain, we can see people of all kinds of backgrounds and beliefs. For many different reasons some people choose to live near to people of similar background and belief. Take David Cameron, for example. This is someone who has led an extraordinarily segregated existence. He and his social group don't travel on the buses we travel on. They go to private hospitals. They travel first-class on planes, they often live behind gates or at the end of long drives, well away from other people or people not like themselves. David Cameron himself went to one of Britain's most expensive schools, where the fees per year are more than most people's salary and where almost everyone came from the same social background as David Cameron, with the same beliefs. He went to a university which continued this, but as it happens, because he seems to have been a little uncomfortable with the very, very limited widening of diversity at his university, he spent a lot of time in an exclusive drinking club, where he and his friends dressed up in old-fashioned clothes, marking them out as quite different from other students, and they went through a variety of private rituals which often involved drinking very large amounts of booze.

The university, Oxford, is interesting at the level of language too: there are hundreds of terms that people of the university learn, whose significance people from outside have no means of knowing: the 'Union' isn't a students' union like other university students' unions, it's the debating society; the main library is called the 'Bod'; the pubs have their own special names – The Eagle and Child is the 'bird and baby'; the colleges have nicknames – St Edmunds Hall is 'Teddy Hall', Christ Church is 'House'. There are posts with names like proctor and scout, and even the streets are subtly renamed – Broad Street is called 'the Broad'. It's all jolly fun, but it serves the basic functions of group language: they are marks of identity and marks of separation. So even as it marks those who know the lingo, it marks those who don't. But we're not talking here about the group identity of the poor or the migrant or the excluded. This is the language of the privileged, and in Cameron's case the super-privileged. He then left university to spend a good deal more time in another extremely exclusive, segregated organisation: his particular political party.

This particular political party has now come to power and is engaged in two bloody wars which don't appear, according to the opinion polls, to have the support of the majority of the people in this country. Maybe we can't quite describe this going to war as 'extremist', but it is violent, and it certainly isn't mainstream, majority thinking.

But when David Cameron is talking about segregated communities, not conforming to mainstream views, and how these give rise to extremist views and violence, I don't think he means his own little group, does he? He's flagging up something else altogether. He's saying that in his view there is something wrong with Muslims living together. That kind of behaviour on the part of Muslims – not his community – leads to terrorism and extremism. Why am I raising this matter of David Cameron's background? Because he was trading in a kind of perverted common sense. He was part of a conversation about 'the other' which he, politicians and newspapers use all the time, a kind of shared meaning which marks out as the difference between 'they' and 'we', 'them' and 'us'.

Look again at the quote I read to you:

> Under the doctrine of state multiculturalism we have encouraged different cultures to live separate lives, apart from each other and the mainstream. We have failed to provide a vision of society to which they feel they want to belong. We have even tolerated these segregated communities behaving in ways that run counter to our values.

It is full of 'we's' and 'they's', so in hearing it or reading it, it tries to position people in either camp. But it's a false 'we' and 'they'. In some respects, I'm similar to David Cameron – I'm white and I too went to his university – but I don't want to be part of his 'we'. On the other hand, he has invented a 'they', a supposed segregation of people somehow not living according to values that he claims belong to the 'we' he is claiming for himself. I find that the values of his segregated community run counter to my values but he doesn't give room in the very grammar of what he is saying for me or you to disentangle ourselves from the binary choice he's given us here. So, ideally in his and his speech-writer's terms, certain people have been recruited into his way of setting out the problem – his map. And yet, as I say, when we look at the nature of his own segregated life, we can see that there is a possible way of looking at the separations and exclusivities of society in a very different way. It's my view that in some ways this kind of invisible storytelling, this unstated narrative in David Cameron's speech, is the most pernicious aspect of it.

Even so, let's run with this notion of segregation. I may not want to use the word but let's ask the question: why do migrants tend to live together?

My background is Jewish and the particular Jews who were my forebears mostly came to this country in the second half of the nineteenth century – in my family's case between 1862 and 1895. They came because they were either escaping violence or feared violence in their countries – Poland and what used to be called Austro-Hungary – now a part of Romania. They were all very poor and most of them had a religion that wasn't followed by many people in Britain at the time, and it was a religion that asked of its followers to eat certain kinds of food prepared in a special way – what is known as kosher.

What's more, these people came into a country that was in two minds as to whether they were welcome or not. On the one hand, they were theoretically free to work anywhere, trade anywhere, go to school anywhere, worship anywhere, though there were secret quotas and exclusions operating – a friend of mine at David Cameron's university told me that his head teacher at his exclusive school did take him to one side on one occasion and explained how they were keeping the numbers of Jewish boys down at the school, and in the fifties it was discovered that posh golf clubs kept a quota too. In the world of ideas and opinions, Jews were viewed in some places and at some times – by no means everywhere – as a dangerous threat. An enemy within. This was partly because they were the old enemy who had killed the Christian God's son, partly because there was a view that circulated that all Jews were rich – even though this lot seemed quite the opposite – and there was also a rumour that Jews killed Christian people's babies at the time of Passover. What's more, it seemed as if some of them were dangerous politically – they seemed to support violent revolution in their own homelands or had links with an enemy power – Germany. In fact, this perceived international danger was something that was very pressing in the last years of the nineteenth century as the great powers did the preliminary jousting before entering into the mass slaughter of the First World War, where some of these dangerous enemies within (the Jews) would end up killing each other in fighting for the very countries who doubted their national allegiances. And incidentally, while we're on the First World War, (which is one of the great symbols of British ceremony, mourning and loss), let's not forget a million and a half Indians along with regiments from Africa and the Caribbean who fought in that war. I say, let's not forget. Perhaps that's too late. They are rarely shown as part of that particular national narrative. Meanwhile, just as we have a Cameron, Sarkozy, Merkel unanimity today about the dangerous enemy within, so at the time my forebears came into this country, France was being rent apart by an affair that involved the false accusation and then the mounting of forged evidence against an army officer who was Jewish. It can be debated whether he was accused because he was a Jew – what is clear is that politicians and newspapers of the time used the affair as an opportunity to found political groups hostile to the minority and to publish great screeds of material explaining the dangers of this particular religious and ethnic community.

We might all want to pause a moment there and think how close this history is to the present-day story of Muslims.

So, when I hear David Cameron getting agitated about segregated communities, though I know full well he's not talking about me, I do think about my forebears living in Whitechapel, Stepney, Bethnal Green and Hackney – where I still live, actually.

And I think about this word 'segregation'. In fact, there are very good reasons why migrants end up living near to people of similar backgrounds and beliefs. You can buy the food you like and the food you might need for religious reasons. If there are enough of you, you can set up the places of worship you need for prayer, birth, marriage and death and initiation into the religion, with classes for the young. If you spread out too much, the trips to the place of worship are too far. There may well be a language question. If you arrive, you're speaking one or several languages that aren't English, but you still need to live and get documents, so the best place to find people who can help you are amongst those who came from where you came from but have been living here for a while and who know what's what.

All this was how it was for my forebears. They set up their own places of worship, some of them for people from their village only; they set up butchers and bakers and grocery shops that sold the meat and food that they liked and needed. And they developed special language books with their own languages, written in the special non-English letters on one side of the page and in English on the other.

But something else happened and always happens when migrants do this. They developed self-confidence. Starting out from being despised not only by many – but by no means all – people in the country they arrived in, but being despised by the leaders of their own religion who were already here, they slowly over some fifty or sixty years moved out of the area they had first settled in, and spread out around the outer London suburbs of east, north and north-west London.

Now, what I've described there is similar to – by no means identical with – patterns of migration of millions of people all over the world, and for some other groups in this country too. And not just over the period of the last twenty or thirty years – as some would have us believe – but over a period stretching back as far as we know.

That's to say, the islands of Britain and Ireland – which, as you probably know, were once one nation – have always been places which people migrated outwards from, people migrated towards and people migrated within. In fact, if we go back far enough, we know that there was a period when no one at all was living where I'm standing now, nor where anyone is living in Britain and Ireland at this very moment. They were covered in ice. When the ice melted, people migrated towards this place. That was about 25,000 years ago.

Now, I'm not going to go through every wave of migration inwards, outwards and within ever since, but it is a study in itself. Let me recommend a book that tells the tale of the migrations inwards – *Bloody Foreigners* by Robert Winder – and while I'm about it a book I haven't read but looked at online: *The Atlas of Human Migration* by Russell King. It's on my list of must-gets.

These books remind us of one key thing about the human condition: we migrate. That's law number one. And law number two is that when we migrate we end up sharing our cultures, no matter how separate or segregated we were at the outset. I'm going to give that side of the matter a name – not multiculturalism but interculturalism.

Now let's break some of that down.

Yes, we do migrate and we do share cultures, but not by any means in the same ways.

One form of migration is the kind that Britain, France, Spain, Holland and

Portugal – with Germany and Belgium tagging along behind – did over several centuries and which has affected human history ever since: the making of empires. And there have been plenty of other empires that have risen and fallen before the ones that the Europeans built. These empires, let's say, are military and colonial, and involved soldiers, sailors and airmen leaving Europe and conquering huge land masses all over the world. This sometimes involved near or full genocide – think of the native peoples of Australia. They also sometimes involved the mass transportation of peoples – the most famous of which was the transatlantic slave trade, which took millions of people from Africa to the Americas and the Caribbean. Some estimate the African arrivants in the Americas and the Caribbean at 12 million people, but many, many more would have been taken from their homes. This affected the lives of people across the huge landmasses of Africa and the so-called new world.

Another kind of migration I'll call 'resistant'. When people are very poor, when they live in overcrowded conditions and can't eat or work or cultivate land, many will try to move. They try to overcome their condition of life by moving. More often than not, the sufferings of these people aren't self-inflicted. They arise out of conditions that have been imposed upon them. One of the most famous of these is what is known as 'The Great Famine', which took place in Ireland between about 1845 and 1852. Though we can say that it was caused by a disease killing the people's staple food, potatoes, the famine itself was caused by the fact that the people who lived where the potatoes were dying weren't allowed to own land. They couldn't cultivate other crops, they couldn't rear animals. The vast majority of them were labourers who weren't paid enough to support themselves and their families. A million people died and a million people migrated out of a population of some eight million. That's an example of resistant migration – getting away from both the starvation and the unfair land laws. More extreme forms of resistant migration are when people flee direct persecution – ethnic, racial, religious or whatever.

In what is sometimes, but not always, a more equitable, fairer way, people have also migrated and/or exchanged their ideas through trade. One way of saying this differently is that human beings have always built boats. That's one of the main reasons why people build them – to take stuff somewhere else and to bring stuff back. At the far end of the journey you may choose to stay long enough to make a family and settle. You've migrated. Human beings have been doing this sort of thing for as long as human beings have settled on seashores and along the sides of rivers.

Let me stop there for the moment. When we study and teach in schools and colleges, we mostly do it with very old tools. I don't just mean pencil and paper and flip charts. The areas we study are divided up as History, English, Biology, Philosophy and the rest, in much the same way it was divided up when I was at school fifty years ago, in the way it was when my father was at school eighty years ago, and as it was for several decades before that. As a consequence, the way we think about the world ends up being divided according to what are really just random divisions. And as a consequence of that, our brains end up being divided too and we start to think that History is somehow different from Geography or different from English literature in some kind of deep, meaningful way.

I don't think so.

And I also think that what actually happens is that some of the most interesting things about ourselves and who we are get missed out.

One example is how we occupy space. I don't mean the space up there – spaceships and all that. I mean the space we live in. Ask yourself the question – have I ever been able to study how come I live where I live, at the same time as studying what I feel about where I live, at the same time as studying how come I have no say in what happens to the spaces I walk about and travel about in? The politics of space, in other words.

Related to this is the subject I've been talking about – migration. Here is a fundamental part of human existence for as long as humans have existed and yet there is no subject called 'Migration'. It crops up in Geography as human settlement. It might crop up in History just as I've just talked about it in relation to the slave trade and the Great Famine, and that's about it. But this doesn't engage with what David Cameron thought he was engaging with (which I dispute): the question of culture – that incredible and wonderful thing that distinguishes us from all other living forms.

So while I'm chatting on, you might want to conjure up for yourself a course in migration and culture. What would you study or teach or research on such a course? How could we do it?

Let's begin with language. Language is what enables human beings to talk and write to each other about what they're going to do and what they have done. It enables them to talk about what they feel and what they feel about each other. It enables us to create things that haven't been created exactly that way before. And – often overlooked – it enables us to think in particular kinds of ways. That is, we carry on what has been called 'inner speech' – a kind of running commentary on what we're doing, who we're thinking about, and even what we're thinking. This inner speech is part of how we position ourselves in relation to other people – am I as good or as bad or as nice or as horrible as that person or that person? And it's part of how we get to grips with anything new – we have to 'make up our minds', as we say, as to how this is going to slot into what we already know – is it going to change what I think, or does it just confirm it?

Now this language I'm using now is one of the most intercultural things we know. In truth, it's not a language, it's a cluster of languages that we could call 'Englishes', according to the great David Crystal in his book *English as a Global Language.*

I'm speaking to you in what is really an oral form of written Standard English. It is, if you like, what is called the prestige dialect or code. It's the language of government, the law, education and administration. If you can't do this dialect, you can't get a job that involves writing in those sectors – government, law, education and administration. You can of course be a cleaner in the buildings that house such people and no one will mind. In fact, there is every chance that as such you might be a member of one of Cameron's segregated communities even as you empty his waste paper basket and vacuum his room.

Back to language and the prestige code: this isn't to say that other Englishes don't exist. It's not to say that other Englishes aren't capable of expressing ideas, thoughts, feelings and culture. And on the matter of interculture, a few moments' study shows us that these different Englishes are no more living in segregated boxes than human beings do. Take one simple out-of-date example. For a brief moment the word 'bling' was used by young people from inner cities. In a matter of months, the word escaped and could be heard in the mouths of DJs, TV presenters and then the population as a whole. We now all know what 'bling' means and on occasions use it – even though the original folks who invented it or brought it in may have long since given up on it.

But of course English doesn't only mingle interculturally with other Englishes. Through the processes of migration (military, colonial, transportation, resistant and trade), whether that is through English speakers migrating outwards and returning or whether it's through peoples out there arriving, or whether it's through tradespeople and cultural workers and artists meeting internationally, what we call English is in fact a massive testimony to all these different forms of migration.

The word 'English' comes attached in some way to the Angles, one of the peoples who came from what is now Schleswig-Holstein in Germany. They were immigrants from a place called Angeln, who were invited in to help the king at the time beat off the invaders coming from what is now Scotland.

These immigrants spoke a Germanic language which developed into what we call Old English or Anglo-Saxon. But I'm not speaking Old English even though a good percentage of the words I'm saying come from Old English. The other big percentage comes from old French, the language that was spoken by some other invaders!, the people from what is now northern France, the Normans, who were themselves descended from invaders from the north, the Vikings. This bit of the story of interculture and migration that I'm telling today is a subject you can study – and when you do, you can take the sentences I'm talking now and underline them in pretty colours showing which words descend from the English and which from the French or indeed which from anywhere else – like say, the Vikings from Scandinavia who settled in Britain and from whom people living here took the words 'take', 'egg', 'sky' and 'window' – which means 'wind-eye' incidentally.

And when I say 'courage' or 'beauty' or 'marvellous' this is thanks to the Norman invasion.

But if I say the names of cloth like 'calico', 'muslin', 'chintz', or words like 'shampoo', 'bungalow', 'verandah', the drink 'punch' and probably the slang word 'cushy' meaning pretty comfy or easy, then these come from the Indian sub-continent as a result of the British colonisation of India.

Meanwhile, the English language has itself spread across the globe in several phases, firstly as part of trade, then colonisation, conquest and empire, then through the rise of new empires or spheres of influence, most notably the USA. As a result of this you can now go to Germany, go to a conference of German scientists, who are all German, and find that the whole conference is being conducted in English. What an extraordinary example of interculture, but then if you did something similar six hundred years ago, people were doing something similar – they were sitting around discussing things, not in their vernacular (the language of their everyday lives), but in the language of dead Italians, Latin. By using something apparently foreign to them, they were able to share culture and ideas.

But interculture isn't only a matter of pure linguistics.

There's a traditional American folk group called the Carter Family. They first recorded what we now call either country music or bluegrass music in 1927. They were poor white people, probably of mostly Irish origin, and they went around south-western Virginia. This was peopled by people such as themselves, Anglo-Irish white people, along with a large minority of African-Americans who had arrived there as part of the last leg of the slave trade to work on the tobacco and cotton plantations.

At the time of the Carter Family singing what have become classic American songs, and using classic styles of guitar picking, there was enforced segregation in the American south. Friendship, sex and marriage between white and black people was not only discouraged; it was dangerous for people to even contemplate it. Even to enter a bar as a white and black person together could result in a beating. However, this doesn't tell the whole story. People will always resist these appalling laws and customs.

I've no idea whether the Carters were racist or not, but they befriended an African-American man called Leslie Riddle, and the man of the family, 'A.P.', as he was known, toured Virginia in and out of largely African-American music joints and with Riddle's help learnt the tunes, learnt the words and just as importantly learnt from him how to play the tunes on the guitar. One of the family, Maybelle, learned to pick tunes with her thumb in a way that no publicly known white guitar-playing singer had ever done before, and as a result this style of playing spread across the US and across the world to make a sound that is familiar to us all. And it all comes from a moment of semi-illegal, dangerous, resistant interculturalism. If you want to hear what I'm talking about, use YouTube and the Carter Family websites. This little known story is there.

But now let me take a shift in this argument. I've talked about interculture as if it is a rather even-handed kind of exchange – and in a way it is. And to my mind this is as good a reply to the David Cameron sound bite as I know. Multiculturalism hasn't failed. We live it as interculture, thank you very much, Dave. If you travelled on the buses we travel on, you'd see it too.

But in fact there is another agenda going on. David Cameron speaks from what we might call the dominant culture. I've already described his cultural origins, but when he speaks, he speaks with centuries of ruling behind him, his family and his party. He and many others (some of whom should know better) speak of a host culture to which migrant cultures assimilate. This implies, and is by some explicitly stated, that the host culture is a kind of permanent, historic, pure culture, while migrant cultures are somehow provisional, less important and need to be modified by assimilating to this more important purer model.

Cameron and others try to wave in front of us all the main signifiers of this host culture, and invoke phrases like 'our democracy', English literature, the rule of law, the English landscape, the Church of England, fish and chips and the various form of English or British high art – music, painting and the like.

I'm going to stick my neck out here. This is a double fib. None of this stuff is purely or only English or British and it is only described this way in order to pull a fast one. That is, it makes the demand that we should assimilate even as they do everything they possibly can to make it impossible for us to do so. Just one example: even as politicians tell us how lamentable it is that there are people living in Britain who haven't learned English, they are making it harder for people to learn English! Grants for learners of English and ESOL teachers themselves are being cut back. But assimilation is a false grail. In the end you can't become David Cameron. You can't have the very segregated culture that he created for himself and his social group. It makes itself exclusive and then blames people for not being part of it.

And more than that: by making 'assimilation' an impossible demand, they turn us into beggars or supplicants sitting up and pleading to come in, and in so doing they keep us at the door in that subservient, apologetic, incomplete position – never quite good enough, always asking to come in, even though what they're asking us to assimilate to is a myth anyway. It's part of how cultural domination is achieved.

I don't think we need to be supplicant, and I'll come to that as my conclusion, but let me first look at the interculturalism of the so-called host culture itself. In other words, even what we are being asked to assimilate to is a mix, a hybrid, an ever-changing mongrel process.

British democracy wasn't invented or created purely or only in England or Britain. The first democratic ideas that circulated and were respected came from ancient Greece, though other peoples the world over developed ways of reaching consensus decisions. Some of the first people in Britain to experiment with democratic forms are those we call Puritans, who developed many of their ideas in conjunction with their co-religionists from Holland, Germany and Switzerland – the Calvinists, Anabaptists, followers of Munzer, and a whole host of movements and sects across Europe and later in America and Australia. The major breakthroughs in democracy mostly came in the USA, France (through revolutionary wars and straight revolution) and later in Australia, while the governments in this country resisted democracy every step of the way, and even then have never agreed to write it down and codify it so that we can all read it and see if we have certain guarantees we can be sure of. The knowledge about this country's democracy is held deep in obscure volumes and in the minds and interpretations of that exclusive, segregated elite, constitutionalists and law lords. Even the terms they use and their rituals are not for the likes of us to understand or learn. When Gerry Adams announced that he wanted to resign from Parliament he was told that he had to go through a strange ritual with names that no one outside a tiny group of people had ever heard of. How quaint, but how segregated!

The Church of England sounds as if it ought to be very English, but of course its most important sacred book, the Bible, is the product almost entirely of Middle-Eastern Jews. The versions of the Bible that people read for hundreds of years were translations from at least three languages, Hebrew, Greek and Latin, and the fifty or so translators of the iconic 1611 text, the so-called King James Bible, interestingly consulted the translations that had been made by other Europeans into their languages. It was a truly international enterprise. The beliefs that are enshrined in that Bible developed far away from Britain, in the areas around the Mediterranean. And the practices and rituals of the Church of England largely but not entirely developed out of rituals developed far from Britain too – mostly in Rome.

And when English literature is invoked as some kind of pure English thread through the culture, I scratch my head and wonder how this can be done.

Let's start at what is supposed to be the first great text of English literature: an epic telling the story of how a warrior saved some people from a terrible monster and then the even more terrible monster's mother, and then a dragon. This is *Beowulf*, written down sometime around the year 1000 of the Christian era. The epic is set in what is now Denmark, Germany, Belgium and Holland – not Britain. And like most literature it draws on ideas and sources beyond these shores – from Scandinavia mostly. But also, at the level of language itself, it is full of Scandinavian and Latin influences and words. It isn't written in some imagined pure old English.

Come forward nearly another four hundred years to the next great name in so-called English literature and we find Chaucer – someone who happily used or borrowed most of his stories in his great book *The Canterbury Tales* from France and Italy, whilst borrowing the shape of the stories from an Arab idea – the frame story. *The Canterbury Tales* are the tales supposedly told by a group of pilgrims wending their way to Canterbury. We hear what each of them looks like and talks like and we hear their conversations before and after they tell their story.

Frame stories seem to have come into Europe via an incredible little book, first appearing in Latin in 1106. It was a re-telling of stories that the author – who called himself Petrus Alphonsus – read in Arabic but which were themselves translations and adaptations from Sanskrit and Persian. What is particularly interesting for me is how uninterested mainstream studies are in this little book. I suspect this is because it is an example of how there is no place for it amongst the old subjects we study and teach. It is a fine example of interculture, a culture that belongs to no one and everyone, so no place for it.

My source for this is a remarkable study called *The Past We Share* by E.L. Ranelagh. In it we can see how the stories of Petrus Alphonsus's little book spread out across Europe to be used and re-used as part of popular literature, sermons, plays and novels from then on.

Then jump forward another two hundred years and we come to the greatest English writer of them all, Shakespeare . . . and yet . . . here was someone who for a good deal of his writing drew on the ideas, images, language and storylines of world literature as it was available to him, living in London in the late 1500s and early 1600s. With Shakespeare there is a whole study around what are called his sources, and a quick glance at the intros to good editions of the plays will break these down for us, while others have reconstructed what might be called Shakespeare's library or reading matter on the basis of it. Here we find Roman comic plays and the famous Greek myths as told by the Roman author Ovid. We find stories from Italy and Denmark, and the technique of the frame story appears in *The Taming of the Shrew* and *A Midsummer Night's Dream*. Some of his ways of writing poetry both in the plays and beyond them came from the Latin or Italian poets – as with his sonnets. Shakespeare was part of an international fervour that was excavating Greek and Roman texts. This movement was, particularly in Italy, inventing new ways of writing, building, sculpting and painting, and it was beginning to challenge the major received wisdoms of the previous six hundred years – in an epoch we call the Renaissance. Even the location of the earth in the universe was questioned and repositioned thanks to an Italian. Hear now the rationalist Edmund in *King Lear* when he comes forward to talk to us after a member of the old aristocracy has said, 'These late eclipses in the sun and moon portend no good to us . . . '

Edmund now says:

This is the excellent foppery of the world, that, when we are sick in fortune, often the surfeit of our own behaviour, we make guilty of our disasters the sun, the moon, and the stars: as if we were villains by necessity; fools by heavenly compulsion; knaves, thieves, and treachers by spherical predominance; drunkards, liars, and adulterers, by an enforc'd obedience of planetary influence; and all that we are evil in, by a divine thrusting on: an admirable evasion of whoremaster man, to lay his goatish disposition to the charge of a star! My father compounded with my mother under the dragon's tail; and my nativity was under Ursa major; so that it follows, I am rough and lecherous. Fut! I should have been that I am, had the maidenliest star in the firmament twinkled on my bastardizing.

It turns out that Edmund the rationalist bastard is indeed a bastard in the other sense, but it's the nature of the play to be staging an argument about this international debate about humans' place in the cosmos.

This is why and how Shakespeare and all these writers belong to the world and belong to all of us. I think we do them a disservice by trying to ring-fence them to the nation. Shakespeare was an internationalist. He and some other writers around him created a brand new art form: the all-moving, many charactered play, full of action, thought, introspection, realistic dialogue and staged debate and argument.

Three hundred years later, people would do something as revolutionary with the invention of cinema and, just like Shakespeare, they plundered world stories and ideas to create their films in the early years of the twentieth century. Where Shakespeare leant heavily on Italy and Latin literature, Hollywood and Disney leant heavily on immigrants from Germany. That all-American movie *Some Like It Hot* was directed by a German immigrant; the English-born Hitchcock borrowed many of his ideas from German cinema of the 1930s and Russian Cinema of the same time and before; and in Disney's case, stories from Germany, Italy and France – think *Pinocchio*, *Snow White* and *Cinderella* – are part of the international intercultural tradition of the folk and fairy story.

And of course, talking of Hollywood and Disney reminds us that the thing people might want to call British culture is in fact thoroughly interfused and intermingled with things American which in turn are themselves the products of migrants.

Look at my jeans. A U.S. idea made with a fabric, denim, which comes from French cloth-makers of Nimes, *de Nimes* . . . denim . . . jeans . . . *bleus de Gênes* or blues from Genoa, because that was where some of the first denim-makers lived and traded.

So I'll finish with a thought about how we view ourselves and what we learn and study and teach.

We can of course be proud of who we are and where we come from. I think that one of the roles of education is to create spaces in which children and young people can explore this. I've just worked with a group of seven-year-olds to write poems to put into a time capsule. I told them about the volcano bags of Montserrat – these are bags that people on the island of Montserrat made and filled with their most precious and necessary things so that if the volcano erupted, they could grab the bag and make for the sea. I suggested that we could do something similar but with words. We started with our names; they had done some research on their names. Why did they have a particular first name or names? Where did they come from? Who are they named after? And where does their family name come from, and what does that mean? So they wrote that down. And then I asked a series of questions: what important object would you like to put in your bag, and why? What memory would you most like to hang on to? Put that in the bag. What piece of helpful advice has anyone given you that you can put in, maybe something your mother or father, uncle or aunt or grandmother or grandfather told you? And you can write that in the language that it was spoken in, of course. What is your nightmare? It could be the thing you most fear or it could be your worst dream. What do you most want, first for you, then for the world? What do you hope for?

Another approach that some of you may be familiar with are language maps, where you put a silhouette of yourself in the middle of the page and then create a set of boxes around your silhouette, each one representing a person or a sphere in your life: your carers, your school, the playground, an important leisure activity, a place of work, and so on. And then in each box you put a significant or interesting or funny part of language that you've picked up in each box. That's your intercultural language map.

But every sphere of ideas and human practice is available to us as ways of looking at our internationalisms – maths, science, philosophy, psychology, architecture, engineering: the lot. In fact, it's an under-researched, under-studied area because we are constantly being framed and re-directed back to a national agenda of which David Cameron's speech was just one of thousands of examples.

So, in conclusion, when I'm talking interculture I'm not trying to take anything away from anyone, but let's not kid ourselves that who we are or what we possess in our minds is some kind of purity either of our own or of the supposed host culture to which we should be assimilating. In fact, the more we learn about it, the less need there is for us to think that there is some kind of core that we should be striving to become part of. Instead, we can discover and enjoy the ways in which we share. And that way, we don't leave ourselves open to being told that multiculturalism has failed. It hasn't failed. It's us.

Culture: It's All in the Mix!

This piece appeared in Defending Multiculturalism: A Guide for the Movement, *edited by Hassan Mahamdallie, published in 2011.*

With David Cameron's words on multiculturalism reverberating round the gutters, now's a good time to take a second look at the word 'culture'. The two main overlapping ways the word is used in everyday conversation are: a) to cover artistic products we consume – plays, films, books, paintings and the like; b) to talk of the way we do things in our everyday lives – our 'kinship' relations, what we eat and how we prepare it, what kind of dwellings, rituals, music, gestures we make and – significantly – what language(s), dialect(s) and accent(s) we speak with.

Underlying many discussions about the second use is the notion that there is a 'host' culture which is distinct, unified, ancient, virtuous and desirable and there are 'other' cultures which at best are 'interesting' or 'lively' but should be made to 'integrate' or become 'assimilated'. As Marxists, we might re-shape that and talk of a 'dominant' or 'hegemonic' culture and talk of 'non-dominant' or 'sub' cultures. Either way, this has its problems, because it presents cultures as if they are discrete chunks. From the right, there has been an effort to claim some kind of pure English or British 'way of life' or 'set of values' which is 'indigenous'. Meanwhile, on our side, we quite rightly celebrate multicultural 'diversity' and 'minority cultures', claiming this as a form of cultural resistance. I think we have to go further than that and celebrate interculturalism – which is ultimately part of internationalism.

Human beings migrate. It is one of the conditions of humanity across time. Many times migration has been in order to colonise and dominate other peoples – military and colonial migration, or transportation migrations where peoples have been taken forcibly across distances. Many times migration has been resistant, to escape persecution, overcrowding and poverty. Other times it has been in a more equitable form of exchange, where peoples have made contact with each other in order to trade goods and/or exchange ideas and art. In all these cases, the consequence is that cultures mix. With colonial migration there has been the spread of the English language, but wherever English has settled it has been re-shaped by the peoples of those places. Transportation has produced the explosion of diverse cultural forms as a consequence of Africans being enslaved across North and South America and the Caribbean, and mixing with natives and Europeans. Resistant migration has resulted in such mixtures as 'the post-colonial novel' or 'Gipsy jazz', while trade migrations have given us Latin phrases like 'et cetera' and, say, modernist architecture.

Such intercultural mixing reaches into a culture which is supposedly both 'host' and somehow immune to this hybridisation. Even as the ruling class uses Britishness or Englishness in order to extend its domination into our minds, it is itself a mish-mash. The early development of 'British' parliamentary democracy owes a good deal to the resistant cultures of dissenting Christians, but this was never purely British. Puritanism was a fusion of European ideas – German, Swiss, Dutch, French, Scots and English. Much of the 'English' landscape was shaped by migrants from continental Europe clearing forests or, much later, draining land. Great 'English' literature like Chaucer is in fact a mix of French, Italian and, in the 'frame story' of *The Canterbury Tales*, Arab influence. Shakespeare's plays are written in Latinate blank verse with plot lines borrowed from Denmark, ancient Greece and ancient Rome, Italy and beyond. Classical music is a trans-European phenomenon and one of the most supposedly 'English' composers – Handel – was German. The 'English' Beatles began and ended with the strains of the blues, Tamla Motown and rock, which themselves were and are cultural hybrids. 'British' education is made up of a mix of Greek, Roman, German, Swiss, French ideas as well as local ones. The Church of England is based on layers of Middle-Eastern religions interfused with structures derived from the religion's Italian establishment. And of course, even the idea of 'nation' is international!

What we do is endlessly assimilate to each other. It's asymmetrical; certain ideas 'dominate', but not as those who dominate describe it. The domination is achieved by inventing the myth of a pure centre whilst making the impossible demand for us to assimilate to it. What's more, this ruling centre props itself up precisely by resisting being the 'other' – by not being the migrant, the Muslim, and so on. In fact, even as members of the ruling centre decry 'segregation', their class politics ensures that it is more difficult to move an inch towards that centre: next year, through cuts in grants and teaching jobs, it will be many times harder for migrants to acquire English. We should of course support all resistant cultures, whilst identifying rulers' lies about their own desirable purity, and celebrating how we defy atomisation, segregation and oppression through all the many ways we mix.

School Rules: the 10 Elements of Successful Arts Education

I wrote this piece in 2012 for Arts Award, managed by Trinity College London in association with Arts Council England, which was launching two new awards, Discover and Explore, for children and young people aged seven and above.

Anyone could be forgiven for thinking that arts education in UK state schools is patchy, and in places confused and arbitrary – the past 15 years have seen waves of anxiety about literacy and maths with attendant concerns about science, modern languages and history.

Using the stick of international league tables, governments try to prove the country's schools and teachers are inadequate and that the solution to the British achievement deficit is more testing, more homework, harder exams, tougher inspection and more selection. Trying to wave the flag for arts education in this climate is like trying to slow a train down by standing in its path.

In this context, advocates for the arts find themselves facing some choices: do we claim that the arts can help children achieve and by extension haul the UK up the league tables? Do we claim for them a unique role in pupils' mental and physical wellbeing? Or do we say that the arts offer some kind of aid to school discipline, enlisting children in team-building?

Should we be linking the creative activities at the heart of the arts with active, inventive learning that can and should take place across the core curriculum? Do we say that the arts are an industry, and that part of the job of education is to train people so they can enter any industry, including the arts? Or should our claim be that old cry of the aesthetes – art for art's sake?

My own view is that the arts are neither superior nor inferior to anything else that goes on in schools. It's just as possible to make arts-focused lessons as weak, oppressive and dull as other subjects. It's just as possible to make those other lessons as enlightening, inventive and exciting as arts work.

The key is in the 'how' – not whether arts education in itself is a good thing but what kinds of approaches can make it worthwhile for pupils. We should think in terms of necessary elements. Pupils should:

1) have a sense of ownership and control in the process of making and doing

2) have a sense of possibility, transformation and change – that the process is not

closed-ended with predictable, pre-planned outcomes, but that unexpected outcomes or content are possible

3) feel safe in the process, that no matter what they do, they will not be exposed to ridicule, relentless assessment and testing, fear of being wrong or making errors

4) feel the process can be individual, co-operative or both, accompanied by supportive and co-operative commentary which is safeguarded and encouraged by teachers

5) feel that there is a flow between the arts, that they are not boxed off from each other according to old and fictitious boundaries and hierarchies

6) feel that they are working in an environment that welcomes their home cultures, backgrounds, heritages and languages into the process with no superimposed hierarchy

7) feel that what they are making or doing matters – that the activity has status within the school and beyond

8) be encouraged and enabled to find audiences for their work whether in the same school, other schools or in the communities beyond the school gate

9) be exposed to the best practice and the best practitioners possible or available in order to see and feel other possibilities

10) be encouraged to think of the arts as including or involving investigation, invention, discovery, play and co-operation, and that these happen both within the actual making and doing but also in the talk, commentary and critical dialogue that goes on around the activity itself.

I believe that if we set out the stall for the arts in this way, we won't find ourselves trying to defend or advocate an art form – say, painting – for what are deemed to be its intrinsic civilising qualities. Instead, we will be advocating a set of humane and democratic educational practices for which the arts provide an amenable home.

Ultimately, I'm not sure that I would (or could) claim that this will enable a pupil to do better at exams, avoid trouble at school or equip her or him with an *esprit de corps*. I would say, however, that conducting arts education with these elements in mind will help pupils explore their own minds and bodies, and the materials around them.

As they work, they will find their minds, bodies and materials changing and as agents of that change they will inevitably change themselves. They will find out things about themselves as individuals – where they come from, how they co-exist with people and places around them – and they will pick up (or create) clues about where they are heading.

This needs to be fought for with a permanent conversation and debate around all the art forms and their possible role in education at every level.

Across the many years I've been involved with arts education, I have seen countless projects, schemes, partnerships and programmes, on and off site, being developed, flowering and then getting phased out. Agencies have come and gone, reports have been written and re-written. To my mind, much of this seems too arbitrary, too inconsistent and too temporary.

The way to take the arts seriously is not to defend this or that art form for its own sake. Pursuing arts activities with humane and democratic principles in mind is where the benefit lies.

Languages of Migration

I gave this talk on 26 November 2014. It was the first annual Public Lecture for the Migration Museum, in partnership with the London School of Economics and Political Science.

Good evening.

Before I start, can we do a quick survey of our lived experiences and close acquaintance with migration? I'm doing this so that we can bring the quick survey with us through the talk. Far too often, the conversation about migration takes place as if people who have experience of migration are somewhere else, outside, over there.

So this mini-questionnaire I'm about to do is the tip of an iceberg, the bottom part of the iceberg being what we might call 'our cultures of migration': cultures that often lie obscured by the dominant rhetoric about migration.

How many people in the room have moved from another country or countries to live and/or work in the UK, short-, medium- or long-term? *[Not me.]*

How many people in the room have at least one parent born in a country other than the UK? *[Me.]*

How many people have at least one grandparent born in a country other than the UK? *[Me.]*

How many people in the room have lived in a country other than the UK for more than a year? *[not me]* for more than five years? *[not me]* for more than ten years? *[Not me.]*

Now, spouses or partners:

How many people have a spouse or partner who comes originally from a non-UK country? *[Not me.]*

How many people have a spouse or partner who has at least one grandparent who comes from a non-UK country? *[Not me.]*

Now, one to include all forms of migration: migration of any kind, some of which isn't called migration, but is called 'moving':

How many people in the room are not living in the same house or flat they lived in as a child? *[Me.]*

I'll come back to this matter of the 'culture of migration' in thinking about my own background later, but let's start in the eye of the storm, the conversations about migration that are going on at this very moment in the world of politics and the media. And in this part of the talk I want to be specific about the language around 'migrants', the language that colours the meaning of the words 'migrant', 'immigrant', 'immigration'.

Here's Barack Obama on 20 November 2014:

> Over the past few years, I have seen the determination of immigrant fathers who worked two or three jobs without taking a dime from the government, and at risk any moment of losing it all, just to build a better life for their kids. I've seen the heartbreak and anxiety of children whose mothers might be taken away from them just because they didn't have the right papers. I've seen the courage of students who, except for the circumstances of their birth, are as American as Malia or Sasha; students who bravely come out as undocumented in hopes they could make a difference in the country they love.
>
> These people – our neighbors, our classmates, our friends – they did not come here in search of a free ride or an easy life. They came to work, and study, and serve in our military, and above all, contribute to America's success.
>
> Tomorrow, I'll travel to Las Vegas and meet with some of these students, including a young woman named Astrid Silva. Astrid was brought to America when she was four years old. Her only possessions were a cross, her doll, and the frilly dress she had on. When she started school, she didn't speak any English. She caught up to other kids by reading newspapers and watching PBS, and she became a good student. Her father worked in landscaping. Her mom cleaned other people's homes. They wouldn't let Astrid apply to a technology magnet school, not because they didn't love her, but because they were afraid the paperwork would out her as an undocumented immigrant – so she applied behind their back and got in. Still, she mostly lived in the shadows – until her grandmother, who visited every year from Mexico, passed away, and she couldn't travel to the funeral without risk of being found out and deported. It was around that time she decided to begin advocating for herself and others like her, and today, Astrid Silva is a college student working on her third degree.
>
> Are we a nation that kicks out a striving, hopeful immigrant like Astrid, or are we a nation that finds a way to welcome her in? Scripture tells us that we shall not oppress a stranger, for we know the heart of a stranger – we were strangers once, too.
>
> My fellow Americans, we are and always will be a nation of

immigrants. We were strangers once, too. And whether our forebears were strangers who crossed the Atlantic, or the Pacific, or the Rio Grande, we are here only because this country welcomed them in, and taught them that to be an American is about something more than what we look like, or what our last names are, or how we worship. What makes us Americans is our shared commitment to an ideal – that all of us are created equal, and all of us have the chance to make of our lives what we will.

That's the country our parents and grandparents and generations before them built for us. That's the tradition we must uphold. That's the legacy we must leave for those who are yet to come.

Here's Tory MP Bernard Jenkin on 24 November 2014, on BBC Radio 4's *Today* programme. He cited Alan Milburn, who spoke of Britain becoming a 'bifurcated nation'. Then he said:

One of the things that's keeping low pay depressed is the endless supply of cheap labour coming in from the EU 8, the eastern European countries, the recent entrants to the European Union . . . This is causing real problems in hospitals, in schools, the provision of public services, shortage of housing . . . We need to address this in the public interest.

By the way, on the programme earlier in the interview, Bernard Jenkin showed his great familiarity with poor people by doubting if the BBC employed people on low pay. Perhaps he doesn't know of the thousands of people working for the BBC as runners, researchers, cleaners, trainees, cafe staff and so on, many of whom are not only people on low pay, but are also migrants or children or grandchildren of migrants. But then why would he know that?

And here's Nigel Farage, who, as we'll hear, has a very intimate acquaintance with migrants. This is from the *Daily Telegraph* of 16 May 2014 as written by Matthew Holehouse, the paper's political correspondent.

Mr Farage was asked to justify claims made earlier this year that he feels 'uncomfortable' and 'awkward' on trains where nobody speaks English and that 'parts of Britain are now a foreign land'.

He said in February: 'I got on the train the other night, it was rush hour, from Charing Cross.

It was a stopper going out and we stopped at London Bridge, New

Cross, Hither Green, it was not till we got past Grove Park that I could hear English being audibly spoken in the carriage. Does that make me feel slightly awkward? Yes it does.'

Mr Farage's wife, Kirsten, is German, and his children are bilingual. Mr Farage said she speaks English outside the home.

'You felt uncomfortable about people speaking foreign languages, despite the fact presumably your own wife does when she phones home to Germany,' said James O'Brien, the host of LBC Radio.

Mr Farage replied: 'I don't suppose she speaks it on the train, you know. That's the point I'm making.'

Mr Farage stood by his view, given in a recent interview, that he would be 'concerned' if he had Romanian neighbours.

'I was asked a question if a group of Romanian men moved in next to you, would you be concerned? If you lived in London I think you would be,' he said. He said the crime statistics relating to Romanian immigrants are 'eye-watering'.

Asked why that would be different to German children moving in next door, he replied: 'You know what the difference is.'

He added: 'We want an immigration policy that is not just based on controlling quantity, but quality.

I'm not demonising anybody. I'm demonising a political class who has had an open door allowing things like this to happen.'

Mr O'Brien claimed there is an 'avalanche of bigotry emerging' from UKIP and it represents 'deeply divisive and racist ideas'. He accused Mr Farage of conflating the trend of primary school children who speak English as a second language with those who cannot speak English at all. Mr Farage said the trend shows the need for tighter immigration controls.

But the former category would include Mr Farage's own children, Mr O'Brien said. 'The point you are making is that the East End is full of children who can't speak English. I want you to recognise that's not true,' he said. 'Most bilingual children in this country are children like yours.'

So from Barack Obama to Bernard Jenkin and Nigel Farage – all using language about migration – but in very different terms.

Obama has chosen to highlight the migrant and invested that word with ideas of struggle, incredibly hard work, sacrifice and bravery. He then went on to picture the reception of the migrant in America as traditional, righteous and historically normal; he posited the idea that everyone is a migrant. He also made a point of drawing on a notion of equality – enshrined in the founding principles of the United States. What was also crucial here was that he was suggesting that these ideas and principles were bigger and more important than illegality, or that at the very least the government could and should overcome the matter of illegality. So, though illegality is often attached to the word 'migrant', Obama suggests that the government could side with the migrant to overcome the illegality or, in language terms, detach illegality from the word 'migrant'.

Needless to say, there are people who are appalled by what Obama has said, and many will take it to 'prove' – 'prove' in quotes – that he is, as they have always said, a foreigner and a Communist Muslim; or is that a Muslim Communist?

From a radical perspective, it's possible to raise an eyebrow at one aspect of the speech. The US is indeed a nation of migrants including the first-nation peoples who migrated into what we call North America any time from about 40,000 years ago. It's a pity they didn't get a mention.

There's also the question of whether America is as different from other countries as Obama suggests. Is there a country in the world that is not a nation of immigrants? Is there any nation in the world that is made up of only the descendants of people who lived in that precise land mass for, what shall we say, 40,000 years? I suspect that Obama was drawing on folk memory and American people's knowledge of family history when he says 'nation of immigrants', rather than making an observation about the history of all human beings everywhere. I'll make that observation instead: we are a world of migrants.

Now for Bernard Jenkin.

Jenkin draws on what some might regard as a radical image, a 'bifurcated nation', meaning the split between rich and poor. Humane though this might seem to be, migrants in his language are not people. He doesn't even use the word 'migrant'. We don't hear a Jenkin equivalent of Obama's Astrid Silva, or the father with three jobs or the woman cleaning in people's homes or the children who are anxious that their mother might be deported. In Bernard Jenkin's language, migrants are 'an endless supply of cheap labour'.

What can we say about this? Well, first off, whatever it is, it's not 'endless'. There are finite numbers involved. It's not a 'supply' because no one is supplying them. And the phrase 'cheap labour' is a handy way of dehumanising people by reducing them to the price of their labour – that is to say, a cost. But labour is a cost purely and only from the point of view of an employer. Working people don't look at their pay slips and say, 'Ah here's my cost.' Now let's remind ourselves of what, according to Jenkin, these costs, these massed economic units do: they 'keep low pay depressed'.

Now I don't know exactly what goes on in boardrooms. I've only ever seen them in documentaries or mocked-up in film and TV. But someone tell me, what are those people doing in there if they're not doing all they can to 'keep low pay depressed'? I thought that this was what shareholders want them to do. In their terms, isn't this keeping the cost of labour down? How, in the Jenkin universe, is the dehumanised mass of labour that Jenkin shakes in front of us able to do that? Aren't they living people who turn up and apply for a job? Throughout most of my childhood and adolescence I heard employers telling a terrible story: they were being brought to their knees by vicious people called trade unionists who did all they could to stop low pay being depressed. Then, the story goes, the heavens opened and we finally got a prime minister who put a stop to all that.

I raise this in order to clarify why it is that Bernard Jenkin of all people would object to 'low pay' being 'depressed'. After all, it's his party which says that the way to having (I quote) a 'resilient economy' is through the wise and necessary implementation of a low-wage policy. So what can his objection be? Or has he just found a bit of populist language for the *Today* programme to attach to the idea he has of migrants?

Then he says that migration is causing problems for the public services. So here, the migrant is attached to an image: the image of overcrowded schools, packed hospital waiting rooms, and tiny huddles of hard-pressed social workers. Now, you and I may have noticed that these particular images have in the last four years been attached to something else altogether – the 'resilient economy' – which, we are told, can only be achieved through Bernard Jenkin's government wisely and sagely cutting back on schools, hospitals and social services.

As Dennis Skinner put it in the House of Commons when the new UKIP MP, Mark Reckless, took his seat this week: 'I have a united nations heart.' Our public services – apparently having problems from migrants, according to Jenkin – also happen to be, and have been, staffed by hundreds of thousands of migrants since the 1950s. So what is it? Staffed or besieged? And if it's besieged, how does cutting the services help?

I suspect that this has much more to do with populism than with logic: the idea of the 'migrant' is attached to blame, as Jenkin makes migrants solely responsible for the effects of the cuts his government implements, and he somehow manages not to attach the word to praise, as Dennis Skinner did, for the decades of hard work running the public services which he claims to want to defend on our behalf.

Now to Farage.

First there is a problem, for him: he claims he couldn't hear English being spoken between London Bridge and Grove Park. I travel all over the London transport systems and the only time I've been in a carriage where there is no English being spoken at all is when a couple of classes of French or German school children fill it up. But that's not what he means, is it? He wants to invoke something that he hopes will appear more sinister.

I very much doubt that he's telling the truth. After all, a great proportion of migrants speak English because English people migrated to their countries. You'll know the old gag about the migrant from one of the countries of the British Empire who is asked why his family live in England and he says, 'We're here because you were there.' Gags like that, it should be said, are part of an alternative and resistant language of migration.

So I suspect that Farage is dabbling in something rather nasty here. He wants to conjure up a picture of a public service taken over and blocked up by foreigners. The reason why you or I are crammed into the train at rush hour, he is saying, is because it's full of migrants. Crowded trains, he suggests, are nothing to do with the resources spent on transport in this country, but entirely down to people who have come to the UK to work, sometimes driving the very train that Farage is sitting on while he curses migrants.

Even so, let's imagine for a moment that Farage is right: that there's a carriage full of people not speaking English. What precisely is the objection here? Should there be a rule about speaking English in public spaces? Should Farage's awkwardness count be respected in law? Has he never been on the Costa Brava or in a cafe in south-west France where you can hear a lot of English being spoken? In his blokey way is he going to point out how 'awkward' that must be for the Spanish and French natives? Or is awkwardness a one-way street?

In fact, it rather seems as if the only awkward thing going on for Farage is that he keeps going on about this stuff about foreigners, even as he lives with a migrant, a migrant who we discover does that suspect thing of speaking another language. And as the interviewer points out, this person almost certainly speaks to her relatives on the phone in that language whilst living in England. But, more importantly, as we gather, unlike the train babble, Mrs Farage does some kind of OK-foreign-language-talking. So we've got a new duality here: bad-language-migrant, good-language-migrant. Let's not look for logic here. This is more populist flame-throwing.

Farage's next bit of language is doing something classic: it's the politician's rhetoric of recruitment. This can be done by using the word 'you' when at very best the politician means 'I'. So apparently, if Romanians moved in, 'you' would be concerned. This is because, says Farage, Romanians commit crimes. Here the word 'migrant' is attached to criminality – one of the main props for selling newspapers for as long as anyone has been identified as a migrant. To sell this one, a politician has to be sure to avoid comparing like with like. Comparing crime figures by nationality doesn't compare like with like. Nationalities come to a country with very different amounts of money in their pockets and CVs in their bags. In this particular case, if we want to find out if there is or is not anything surprising or distinctive going on, a comparison might be fairer between, say, different groups of poor, young single males. Even so, criminality is not an objective measure. It's a measure as done by the police. Since the Stephenson report, it is now public knowledge that how and why the police make arrests is not an unbiased matter.

But Farage's purpose is to avoid nuance: keep it short – attach the word 'migrant' to criminality.

And then he performs another old dodge of the anti-migrant: the verbal nudge-nudge. When asked why a Romanian moving in next door would be different from someone like Mrs Farage moving in, he says, 'You know what I mean.'

This nudge-nudge phrasing is ideal if you don't want to be accused of being racist. While saying everything, it appears to say nothing. It makes the listener responsible for the racism. The bad migrant, the invading neighbour is here attached to whatever bad thoughts might be swirling around in your mind. Given that newspapers have worked overtime for well over a hundred years suggesting that migrants have a particular interest (on account of being migrant) in committing unspeakable crimes, we might ask why wouldn't I do as Farage suggests and nudge-nudge 'know what he means'. In fact, some of us don't. We resist the nudge.

And then, back with the foreign-language question, it's clear that Farage would rather make the linguistic complexity of the migration very simple: foreigners speak foreign. And yet he must be intimately acquainted with how nuanced these things can be, how his wife has come, we might suspect, to be very fluent in English, how their children are growing up bilingual, how he too perhaps has some grasp of his partner's language. How, as a family, they mingle words and expressions across at least two languages. And if he wanted to be honest, he could find out in a matter of minutes that this is precisely the situation that prevails in most migrant households: a mixture of language use across two or more languages. Far from this being strange or problematical, this is what happens in billions of households all over the world. What is strange and problematical is that Farage appears to think that it's strange or problematical. 'Appears to.' Surely it isn't problematical down at the Farages, so why is he saying that it is for others? Because the script of anti-migration-speak says to Farage, 'Go on about foreigners talking foreign. Attach migrants to the idea that they get together in huddles precisely in order to stop you understanding what they're saying. Suggest, without saying so, that as migrants are attached to criminality, then you good English folks within earshot are entitled to think that the reason why foreigners talk foreign on our trains is so that they can plan to burgle your house, without you English people knowing about it. After all, before there were migrants, no one went burglaring.'

There was, Farage implies, a time when there was a pre-migrant London and this never-existing pre-migrant London was a burglar-free zone.

So, by comparing Obama's rhetoric with that of Jenkin and Farage, we can see that politicians have options on how to speak about migrants.

But so far, this talk has hardly touched on another matter in the language of migration: the voice of the migrants.

Let me get personal and, as I do so, I hope you'll compare your family and historical experiences of migration.

My father was born in the United States. He came to London when he was two. His father, who was born in Poland, stayed in the U.S. along with two of my father's brothers who had been born in London. My father's mother was born in England. Her mother and father were born in Poland. I don't expect you to remember any of that. Indeed, in many migrant families, even family members find it hard to remember this sort of thing. It's the stuff of a hundred stories, coincidences, losses, and strange meetings.

Poland for many Jewish emigrants was known in Yiddish as '*der Heim*', which literally means 'home' but it came to mean 'the homeland' or something more vague like 'back there'. Again, the culture of migration creates popular shorthand phraseology that doesn't tally neatly with the concerns of politicians with their cricket-supporting tests and nationality exams. In the case of the term '*der Heim*' it's transnational; Jews of many different nationalities all over the world called it that. The language of migration crosses many borders.

In this passage I'm about to read you'll hear the Yiddish words for grandfather, which is '*zeider*', grandmother, which is '*bubbe*', and a crazy person, which is '*meshuggene*'. Part of the language of migrants is that they often talk in many tongues like this. Here's my father writing:

> We would stand by the edge of the grubby old public swimming pool drying ourselves, my *zeider* and I. As likely as not he would tell me once again about how he would go swimming back in *der Heim* somewhere in Poland. I would listen to this fragment of his boyhood. Always I saw him in some Arcadian setting of endless pine trees and velvet grass sloping down to a still lake. It was always early morning. He would emerge from a log cabin, run to the water and fracture its stillness with strong strokes. He would go on swimming till he was lost to view. There were no other people, no other houses, no other movements. It was an idyll I clung to from which I had banished pogroms and poverty and the fearful little community huddled over their prayers and sewing machines. That was my story not his. And when we went on day trips to Southend, east London's seaside, in his sixties he would set out to swim the length of the pier and back, a mile or so each way. My *bubbe* without fail went through the identical torments of anxiety. 'The *meshuggene*! He's gone out too far again.' I was free from all such fears. For he was always the intrepid boy swimmer in the pure lake who always came back. And he did. And even in death still does.

So, my father carried about an image of another place, a mythic place of origin, which he shared with me and my brother through language.

And there's this:

> *Zeider*'s jokes baffled me at first and I would have to put on a phony laugh at stories I wasn't ready for. He once told me of the great sage Rabbi Nachman. I've heard it in dozens of versions since. The old rabbi was on his deathbed, and his devoted disciples gathered round and took their last chance to ask him the great question.
>
> 'Rabbi Nachman, tell us what is life?'
>
> They waited for a long time, fearful that they would not hear a reply. At long last the rabbi gasped out, 'Life – is like a fish.'
>
> Baffled, they hastily conferred and came back to his bedside.
>
> 'Rabbi Nachman, why is life like a fish?'
>
> The old man looked at them. 'So? It's not like a fish.'
>
> *Zeider* gave the rabbi's reply the tone of impatient irritation. How

was this a joke? The adults loved it. Relished it and would repeat, 'So? It's not like a fish', and fall about. In due course I came to laugh too.

What do stories like this tell us?

Lines of language, thought and culture that persist across countries and across time. No matter what Jenkin and Farage say, the word 'migrant' in my mind is much more attached to these lines than to the lines they want to make.

And though there's nothing wrong with sentiment and nostalgia, from my position of comfort it's easy to forget that some of these lines are stories of persecution, separation, hardship, humiliation or worse.

In my father's writing, there are memories of relatives talking about Cossacks charging at people in Russia, but also of standing between his mother and grandfather on a demonstration during the General Strike of 1926. A few months ago, my stepmother came to the house with a little plastic jar full of odds and ends that had belonged to my father, some dating back to the 1920s. In amongst them was a small brass brooch in the shape of a miner's lamp. I looked it up on the internet and discovered that such brooches were sold to support the miners' families who were on strike or locked out after everyone else went back to work during and after the General Strike. I can't be certain, but it probably belonged to his mother or grandfather.

When I hear that the word 'migrant' has to be tested for its owner's allegiance to Britain, I think that that's only one kind of allegiance. Isn't there an allegiance to the people around us? I have to spell it out for myself – perhaps for you, or perhaps not. Here are these people standing behind me, with their memories of a real or mythic *Heim*, telling mythic jokes about Rabbi Nachman and buying a brooch to send money to South Wales or Yorkshire or Lanarkshire for families who, according to the migrant-versus-native-Briton scenario, lived lives utterly different from my relatives, or indeed, according to the propaganda of the day, were utterly opposed to each other. Of the two main stereotypes attached to Jews of the time – 'as rich as Baron Rothschild' or as 'poor, stingy, filthy, greasy and jabbering' as in William Makepeace Thackeray's poem 'The White Squall' – neither would have included buying a brooch for hungry miners' families.

As I am doing right now, I write about such things. Because of that, I, like other writers, become magnets for other people's tales.

My second cousin wrote to me a few years ago to say that his mother's second husband had left behind some papers. In the papers there were letters and cards that had been sent from Poland and France during the Second World War. They were in German.

461

Sender:
Exp.
Rosen, 11 rue Mellaise Niort (Deux Sèvres) France
Addressee: Monsieur
Max Rosen
96, West Cedar St. Boston (Mass)
S.A.

Niort, March 23, 1940

My dears,

Only today did I receive your dear letter dated February 29. I hope that you already received my card dated March 18. We are glad to hear that you are in good health and I can tell you the same from us. We were very pleased to receive your letter and we thank you very much. I just learned from you that dear Bella is no more in Biala. I tried to make inquiries but unfortunately I can't get any information. I am very surprised that you have not yet received any news from Poland. You live in a neutral country, therefore it is much easier for you to find out something about our sisters in Poland. Who knows whether they are still alive. I am giving you the following addresses. Write immediately. Also let me know right away whether you received this card. You may also write to me in Yiddish. Tea Weinstock in Opoczno, ziemia Radomska. – Stella Rechnitz, ulica Zeromskiego No. 17 in Dombrowa-Górnicza, bei Sosnowiec Poland.

I learned that it is best to write in Polish to Poland, and up to 25 words, not more.

If you receive a letter from Poland, only send me a copy.

Nothing else new, as I am awaiting good news.

Best regards,
Your brother, brother-in-law
Oscar

My dear wife also sends you many regards and wishes you the best. Awaiting immediate answers, as it takes very long.

. . . and a hand-written registered postcard with German stamps, airmail stamp, and a German military censorship stamp:

Sender:
Bernard Rechnitz Dombrowa 6/S Schlesischestr. 14
Addressee: Mr.
Max Rosen Boston-Mass West Cedar 96 U.S.A.
Dombrowa, January 22, 1941

Dear Brother,

I have written to you several times and urged you fervently to take in my only child. Michal/ Marolka / Rechnitz in Joszkar – 6 Ta, Maryjskoja U.S.S.R. pocstowy Jasscryk No. 8 barack / 7. Sowjet Union.

He was sent way from Lemberg and only America can rescue him. Therefore I am fervently asking you to take the necessary steps immediately. Many thousands have already gone to America. I am asking you again and fulfill my request. I have sent you my son's birth certificate. Born November 16, 1923 in Dombrowa 6/S.

What are you doing my dears? Kisses to you and your dear wife.

Maybe for now you can send him a few dollars? I beg you very much.

. . . and a hand-written postcard with German stamps and airmail stamp

Sender:
Bernard Rechnitz Dombrowa 6/S Schlesischestr. 14
Addressee: Mr.
Max Rosen Boston-Mass West Cedar 96 U.S.A.
Dombrowa, February 11, 1941

Dear Brother,

I hope you have already taken the steps to take in my son. Maybe you could adopt him to make this work?

Dear brother, I urge you. For now send him a few dollars and packages with food because he has nothing. I fervently urge you to send something as soon as possible. Don't be upset with me but only you . . . [remainder of the sentence is obscured by airmail stamp]

Kisses to you and to your dear wife and children.

Your sister Stella

So, to be clear here, the letters survived because they were passed from the recipient, Max Rosen, to his son Ted, who left them with his divorced wife. She left them with her second husband and when he died they were passed on to his stepson, my second cousin, Ted Junior. I asked Ted Junior why his father hadn't kept them. 'My theory,' he said, 'is because they were all ashamed that none of the senders of the letters, Stella, Bernard, Bella and Tea in Poland and Oscar and his wife in France survived beyond 1944.'

In France the prefects and sub-prefects made lists of foreign-born Jews – recent migrants, that is – and handed them to the occupying power: an example of how the official language of migration can be used. Oscar and his wife were rounded up in Nice and sent to Paris, to the transit camp of Drancy, then to Auschwitz. Michael did survive – migration saved his life – another connotation which can be attached to the word 'migrant' – 'life-saving'. He spent all his working life as a London cab driver and lives in Stanmore. When we sent him these letters, he said that he had always wondered who sent him 50 dollars while he was in a Russian prison camp in Siberia and now he knew. It must have come from his cousin Max. Fragments of language preserved in letters across decades, suddenly solving old mysteries.

A few years ago, I was sitting in a classroom in Hackney and we were talking about the different languages we spoke and the different countries that people came from.

A child spoke to the teacher and I wrote down what he said:

He doesn't speak English miss.
He comes from the Congo miss.
I translate for you, miss.
He says that the bad men take his grandfather, miss.
He says that the bad men take his grandmother, miss.
He says that the bad men take his dad, miss.
He says that the bad men take his mum, miss.
He doesn't say how he got here, miss.
He can't say how he got here, miss.

I'll finish with what we might take as the mother of all interviews about migrants. It provided the key word 'swamp' which, along with synonyms not used by Margaret Thatcher on this occasion – like 'flood' and 'swarm' – has provided metaphors for a thousand articles and speeches since. It was January 1978 and Margaret Thatcher connected 'swamped' with the words 'people are really rather afraid', followed a moment later with 'fear', and people being 'rather hostile to those coming in'.

I think this is all I remembered from the interview, but going back over it, I find that I've forgotten a great deal. It was also here that Margaret Thatcher invoked the superiority of the British – 'British characteristics that have done so much for the world' – and the essential item in the anti-migrant's tool box: the contrast between the word 'migrant' and the word 'people', as in 'The moment the minority threatens to become a big one, people get frightened.' For a flicker of a second we could be forgiven here for thinking that the minority aren't people. Or that the normal and good thing to be is 'people' and the strange, scary thing is to be is a 'minority'.

Whether intentionally or not, this language structure has been repeated a thousand times since. In the sentence, the 'people' are not the 'minority'. If you're going to play with contrasts and opposites, the linguistic counterpart to a 'minority' is a 'majority'. It's not 'people'. So we are shown, without it being said explicitly, that the minority are not people. As I've suggested, this kind of sentence's comrade in arms is any that finds ways of reducing or distorting migrants into objects, as with 'the endless supply of cheap labour'. Bernard Jenkin, you'll remember, counterposed that phrase with 'the public interest'.

What both Thatcher and Jenkin do with their language is to deliberately not give us a picture of a majority-minority making up a whole population, a whole people. They use all-inclusive words like 'people' and 'public interest' at the very same moment they are suggesting that there is a particular kind of non-human creature who is not part of that inclusiveness. In logical terms it's an absurdity: migrants are part of the 'people'. Migrants are part of the 'public interest'. Everywhere, that is, apart from in these kinds of sentences.

The British political scene is changing. Mark Reckless implied and then 'unimplied' that he thinks it would be desirable or necessary to deport migrants. Having flagged this up as a possibility, his head office denied it. It's OK, the deed was done. The word 'migrant' was attached to the idea of deportation. If I was someone who says there are too many migrants, then the logical next step from there is to say that some of them must be got rid of, removed. If I was then wondering who would be the most likely party to do the removing then, surely, I would now know that it would be Mark Reckless's party, even if that party did deny it, eh, nudge nudge.

Because they've denied it, we can't quiz them on how precisely these deportations would be handled. What do they have in mind? snatch squads? armed guards? armoured trains? transit camps?

465

But this is an inadmissible conversation. It lies in the land behind and beyond the language of migration. In some ways, because it's not said, it's the most powerful use of language of all.

It's in some people's heads.

Arts in Schools

I gave this talk at the Royal Academy on 5 May 2019.

Let's begin by looking at these two pictures. The one on the left is called *Thor battering the Midgard Serpent* and the one on the right is called *Prospero summons Ariel: a scene from Shakespeare's Tempest*.

They belong right here in the Royal Academy. Thanks to the RA for reproducing them.

They're both by the artist Henry Fuseli. He lived from 1741 to 1825.

He was born in Zürich, Switzerland, the second of 18 children.

In 1765, he visited England, where he supported himself for some time by miscellaneous writing. Eventually, he became acquainted with Sir Joshua Reynolds, to whom he showed his drawings. Following Reynolds's advice, he decided to devote himself entirely to art. In 1770 he made an art pilgrimage to Italy, where he remained until 1778, changing his name from Füssli to the more Italian-sounding Fuseli.

Early in 1779 he returned to Britain. In 1788 he married Sophia Rawlins (originally one of his models), and he soon after became an associate of the Royal Academy. The early feminist Mary Wollstonecraft, whose portrait he had painted, planned a trip with him to Paris, and pursued him determinedly, but after Sophia's intervention the Fuselis' door was closed to her for ever. Fuseli later said, 'I hate clever women. They are only troublesome.' In 1790 he became a full Academician, presenting *Thor battering the Midgard Serpent* as his diploma work. In 1799 Fuseli was appointed professor of painting to the Academy. Four years later he was chosen as Keeper, and resigned his professorship, but resumed it in 1810, continuing to hold both offices until his death. What has this got to do with anything we're discussing today?

Well, one of my key words for this talk is 'interpretation'.

We might say that all art, and all commentary about art, involves interpretation. By filling you in on a few details about Fuseli I have already affected your interpretation of the pictures. I'm guessing that now I've told you Fuseli's dates, some of you are slotting the pictures into your mind's filing systems to do with the years around 1800, and other artists you know of. You might be thinking about Switzerland, or about Joshua Reynolds. You might be thinking about what dangers – or perhaps what delights – encounters with clever women placed in his way. Or what a jerk he was to say that thing about clever women.

There's another aspect about these two pictures that I can mention: as with thousands of others in the western traditions, Fuseli has used the medium of graphic art to interpret two works of literature.

I'm guessing that most people here will be familiar with at least something of the literature that Fuseli has interpreted in these pictures. Thor is very popular these days because he's one of *The Avengers*. In another form, he was the Norse God of War. His name was taken to make Thursday – Thor's day.

The other day I watched the *Graham Norton Show* and Chris Hemsworth, who plays Thor in *The Avengers*, was on the couch talking about how he has collected three or four of the hammers that he's wielded in the films. Also on the couch was Paul Rudd who plays Ant-Man in other movies, Kit Harrington who plays Jon Snow in the TV film series *Game of Thrones*, and Julianne Moore who plays all sorts of people in many different types of film. (I wonder if Fuseli would have thought her clever and troublesome.) Kit Harrington said that he has a giant statue of himself which he doesn't know what to do with. Graham Norton said he could bury it in the garden and years later people might come along and find it, and wonder what had been going on. Thor said that he tries to put the hammers on the mantelpiece but his wife takes them away. He then said his son picked up one of the hammers and asked him if it was a toy. 'No,' said Thor, 'that's the real one.'

So, the Norse myth was meeting Marvel Comics meeting *Game of Thrones*, and the relative reality or unreality of film-set props from the Hollywood version of the Norse myth. There are a lot of intertwined narratives going on there.

I'm not sure how the Norse myths made their way into Fuseli's consciousness. I knew them well from one of my favourite books as a child, an anthology of the tales by Barbara Leonie Picard. I can retell – or interpret – them because of my memory of them. In fact, when I've been put on the spot by my children to make up a story, I've secretly plundered the myths for storylines and motifs. Rather as Hollywood does, and – if there's time – schools can help children do: be like Shakespeare – steal a story, adapt it, change the setting, switch the gender of one of the lead characters, add in a sub-plot and you've got a hit. My favourite Norse myth when I was a boy was the one sometimes known as the *Binding of Fenrir*. Fenrir is a giant wolf, and a key moment in the story involves a test of courage: the god Tyr puts his hand in Fenrir's mouth as evidence of the gods' good faith in binding Fenrir with what looks like nothing more than a garland of flowers. I won't spoil the story other than to tell you that Tyr's name was taken to give us Tuesday – Tyr's day.

These little interconnected anecdotes tell me that stories don't just begin and end. They exist in chains of memories, retellings and interpretations even to the point where some end up on our tongues every day – quite literally as days of the week.

Fuseli painted his *Thor* picture in 1790 and it was, as you heard, the one that enabled him to become an Academician right here.

Let's look at *The Tempest*.

Here we can see Prospero in the middle and the two natives – and two slaves – Ariel and Caliban.

Can we take it that that's Prospero's daughter standing behind Prospero there? She's called Miranda, who gives us the famous phrase 'Brave new world' – which in the play is a line of great irony as the world she is looking at is neither 'brave' nor 'new'. It's made up of people full of old-world cowardices, rivalries and treacheries.

In both pictures Fuseli has interpreted stories.

This was a high-status activity.

Because Fuseli was so good at it, according to contemporary tastes and attitudes, it enabled him to be accepted in the top artistic institution of the day: the one we are in right now.

I'll ask a rhetorical question here: if what Fuseli was doing was a high-status activity then, why isn't it a high-status activity now in education?

What else might we say about these pictures? Do you think both have a heroic tone? These heroes (both in their own ways magical beings – can we say 'supermen'?) have been positioned centre stage, mid-action, one striking down the serpent, the other commanding his slaves, the heavens and the seas.

If you know *The Tempest* or the Norse myths you'll know that other scenes and interpretations are available. The myths offer us the figure of Loki who as the god of fire can create mischief and wreak havoc. *The Tempest* gives voice and space to a native's slave revolt, which draws into the rebellion the servants of the aristocrats who are occupying the island. Several times I've put Caliban's words 'This island's mine' into poetry anthologies, and I've written about Caliban in my book for young people about Shakespeare.

These are all interpretations of mine.

I've just demonstrated in the first minutes of this talk how looking at these pictures has set off trails of thoughts and opinions about the Norse myths and *The Tempest*.

My central argument today is to say that:

a) what Fuseli has done here by painting scenes from literature,

b) what I've done in the past with the stories that Fuseli has drawn on

and

c) what I've done right now, musing on how these stories exist in me and in popular culture

…are the kinds of activities that are being squeezed out of primary and secondary education.

How is this being done?

It's mostly as a consequence of what the government calls 'accountability'. Schools are locked into a system of testing, inspections and league tables. These are all high stakes because the governance of a school depends on them: children's scores in tests are aggregated and tracked over time. If a decision is made that the school is inadequate, it can be forced out of local-authority control and become an academy. Or, if it's already an academy it can be forced to become another academy.

No matter what one thinks of this as a way of managing schools and managing standards, you can see that the whole apparatus rests on testing children.

It's legitimate then to look at the tests themselves and ask some questions. I'll restrict this for the moment to primary-school children.

First: What kinds of knowledge do the tests test?

Secondly: What kinds of effect on education do these tests have?

This may sound tautological but I'll start by saying that the tests only test what is testable according to the kinds of test they are. By this I mean that they are pencil-and-paper tests which ask children questions for which there are only right and wrong answers.

This tells us straight away that there are whole areas of knowledge that are excluded. (Just to be clear, I mean knowledge that is both know-what and know-how.)

I'm sure you could think of some too. Here are mine:

How to save someone's life
How to feed someone
How to be compassionate
How to co-operate with others
How to be brave in the face of people being over-bearing, bullying or who persecute you
How to hold two equally valid ideas in your head at the same time
How to plan.

More specifically, if you look closely at the questions on a SATs paper you'll see that, quite specifically, there is only one possible answer for any one question. This is from last year's SATs paper for 10- and 11-year-olds. The children were asked to read a poem. They were then asked:

> The experience of the last line could best be described as: amusing, or shocking, or puzzling, or comforting?

The marking guide that the teachers use to mark the test show that only one of these words is 'right'. Notice that in the question there's a passive construction: 'could best be described'. Could best be described by whom? Who is this Best-Describer Person? On what basis does Best-Describer

Person come to their conclusions? I'm getting a picture here of a great god Best-Describer roaming the world of poetry tests who always knows best. Perhaps Fuseli could draw it for me.

It is through passive constructions like 'best be described' that passivity is taught. The passive teaches passivity. Children are asked to accept that an unknown, unchallenged and unchallengeable authority runs poetry.

Hey, I thought it was poets who run poetry, but what do I know?

Actually, when I read the test question, I had two subversive thoughts: first, that none of the words on offer 'best described' the last line. I could think of some others that I think are better. But as it was me doing the test (in my mind) I remembered the rule: I must not think of other words. I must not think of other words.

My other thought was, those words on offer in the question could – at a push – all describe the last line. That's what poetry is like. The words in a poem slide about, full of ambiguity, suggesting one thing which, if true, might suggest something else which might suggest something else, on down a chain of meaning.

In fact, nearly 90 years ago, William Empson wrote a book which showed us just how ambiguous poetry can be and often is.

Poetry is not a store of right and wrong facts. To treat it as such – which this SATs test does – is to distort and wreck poetry.

The reader of a poem is not someone who takes specific lumps of meaning out of a poem as if they are taking eggs out of an egg box. If I take that metaphor further, I'd say, well if they are eggs, you can't actually use the egg for much until you open the egg up and cook it according to your taste and culture. What are you going to have: scrambled, poached, fired, boiled, omelette?

In other words, interpretation. We make meanings.

That's just one question.

Multiply that many times – not just in terms of that test. Think now of the second of my questions:

What kinds of effect on education do these tests have?

One direct effect is that children spend hours and hours and hours doing practice testing. In other words, the test method (or test way of thinking) is instilled into children as being the best way, the only way, the authoritative way of doing things.

Here's my 'Guide to Education'.

You get education in schools.
To find out how much education you get,

the government gives you tests.
Before you do the tests
the government likes it if you are put on
different tables that show how well or badly
you are going to do in the tests.
The tests test whether they
have put you on the right table.
The tests test whether you know what you're
supposed to know.

But
don't try to get to know any old stuff like
'What is earwax?' or 'How to make soup'.
The way to know things you're supposed to know
is to do pretend tests.
When you do the pretend tests
you learn how to think in the way that tests
want you to think.
The more practice you do,
the more likely it is that you won't make the mistake
of thinking in any other way other than in
the special test way of thinking.

Here's an example:
The apples are growing on the tree.
What is growing on the tree?
If you say, 'leaves', you are wrong.
It's no use you thinking that when apples are on a tree
there are usually leaves on the tree too.
There is only one answer. And that is 'apples'.
All other answers are wrong.

If you are the kind of person that thinks 'leaves' is a
good answer, doing lots and lots and lots of practice tests
will get you to stop thinking that 'leaves' is a good answer.

Doing many, many practice tests will also make it
very likely that there won't be time for you to go out

and have a look at an apple tree to see what else grows on apple trees. Like ants. Or mistletoe.

Education is getting much better these days because there is much more testing.

Remember, it's 'apples' not 'leaves'.

But there's another effect:

i) how this kind of testing,

ii) the preparation for this kind of testing

and

iii) the accountability model of testing, inspection and league tables

…are transforming the timetable.

Here are some observations from some teachers I asked:

'My college has cut A-level Dance, Film Studies, Music… more pressure on working-class students to take business-type subjects, and more academies with sixth forms hanging on to A-level students.'

'Our college has cut BTEC Music, and A-level Music, Dance, Drama, Textiles and Graphic Design. Combination of factors including low recruitment (as a knock-on from smaller number of students taking up creative subjects at GCSE) but probably other factors too.'

'I'm not a teacher but my Year 4 son's English is only marked for spelling, grammar and neat handwriting. Ideas and creativity are never commented on so it's hard for me to persuade him it's worth bothering. And art projects seem designed only to provide classroom decoration. Kids are given very specific instructions, so are basically just colouring in.'

'As a child aged 10 we did pottery with a kiln and glazes, acrylic moulding, cutting and polishing, water colours, woodworking, marbled paper-making and calligraphy. My daughter at the same age does colouring in. They made something out of air-dried clay but it broke by the time she got home.'

'They brought in EBacc which excluded the Arts, and Progress 8 which all but eliminated them. The schools that have struggled the most to retain the Arts are the same ones that struggle to achieve the limiting data figures that are supposedly so important. The greatest threat they have is one that has been wielded across all disadvantaged areas: if you don't meet the data targets then Ofsted will tell you you're failing your students, place you in special measures and the DfE sell you off to the highest bidder.'

'I work in a special school and have been pressured to cut out creative arts almost completely. A few years ago, my timetable included plays, music, art, reading and writing for pleasure, and fun poetry. Now my managers want evidence of progressive writing and worksheets, as these can be assessed for data.'

'My secondary school, in a socially deprived area of Newcastle, now has NO music at KS3 or 4 and no music teachers employed, for the first time in my 23 years there...'

'In 2014 three pupils took A-level Music. One was my son. Two others transferred in from elsewhere. By 2014 A-level Music was cut altogether. Because of this my younger son went to a large non-selective state sixth-form college to do music. This establishment has now cut it. The other large state sixth-form college in our town to offer A-level Music still offers it but it is highly selective. Neither one of my boys would have done well there yet one is currently working in the creative industries as a musician/creative, and the other is doing a music degree at university. They got their A-level Music qualifications 'just in the nick of time'. They would not have the same opportunities if they were a year or two younger.'

'My secondary school tries to still offer creative arts at GCSE and

A-level, and to offer extra-curricular music and drama. But due to pressure mainly from the English department, students in Years 11 and 13 were banned from taking part in productions. The last year they were allowed to take part, when they missed part of an English lesson for the dress rehearsal, they were told when they got back to the lesson how many marks they were likely to have lost. No credit given for the benefits to their English development of taking part in a performance.'

'In Year 11 students not achieving targets just get Maths, English and Science lessons.'

'I'm a secondary art teacher and we have had KS3 art lessons reduced from 50 minutes a week to an hour a fortnight. Additionally from next year there will be a two-year Key Stage 3; in total this means that students will receive 36 hours of art if they don't opt for it at GCSE. They will also have a two-year GCSE which means that they will complete their GCSE in Year 10. Obviously as students mature they are capable of higher-level skills. I'm not looking forward to being invited to explain why the results are poorer than previous years…'

So what are these children and school students missing out on?

Or put this another way: what can arts in education, arts in schools, offer children and school students?

In an ideal world they can offer:

trial and error without fear of failure;

a chance to explore materials or aspects of the material world, whether that's

your own voice – through e.g. singing and speaking

your body – through movement, dance and acting

or materials like clay, wood, iron, plastic, stone, glass

or materials like pencil, charcoal, paint, pen, ink, paper, canvas, film, video

or language which can only manifest itself materially through voice, print, digitally produced signs, and so on.

Every artistic act starts with possibilities for change, it enacts change, it changes materials, it offers possibilities to the maker and to the viewer.

By the way, I tried to express this idea with a little poem:

Take a brush:
the sky is green
the grass is blue
you are purple
the house is silver
the river is gold
the sun is black
the world has changed.
Did you do that?

What I didn't express in the poem is that in changing things we change ourselves. We are never the same as we were.

We discover that we are not passive receptacles, we discover that we have the potential to change things.

A good deal of art involves co-operation of some sort – some more than others.

A good deal of art involves us seeing things as others see them. It often involves making comparisons between how we see things and how others see them. The events of the 20th century tell us that this is desperately necessary if we are to avoid destroying each other or the planet or both.

And let me come back to that word 'interpretation'. All art – not just Fuseli and the rest who interpret across art forms – involves some kind of transformation of what's already there, whether that's language or all the different kinds of materials I mentioned earlier.

But interpretation is also a totally valid practice that takes place off the back of art.

This is not the ritual of what the exam boards call retrieval, inference, chronology and presentation.

Interpretation involves using the available resources of our experience and, more specifically, our experience of other art forms and texts.

One of the key parts of this is what we might call 'storying'. You show me a story – or fragments of a story – as with Fuseli's pictures – and I'll tell you a story. This exchange of stories that goes on every day of our lives is how we form the foundation of our abstract thoughts. In fact, it's not just storying, it's analogising. In order to story off the back of one story, I have to select one aspect from the story in front of me, and compare it with one aspect of a story that is in the story library in my mind. I make analogies. The moment I make analogies, I am beginning to categorise, generalise and classify.

I would suggest that that is precisely what Fuseli has done here. He has categorised Prospero or Thor as a type – as selected from Fuseli's library of types sitting in his head.

Categories, generalisations and classifications are highly prized in education – at least at the level of being told what they are, as when we are asked to read and learn: 'The following are types of erosion, the following are types of triangle, the following are types of figurative language.'

But what value do we put on the ability to do this through interpretation, through storying and through the arts?

Many thanks to the Royal Academy for permission to reproduce the two Fuseli works in this book. Here are the permission details:

Object ID: 03/995
Picture Library number: PL000552
Henry Fuseli R.A.
Title: *Thor battering the Midgard Serpent*
1790
Oil on canvas
Height: 133 cm, Width: 94.6 cm
Photo credit: ©Royal Academy of Arts, London; photographer: John Hammond

Object ID: 06/147
Picture Library number: PL003659
Title: *Prospero summons Ariel: a scene from Shakespeare's Tempest*
Artist/designer: Henry Fuseli R.A. (1741-1825)

Engraved by William Bromley A.R.A. (1769-1842)

Published by F. and C. Rivington

From A. Chalmers (ed.), *The plays of William Shakspeare*, London 1805, vol. I, facing p.17

Date: 1 January 1803
Etching with engraving
Height: 15.8 cm Width: 8.7 cm
Photo credit: ©Royal Academy of Arts, London

Other Books by Michael Rosen

In 1997 I completed a Ph.D. on the subject of authoring a piece of children's literature - a book of poems that was eventually published as *You Wait Till I'm Older Than You* (Puffin). In the thesis I tried to put to one side mystical and Romantic ideas around creating poetry and instead, locate the whole process in reality.

POETRY AND STORIES FOR PRIMARY AND LOWER SECONDARY SCHOOLS

MICHAEL ROSEN

This is a short guide for teachers on how to teach poetry – reading, responding and writing. It is full of ideas on where and how to start, descriptions of why it's such a valuable activity. It's for you to use, adapt and change as you think best for the school and students you have in front of you.

WHY WRITE? WHY READ?

MICHAEL ROSEN

This booklet gathers together some recent talks and blogs on writing and reading, for use by teachers, librarians, parents, or anyone interested in engaging children and students in reading and writing, analysing why and how we do both.

WRITING FOR PLEASURE

MICHAEL ROSEN

This booklet is the third in a series about reading, writing and responding to literature. It focuses on how to make writing pleasurable and interesting and would be ideal as part of teacher training, staff discussion, curriculum development or just for reading and using.

READING FOR PLEASURE

MICHAEL ROSEN

This is a short guide for teachers on how to help a school put in place a reading for pleasure policy. To support this policy the guide also takes a close look at how children read – what do they think as they read? I've also included some plans from teachers putting reading for pleasure policies in place. It's for you to use, adapt and change as you think best for the school and students you have in front of you.

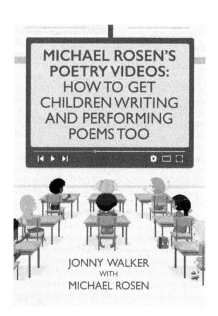

MICHAEL ROSEN'S POETRY VIDEOS: HOW TO GET CHILDREN WRITING AND PERFORMING POEMS TOO

JONNY WALKER
WITH
MICHAEL ROSEN

This is a guide for teachers on how to support children to write and perform poems that matter to them – it shares creative ways to harness the classroom potential of the 'Kids' Poems and Stories with Michael Rosen' YouTube channel. It is a practical and supportive handbook, put together by a practising teacher, and it suggests some ways that fellow teachers can create enriching writing communities with and for their students.

Further details on all these self-published books, including where they can be ordered from, can be found on my website:

www.michaelrosen.co.uk/books

Lightning Source UK Ltd.
Milton Keynes UK
UKHW010645240222
399180UK00003B/302